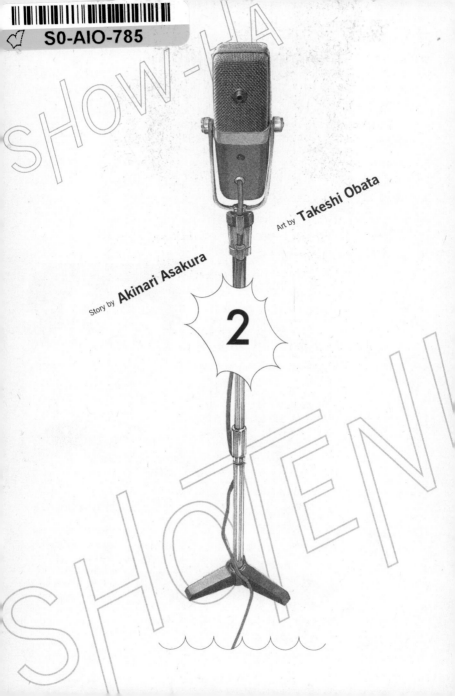

SHOW-HA SHOTEN!

2

Story by **Akinari Asakura**

Art by **Takeshi Obata**

Story

Azemichi Shijima is a first-year high school student. Under the nom de plume "Everday Shijimi," he submits winning answers to joke prompts on radio and TV shows. But despite his incredible comedic sensibility, he's too timid to speak in front of others in person. One day, he meets a student named Taiyo Higashikata who wants to take part in the stand-up comedy competition at the school's culture festival. Taiyo has a gift for performing, but he doesn't know how to write good material.

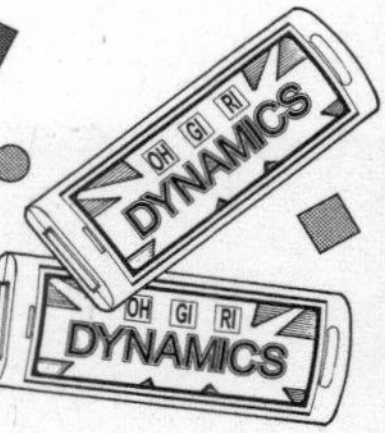
OH GI RI
DYNAMICS
OH GI RI
DYNAMICS

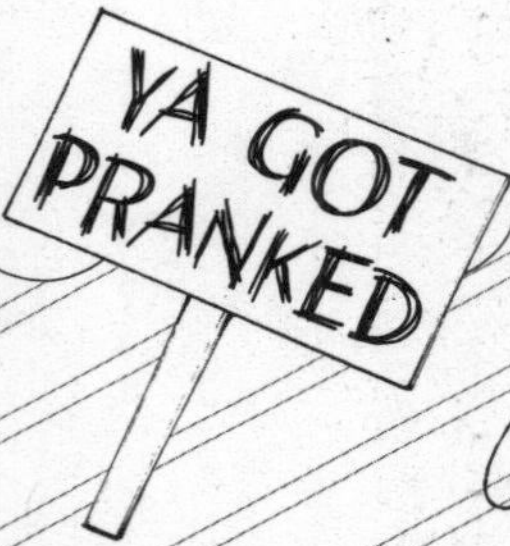
YA GOT PRANKED

Character

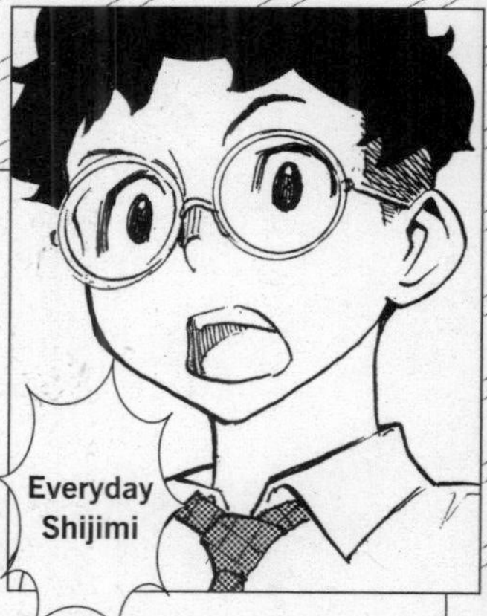
Everyday Shijimi

Azemichi Shijima

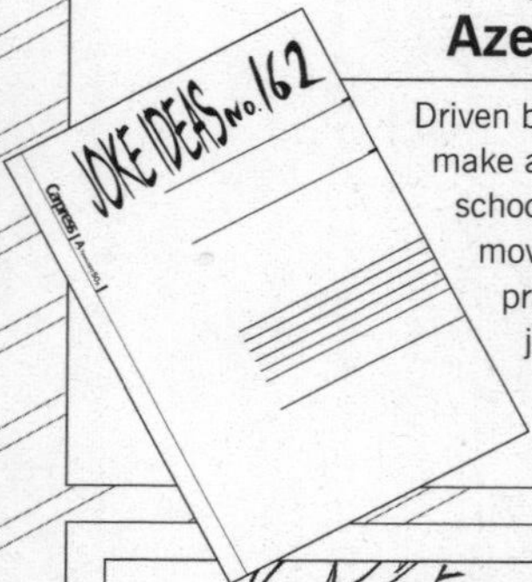
JOKE IDEAS No.162

Driven by regret that he couldn't make a girl from middle school laugh when she was moving away, he started practicing comedy. Writes jokes under the name "Everyday Shijimi." Gets stage fright.

Taiyo Higashikata

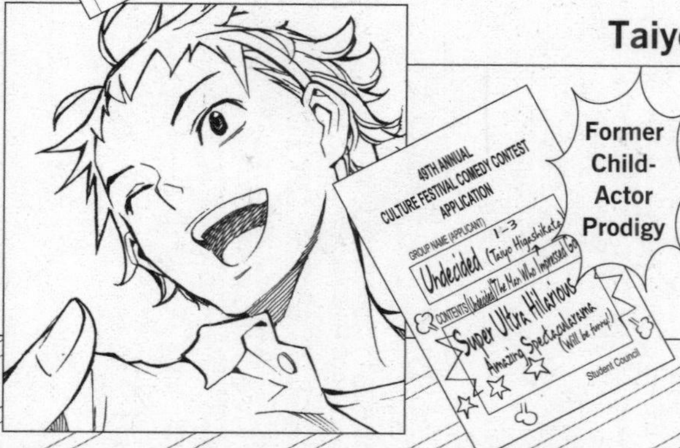
49TH ANNUAL
CULTURE FESTIVAL COMEDY CONTEST
APPLICATION
GROUP NAME (APPLICANT)
1-3
Undecided (Taiyo Higashikata)
CONTENTS (Undecided) The Man Who Impressed Go
Super Ultra Hilarious
Amazing Spectacularama
(Will be funny!)
Student Council
Former Child-Actor Prodigy

A former child-actor prodigy with a gift for performing. After his previous comedy partner passed away, he inherited the dream of rising to the top of the comedy world.

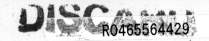

When Taiyo learns that Azemichi is Everyday Shijimi, he invites him to be his partner in the contest. Despite having been written on the fly, their sketch is a hit, and the duo experience the elation of their first true wave of laughter. For Azemichi, it's the motivation he needs to finally dedicate himself to being a comedian. Next, they're setting their sights on rising to the very pinnacle of comedy!

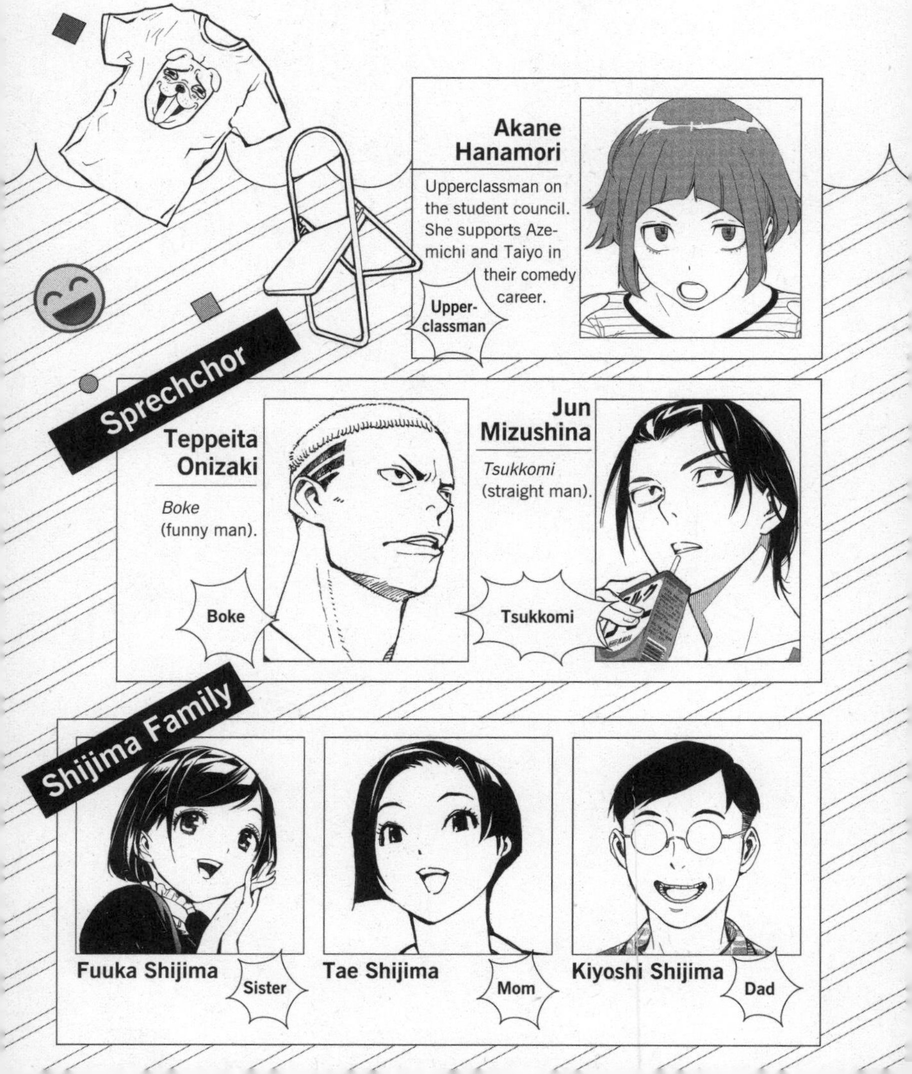
Akane Hanamori
Upperclassman on the student council. She supports Azemichi and Taiyo in their comedy career.
Upperclassman
Sprechchor
Jun Mizushina
Tsukkomi (straight man).
Tsukkomi
Teppeita Onizaki
Boke (funny man).
Boke
Shijima Family
Fuuka Shijima
Sister
Tae Shijima
Mom
Kiyoshi Shijima
Dad

Contents 2

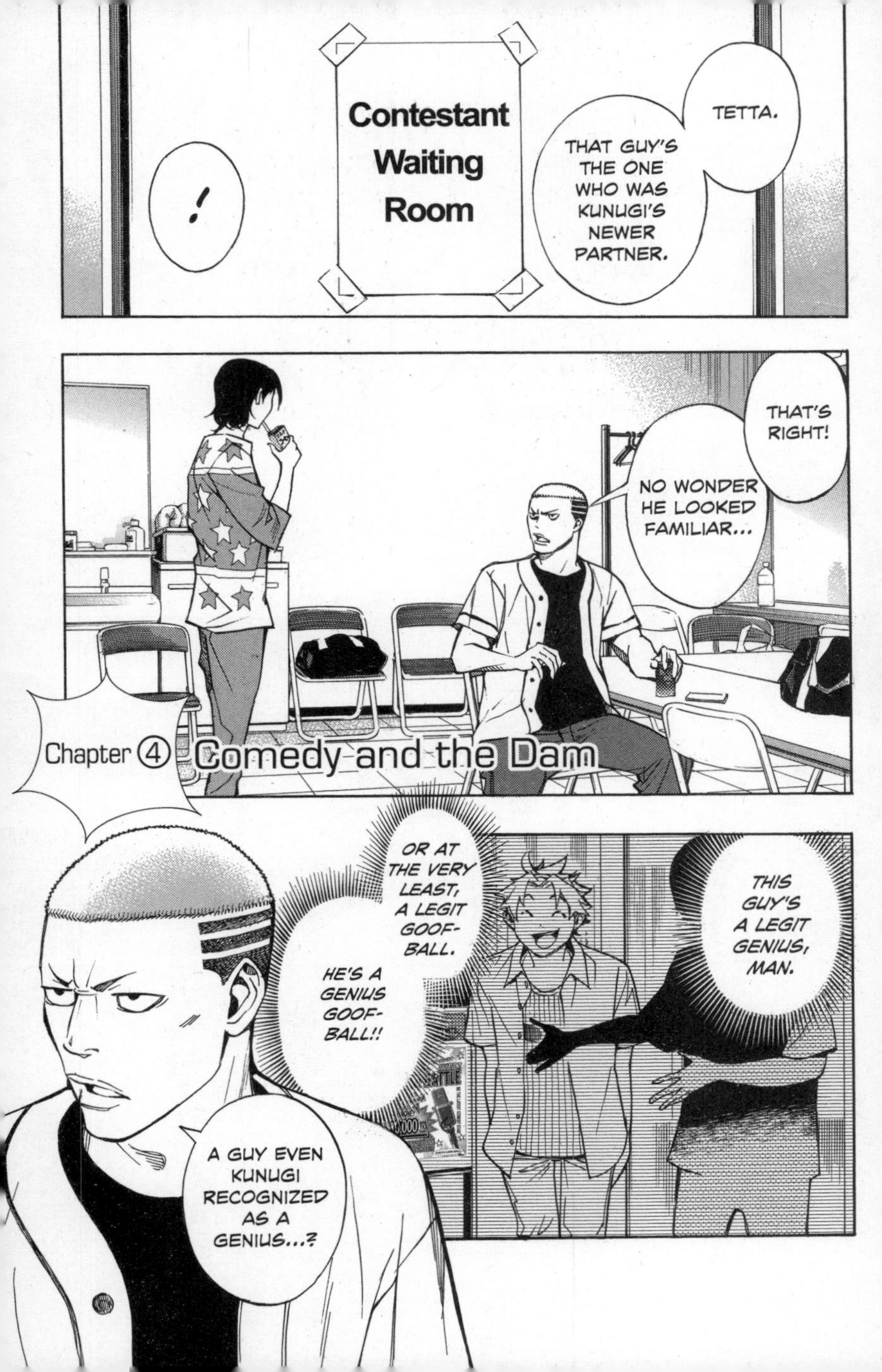
TETTA.
THAT GUY'S THE ONE WHO WAS KUNUGI'S NEWER PARTNER.
Contestant Waiting Room
!
THAT'S RIGHT!
NO WONDER HE LOOKED FAMILIAR...
Chapter ④ Comedy and the Dam
THIS GUY'S A LEGIT GENIUS, MAN.
OR AT THE VERY LEAST, A LEGIT GOOF-BALL.
HE'S A GENIUS GOOF-BALL!!
A GUY EVEN KUNUGI RECOGNIZED AS A GENIUS...?

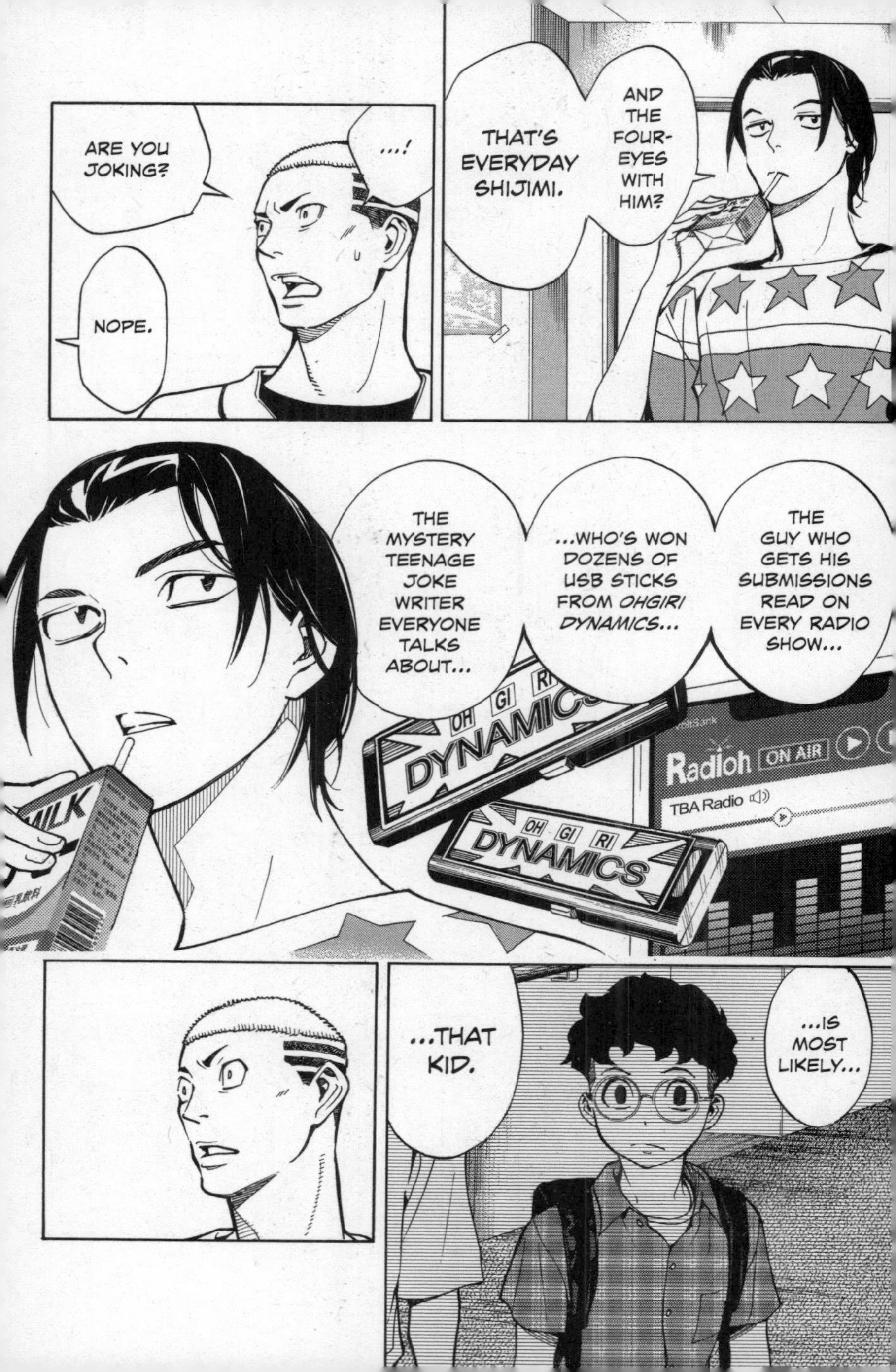
AND THE FOUR-EYES WITH HIM?
THAT'S EVERYDAY SHIJIMI.
...!
ARE YOU JOKING?
NOPE.
THE GUY WHO GETS HIS SUBMISSIONS READ ON EVERY RADIO SHOW...
...WHO'S WON DOZENS OF USB STICKS FROM *OHGIRI DYNAMICS*...
THE MYSTERY TEENAGE JOKE WRITER EVERYONE TALKS ABOUT...
OH GI RI DYNAMICS
OH GI RI DYNAMICS
Radioh ON AIR
TBA Radio
MILK
...IS MOST LIKELY...
...THAT KID.

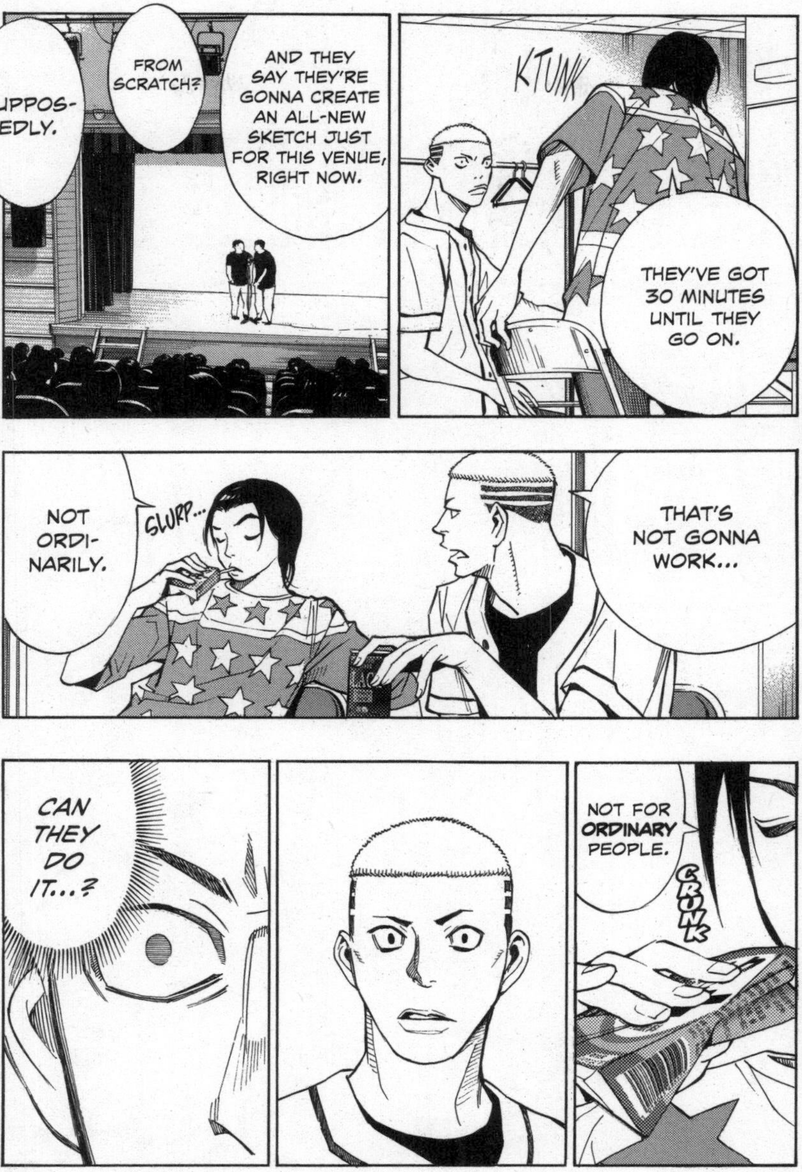
KTUNK
THEY'VE GOT 30 MINUTES UNTIL THEY GO ON.
AND THEY SAY THEY'RE GONNA CREATE AN ALL-NEW SKETCH JUST FOR THIS VENUE, RIGHT NOW.
FROM SCRATCH?
SUPPOS-EDLY.
THAT'S NOT GONNA WORK...
SLURP...
NOT ORDI-NARILY.
NOT FOR **ORDINARY** PEOPLE.
CRUNK
CAN THEY DO IT...?

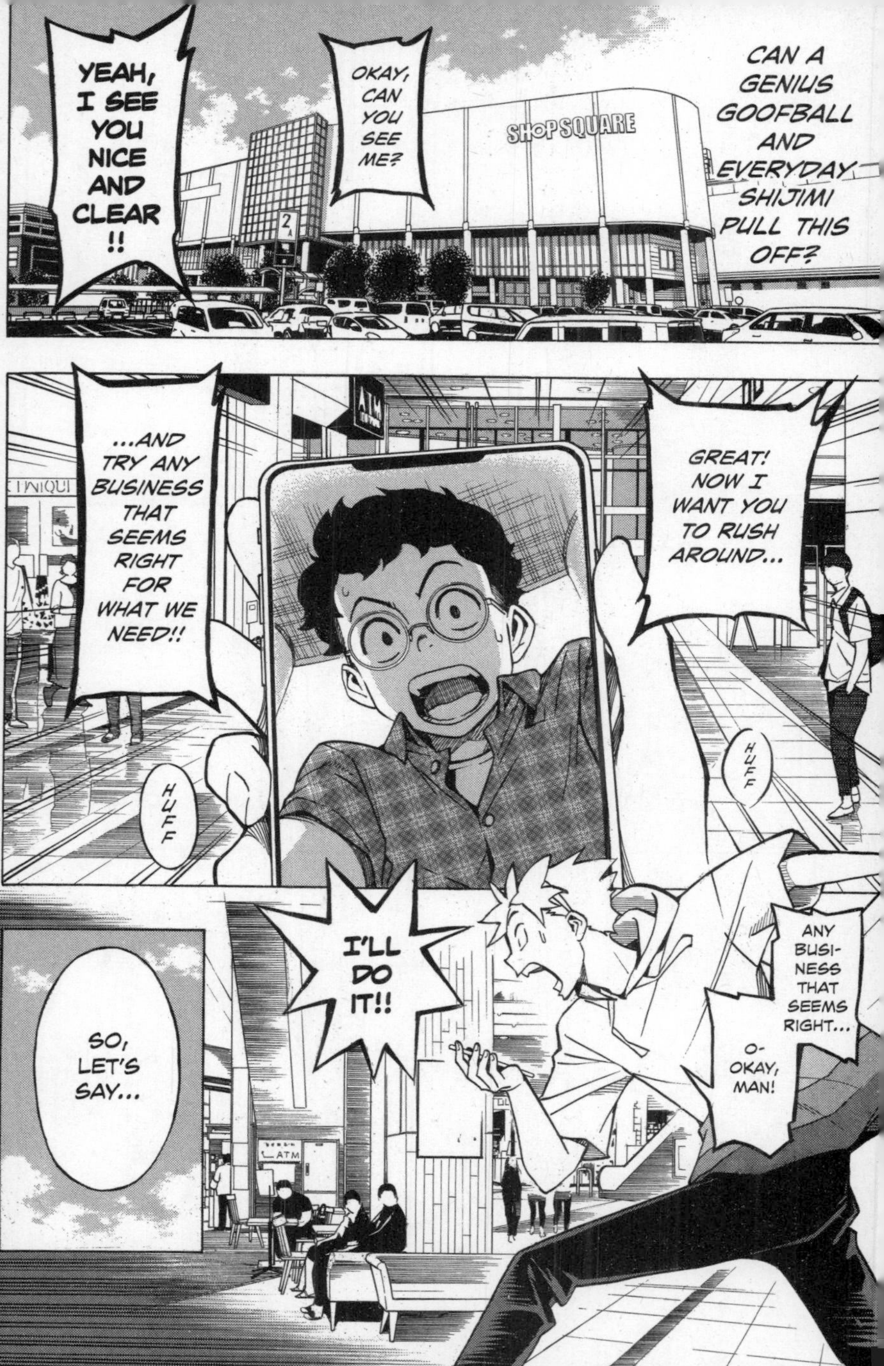
CAN A GENIUS GOOFBALL AND EVERYDAY SHIJIMI PULL THIS OFF?
OKAY, CAN YOU SEE ME?
YEAH, I SEE YOU NICE AND CLEAR!!
SHOPSQUARE
GREAT! NOW I WANT YOU TO RUSH AROUND...
...AND TRY ANY BUSINESS THAT SEEMS RIGHT FOR WHAT WE NEED!!
HUFF
HUFF
ANY BUSI-NESS THAT SEEMS RIGHT...
O-OKAY, MAN!
I'LL DO IT!!
SO, LET'S SAY...

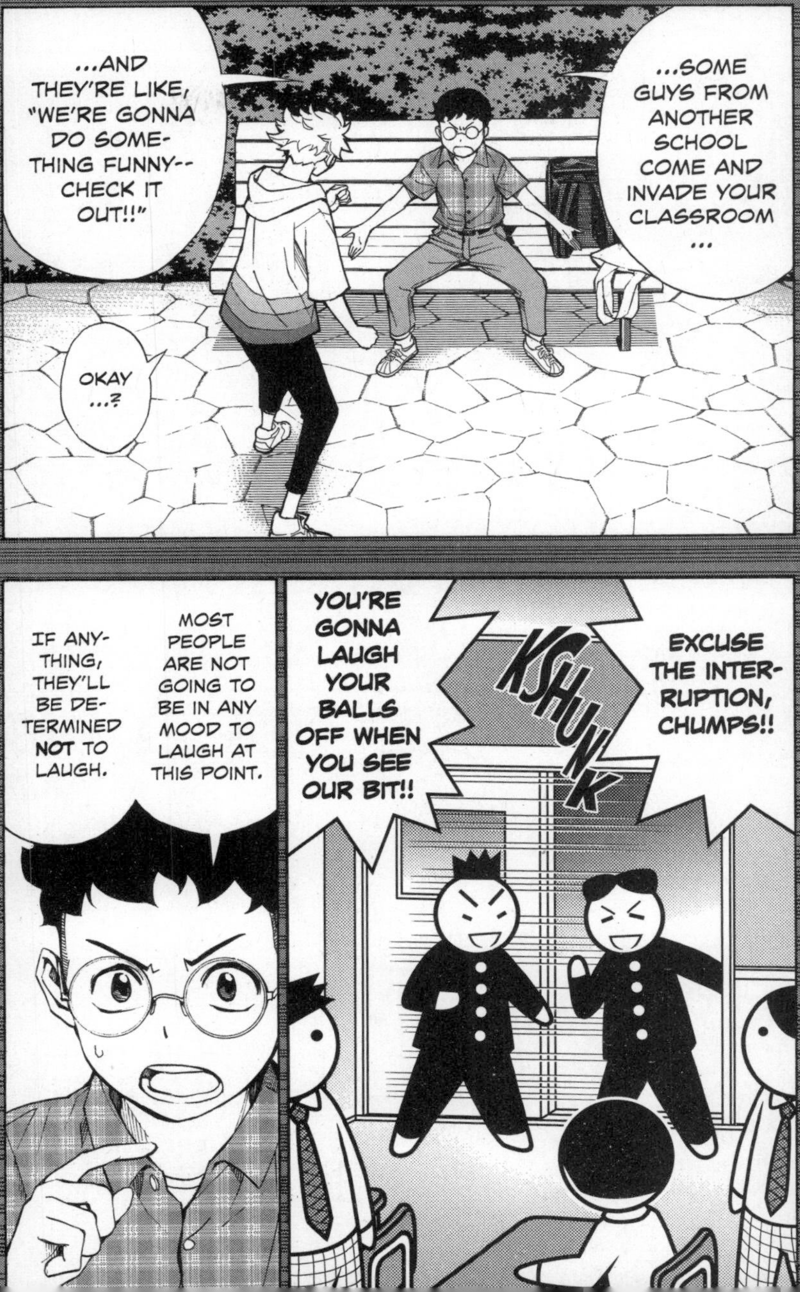
...SOME GUYS FROM ANOTHER SCHOOL COME AND INVADE YOUR CLASSROOM ...
...AND THEY'RE LIKE, "WE'RE GONNA DO SOME-THING FUNNY-- CHECK IT OUT!!"
OKAY ...?
EXCUSE THE INTER-RUPTION, CHUMPS!!
KSHUNK
YOU'RE GONNA LAUGH YOUR BALLS OFF WHEN YOU SEE OUR BIT!!
MOST PEOPLE ARE NOT GOING TO BE IN ANY MOOD TO LAUGH AT THIS POINT.
IF ANY-THING, THEY'LL BE DE-TERMINED **NOT** TO LAUGH.

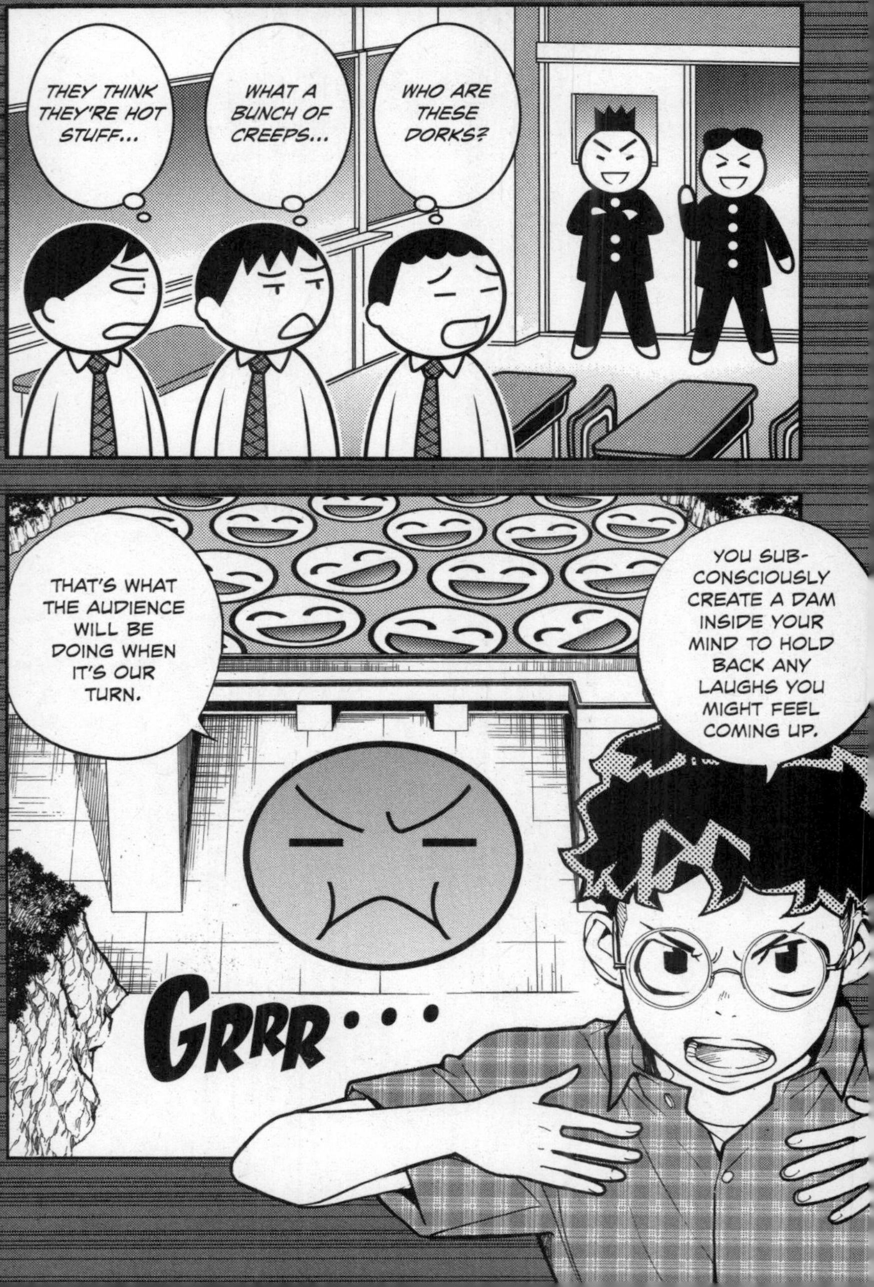
WHO ARE THESE DORKS?
WHAT A BUNCH OF CREEPS...
THEY THINK THEY'RE HOT STUFF...
YOU SUB-CONSCIOUSLY CREATE A DAM INSIDE YOUR MIND TO HOLD BACK ANY LAUGHS YOU MIGHT FEEL COMING UP.
THAT'S WHAT THE AUDIENCE WILL BE DOING WHEN IT'S OUR TURN.
GRRR...

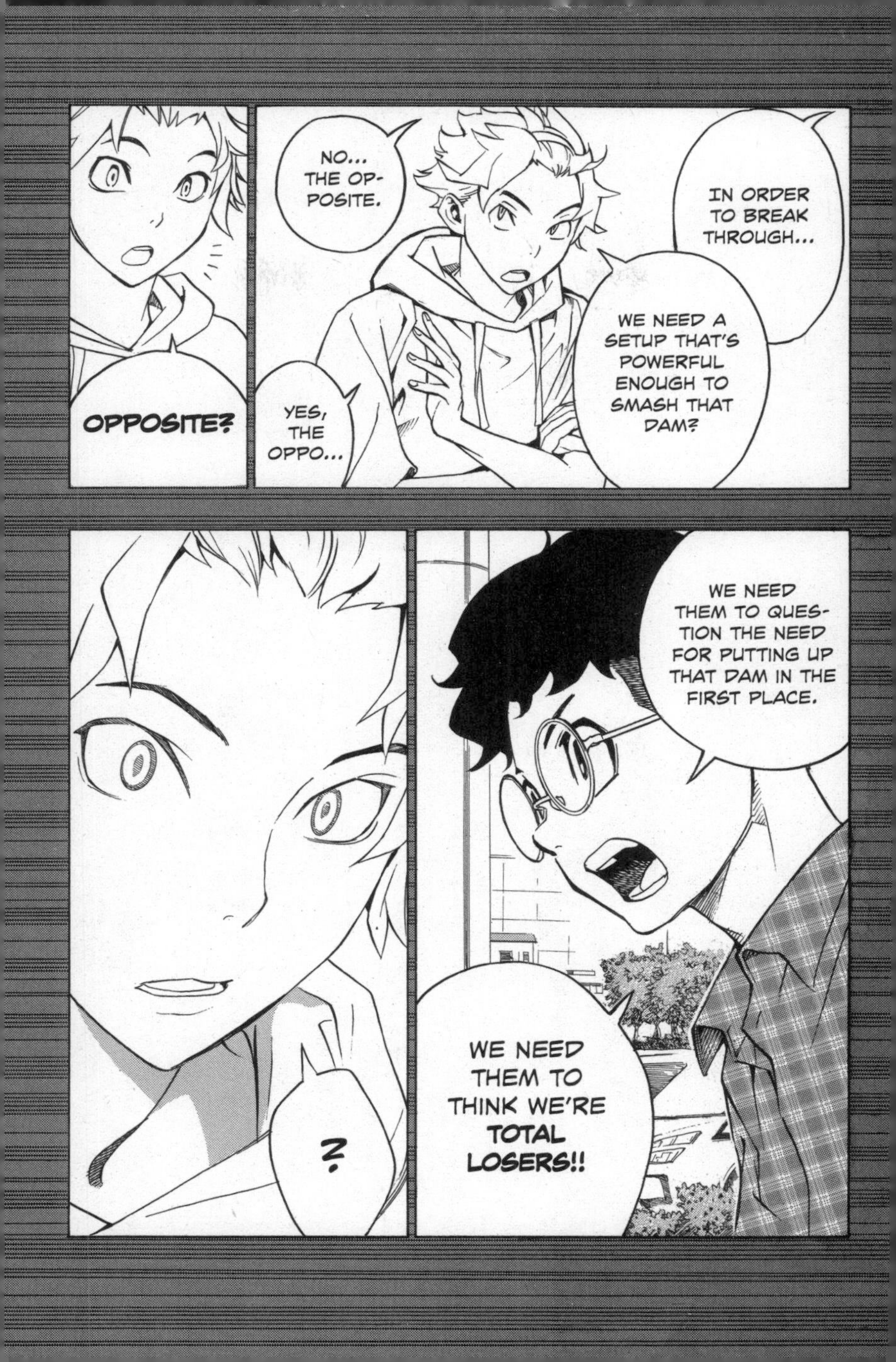
IN ORDER TO BREAK THROUGH...
WE NEED A SETUP THAT'S POWERFUL ENOUGH TO SMASH THAT DAM?
NO... THE OP-POSITE.
YES, THE OPPO...
OPPOSITE?
WE NEED THEM TO QUES-TION THE NEED FOR PUTTING UP THAT DAM IN THE FIRST PLACE.
WE NEED THEM TO THINK WE'RE TOTAL LOSERS!!
?

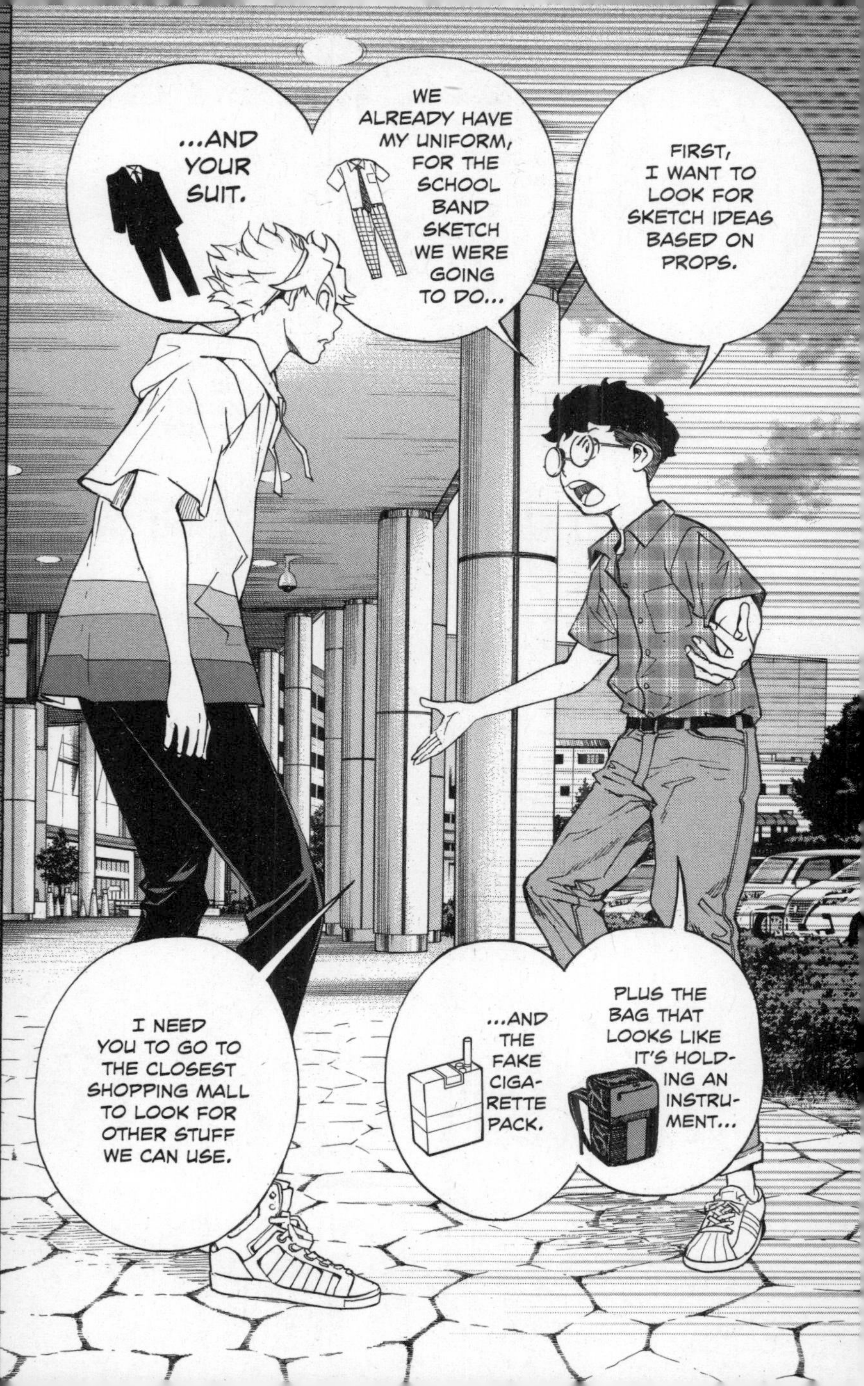
FIRST, I WANT TO LOOK FOR SKETCH IDEAS BASED ON PROPS.
WE ALREADY HAVE MY UNIFORM, FOR THE SCHOOL BAND SKETCH WE WERE GOING TO DO...
...AND YOUR SUIT.
PLUS THE BAG THAT LOOKS LIKE IT'S HOLDING AN INSTRUMENT...
...AND THE FAKE CIGARETTE PACK.
I NEED YOU TO GO TO THE CLOSEST SHOPPING MALL TO LOOK FOR OTHER STUFF WE CAN USE.

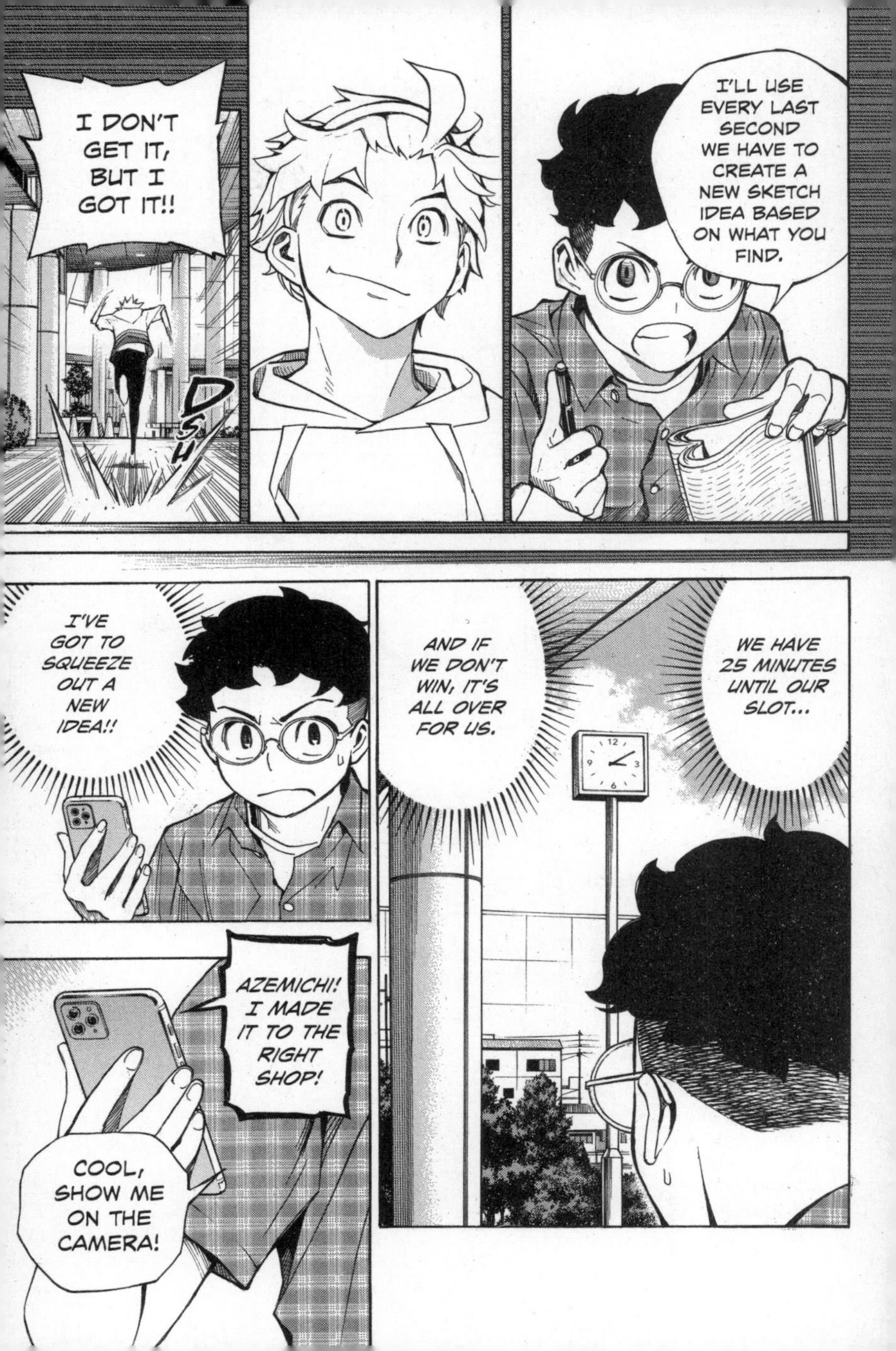
I'LL USE EVERY LAST SECOND WE HAVE TO CREATE A NEW SKETCH IDEA BASED ON WHAT YOU FIND.
I DON'T GET IT, BUT I GOT IT!!
DSH
WE HAVE 25 MINUTES UNTIL OUR SLOT...
AND IF WE DON'T WIN, IT'S ALL OVER FOR US.
I'VE GOT TO SQUEEZE OUT A NEW IDEA!!
AZEMICHI! I MADE IT TO THE RIGHT SHOP!
COOL, SHOW ME ON THE CAMERA!

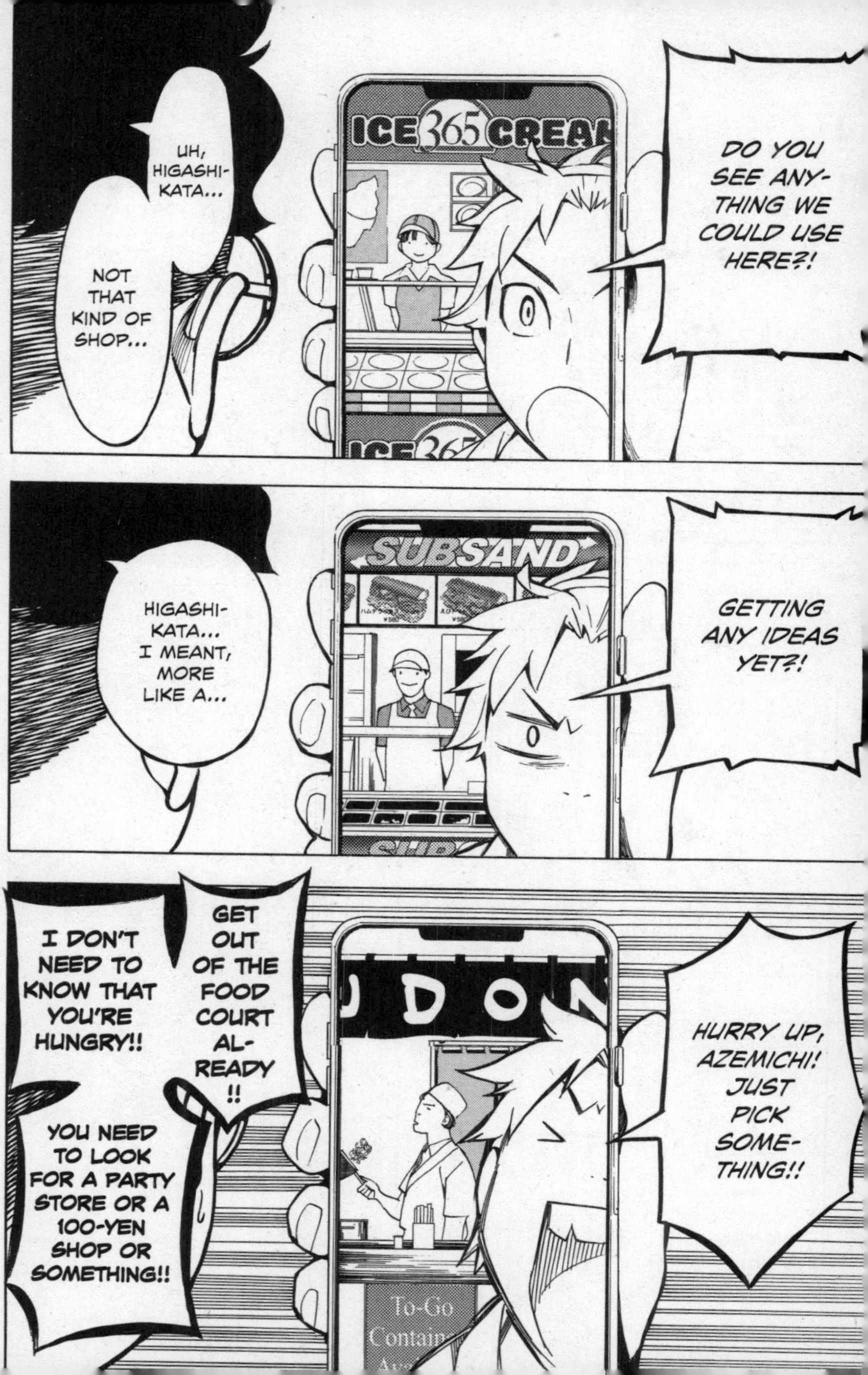
DO YOU SEE ANYTHING WE COULD USE HERE?!
UH, HIGASHIKATA...
NOT THAT KIND OF SHOP...
SUBSAND
GETTING ANY IDEAS YET?!
HIGASHIKATA... I MEANT, MORE LIKE A...
HURRY UP, AZEMICHI! JUST PICK SOMETHING!!
GET OUT OF THE FOOD COURT ALREADY!!
I DON'T NEED TO KNOW THAT YOU'RE HUNGRY!!
YOU NEED TO LOOK FOR A PARTY STORE OR A 100-YEN SHOP OR SOMETHING!!

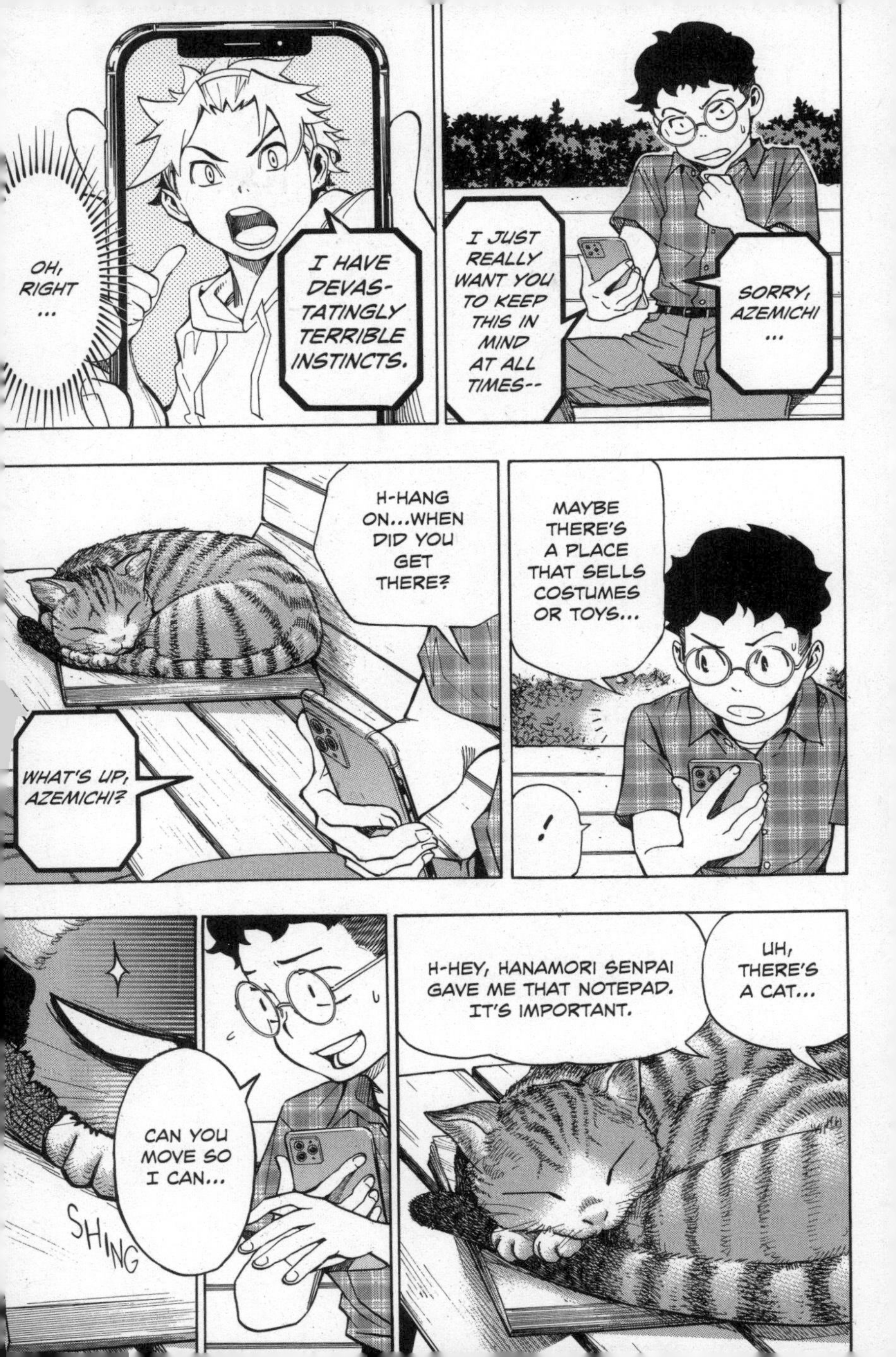
I JUST REALLY WANT YOU TO KEEP THIS IN MIND AT ALL TIMES--
SORRY, AZEMICHI...
I HAVE DEVAS-TATINGLY TERRIBLE INSTINCTS.
OH, RIGHT...
MAYBE THERE'S A PLACE THAT SELLS COSTUMES OR TOYS...
!
H-HANG ON...WHEN DID YOU GET THERE?
WHAT'S UP, AZEMICHI?
UH, THERE'S A CAT...
H-HEY, HANAMORI SENPAI GAVE ME THAT NOTEPAD. IT'S IMPORTANT.
CAN YOU MOVE SO I CAN...
SHING

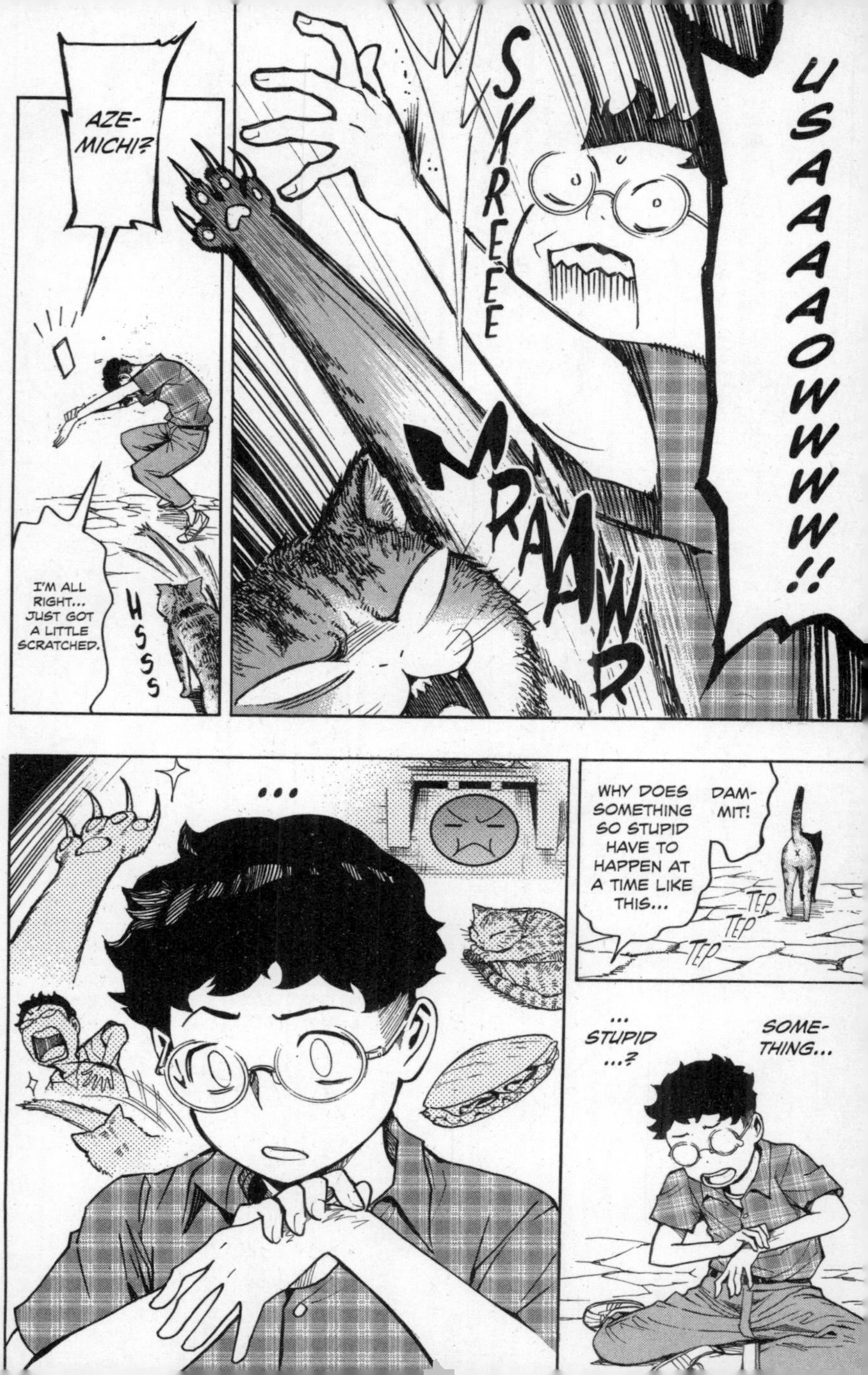
USAAAAAOWWWWWW!!
SKREEE
MRAAAWR
AZE-MICHI!?
I'M ALL RIGHT... JUST GOT A LITTLE SCRATCHED.
HSSS
DAM-MIT!
WHY DOES SOMETHING SO STUPID HAVE TO HAPPEN AT A TIME LIKE THIS...
TEP TEP TEP
SOME-THING...
...STUPID...?
...

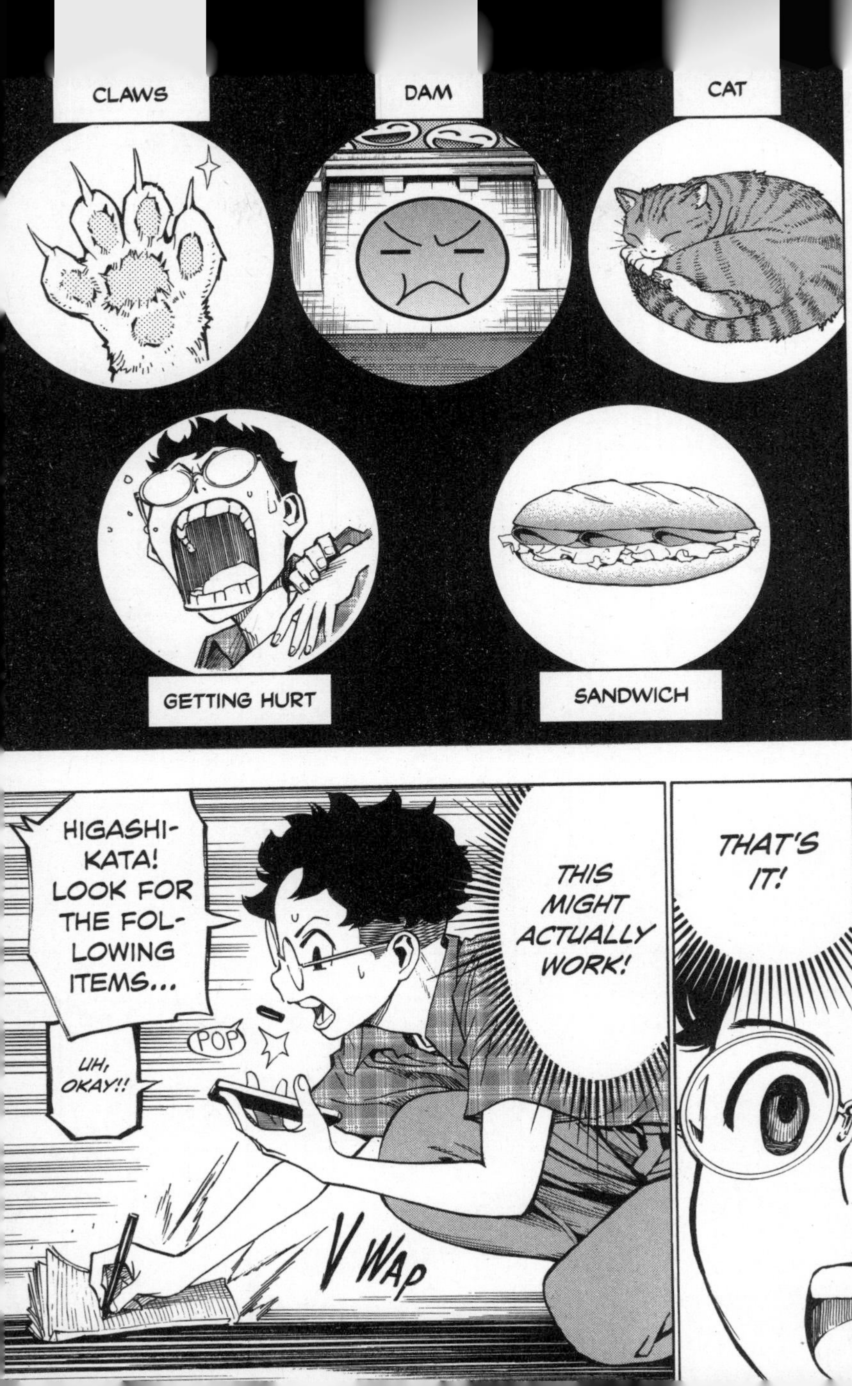
CAT
DAM
CLAWS
SANDWICH
GETTING HURT
THAT'S IT!
THIS MIGHT ACTUALLY WORK!
HIGASHI-KATA! LOOK FOR THE FOL-LOWING ITEMS...
POP
UH, OKAY!!
V WAP

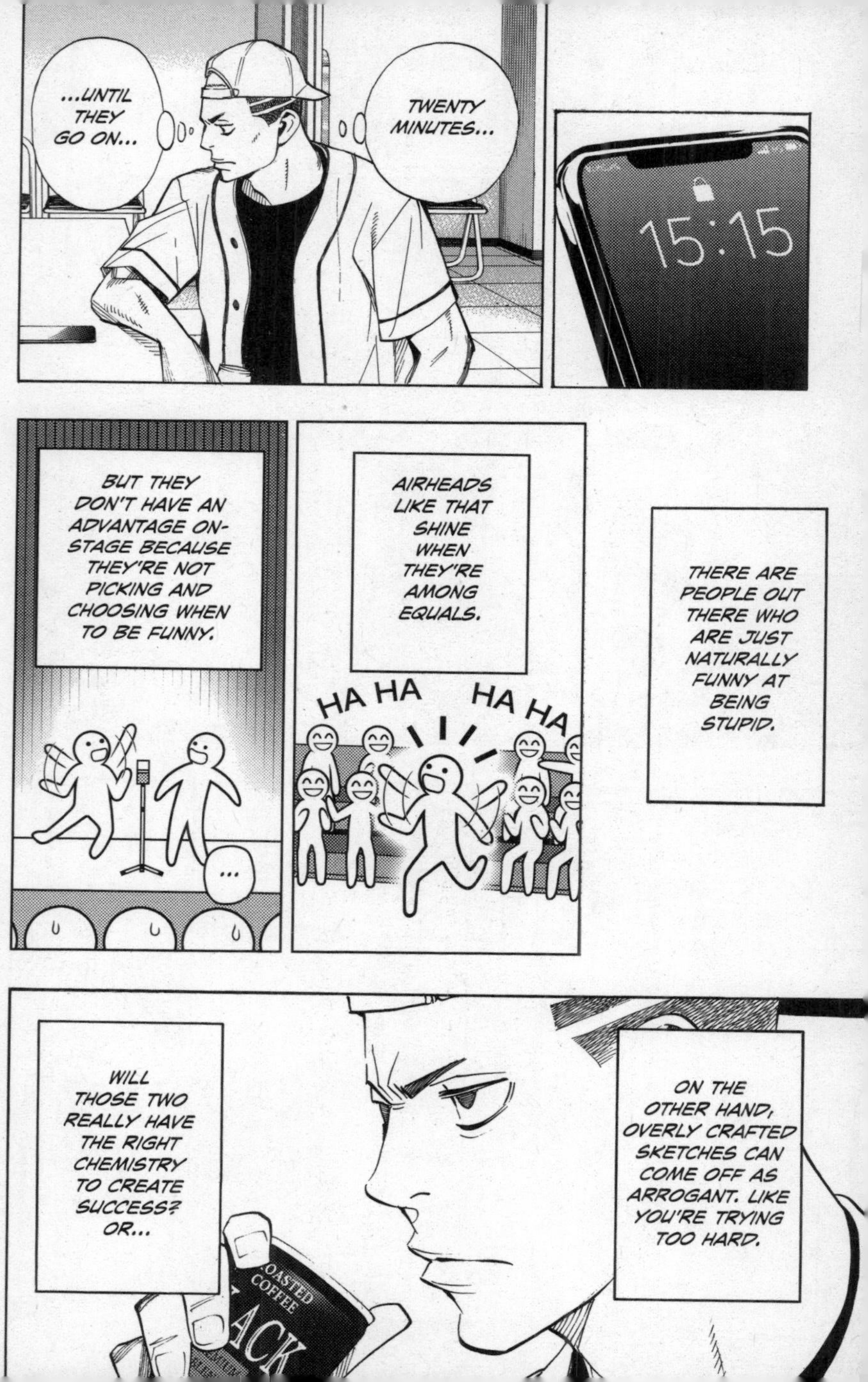
15:15
TWENTY MINUTES...
...UNTIL THEY GO ON...
THERE ARE PEOPLE OUT THERE WHO ARE JUST NATURALLY FUNNY AT BEING STUPID.
AIRHEADS LIKE THAT SHINE WHEN THEY'RE AMONG EQUALS.
HA HA
HA HA
BUT THEY DON'T HAVE AN ADVANTAGE ON-STAGE BECAUSE THEY'RE NOT PICKING AND CHOOSING WHEN TO BE FUNNY.
...
ON THE OTHER HAND, OVERLY CRAFTED SKETCHES CAN COME OFF AS ARROGANT. LIKE YOU'RE TRYING TOO HARD.
WILL THOSE TWO REALLY HAVE THE RIGHT CHEMISTRY TO CREATE SUCCESS? OR...
COFFEE

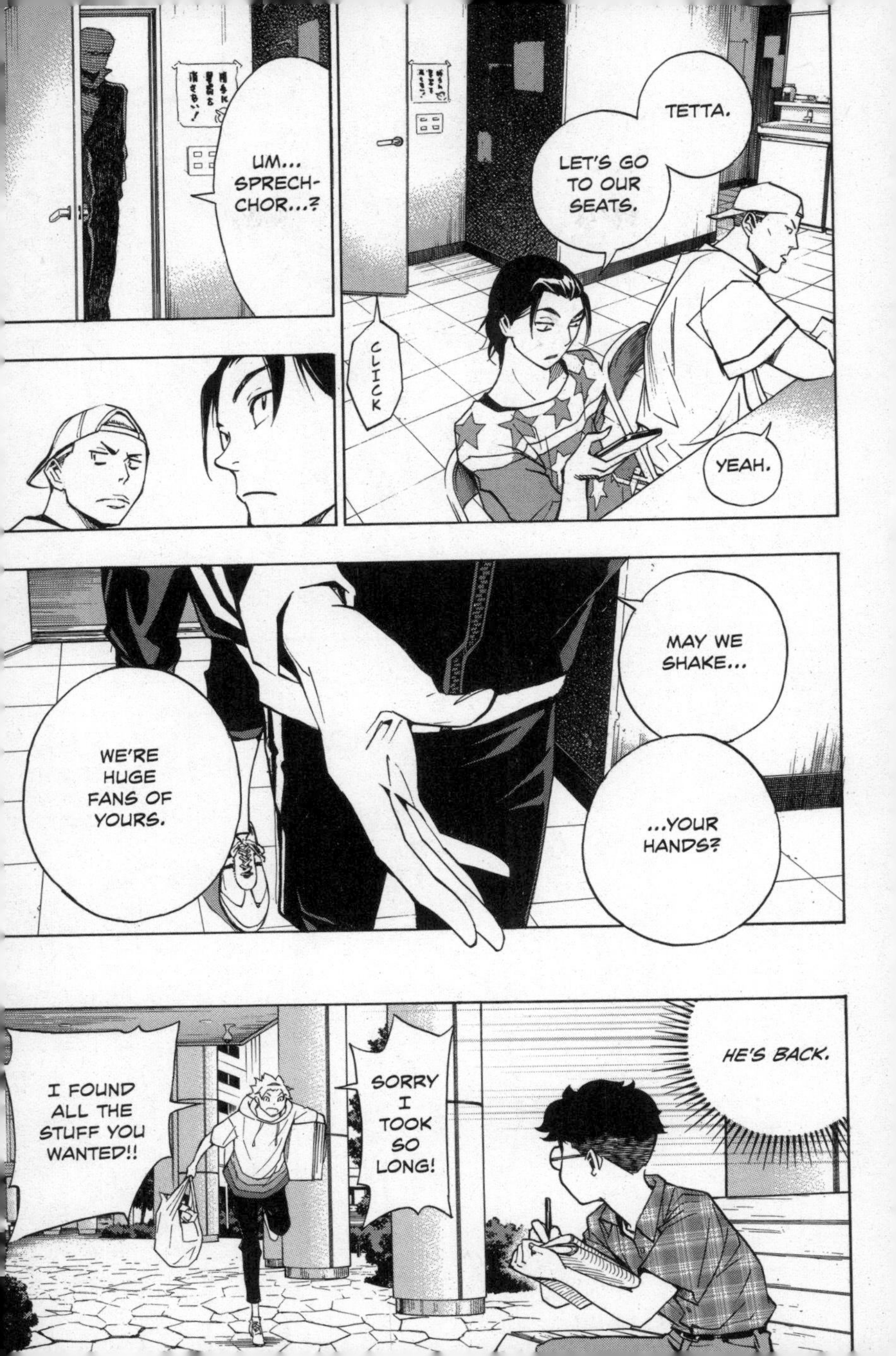
TETTA.
LET'S GO TO OUR SEATS.
CLICK
YEAH.
UM... SPRECH-CHOR...?
MAY WE SHAKE...
...YOUR HANDS?
WE'RE HUGE FANS OF YOURS.
HE'S BACK.
SORRY I TOOK SO LONG!
I FOUND ALL THE STUFF YOU WANTED!!

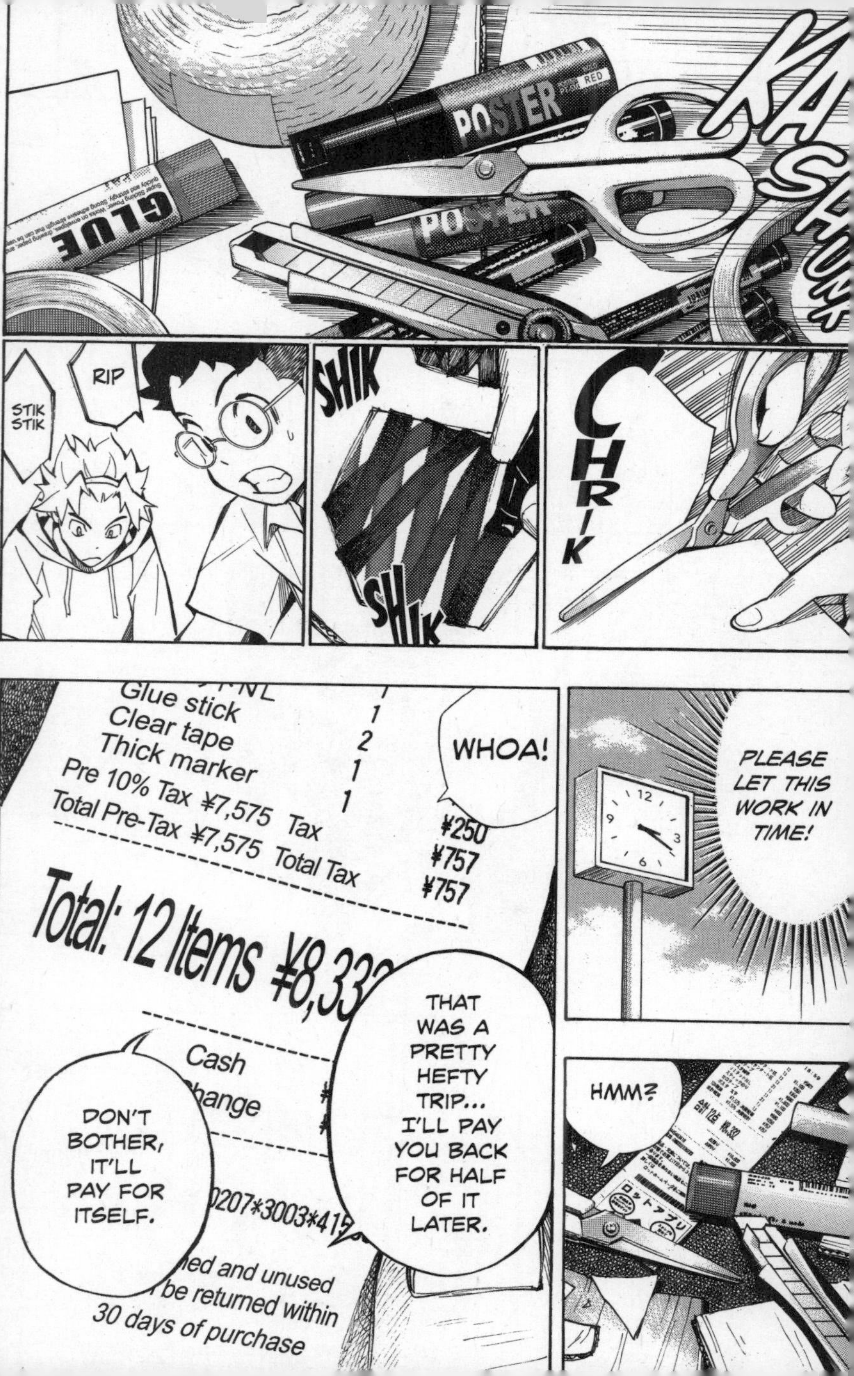
KASHUNK
GLUE
POSTER
RED
POSTER
CHRIK
SHIK
SHIK
RIP
STIK
STIK
PLEASE LET THIS WORK IN TIME!
HMM?
Glue stick 1
Clear tape 2
Thick marker 1
Pre 10% Tax ¥7,575 Tax 1
¥250
Total Pre-Tax ¥7,575 Total Tax ¥757
¥757
Total: 12 Items ¥8,33
Cash
Change
0207*3003*41
ned and unused
be returned within
30 days of purchase
WHOA!
THAT WAS A PRETTY HEFTY TRIP... I'LL PAY YOU BACK FOR HALF OF IT LATER.
DON'T BOTHER, IT'LL PAY FOR ITSELF.

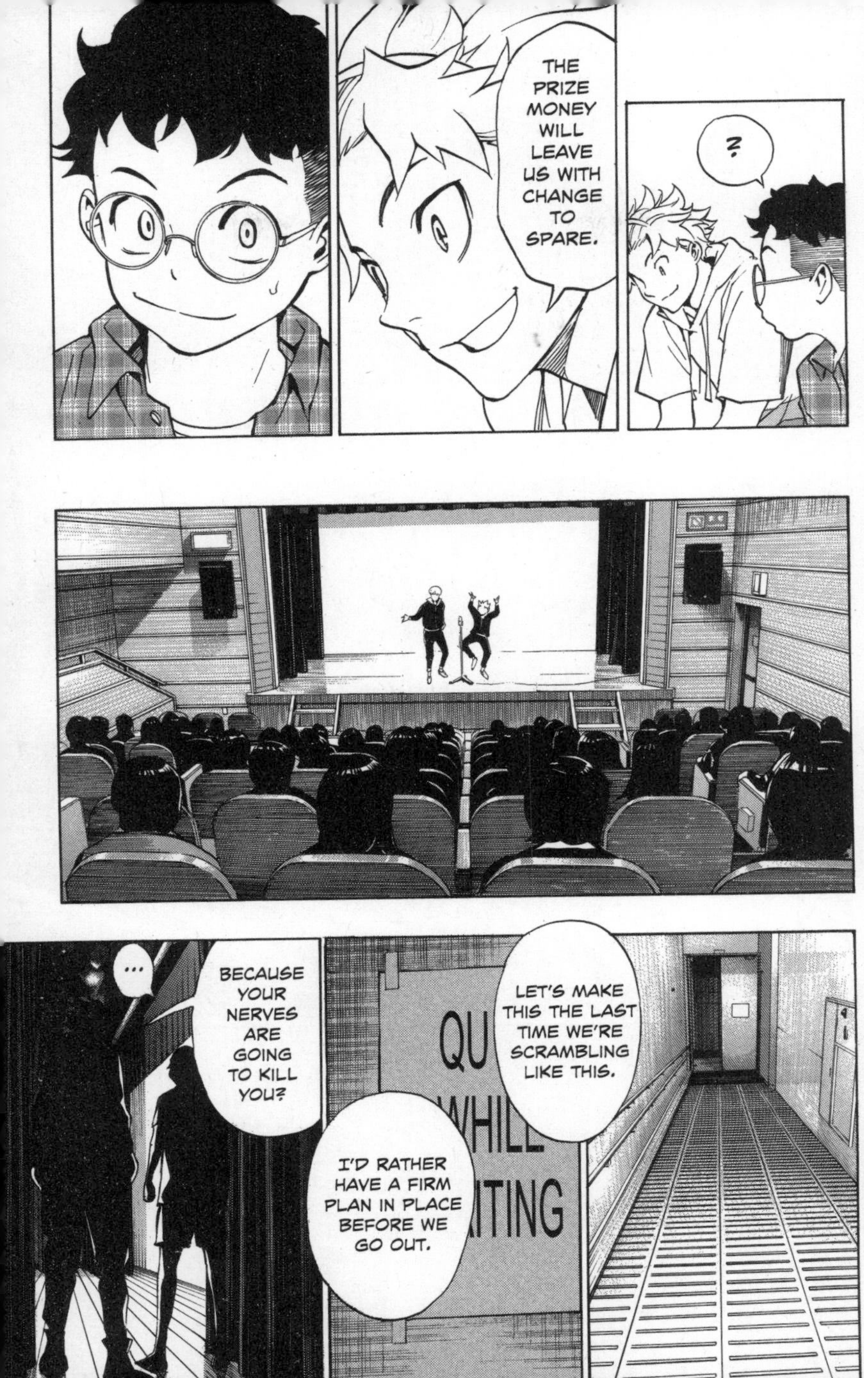
?
THE PRIZE MONEY WILL LEAVE US WITH CHANGE TO SPARE.
LET'S MAKE THIS THE LAST TIME WE'RE SCRAMBLING LIKE THIS.
I'D RATHER HAVE A FIRM PLAN IN PLACE BEFORE WE GO OUT.
...
BECAUSE YOUR NERVES ARE GOING TO KILL YOU?

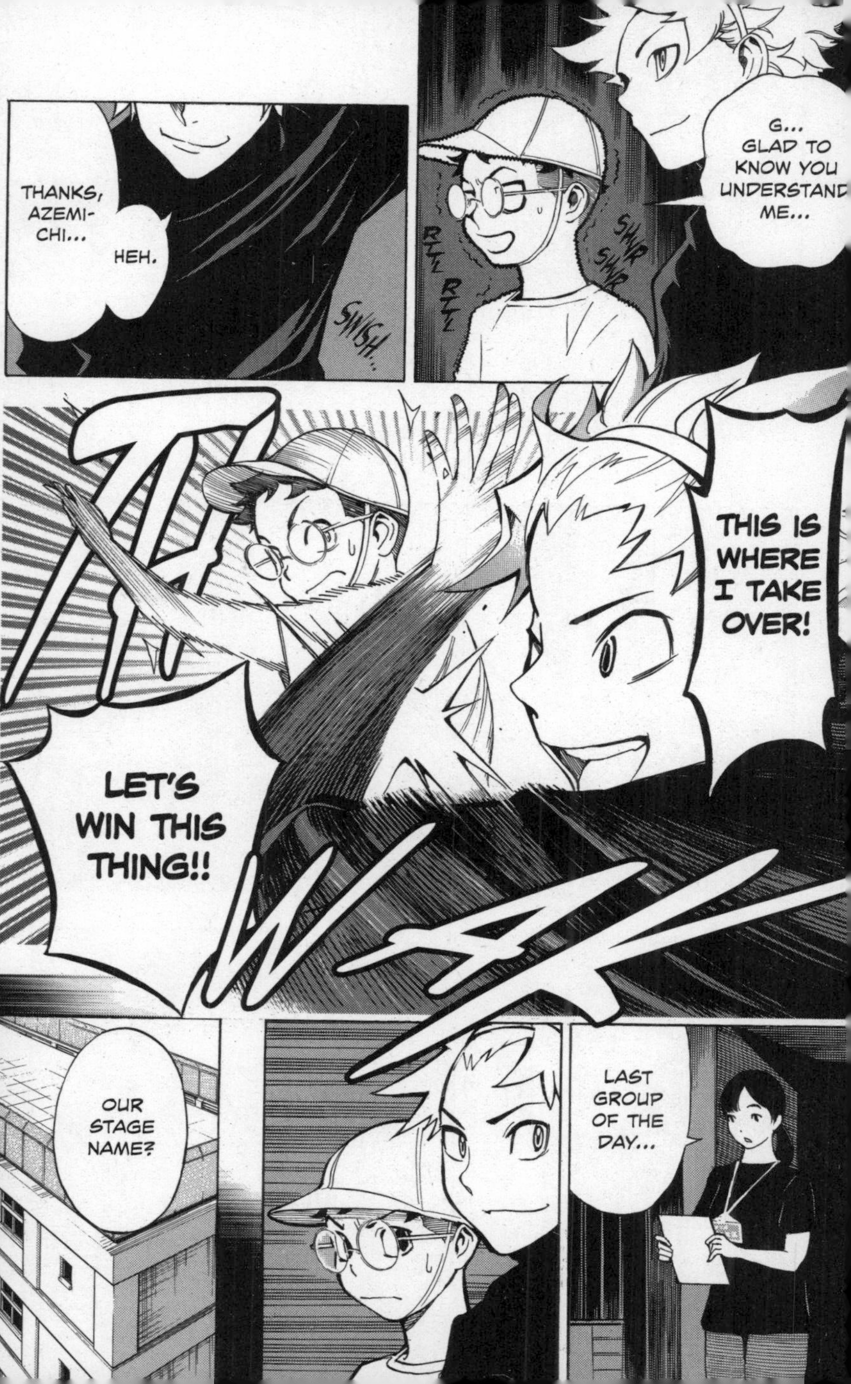
G... GLAD TO KNOW YOU UNDERSTAND ME...
SHIR SHIR
RTTL RTTL
THANKS, AZEMI-CHI...
HEH.
SWISH...
THIS IS WHERE I TAKE OVER!
LET'S WIN THIS THING!!
LAST GROUP OF THE DAY...
OUR STAGE NAME?

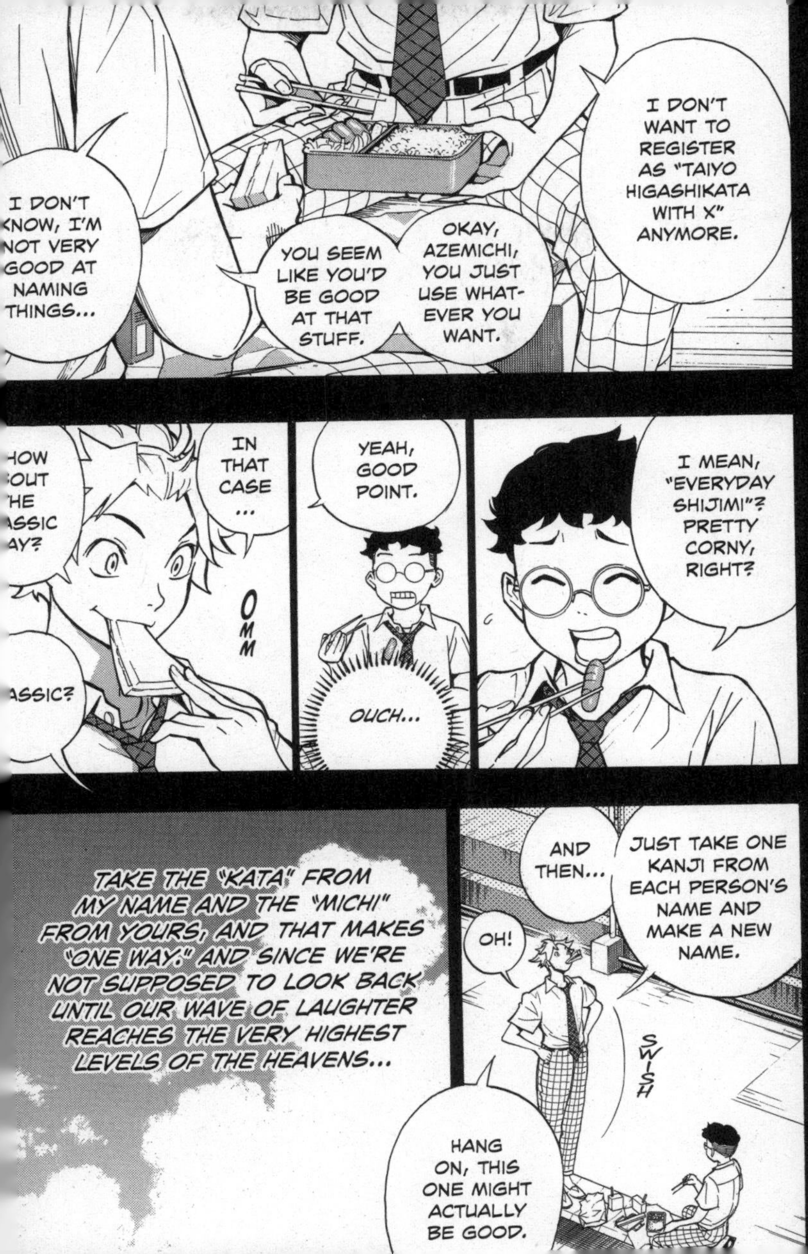
I DON'T WANT TO REGISTER AS "TAIYO HIGASHIKATA WITH X" ANYMORE.
OKAY, AZEMICHI, YOU JUST USE WHATEVER YOU WANT.
YOU SEEM LIKE YOU'D BE GOOD AT THAT STUFF.
I DON'T KNOW, I'M NOT VERY GOOD AT NAMING THINGS...
I MEAN, "EVERYDAY SHIJIMI"? PRETTY CORNY, RIGHT?
YEAH, GOOD POINT.
OMM
OUCH...
IN THAT CASE ...
HOW OUT THE ASSIC AY?
ASSIC?
JUST TAKE ONE KANJI FROM EACH PERSON'S NAME AND MAKE A NEW NAME.
AND THEN...
OH!
SWISH
HANG ON, THIS ONE MIGHT ACTUALLY BE GOOD.
TAKE THE "KATA" FROM MY NAME AND THE "MICHI" FROM YOURS, AND THAT MAKES "ONE WAY." AND SINCE WE'RE NOT SUPPOSED TO LOOK BACK UNTIL OUR WAVE OF LAUGHTER REACHES THE VERY HIGHEST LEVELS OF THE HEAVENS...

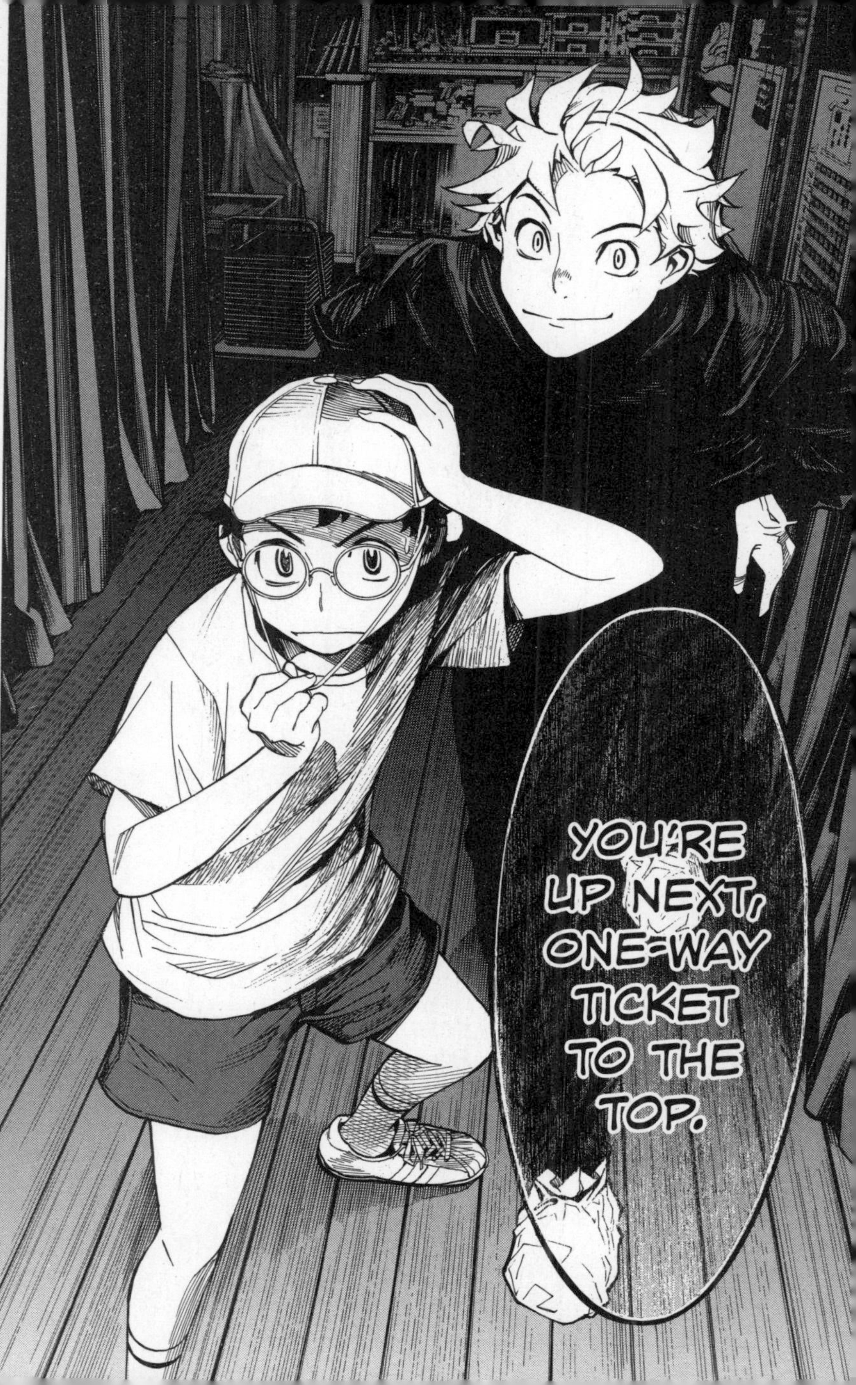
YOU'RE UP NEXT, ONE-WAY TICKET TO THE TOP.

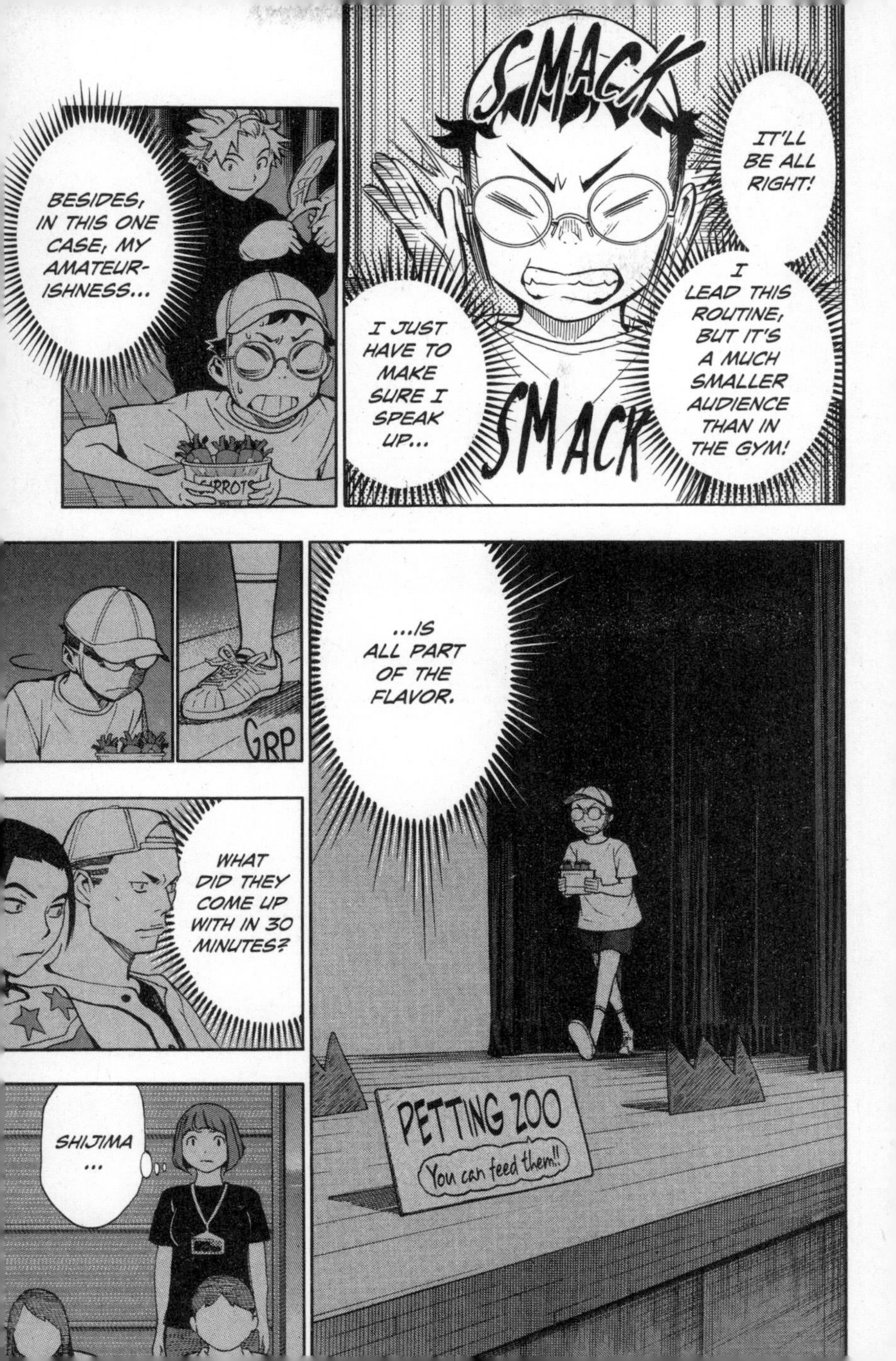
SMACK
IT'LL BE ALL RIGHT!
I LEAD THIS ROUTINE, BUT IT'S A MUCH SMALLER AUDIENCE THAN IN THE GYM!
I JUST HAVE TO MAKE SURE I SPEAK UP...
SMACK
BESIDES, IN THIS ONE CASE, MY AMATEUR-ISHNESS...
...IS ALL PART OF THE FLAVOR.
PETTING ZOO
You can feed them!!
GRP
WHAT DID THEY COME UP WITH IN 30 MINUTES?
SHIJIMA ...

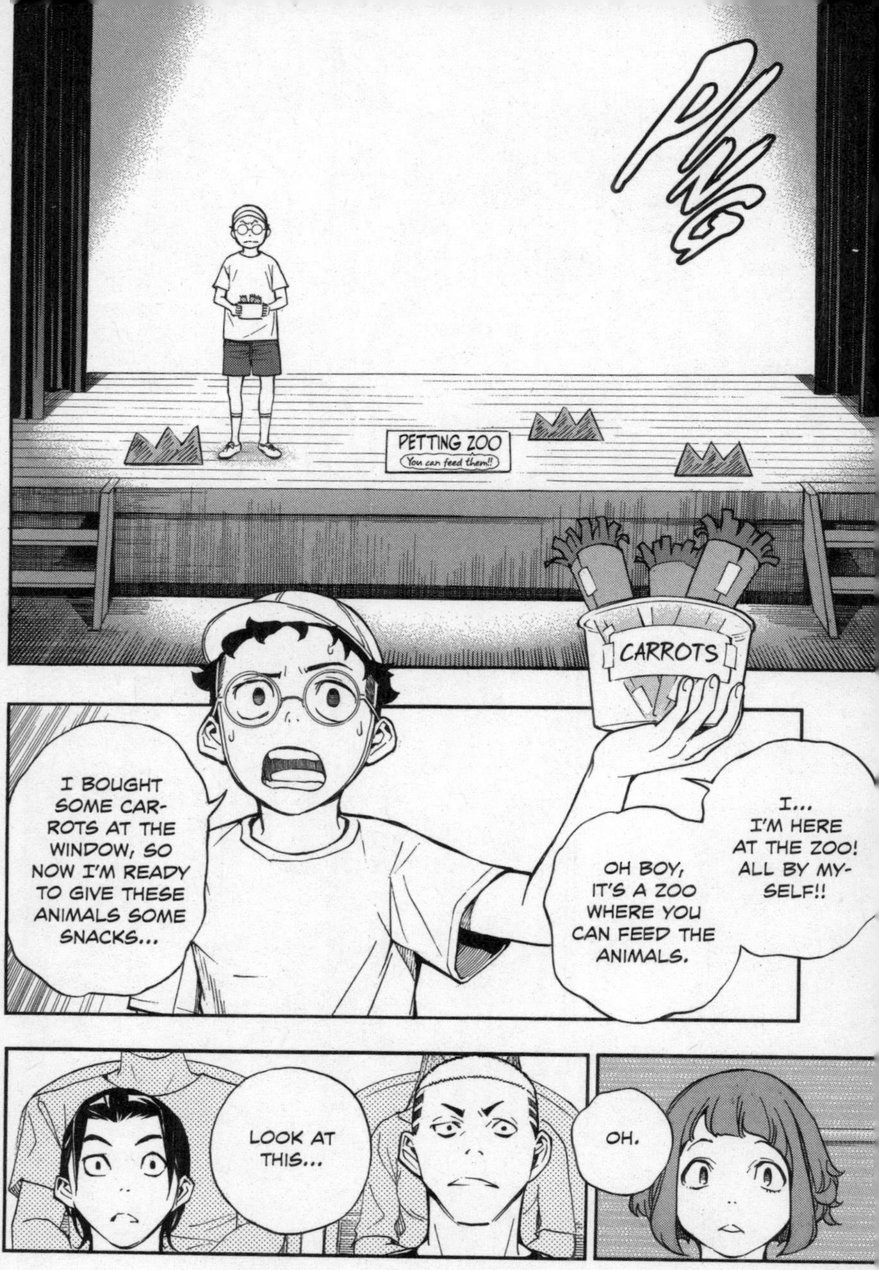
PLING
PETTING ZOO
You can feed them!!
CARROTS
I... I'M HERE AT THE ZOO! ALL BY MYSELF!!
OH BOY, IT'S A ZOO WHERE YOU CAN FEED THE ANIMALS.
I BOUGHT SOME CARROTS AT THE WINDOW, SO NOW I'M READY TO GIVE THESE ANIMALS SOME SNACKS...
OH.
LOOK AT THIS...

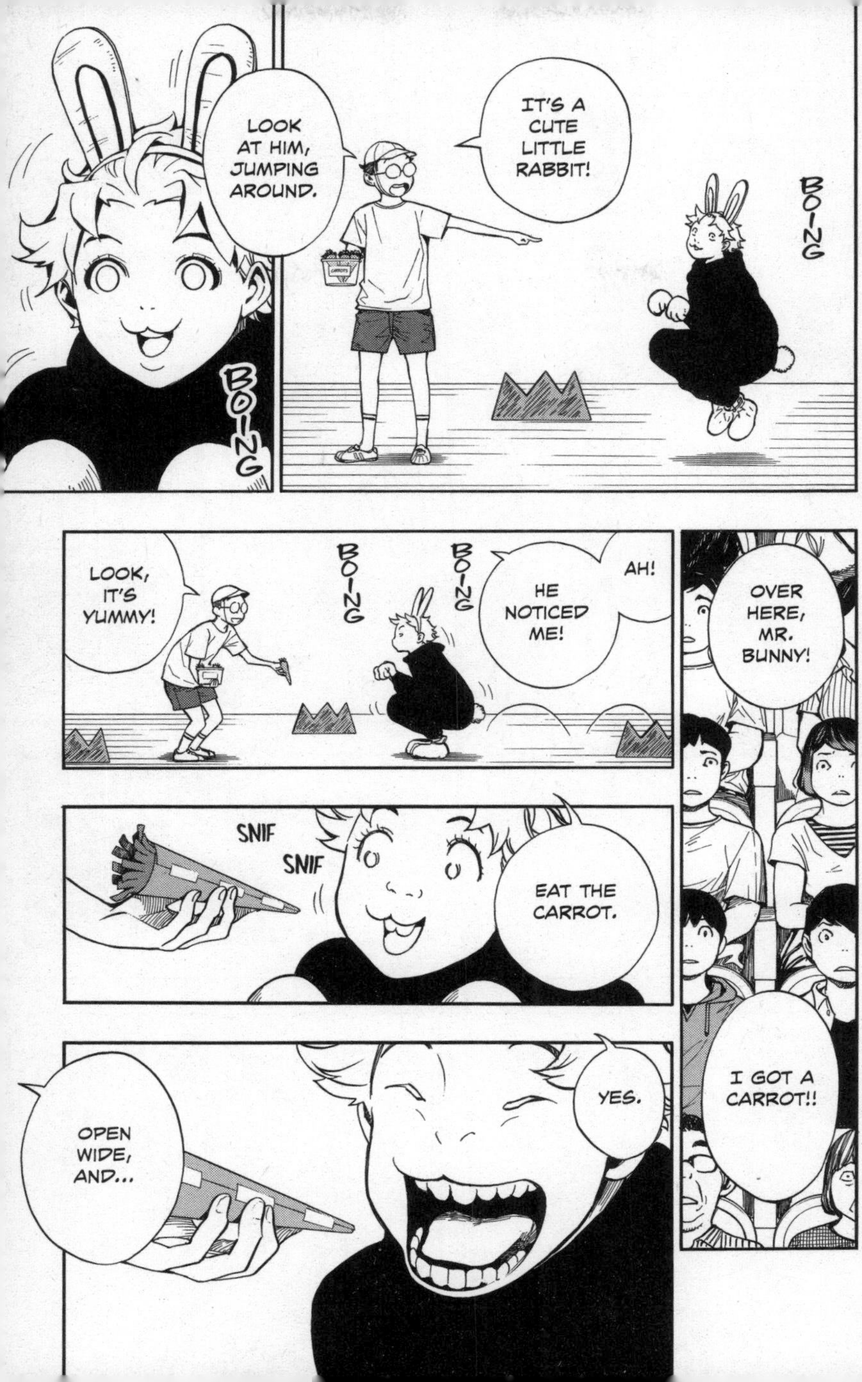
BOING
IT'S A CUTE LITTLE RABBIT!
LOOK AT HIM, JUMPING AROUND.
BOING
OVER HERE, MR. BUNNY!
I GOT A CARROT!!
AH!
HE NOTICED ME!
BOING
BOING
LOOK, IT'S YUMMY!
EAT THE CARROT.
SNIF
SNIF
YES.
OPEN WIDE, AND...

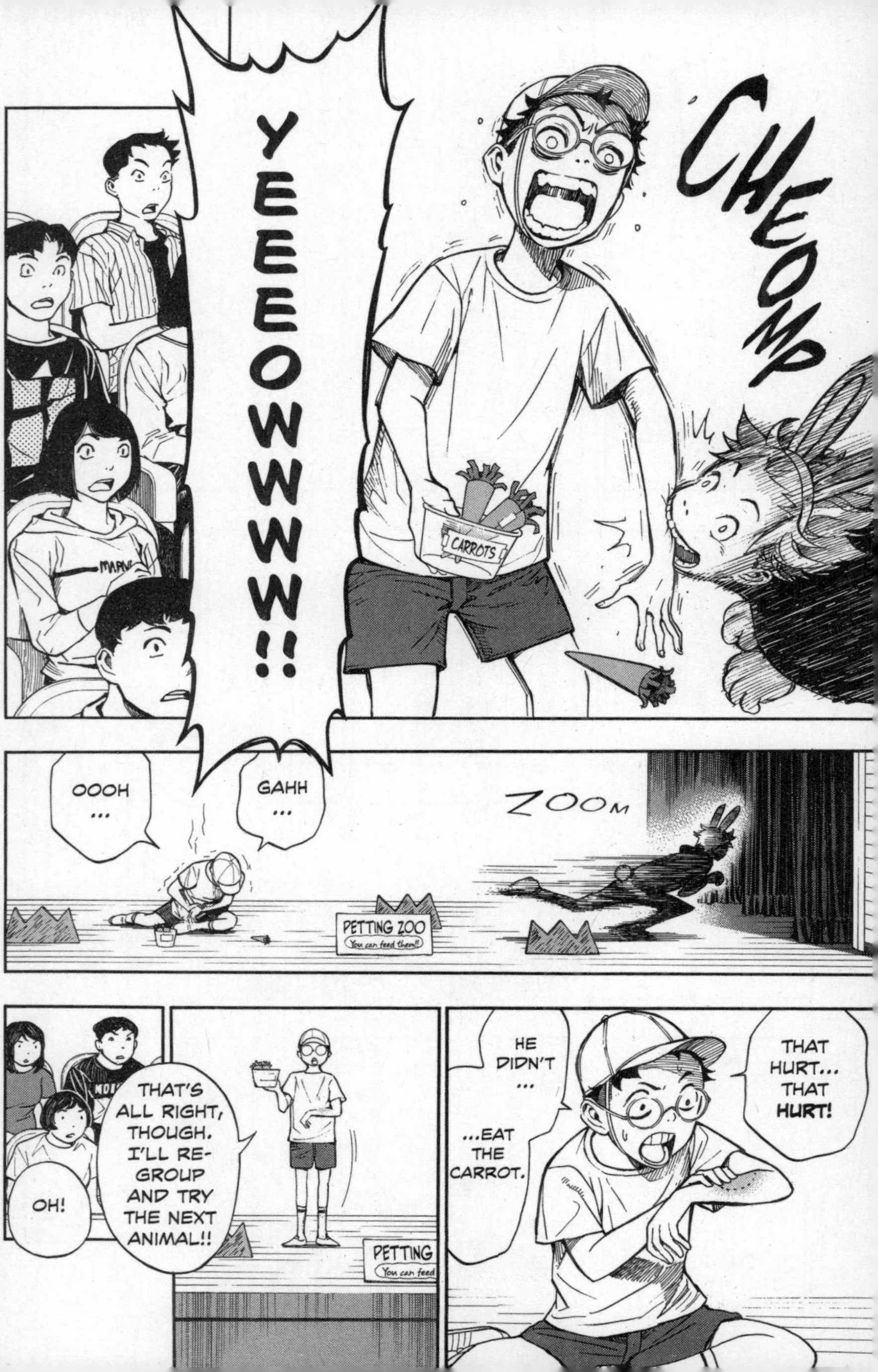
CHEOMP
YEEEOWWWWW!!
CARROTS
ZOOM
GAHH ...
OOOH ...
PETTING ZOO
You can feed them!!
THAT HURT... THAT **HURT!**
HE DIDN'T ...
...EAT THE CARROT.
THAT'S ALL RIGHT, THOUGH. I'LL RE-GROUP AND TRY THE NEXT ANIMAL!!
PETTING
You can feed
OH!

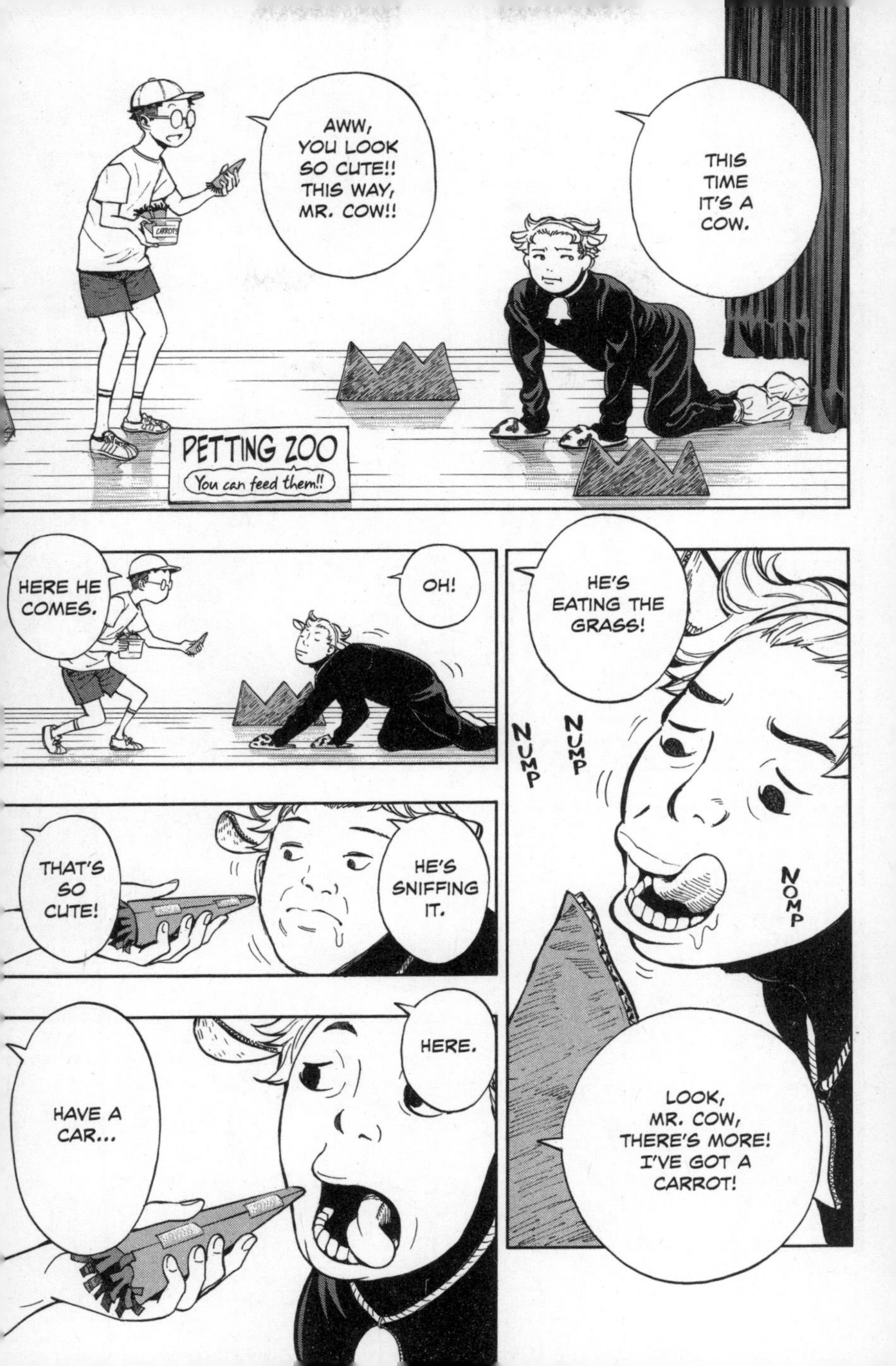
THIS TIME IT'S A COW.
AWW, YOU LOOK SO CUTE!! THIS WAY, MR. COW!!
CARROTS
PETTING ZOO
You can feed them!!
HE'S EATING THE GRASS!
NUMP NUMP
NOMP
LOOK, MR. COW, THERE'S MORE! I'VE GOT A CARROT!
OH!
HERE HE COMES.
HE'S SNIFFING IT.
THAT'S SO CUTE!
HERE.
HAVE A CAR...

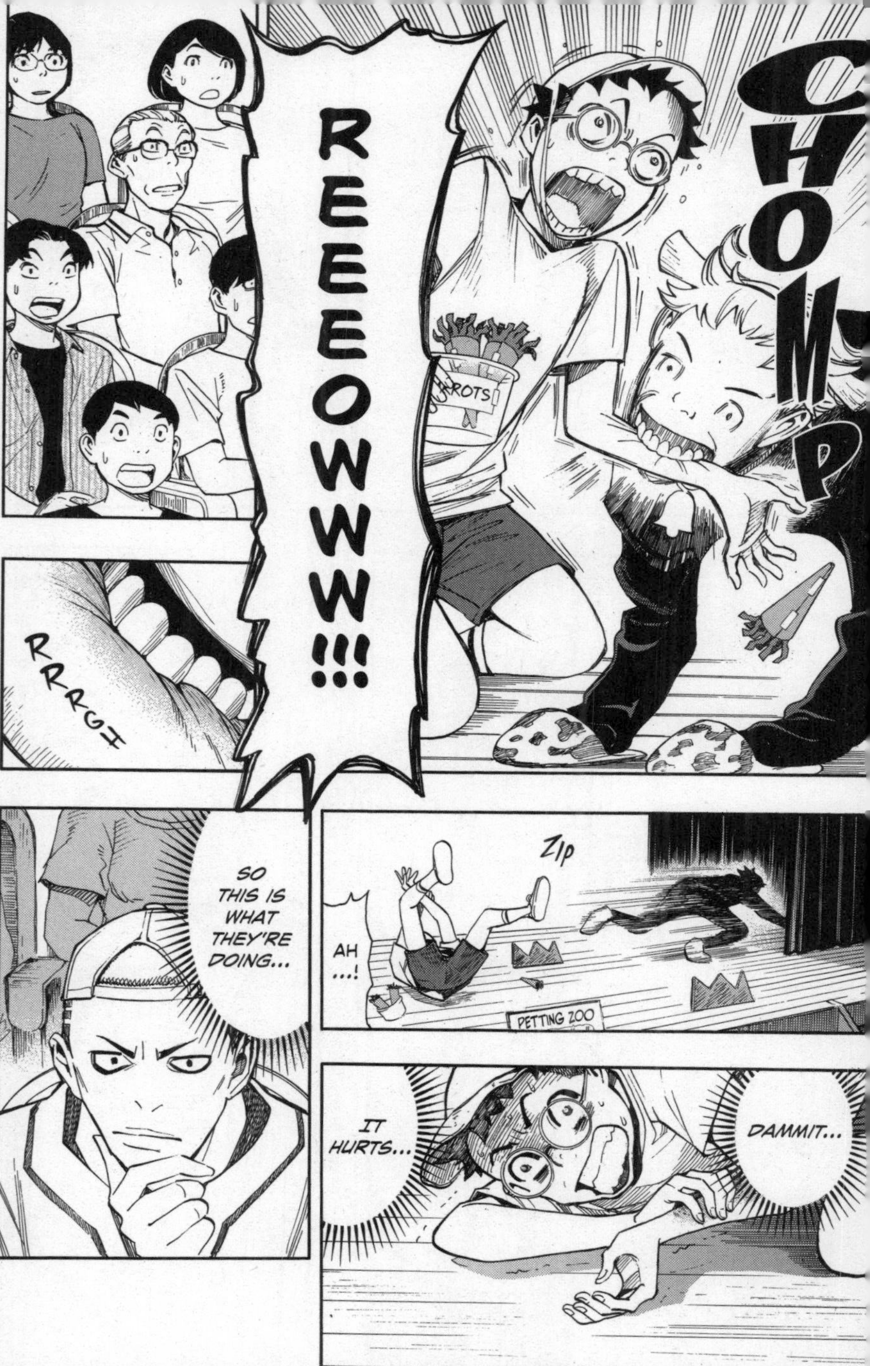
CHOMP
REEEOWWW!!!
RRRGH
ZIP
AH ...!
PETTING ZOO
DAMMIT...
IT HURTS...
SO THIS IS WHAT THEY'RE DOING...

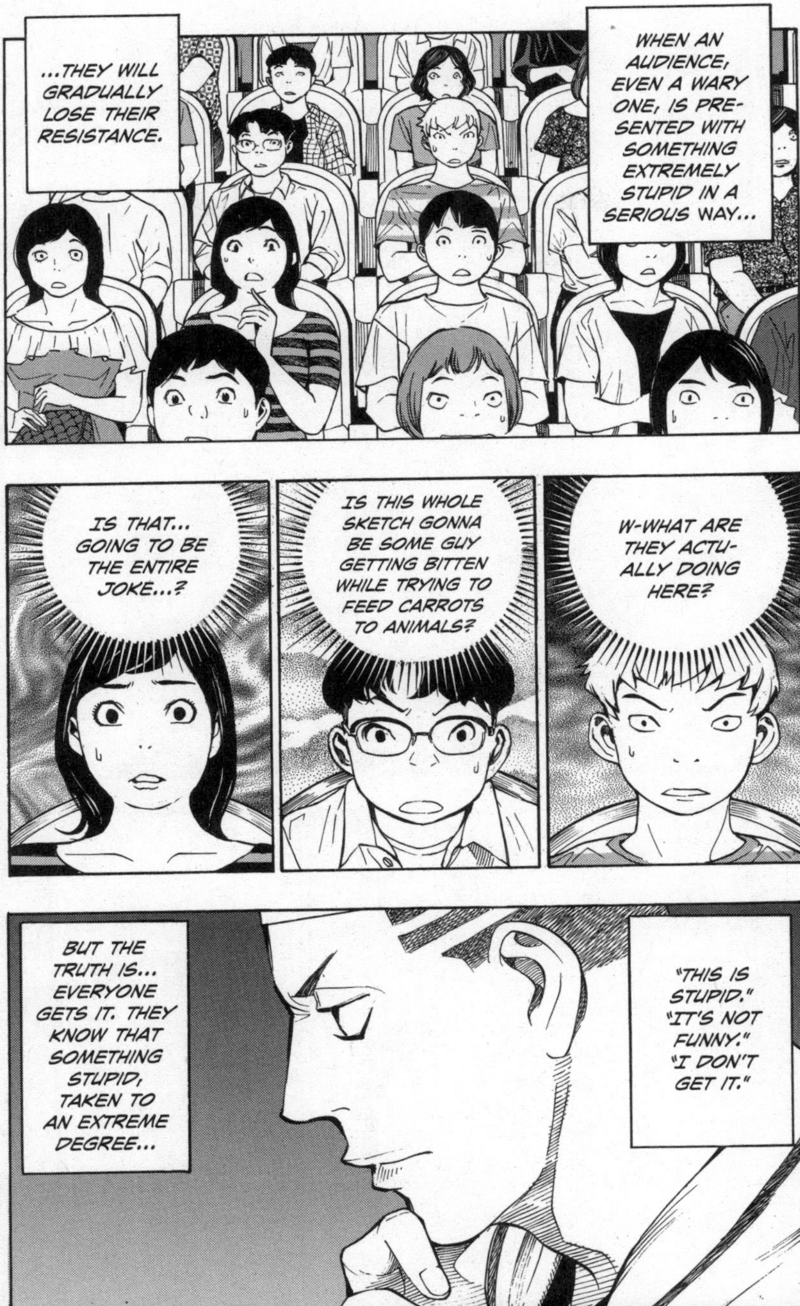
WHEN AN AUDIENCE, EVEN A WARY ONE, IS PRE-SENTED WITH SOMETHING EXTREMELY STUPID IN A SERIOUS WAY...
...THEY WILL GRADUALLY LOSE THEIR RESISTANCE.
W-WHAT ARE THEY ACTU-ALLY DOING HERE?
IS THIS WHOLE SKETCH GONNA BE SOME GUY GETTING BITTEN WHILE TRYING TO FEED CARROTS TO ANIMALS?
IS THAT... GOING TO BE THE ENTIRE JOKE...?
"THIS IS STUPID." "IT'S NOT FUNNY." "I DON'T GET IT."
BUT THE TRUTH IS... EVERYONE GETS IT. THEY KNOW THAT SOMETHING STUPID, TAKEN TO AN EXTREME DEGREE...

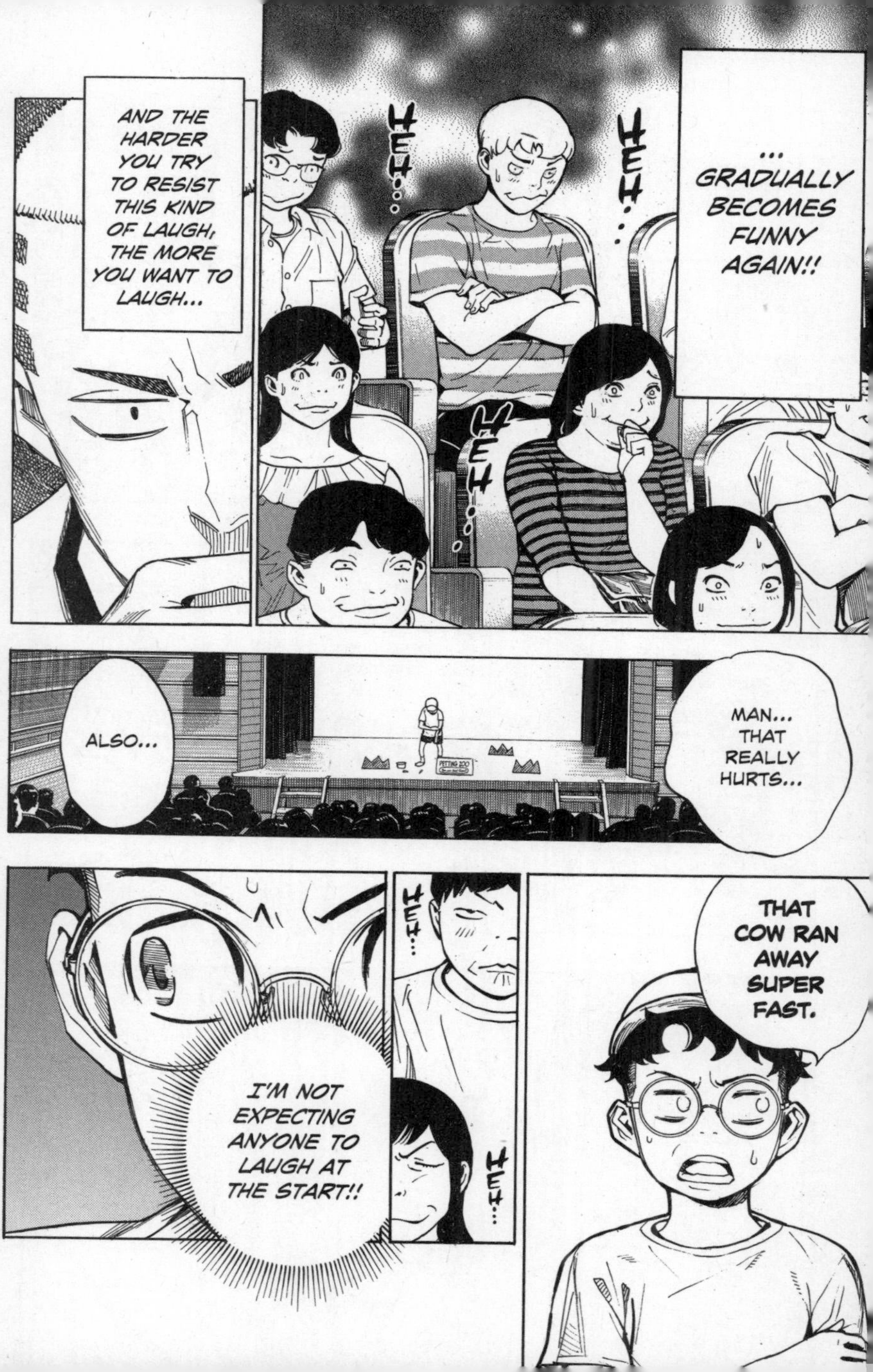
...GRADUALLY BECOMES FUNNY AGAIN!!
HEH...
HEH...
HEH...
AND THE HARDER YOU TRY TO RESIST THIS KIND OF LAUGH, THE MORE YOU WANT TO LAUGH...
MAN... THAT REALLY HURTS...
PETTING ZOO
ALSO...
THAT COW RAN AWAY SUPER FAST.
HEH...
HEH...
I'M NOT EXPECTING ANYONE TO LAUGH AT THE START!!

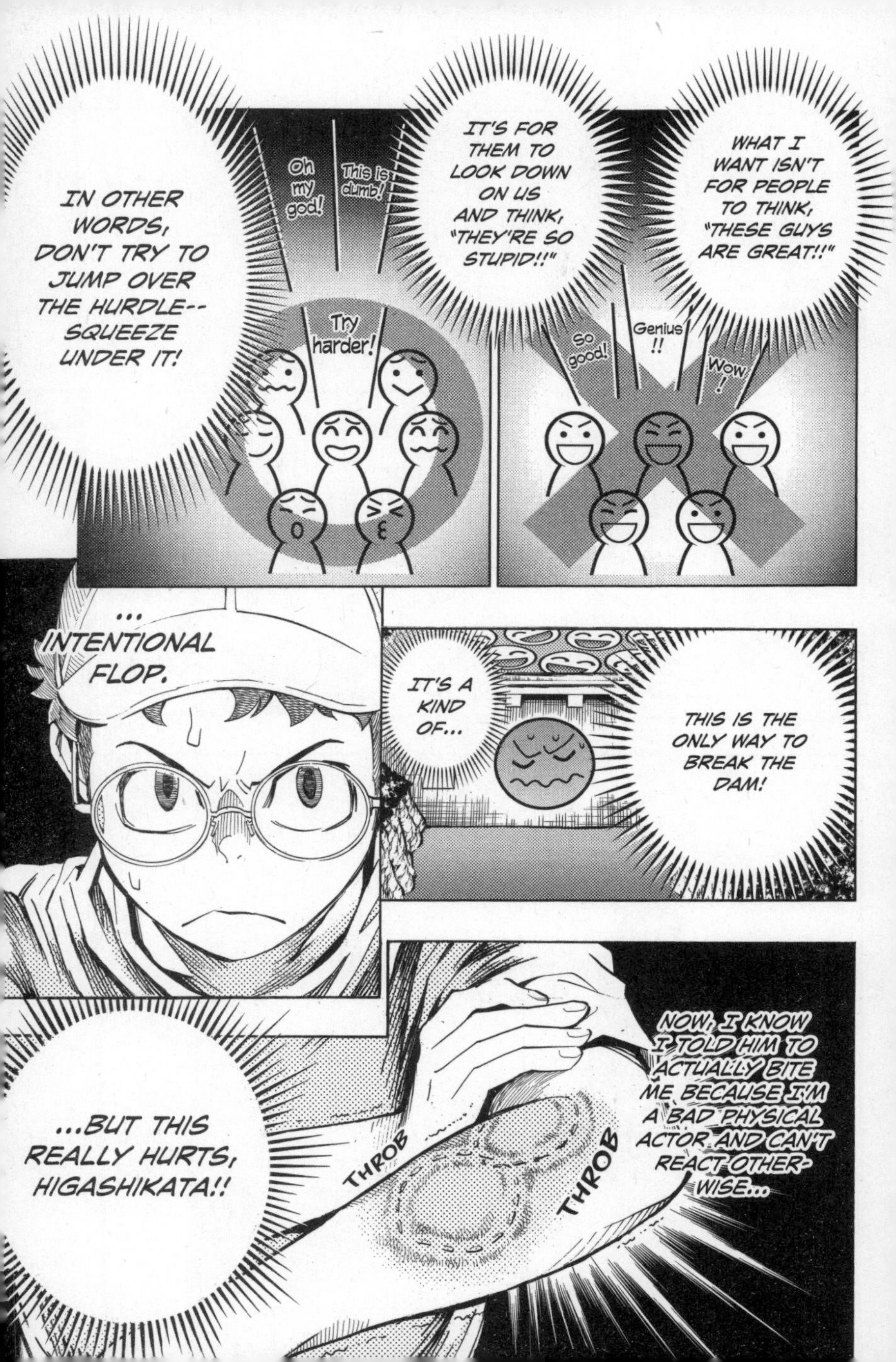
WHAT I WANT ISN'T FOR PEOPLE TO THINK, "THESE GUYS ARE GREAT!!"
Wow!
Genius!!
So good!
IT'S FOR THEM TO LOOK DOWN ON US AND THINK, "THEY'RE SO STUPID!!"
This is dumb!
Oh my god!
Try harder!
IN OTHER WORDS, DON'T TRY TO JUMP OVER THE HURDLE-- SQUEEZE UNDER IT!
THIS IS THE ONLY WAY TO BREAK THE DAM!
IT'S A KIND OF...
... INTENTIONAL FLOP.
NOW, I KNOW I TOLD HIM TO ACTUALLY BITE ME BECAUSE I'M A BAD PHYSICAL ACTOR AND CAN'T REACT OTHER-WISE...
THROB
THROB
...BUT THIS REALLY HURTS, HIGASHIKATA!!

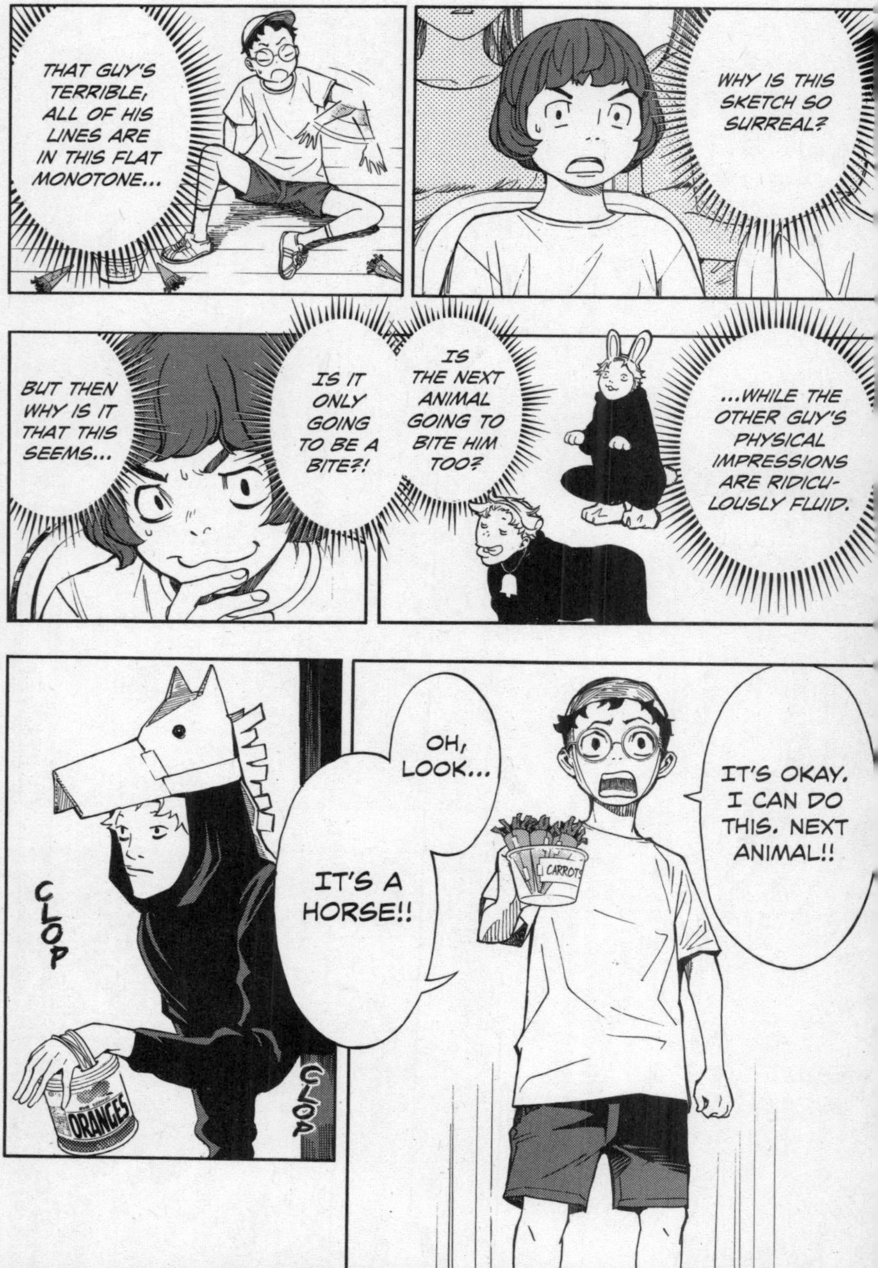
WHY IS THIS SKETCH SO SURREAL?
THAT GUY'S TERRIBLE, ALL OF HIS LINES ARE IN THIS FLAT MONOTONE...
...WHILE THE OTHER GUY'S PHYSICAL IMPRESSIONS ARE RIDICU-LOUSLY FLUID.
IS THE NEXT ANIMAL GOING TO BITE HIM TOO?
IS IT ONLY GOING TO BE A BITE?!
BUT THEN WHY IS IT THAT THIS SEEMS...
IT'S OKAY. I CAN DO THIS. NEXT ANIMAL!!
CARROTS
OH, LOOK...
IT'S A HORSE!!
CLOP
CLOP
ORANGES

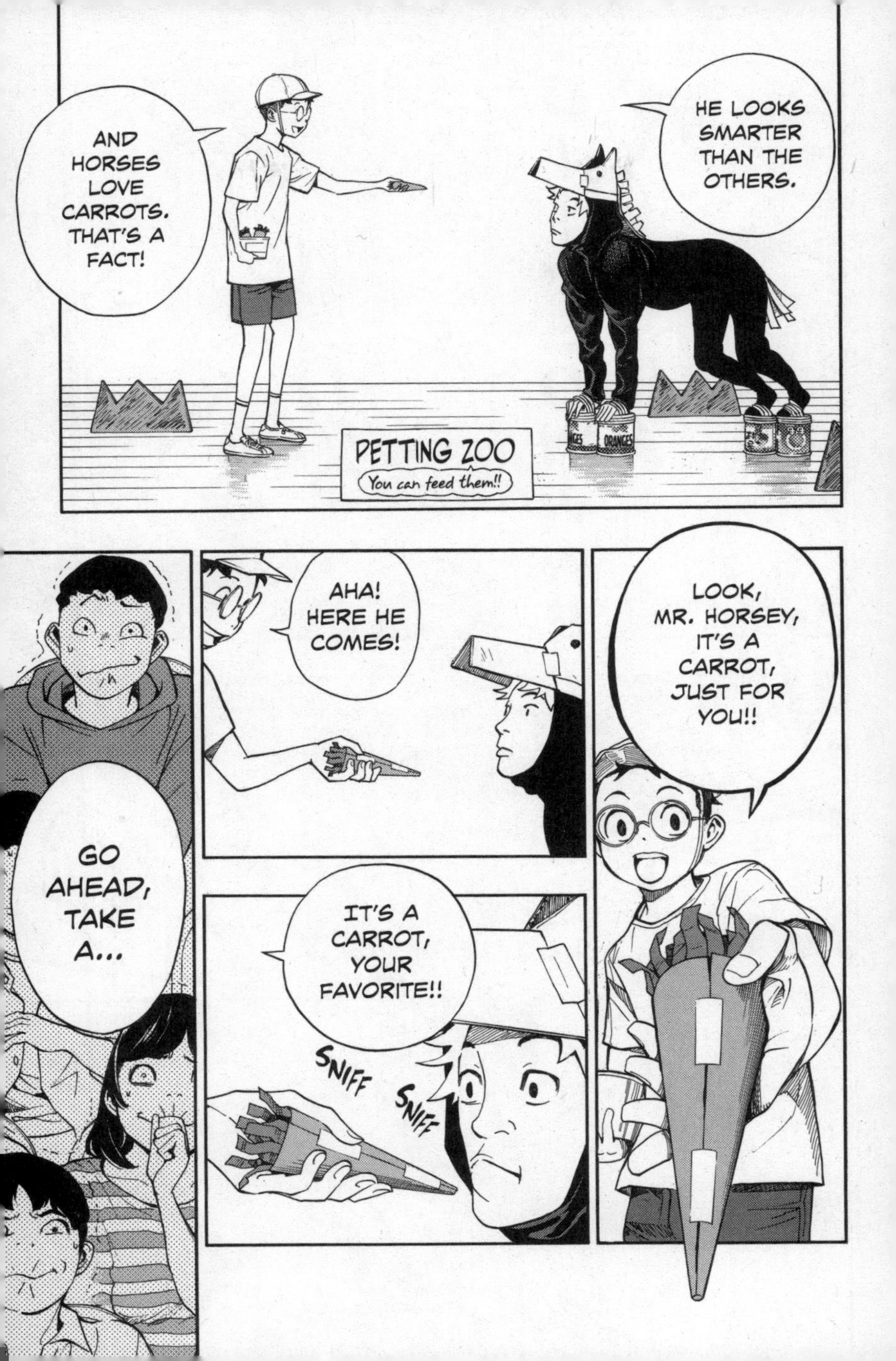
HE LOOKS SMARTER THAN THE OTHERS.
AND HORSES LOVE CARROTS. THAT'S A FACT!
ORANGES
PETTING ZOO
You can feed them!!
LOOK, MR. HORSEY, IT'S A CARROT, JUST FOR YOU!!
AHA! HERE HE COMES!
IT'S A CARROT, YOUR FAVORITE!!
SNIFF
SNIFF
GO AHEAD, TAKE A...

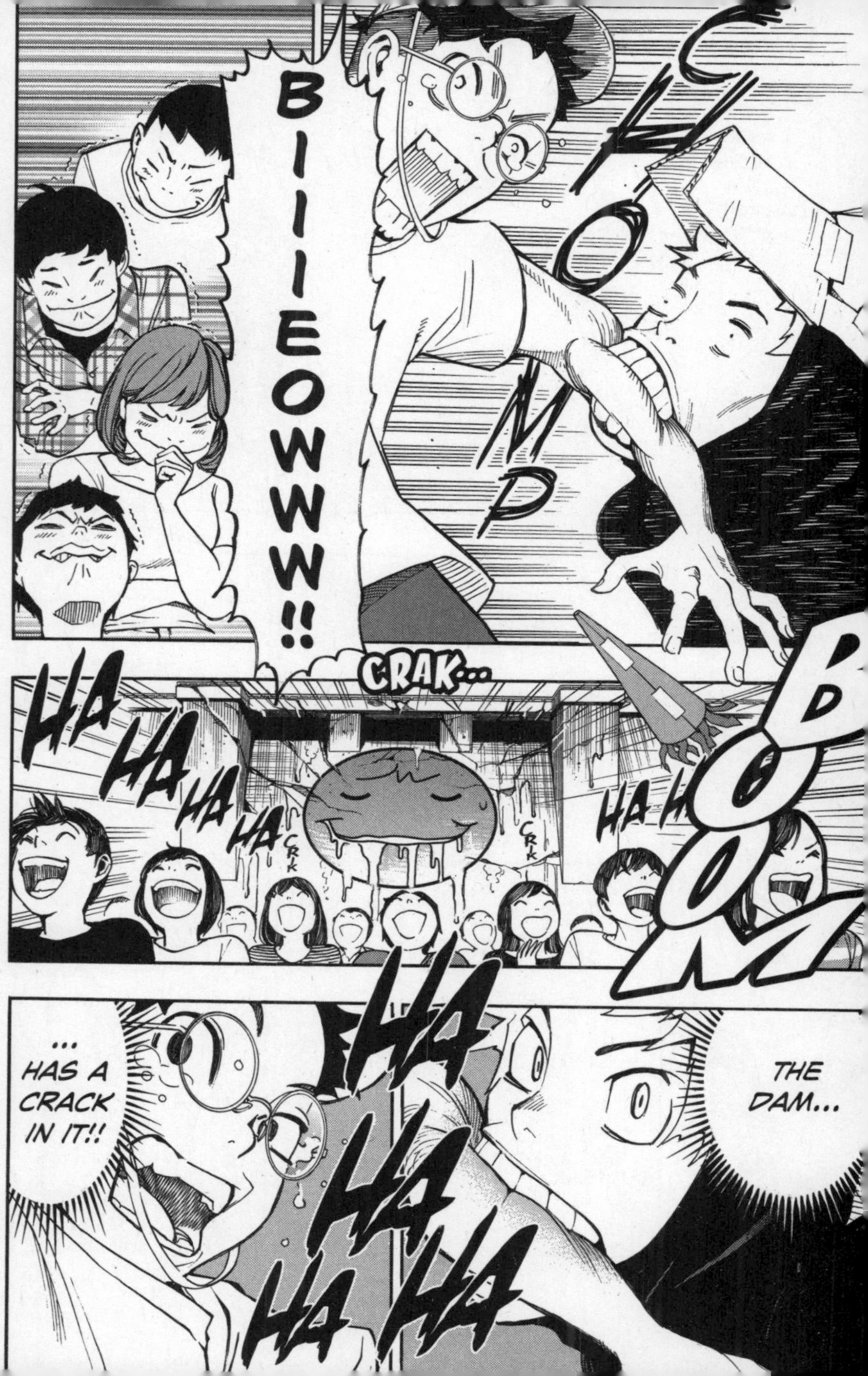
CHOMP
BIIIEOWWW!!
CRAK...
BOOM
HA HA HA HA
CRIK
CRIK
THE DAM...
... HAS A CRACK IN IT!!
HA HA HA HA HA HA

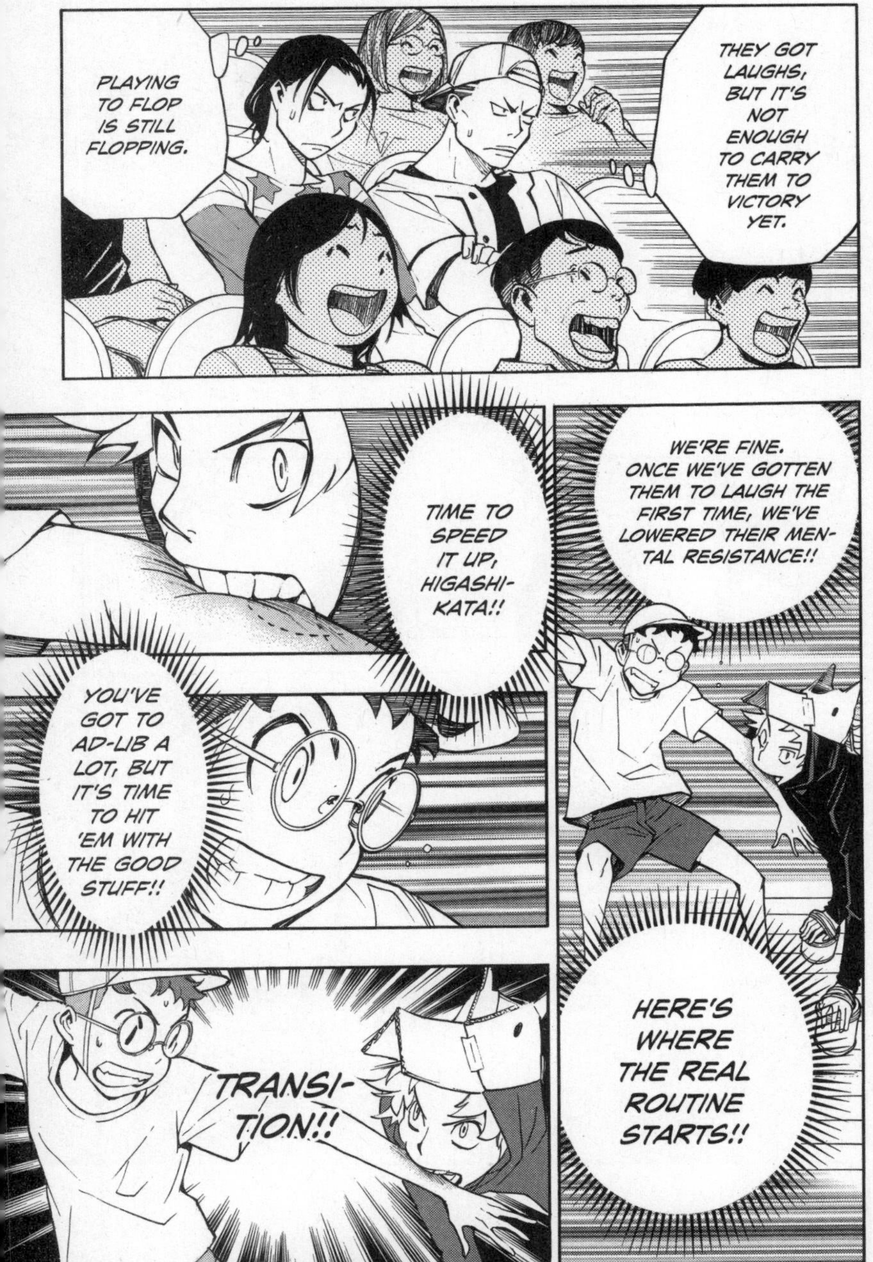
THEY GOT LAUGHS, BUT IT'S NOT ENOUGH TO CARRY THEM TO VICTORY YET.
PLAYING TO FLOP IS STILL FLOPPING.
WE'RE FINE. ONCE WE'VE GOTTEN THEM TO LAUGH THE FIRST TIME, WE'VE LOWERED THEIR MEN-TAL RESISTANCE!!
HERE'S WHERE THE REAL ROUTINE STARTS!!
TIME TO SPEED IT UP, HIGASHI-KATA!!
YOU'VE GOT TO AD-LIB A LOT, BUT IT'S TIME TO HIT 'EM WITH THE GOOD STUFF!!
TRANSI-TION!!

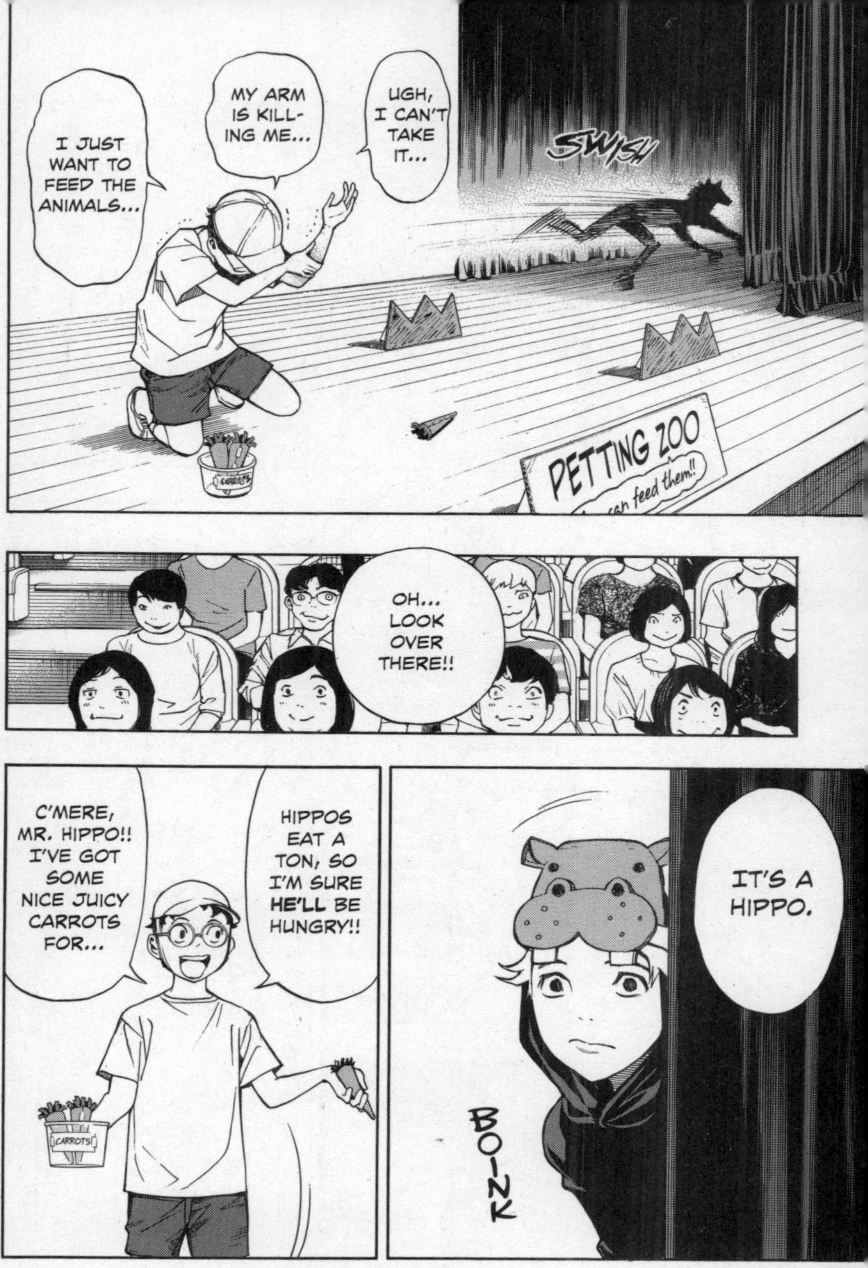
SWISH
UGH, I CAN'T TAKE IT...
MY ARM IS KILLING ME...
I JUST WANT TO FEED THE ANIMALS...
PETTING ZOO
can feed them!!
CARROTS
OH... LOOK OVER THERE!!
IT'S A HIPPO.
BOINK
HIPPOS EAT A TON, SO I'M SURE HE'LL BE HUNGRY!!
C'MERE, MR. HIPPO!! I'VE GOT SOME NICE JUICY CARROTS FOR...
CARROTS

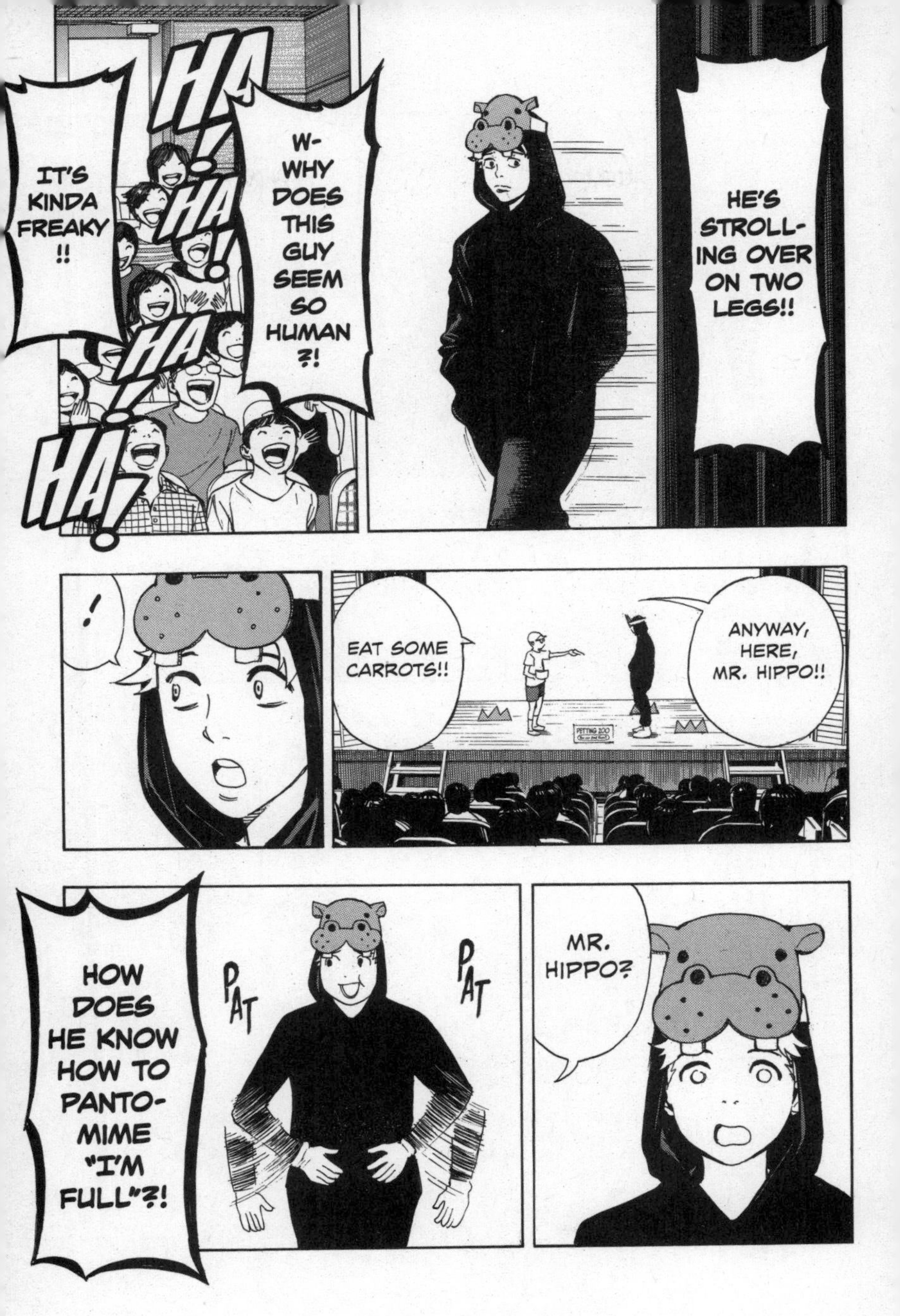
HE'S STROLLING OVER ON TWO LEGS!!
W-WHY DOES THIS GUY SEEM SO HUMAN?!
IT'S KINDA FREAKY!!
HA! HA! HA! HA!
ANYWAY, HERE, MR. HIPPO!!
EAT SOME CARROTS!!
PETTING ZOO
!
MR. HIPPO?
PAT PAT
HOW DOES HE KNOW HOW TO PANTOMIME "I'M FULL"?!

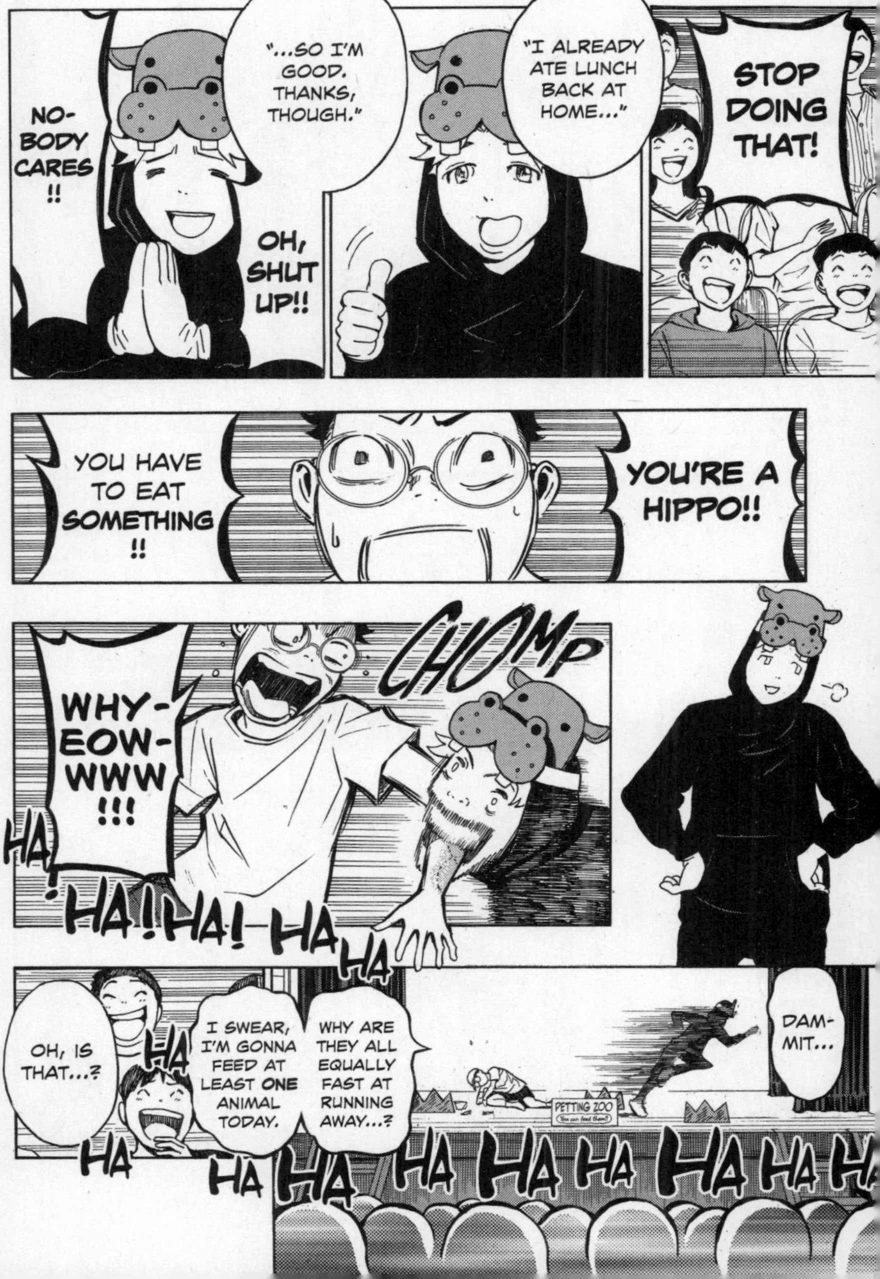
STOP DOING THAT!
"I ALREADY ATE LUNCH BACK AT HOME..."
"...SO I'M GOOD. THANKS, THOUGH."
OH, SHUT UP!!
NO-BODY CARES!!
YOU'RE A HIPPO!!
YOU HAVE TO EAT SOMETHING!!
CHOMP
WHY-EOW-WWW!!!
HA! HA! HA! HA HA
DAM-MIT...
PETTING ZOO
You can feed them!
WHY ARE THEY ALL EQUALLY FAST AT RUNNING AWAY...?
I SWEAR, I'M GONNA FEED AT LEAST ONE ANIMAL TODAY.
OH, IS THAT...?
HA HA HA HA HA HA HA HA HA HA HA HA

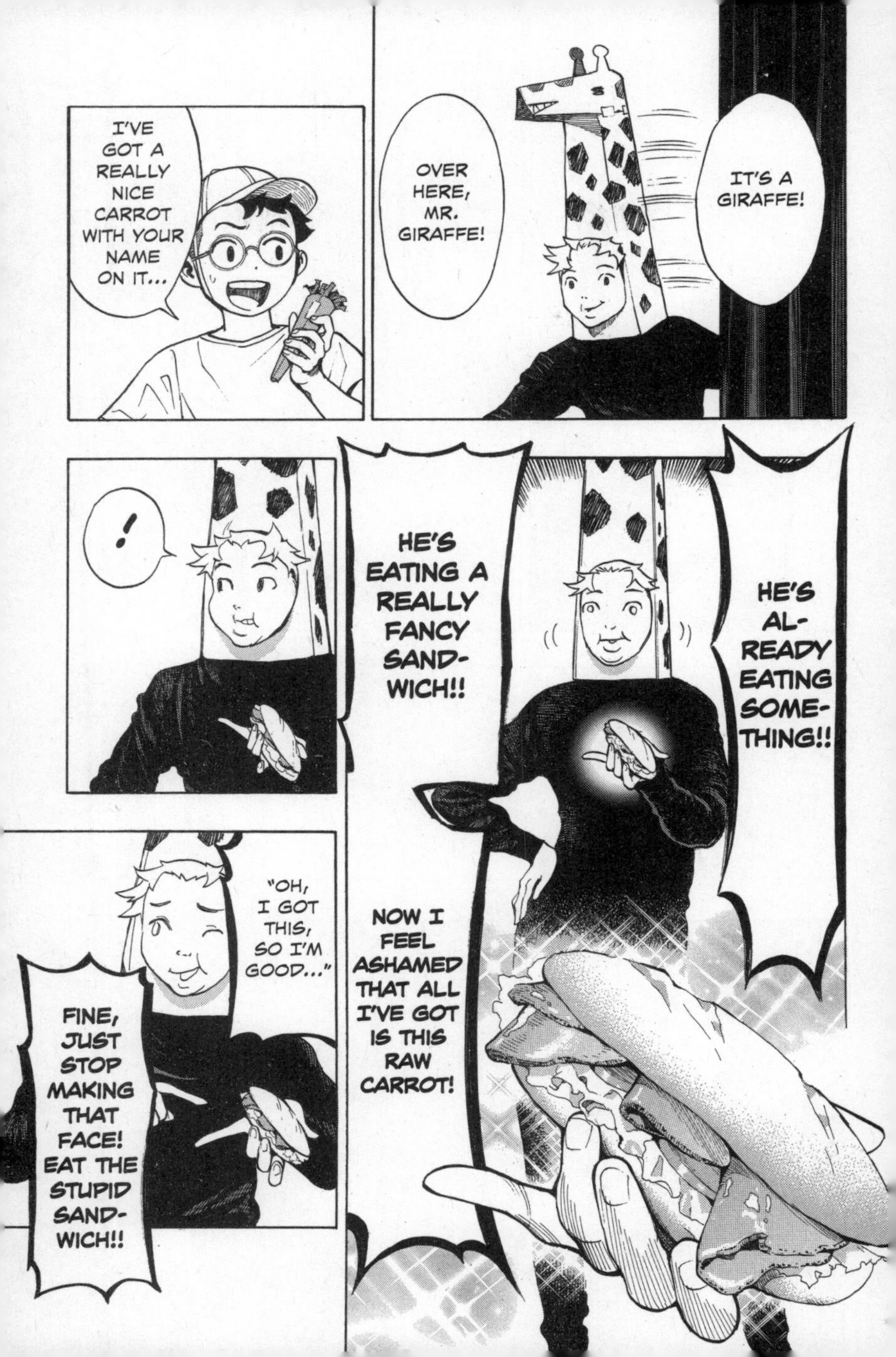
IT'S A GIRAFFE!
OVER HERE, MR. GIRAFFE!
I'VE GOT A REALLY NICE CARROT WITH YOUR NAME ON IT...
HE'S AL-READY EATING SOME-THING!!
HE'S EATING A REALLY FANCY SAND-WICH!!
NOW I FEEL ASHAMED THAT ALL I'VE GOT IS THIS RAW CARROT!
!
"OH, I GOT THIS, SO I'M GOOD..."
FINE, JUST STOP MAKING THAT FACE! EAT THE STUPID SAND-WICH!!

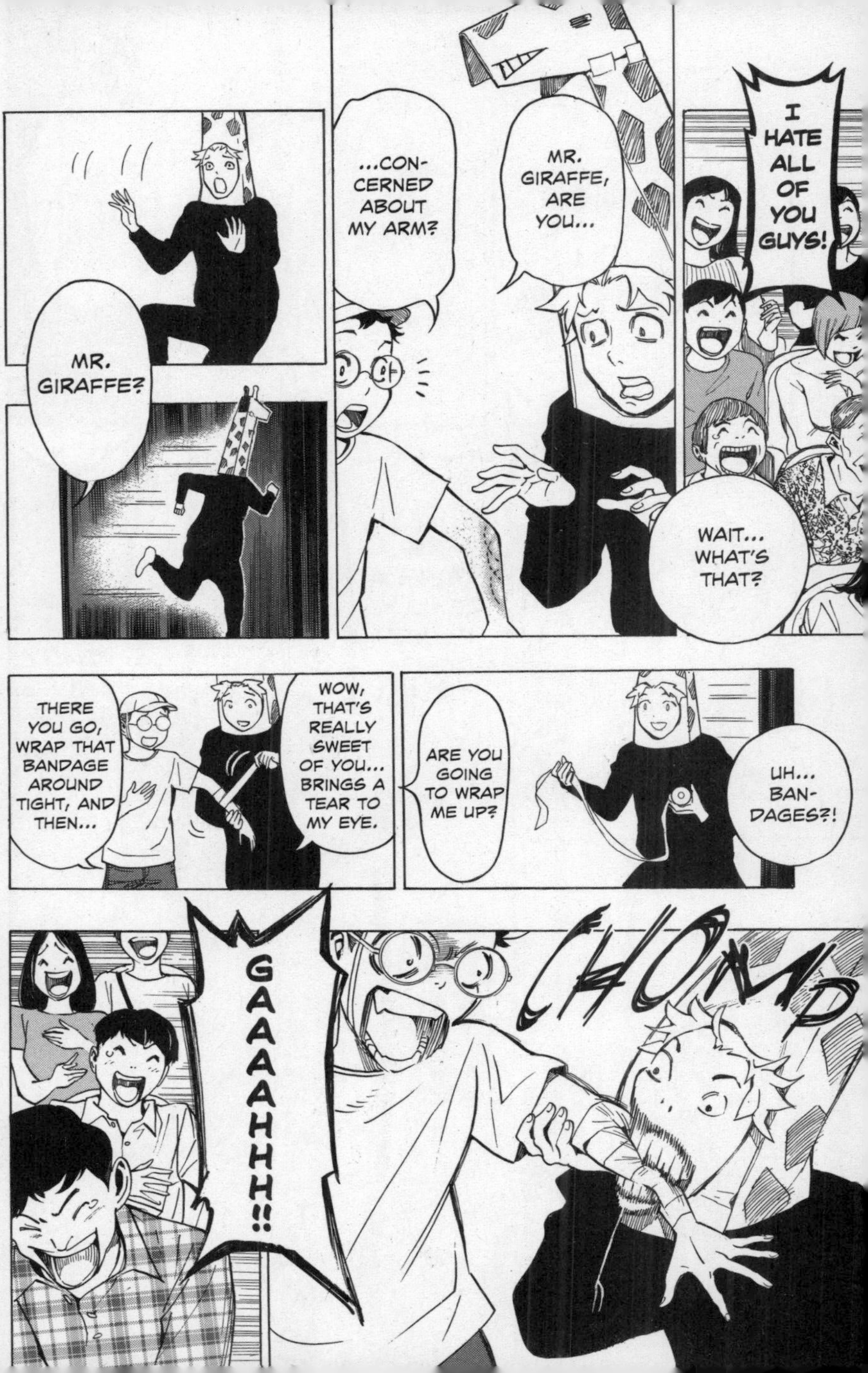
I HATE ALL OF YOU GUYS!
WAIT... WHAT'S THAT?
MR. GIRAFFE, ARE YOU...
...CONCERNED ABOUT MY ARM?
MR. GIRAFFE?
UH... BANDAGES?!
ARE YOU GOING TO WRAP ME UP?
WOW, THAT'S REALLY SWEET OF YOU... BRINGS A TEAR TO MY EYE.
THERE YOU GO, WRAP THAT BANDAGE AROUND TIGHT, AND THEN...
CHOMP
GAAAAAHHH!!

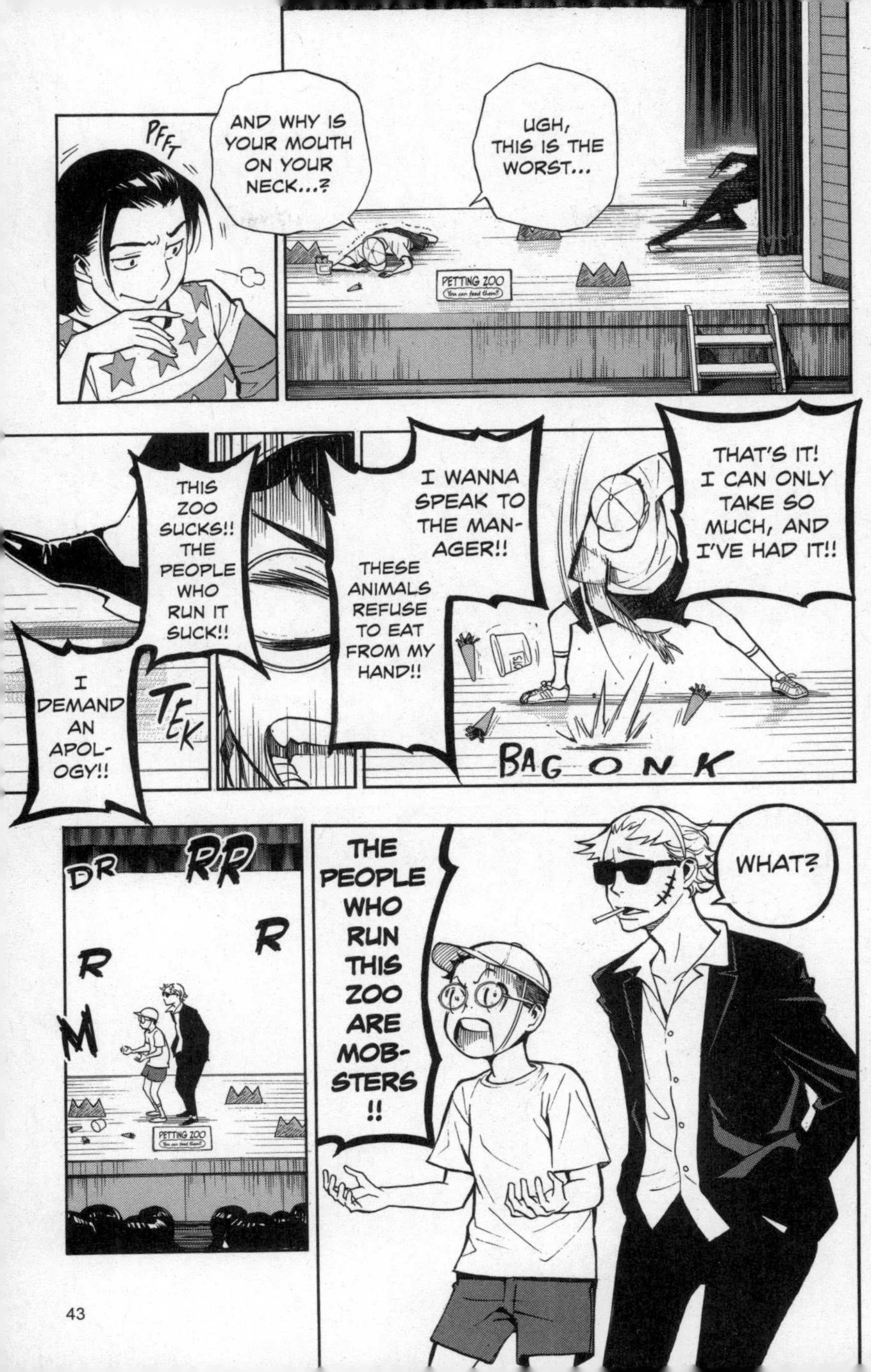
UGH, THIS IS THE WORST...
PETTING ZOO
You can feed them!!
PFFT
AND WHY IS YOUR MOUTH ON YOUR NECK...?
THAT'S IT! I CAN ONLY TAKE SO MUCH, AND I'VE HAD IT!!
BAGONK
I WANNA SPEAK TO THE MAN-AGER!!
THESE ANIMALS REFUSE TO EAT FROM MY HAND!!
THIS ZOO SUCKS!! THE PEOPLE WHO RUN IT SUCK!!
TEK
I DEMAND AN APOL-OGY!!
WHAT?
THE PEOPLE WHO RUN THIS ZOO ARE MOB-STERS!!
DRRRRRM
PETTING ZOO

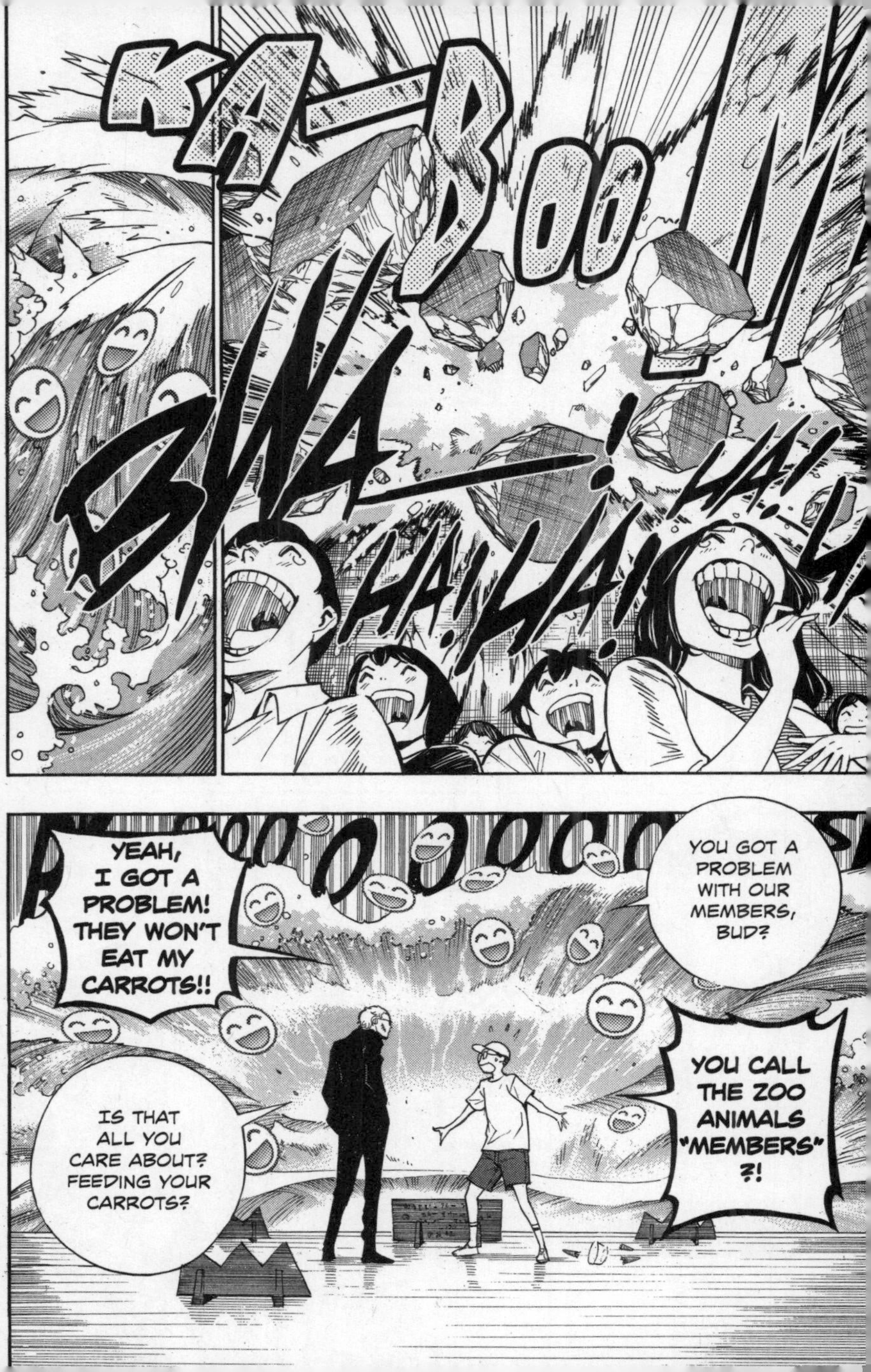
KA-BOOM!
BWA!
HA! HA! HA! HA!
YOU GOT A PROBLEM WITH OUR MEMBERS, BUD?
YEAH, I GOT A PROBLEM! THEY WON'T EAT MY CARROTS!!
YOU CALL THE ZOO ANIMALS "MEMBERS"?!
IS THAT ALL YOU CARE ABOUT? FEEDING YOUR CARROTS?

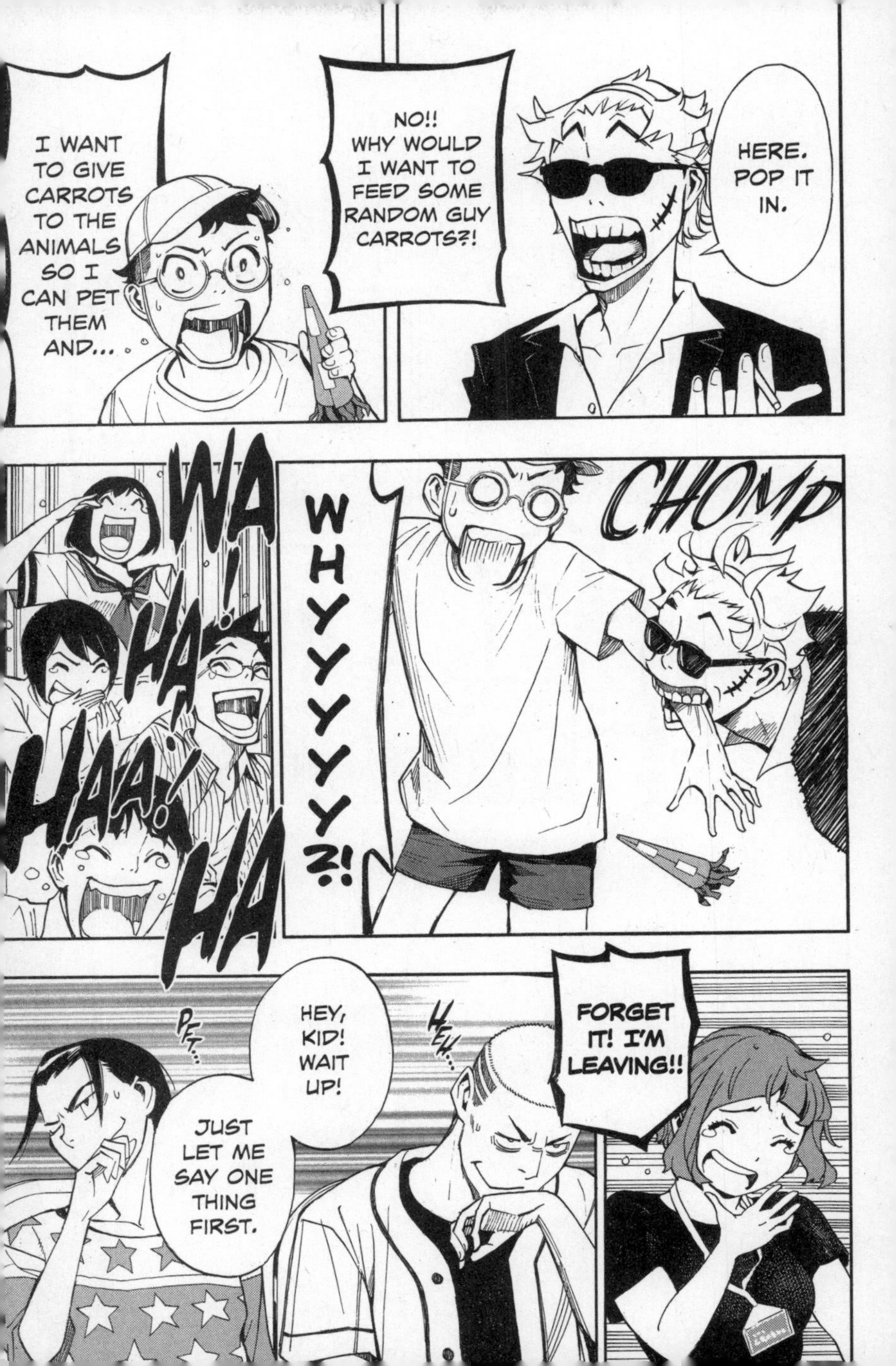
HERE. POP IT IN.
NO!! WHY WOULD I WANT TO FEED SOME RANDOM GUY CARROTS?!
I WANT TO GIVE CARROTS TO THE ANIMALS SO I CAN PET THEM AND...
CHOMP
WHYYYYYY?!
WA HA! HA! HAA! HA HA
FORGET IT! I'M LEAVING!!
HEH...
HEY, KID! WAIT UP!
PFT...
JUST LET ME SAY ONE THING FIRST.

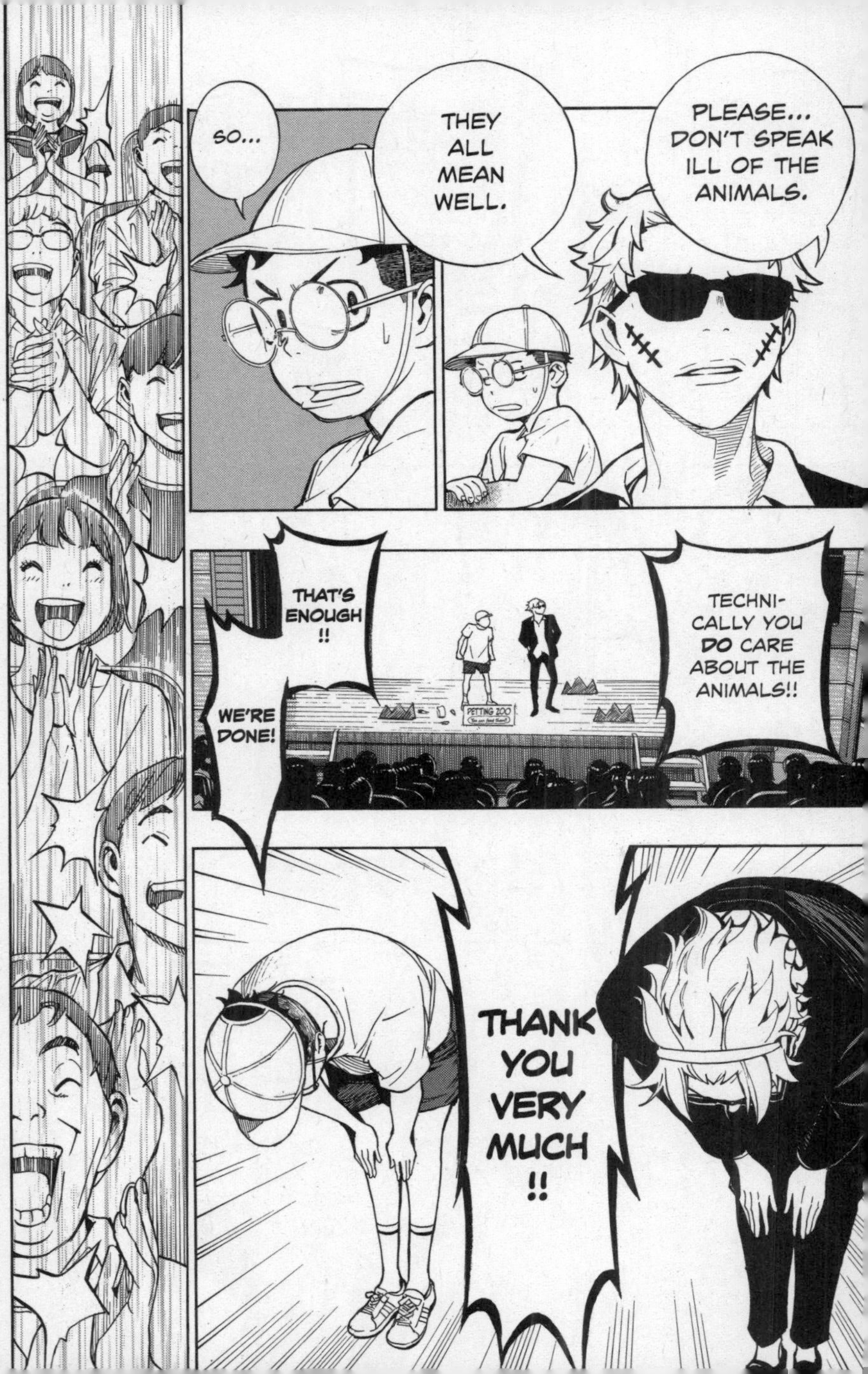
PLEASE... DON'T SPEAK ILL OF THE ANIMALS.
THEY ALL MEAN WELL.
SO...
TECHNI-CALLY YOU DO CARE ABOUT THE ANIMALS!!
THAT'S ENOUGH!!
WE'RE DONE!
PETTING ZOO
THANK YOU VERY MUCH!!

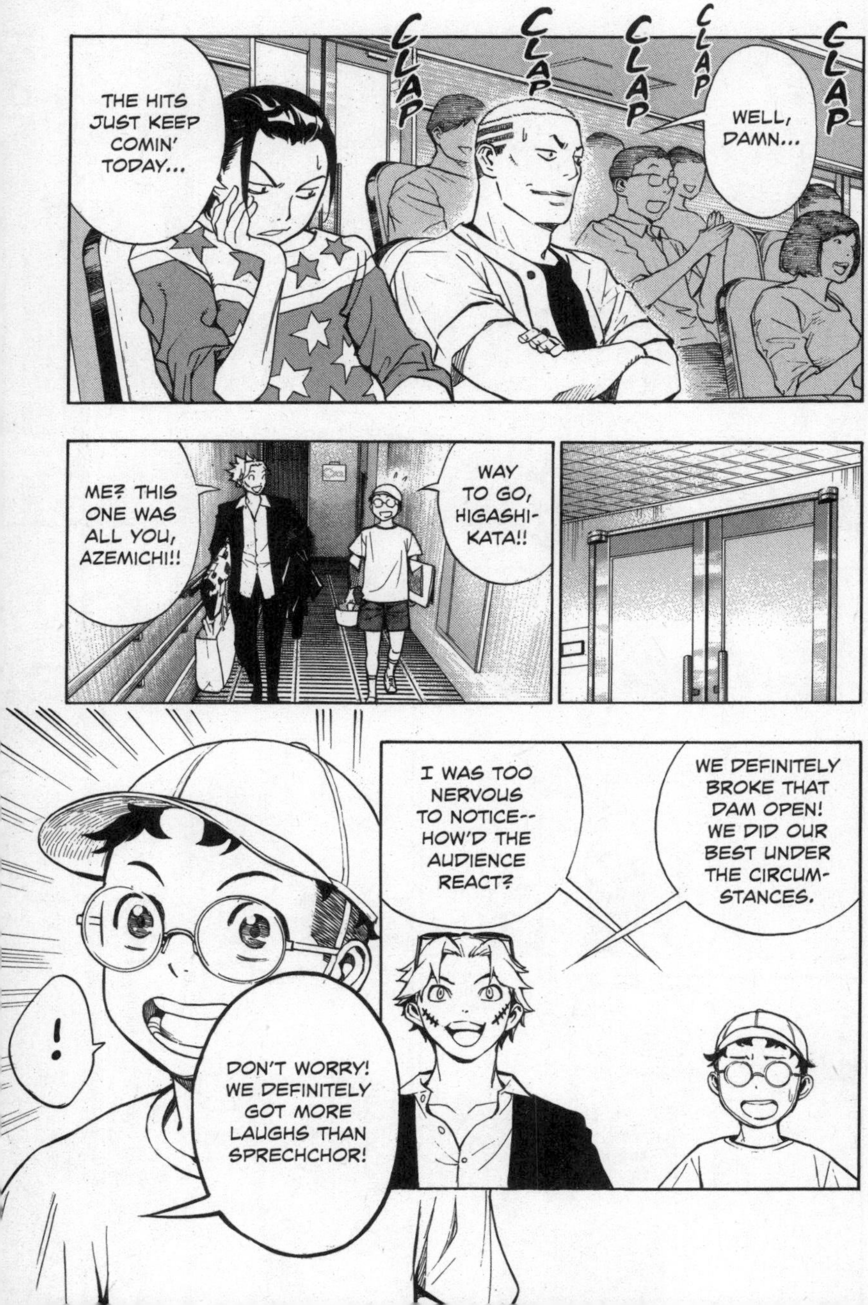
CLAP
CLAP
CLAP
CLAP
CLAP
WELL, DAMN...
THE HITS JUST KEEP COMIN' TODAY...
WAY TO GO, HIGASHI-KATA!!
ME? THIS ONE WAS ALL YOU, AZEMICHI!!
WE DEFINITELY BROKE THAT DAM OPEN! WE DID OUR BEST UNDER THE CIRCUM-STANCES.
I WAS TOO NERVOUS TO NOTICE-- HOW'D THE AUDIENCE REACT?
!
DON'T WORRY! WE DEFINITELY GOT MORE LAUGHS THAN SPRECHCHOR!

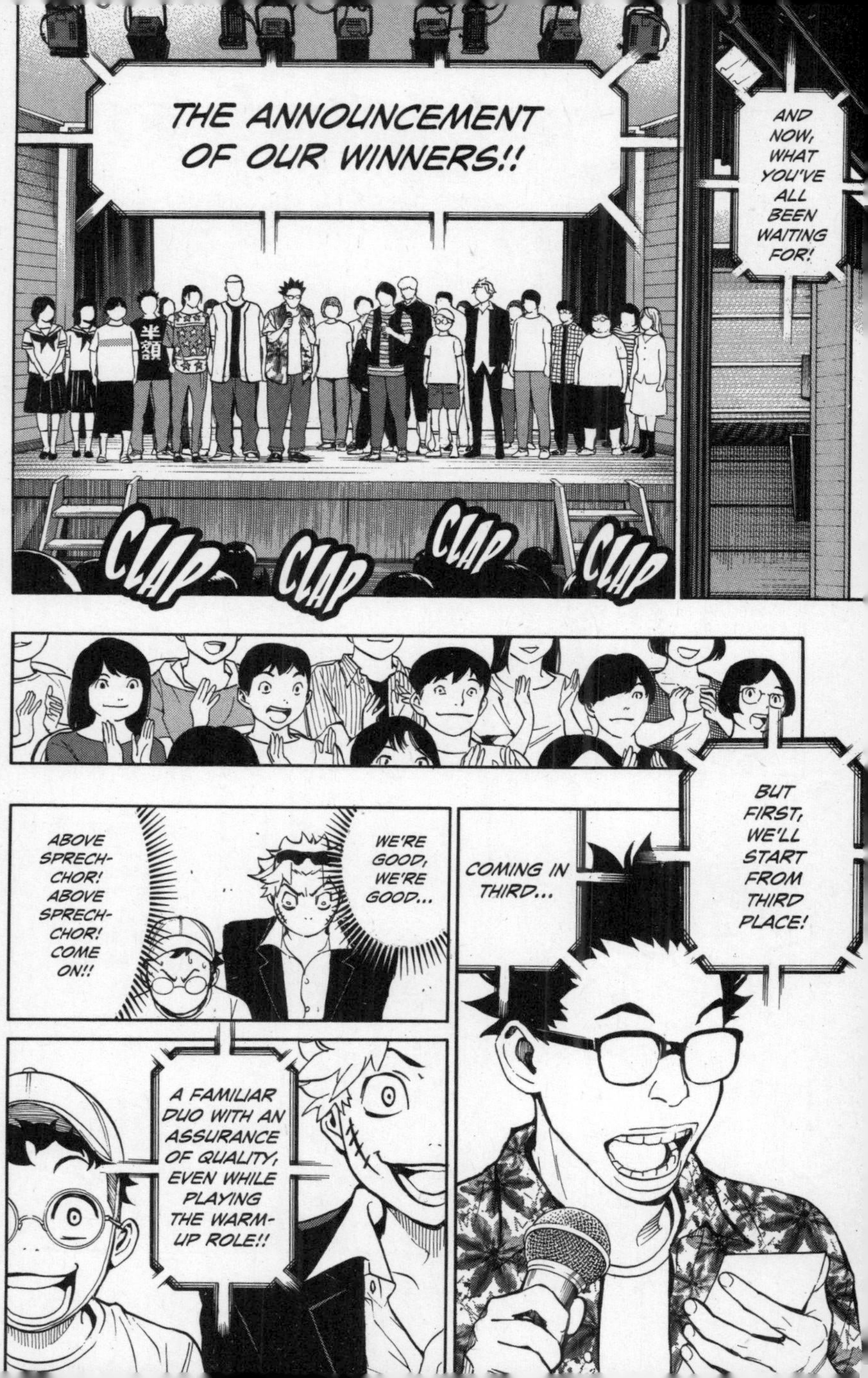
AND NOW, WHAT YOU'VE ALL BEEN WAITING FOR!
THE ANNOUNCEMENT OF OUR WINNERS!!
CLAP CLAP CLAP CLAP
BUT FIRST, WE'LL START FROM THIRD PLACE!
COMING IN THIRD...
WE'RE GOOD, WE'RE GOOD...
ABOVE SPRECH-CHOR! ABOVE SPRECH-CHOR! COME ON!!
A FAMILIAR DUO WITH AN ASSURANCE OF QUALITY, EVEN WHILE PLAYING THE WARM-UP ROLE!!

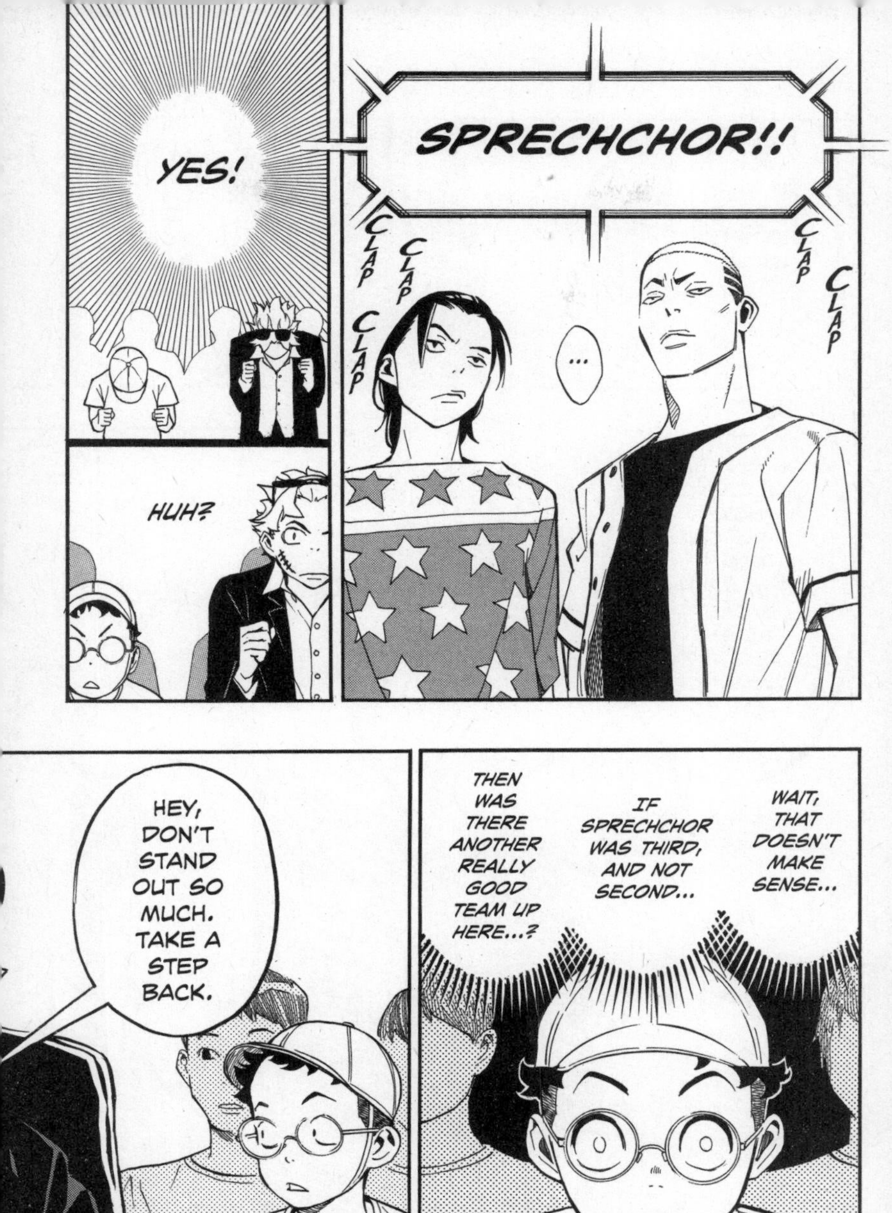
SPRECHCHOR!!
CLAP CLAP
CLAP CLAP
...
CLAP CLAP
YES!
HUH?
WAIT, THAT DOESN'T MAKE SENSE...
IF SPRECHCHOR WAS THIRD, AND NOT SECOND...
THEN WAS THERE ANOTHER REALLY GOOD TEAM UP HERE...?
HEY, DON'T STAND OUT SO MUCH. TAKE A STEP BACK.

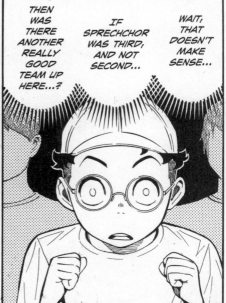

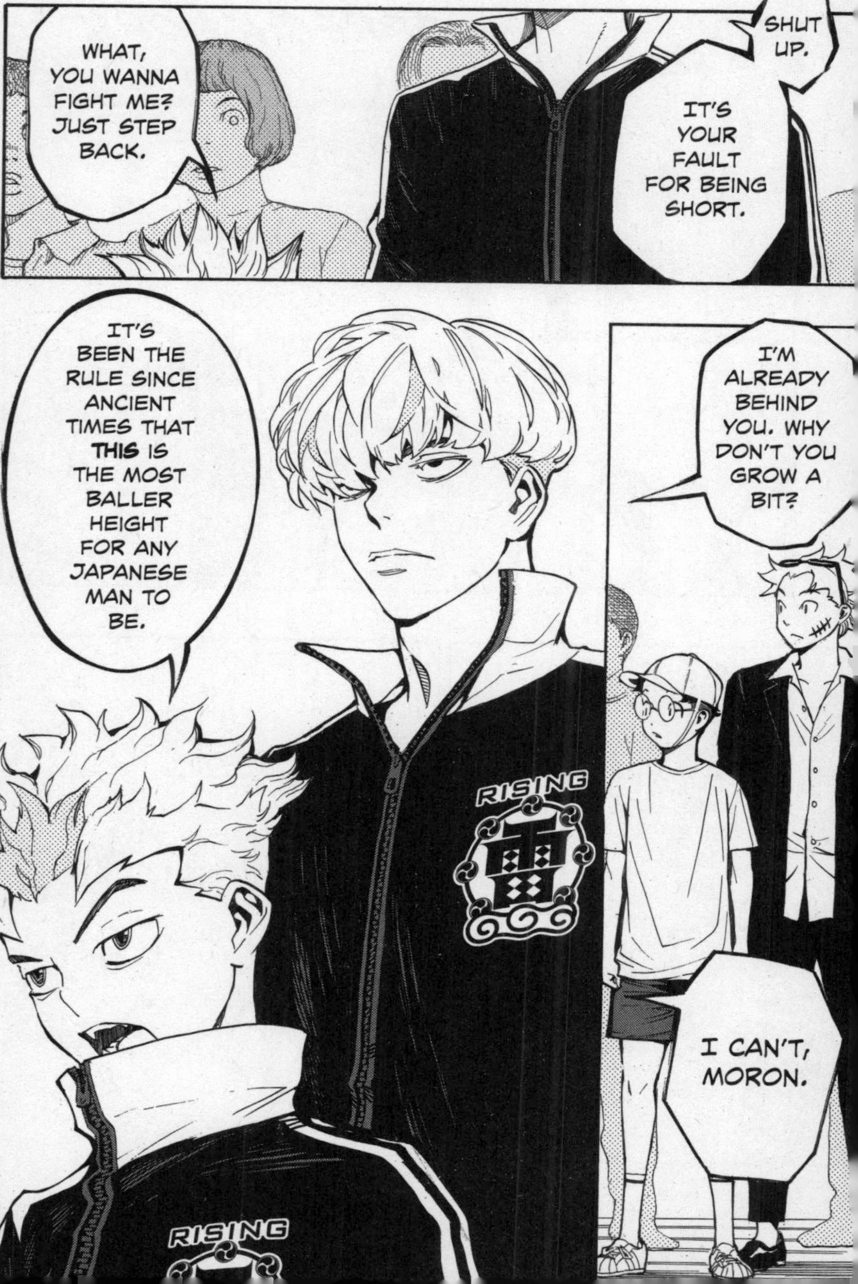
SHUT UP.
IT'S YOUR FAULT FOR BEING SHORT.
WHAT, YOU WANNA FIGHT ME? JUST STEP BACK.
I'M ALREADY BEHIND YOU. WHY DON'T YOU GROW A BIT?
I CAN'T, MORON.
IT'S BEEN THE RULE SINCE ANCIENT TIMES THAT **THIS** IS THE MOST BALLER HEIGHT FOR ANY JAPANESE MAN TO BE.
RISING
RISING

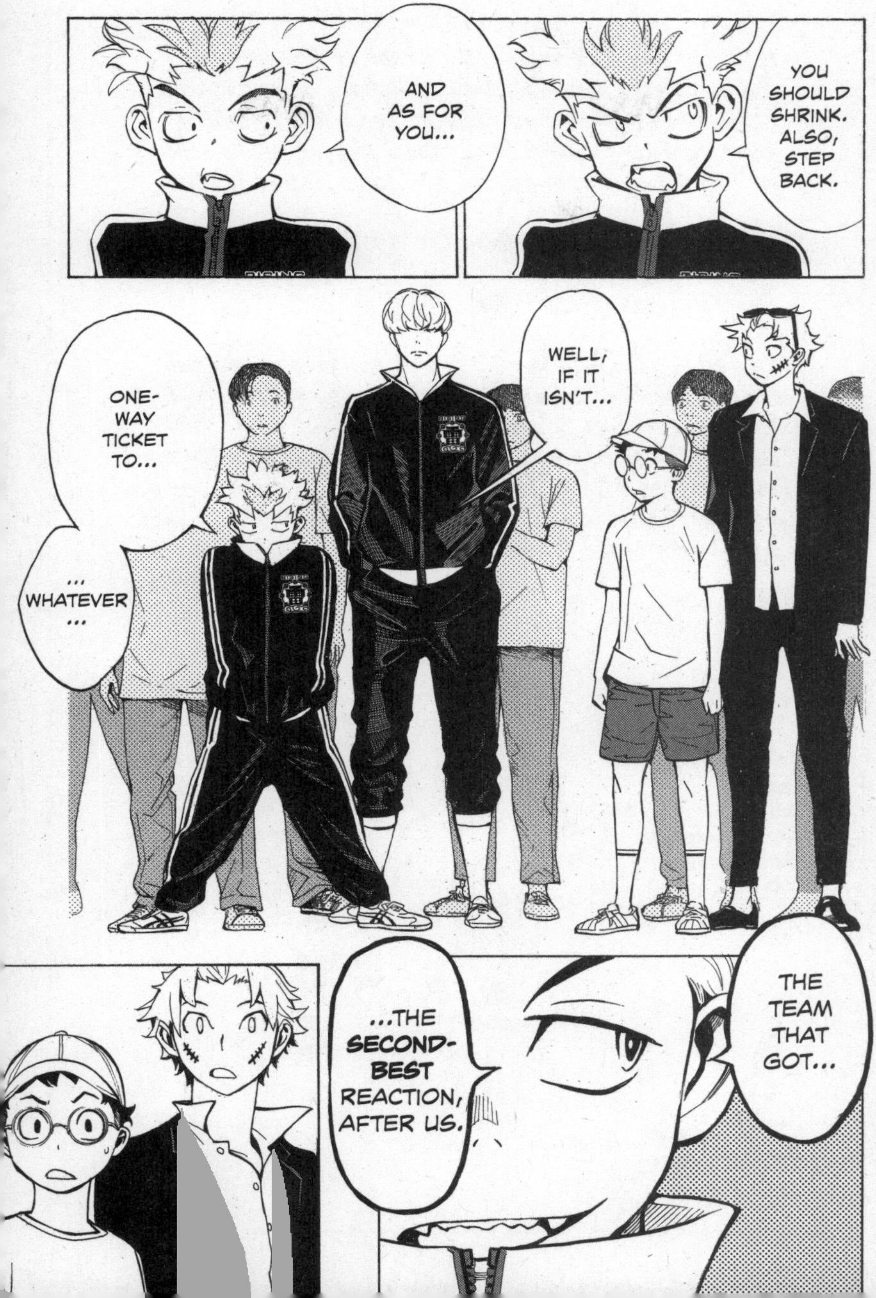
YOU SHOULD SHRINK. ALSO, STEP BACK.
AND AS FOR YOU...
WELL, IF IT ISN'T...
ONE-WAY TICKET TO...
...WHATEVER...
THE TEAM THAT GOT...
...THE SECOND-BEST REACTION, AFTER US.

Hello. I'm Akinari Asakura, the writer of this manga. Thank you very much for checking out the second volume. I mentioned that me and "Jicchan" had a bitter first experience performing. In our third year of middle school, we started practicing manzai, for some bizarre reason.

"Why would you do something like that?"

"Where do you expect to take this?"

We had no plan between the two of us, but for whatever reason, we were obsessed with rehearsing a routine that we could perform. It seems stupid now, but it was really just a sign of how much we loved comedy. We felt like the material was strong, but sadly, it had to be shelved...or so I thought all those years ago. But perhaps it will see the light of day in the future...?

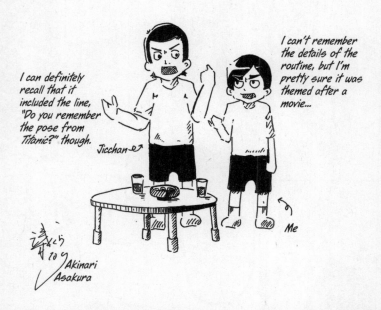

I can't remember the details of the routine, but I'm pretty sure it was themed after a movie...
I can definitely recall that it included the line, "Do you remember the pose from Titanic?" though.
Jicchan
Me
Akinari Asakura

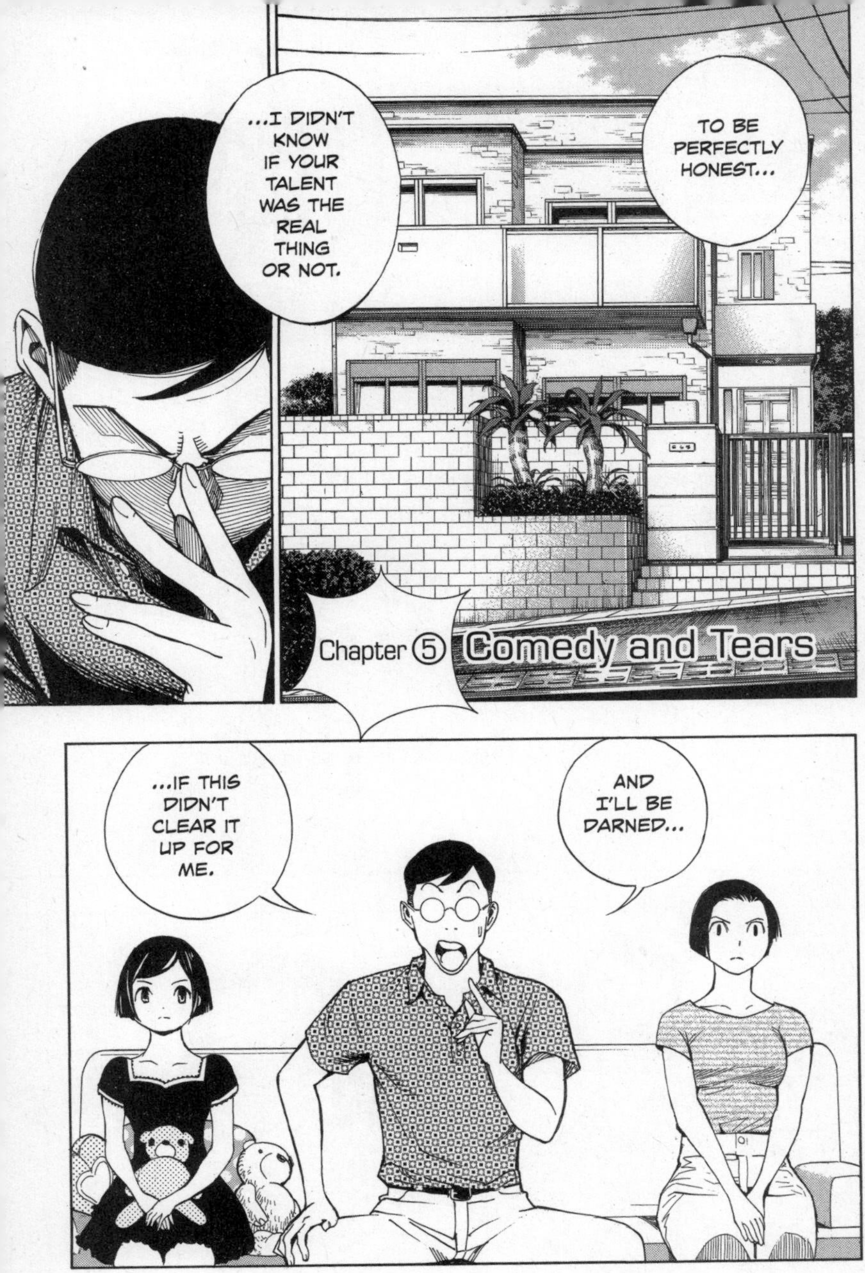
TO BE PERFECTLY HONEST...
Chapter 5 Comedy and Tears
...I DIDN'T KNOW IF YOUR TALENT WAS THE REAL THING OR NOT.
AND I'LL BE DARNED...
...IF THIS DIDN'T CLEAR IT UP FOR ME.

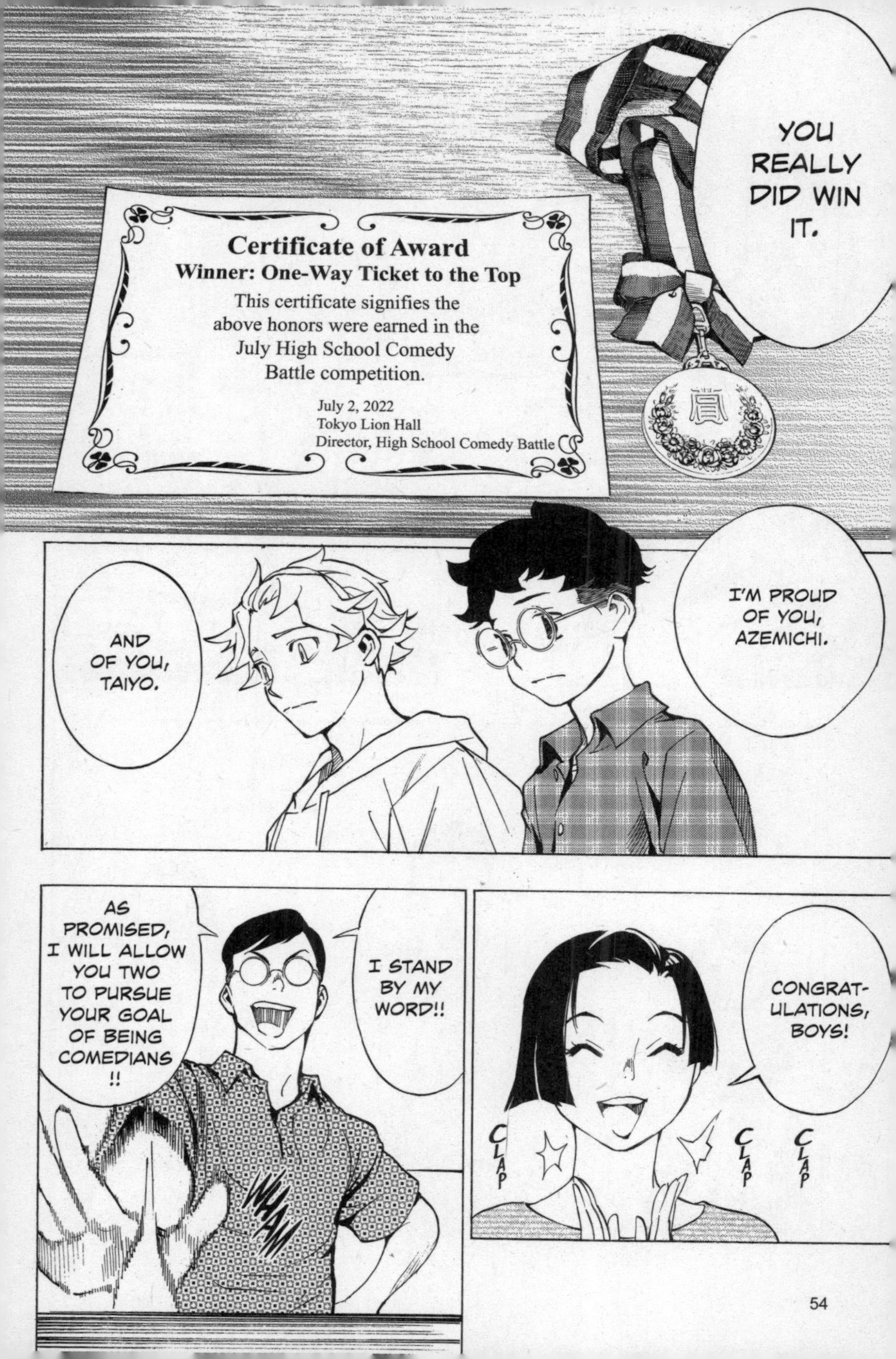
YOU REALLY DID WIN IT.
Certificate of Award
Winner: One-Way Ticket to the Top
This certificate signifies the above honors were earned in the July High School Comedy Battle competition.
July 2, 2022
Tokyo Lion Hall
Director, High School Comedy Battle
I'M PROUD OF YOU, AZEMICHI.
AND OF YOU, TAIYO.
CONGRAT-ULATIONS, BOYS!
CLAP
CLAP
CLAP
I STAND BY MY WORD!!
AS PROMISED, I WILL ALLOW YOU TWO TO PURSUE YOUR GOAL OF BEING COMEDIANS!!
WHAM

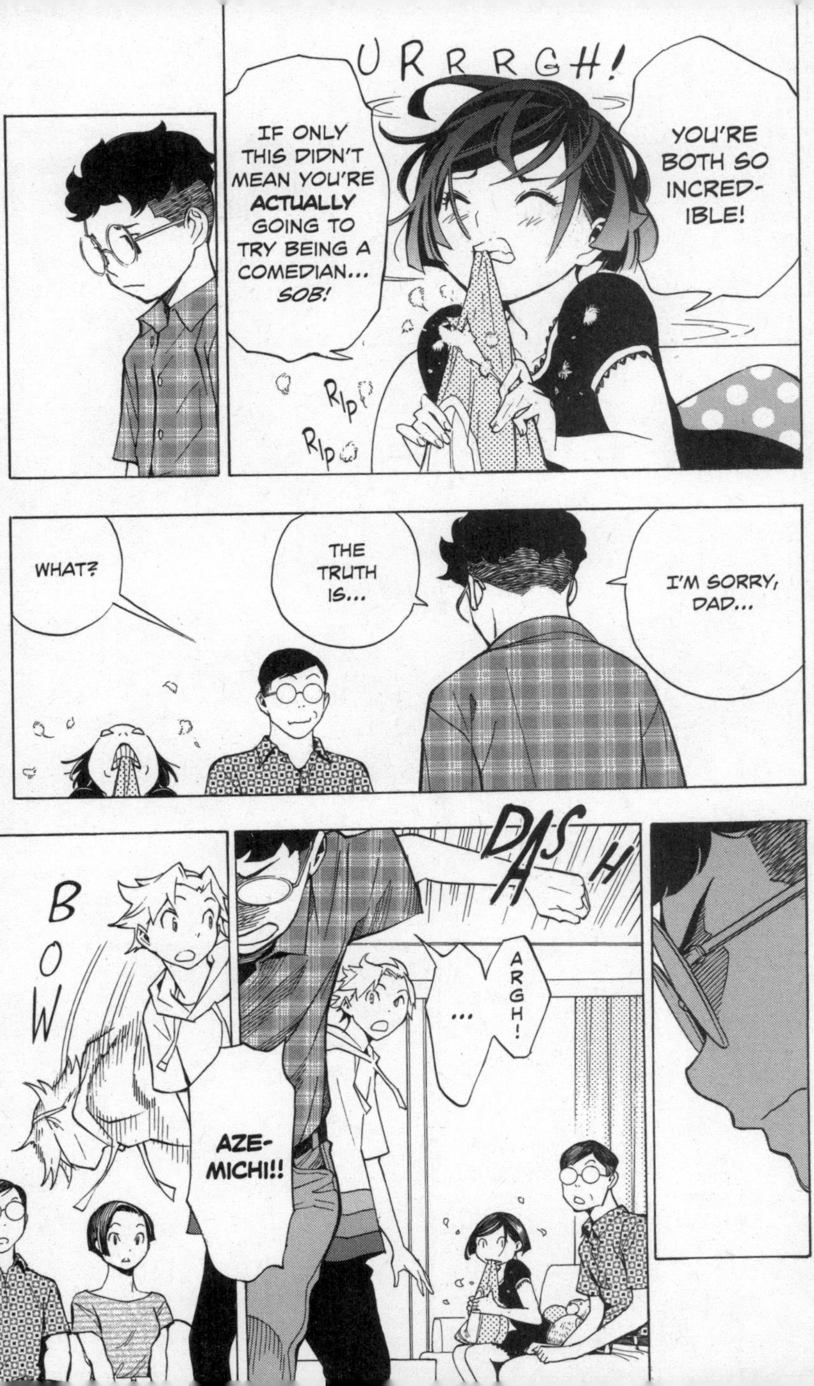
URRRGH!
YOU'RE BOTH SO INCRED-IBLE!
IF ONLY THIS DIDN'T MEAN YOU'RE **ACTUALLY** GOING TO TRY BEING A COMEDIAN... *SOB!*
RIP
RIP
I'M SORRY, DAD...
THE TRUTH IS...
WHAT?
DASH
ARGH!
...
AZE-MICHI!!
BOW

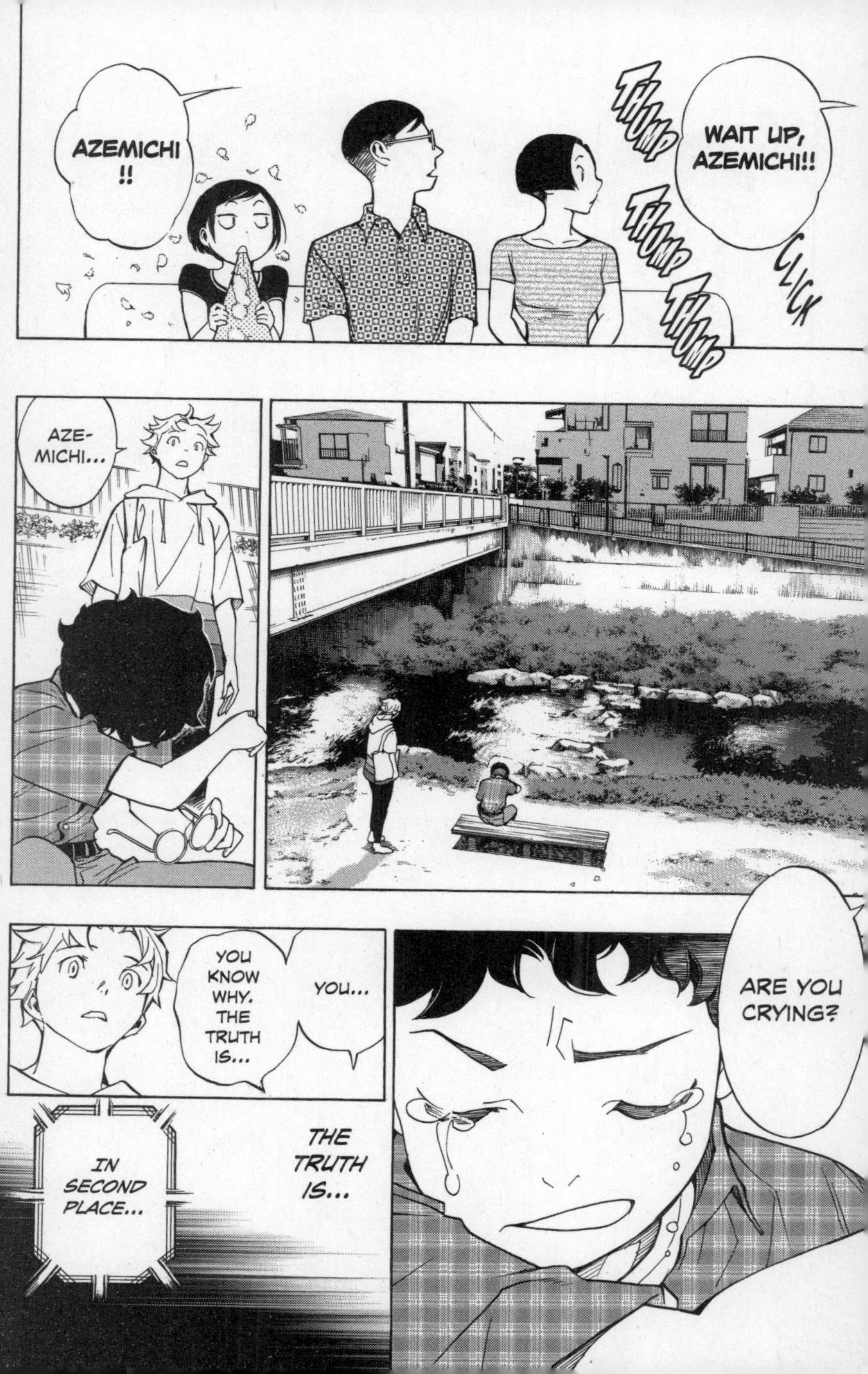
WAIT UP, AZEMICHI!!
CLICK
THUMP THUMP THUMP
AZEMICHI !!
AZE-MICHI...
ARE YOU CRYING?
YOU...
YOU KNOW WHY. THE TRUTH IS...
THE TRUTH IS...
IN SECOND PLACE...

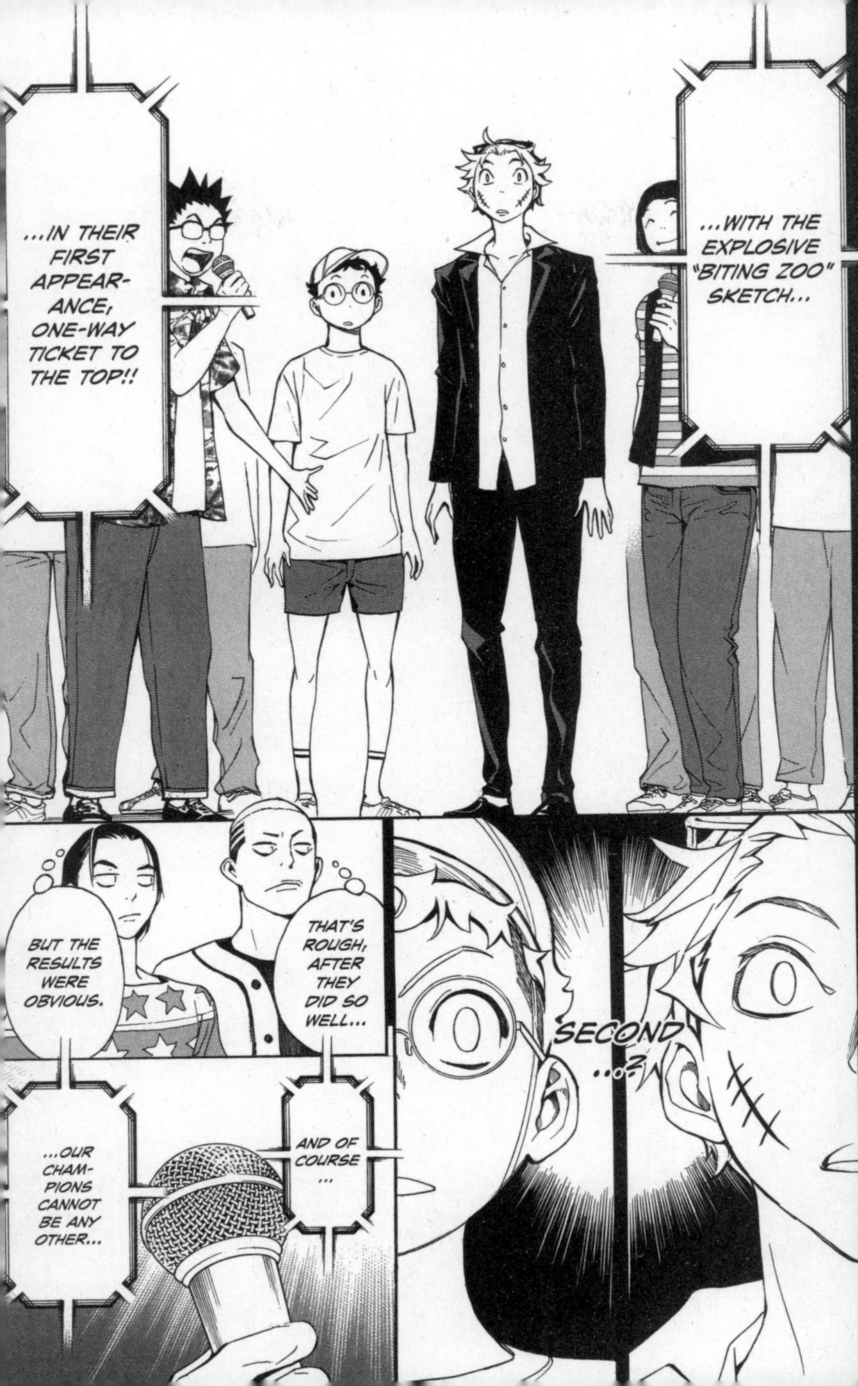
...WITH THE EXPLOSIVE "BITING ZOO" SKETCH...
...IN THEIR FIRST APPEARANCE, ONE-WAY TICKET TO THE TOP!!
SECOND...?
THAT'S ROUGH, AFTER THEY DID SO WELL...
BUT THE RESULTS WERE OBVIOUS.
AND OF COURSE...
...OUR CHAMPIONS CANNOT BE ANY OTHER...

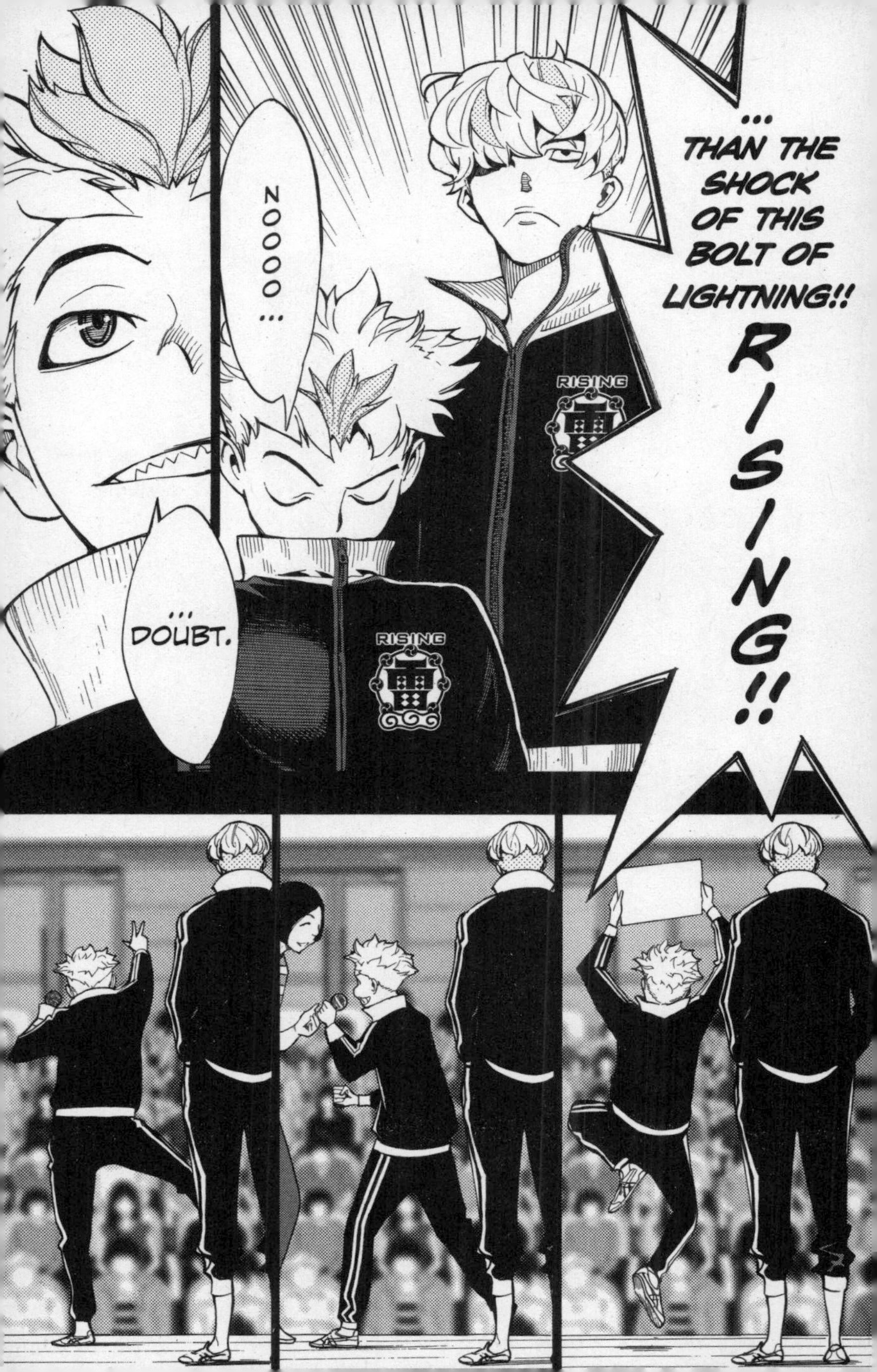
... THAN THE SHOCK OF THIS BOLT OF LIGHTNING!!
RISING!!
NOOOO...
... DOUBT.

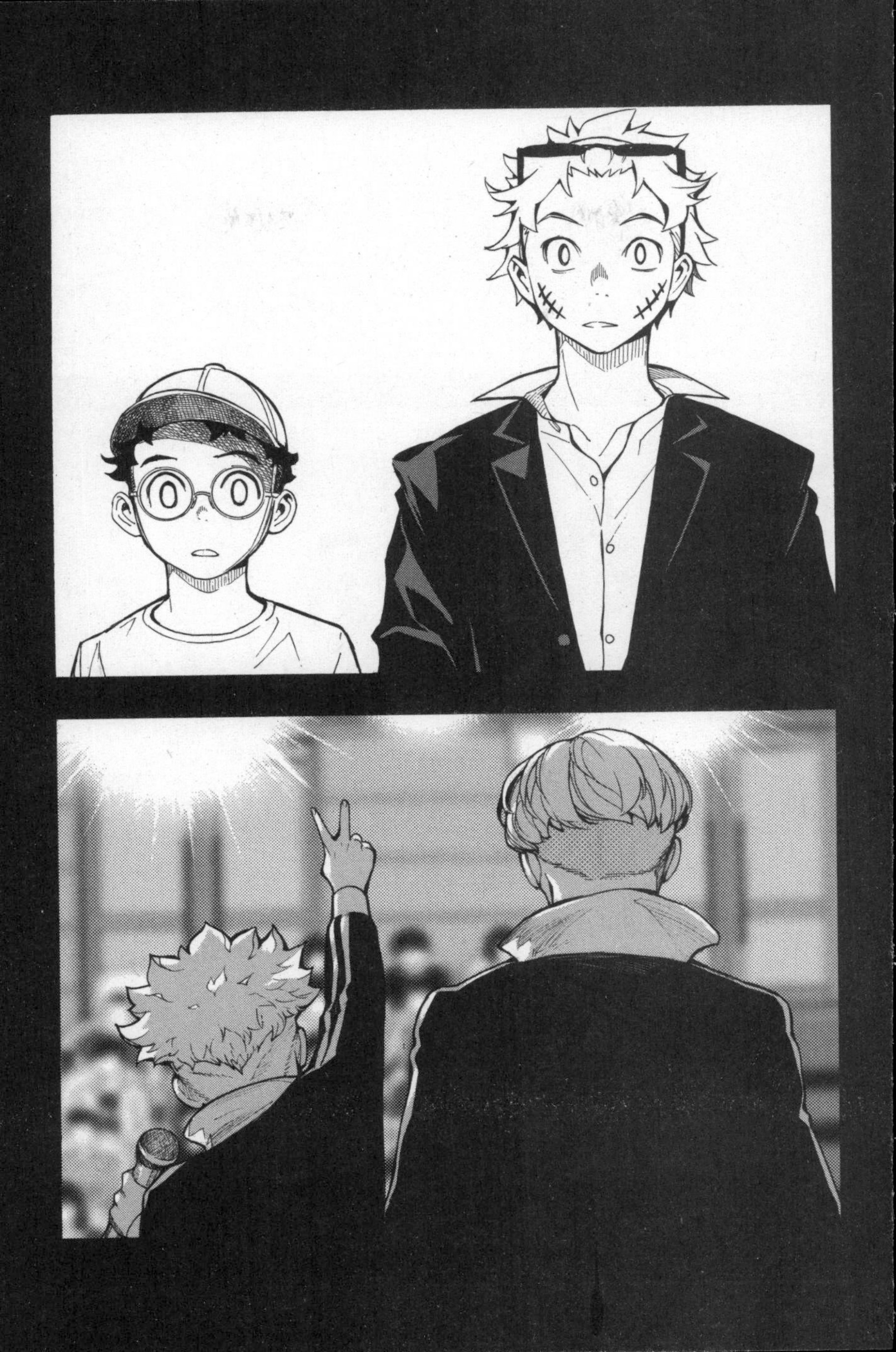

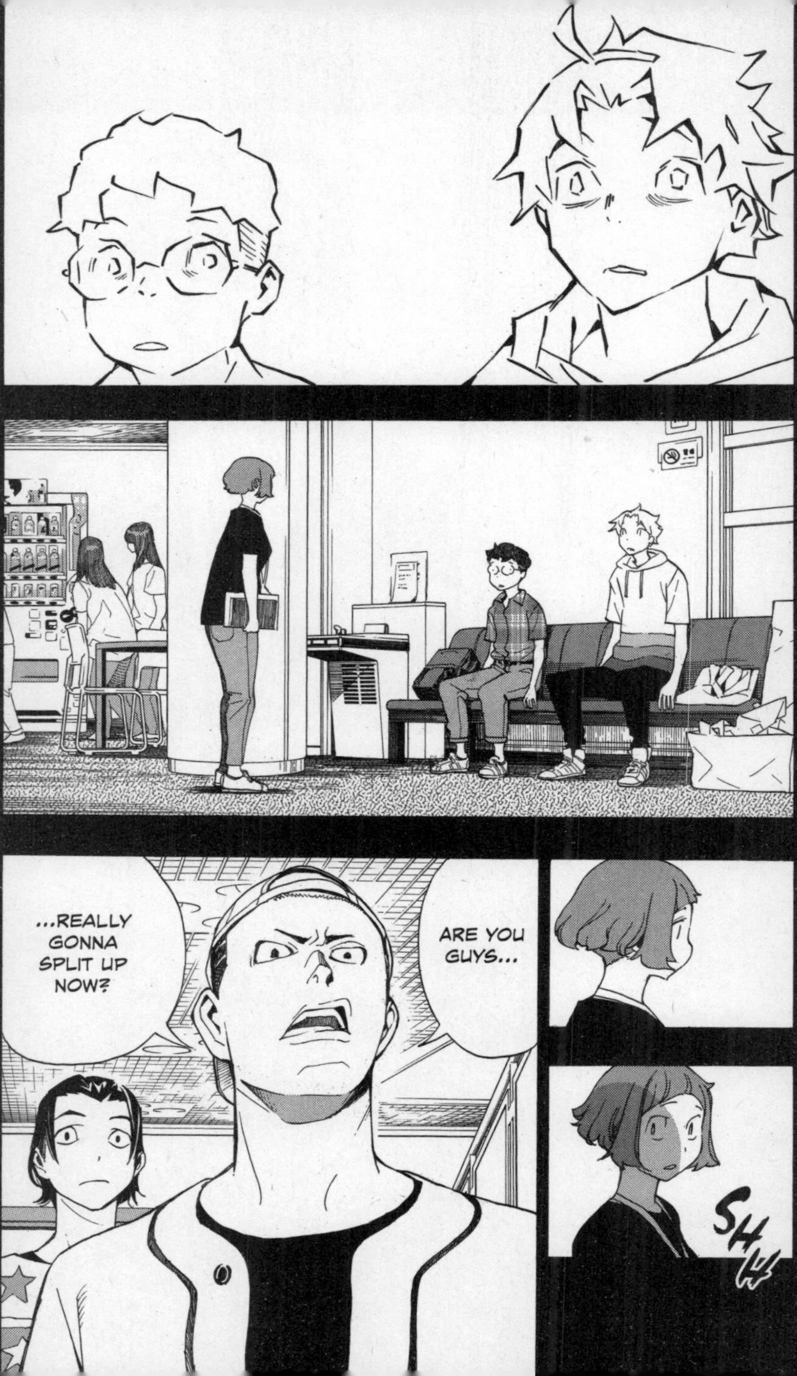
ARE YOU GUYS...
...REALLY GONNA SPLIT UP NOW?
SH

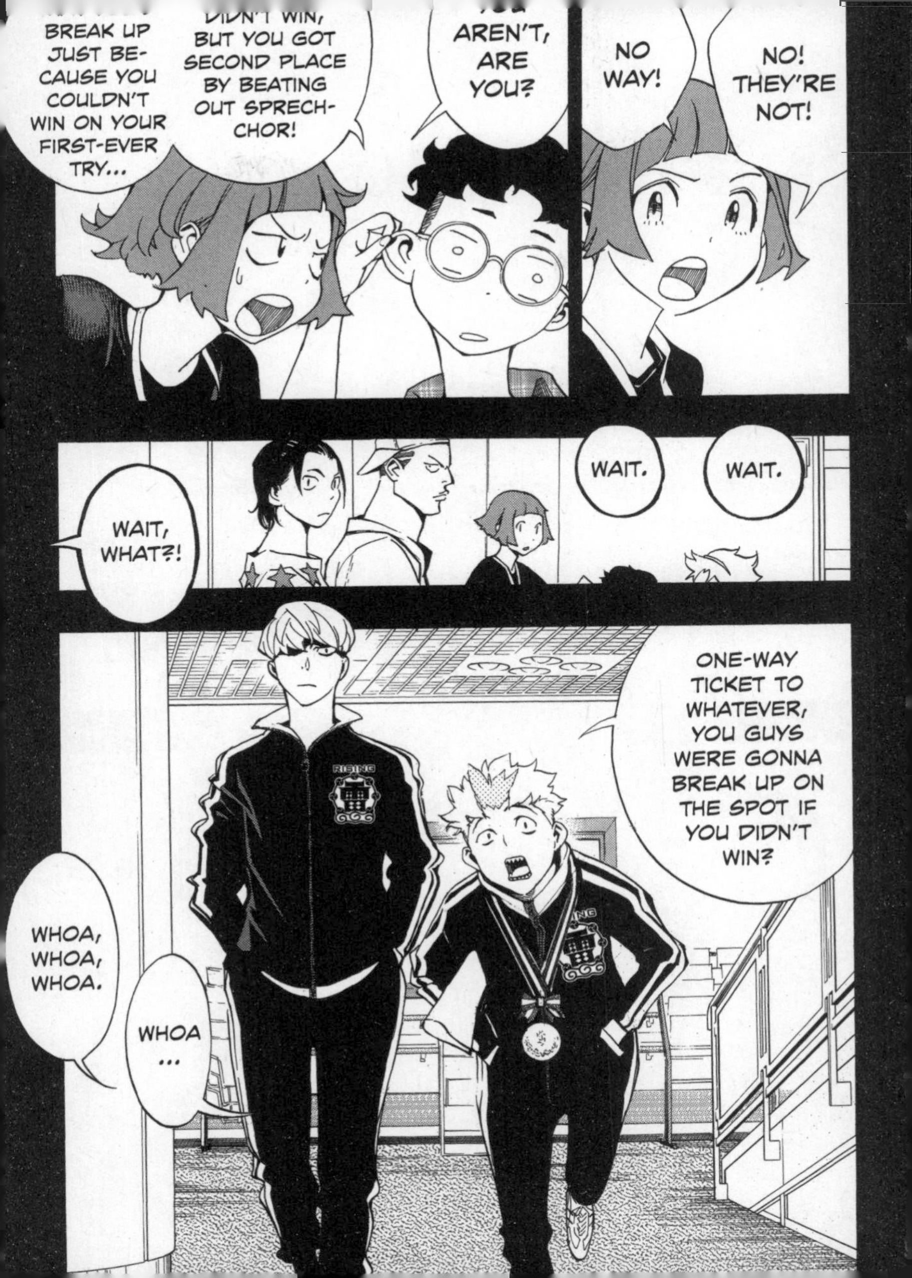
NO! THEY'RE NOT!
NO WAY!
AREN'T, ARE YOU?
DIDN'T WIN, BUT YOU GOT SECOND PLACE BY BEATING OUT SPRECH-CHOR!
BREAK UP JUST BE-CAUSE YOU COULDN'T WIN ON YOUR FIRST-EVER TRY...
WAIT.
WAIT.
WAIT, WHAT?!
ONE-WAY TICKET TO WHATEVER, YOU GUYS WERE GONNA BREAK UP ON THE SPOT IF YOU DIDN'T WIN?
RISING
WHOA, WHOA, WHOA.
WHOA ...

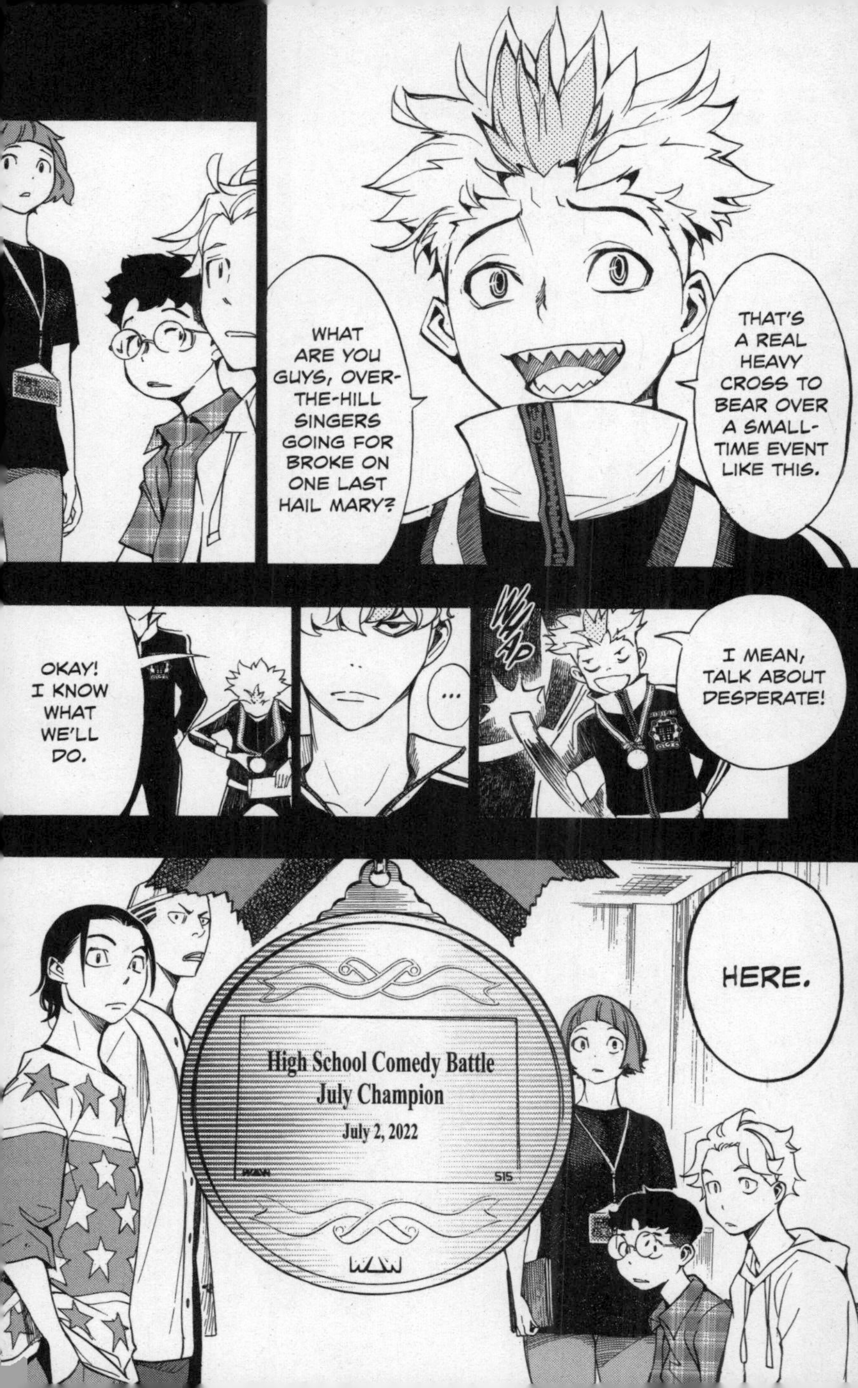

THAT'S A REAL HEAVY CROSS TO BEAR OVER A SMALL-TIME EVENT LIKE THIS.
WHAT ARE YOU GUYS, OVER-THE-HILL SINGERS GOING FOR BROKE ON ONE LAST HAIL MARY?
I MEAN, TALK ABOUT DESPERATE!
WHAP
...
OKAY! I KNOW WHAT WE'LL DO.
HERE.
High School Comedy Battle
July Champion
July 2, 2022
WAW
515
WAW

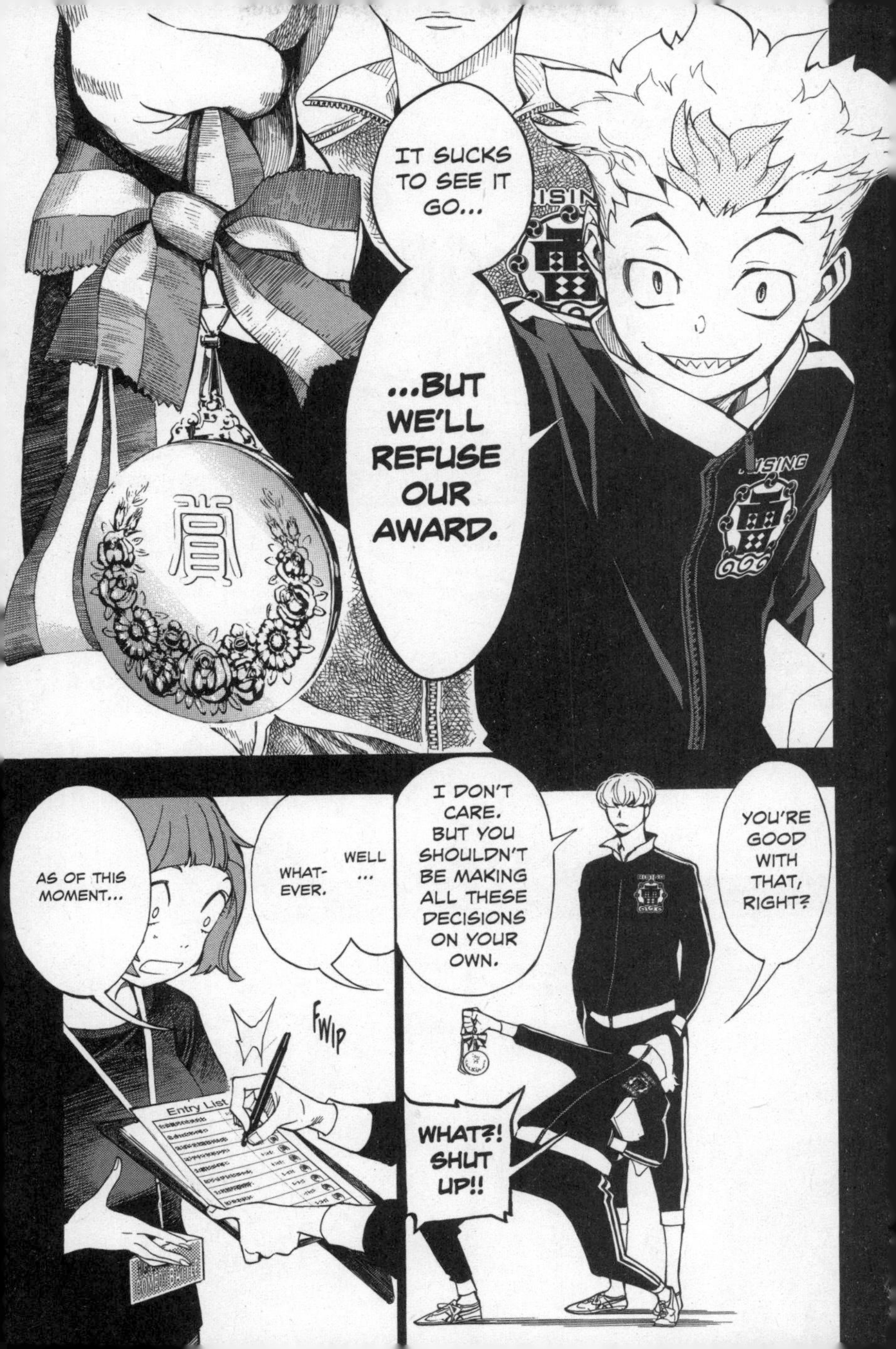
IT SUCKS TO SEE IT GO...
...BUT WE'LL REFUSE OUR AWARD.
YOU'RE GOOD WITH THAT, RIGHT?
I DON'T CARE. BUT YOU SHOULDN'T BE MAKING ALL THESE DECISIONS ON YOUR OWN.
WHAT?! SHUT UP!!
WELL ...
WHAT-EVER.
AS OF THIS MOMENT...
FWIP
Entry List

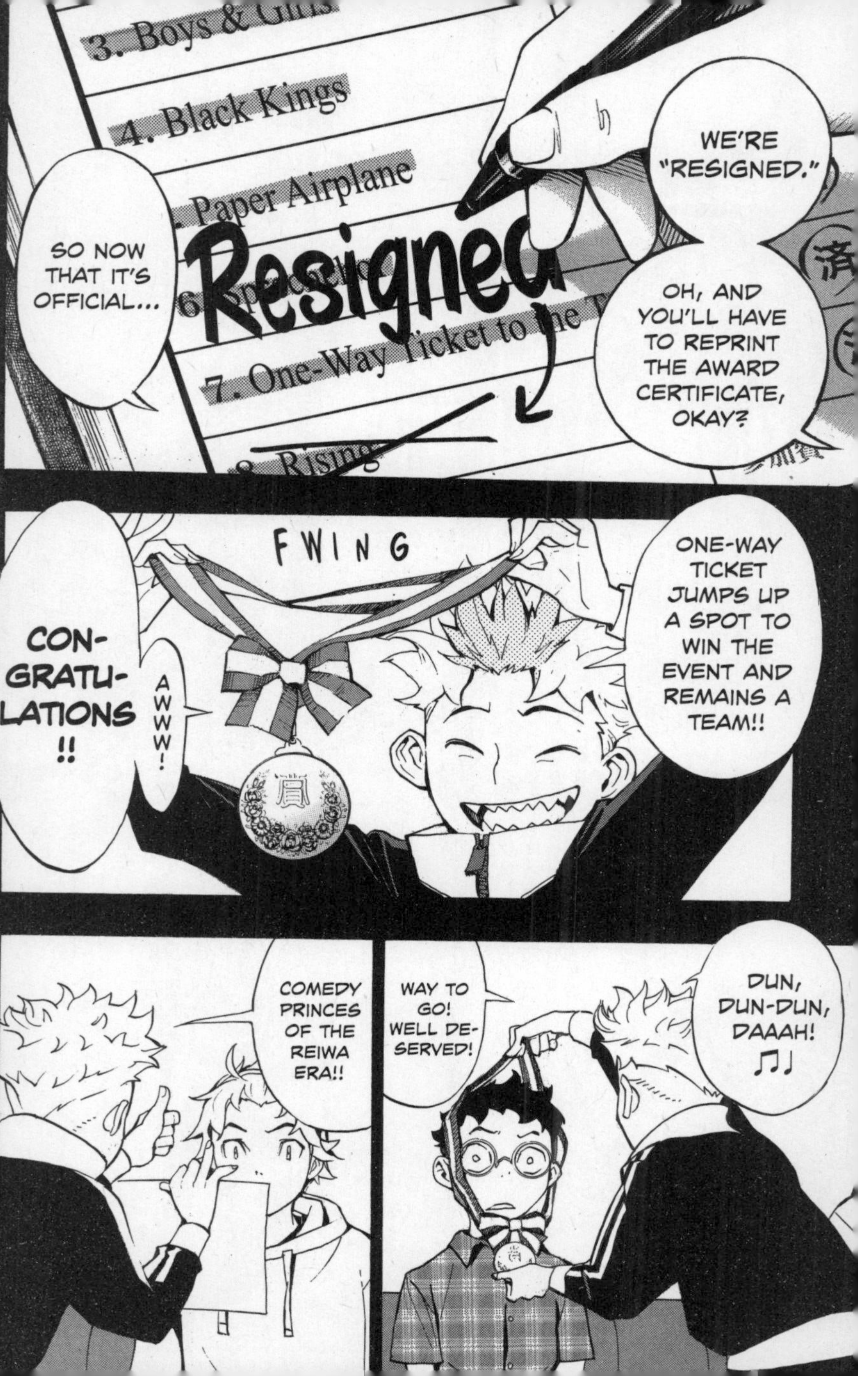
3. Boys &
4. Black Kings
Paper Airplane
WE'RE "RESIGNED."
Resigned
7. One-Way Ticket to
OH, AND YOU'LL HAVE TO REPRINT THE AWARD CERTIFICATE, OKAY?
SO NOW THAT IT'S OFFICIAL...
Rising
ONE-WAY TICKET JUMPS UP A SPOT TO WIN THE EVENT AND REMAINS A TEAM!!
FWING
AWWW!
CON-GRATU-LATIONS!!
DUN, DUN-DUN, DAAAH! ♫♩
WAY TO GO! WELL DE-SERVED!
COMEDY PRINCES OF THE REIWA ERA!!

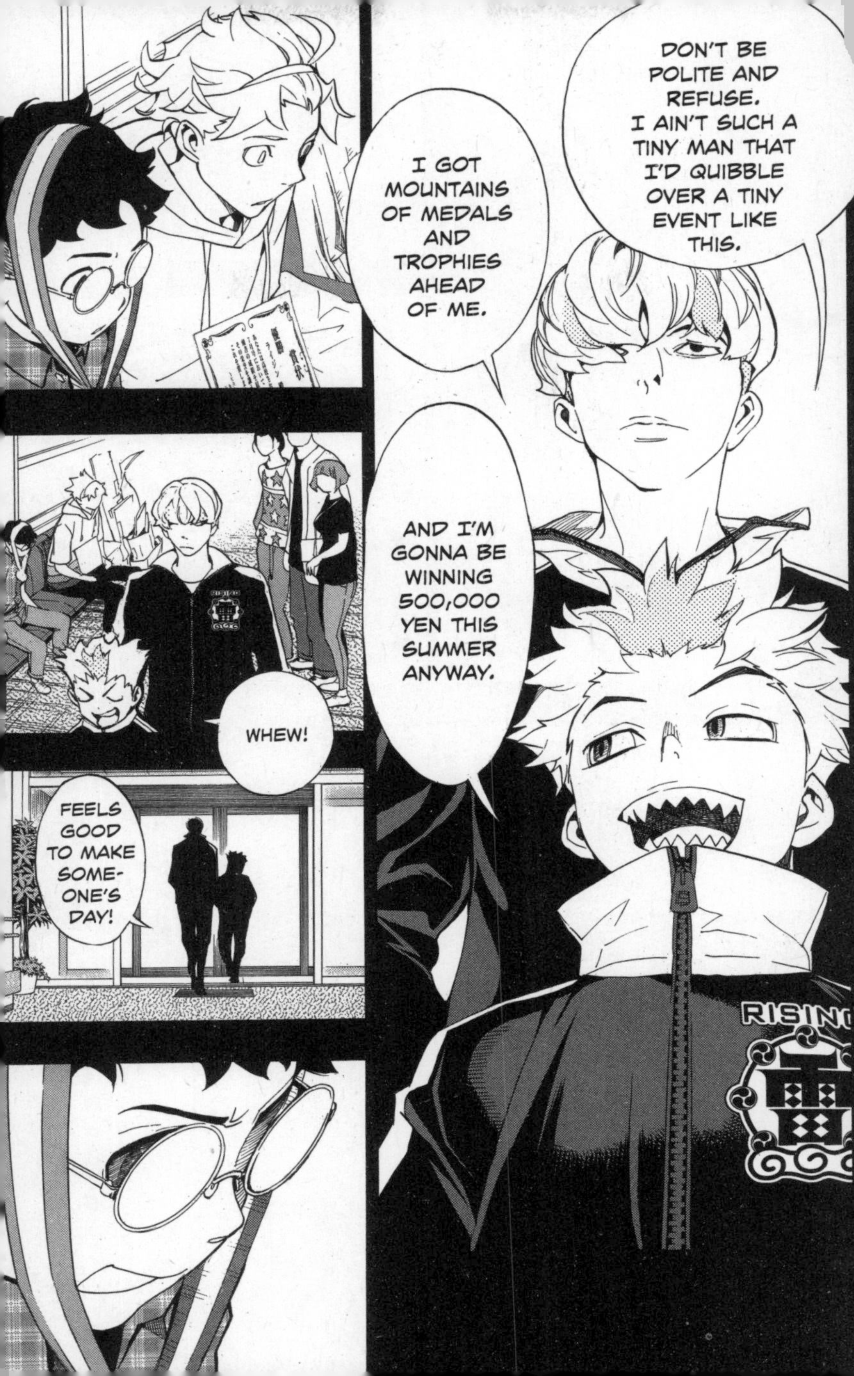
DON'T BE POLITE AND REFUSE. I AIN'T SUCH A TINY MAN THAT I'D QUIBBLE OVER A TINY EVENT LIKE THIS.
I GOT MOUNTAINS OF MEDALS AND TROPHIES AHEAD OF ME.
AND I'M GONNA BE WINNING 500,000 YEN THIS SUMMER ANYWAY.
WHEW!
FEELS GOOD TO MAKE SOME-ONE'S DAY!

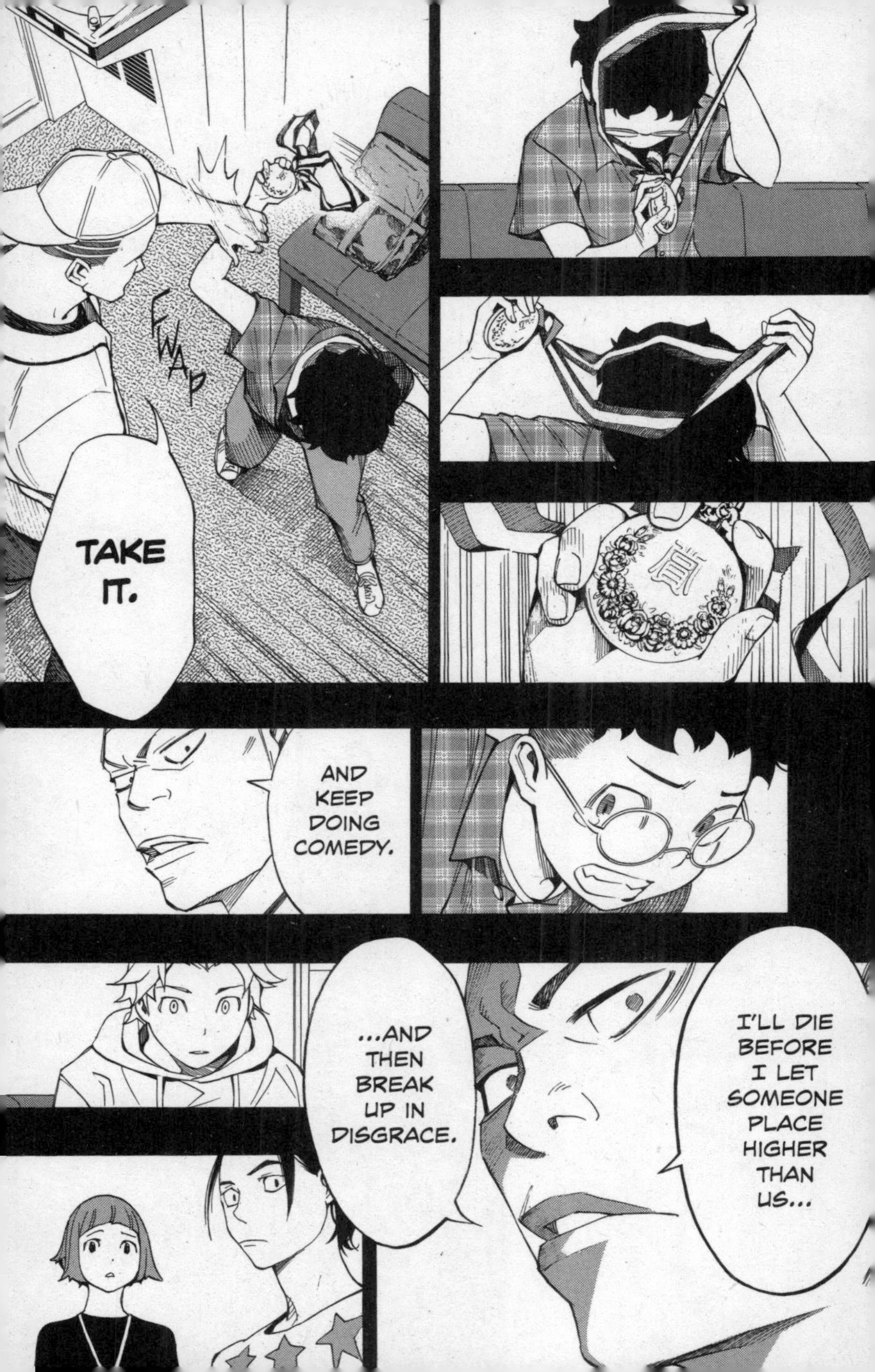
FWAP
TAKE IT.
AND KEEP DOING COMEDY.
I'LL DIE BEFORE I LET SOMEONE PLACE HIGHER THAN US...
...AND THEN BREAK UP IN DISGRACE.

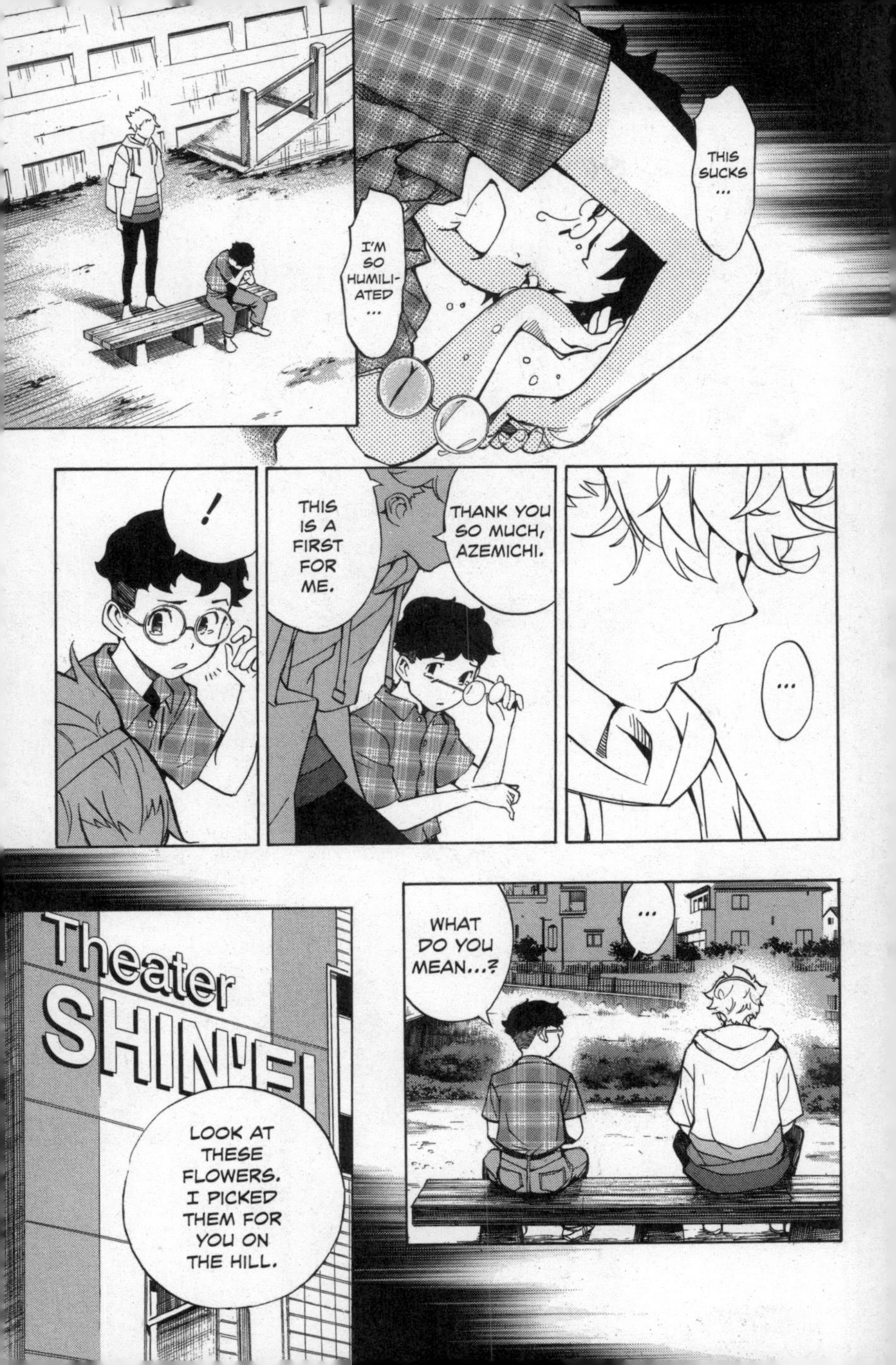
THIS SUCKS ...
I'M SO HUMILIATED ...
...
THANK YOU SO MUCH, AZEMICHI.
THIS IS A FIRST FOR ME.
!
...
WHAT DO YOU MEAN...?
Theater SHIN'EI
LOOK AT THESE FLOWERS. I PICKED THEM FOR YOU ON THE HILL.

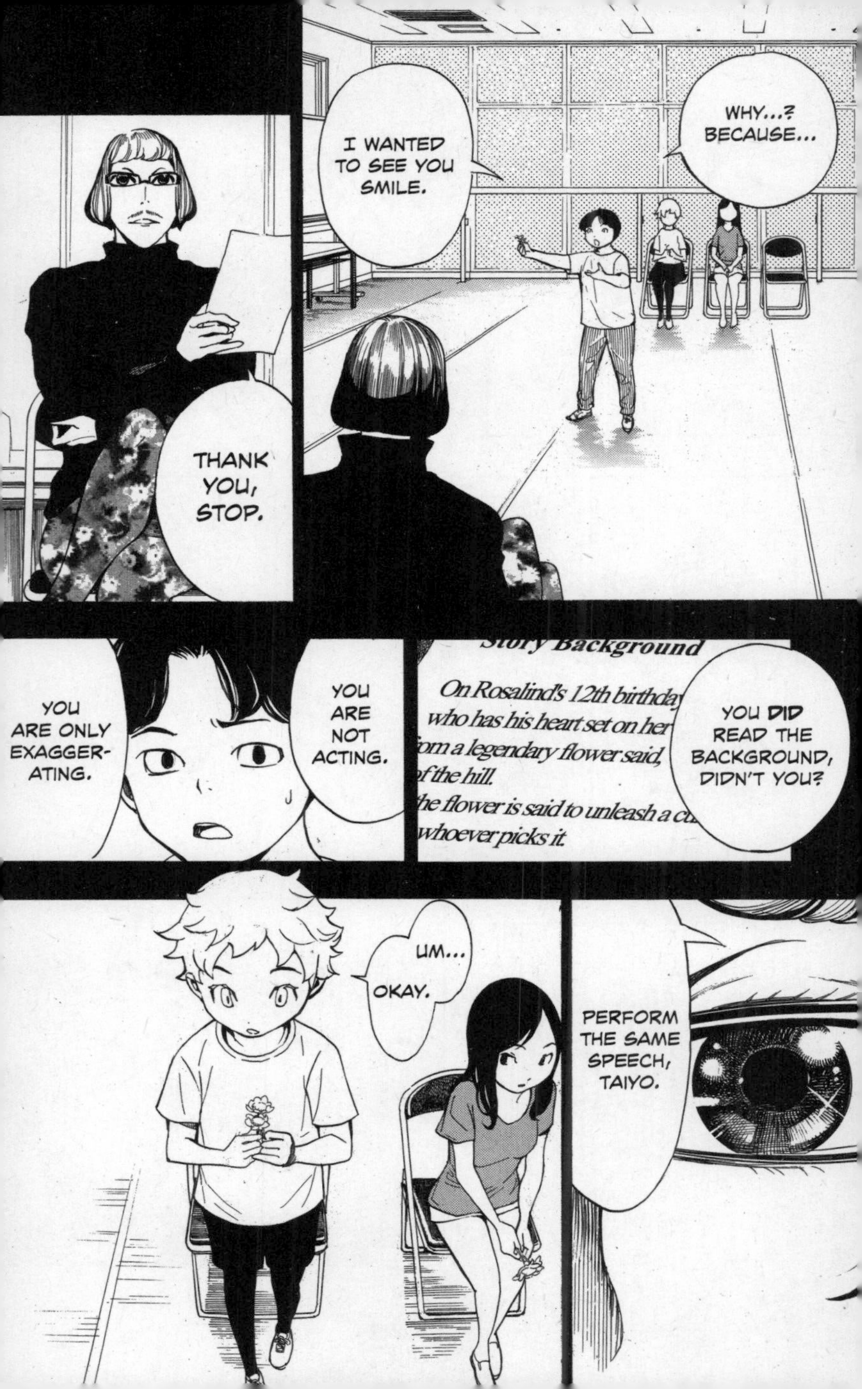
WHY...? BECAUSE...
I WANTED TO SEE YOU SMILE.
THANK YOU, STOP.
Story Background
On Rosalind's 12th birthday
who has his heart set on her
a legendary flower said,
the hill.
the flower is said to unleash a
whoever picks it.
YOU DID READ THE BACKGROUND, DIDN'T YOU?
YOU ARE NOT ACTING.
YOU ARE ONLY EXAGGERATING.
PERFORM THE SAME SPEECH, TAIYO.
UM...
OKAY.

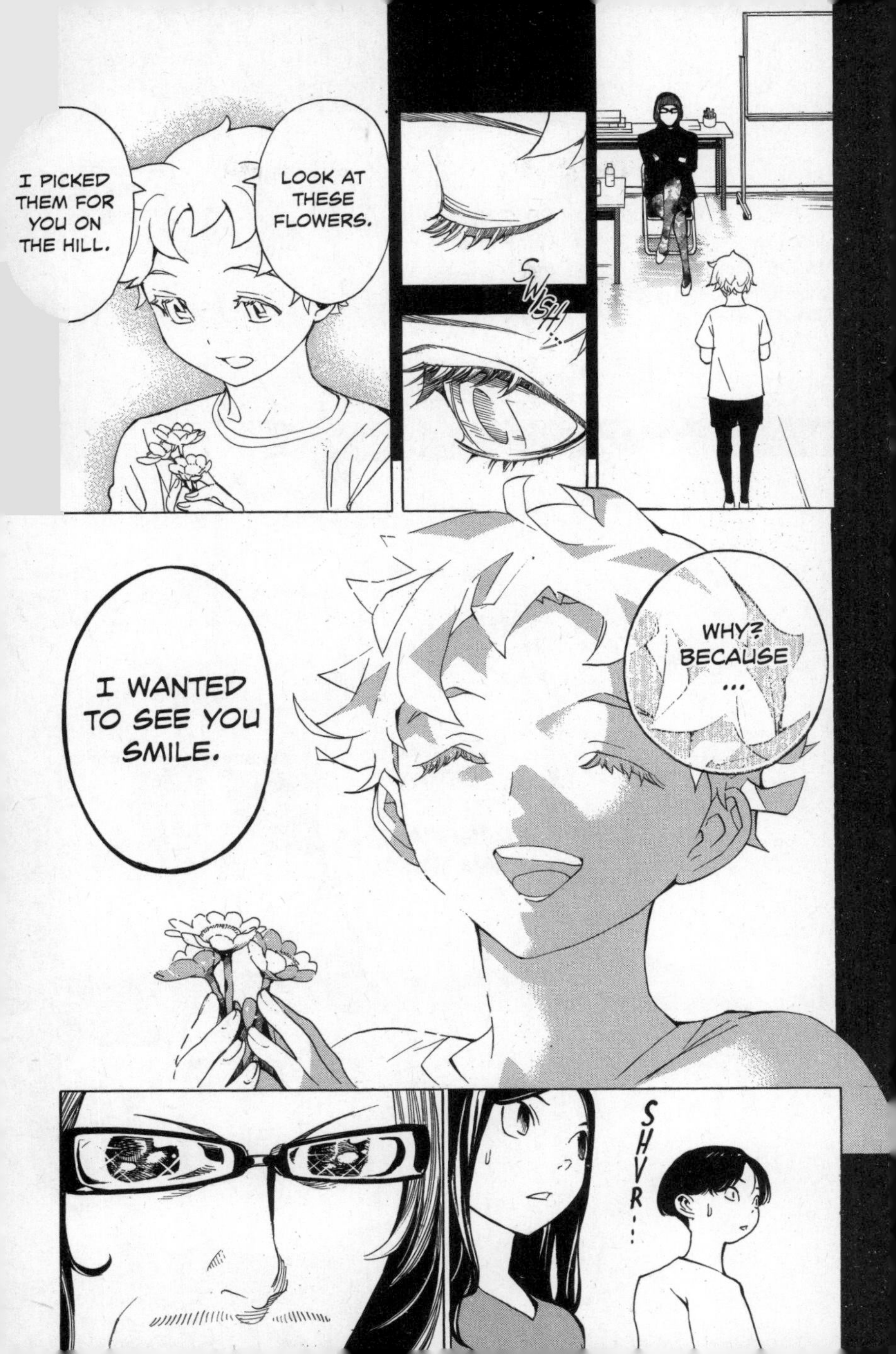
SWISH...
LOOK AT THESE FLOWERS.
I PICKED THEM FOR YOU ON THE HILL.
WHY? BECAUSE ...
I WANTED TO SEE YOU SMILE.
SHVR...

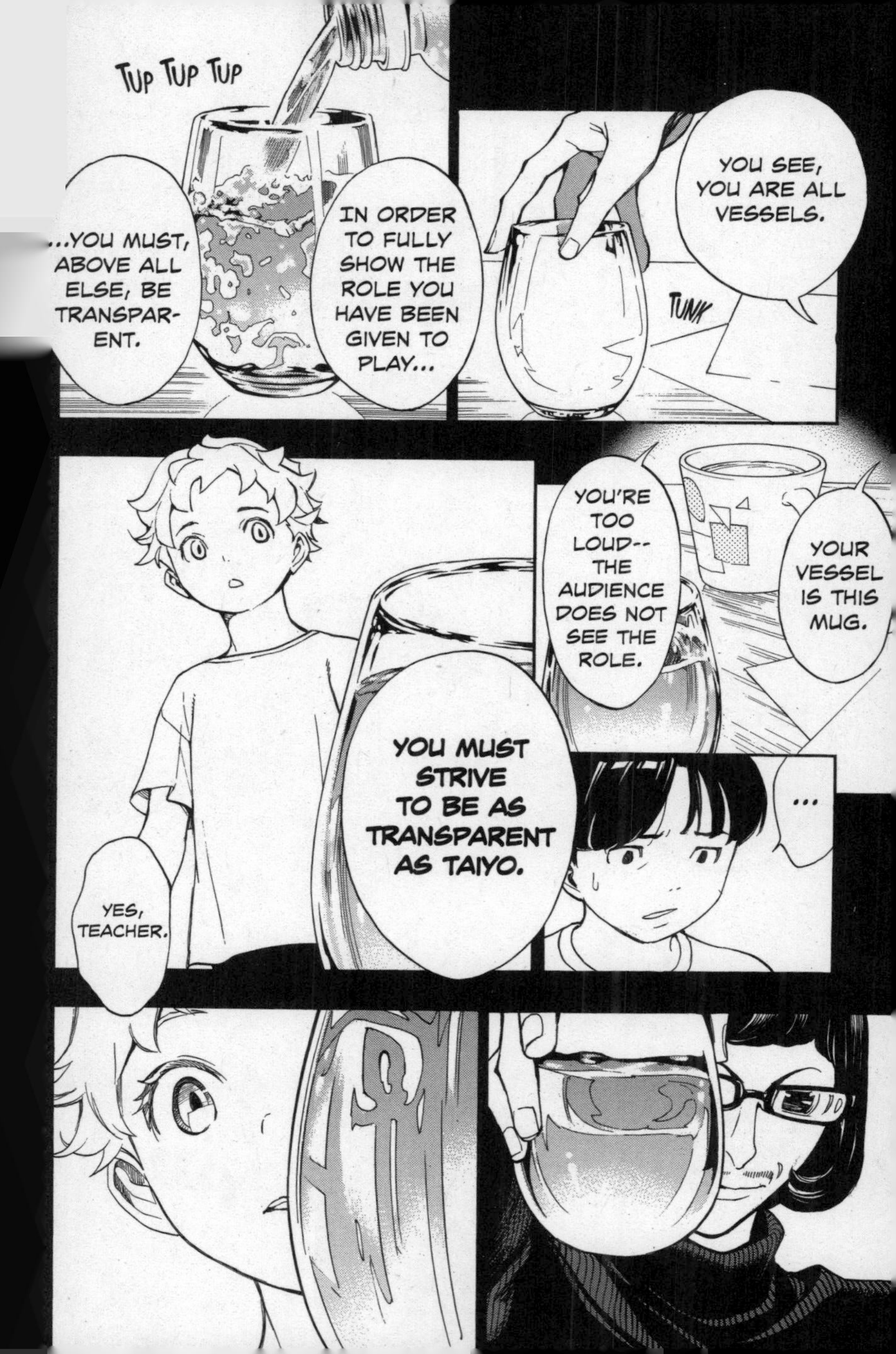
YOU SEE, YOU ARE ALL VESSELS.
TUNK
TUP TUP TUP
IN ORDER TO FULLY SHOW THE ROLE YOU HAVE BEEN GIVEN TO PLAY...
...YOU MUST, ABOVE ALL ELSE, BE TRANSPAR-ENT.
YOUR VESSEL IS THIS MUG.
YOU'RE TOO LOUD-- THE AUDIENCE DOES NOT SEE THE ROLE.
...
YOU MUST STRIVE TO BE AS TRANSPARENT AS TAIYO.
YES, TEACHER.

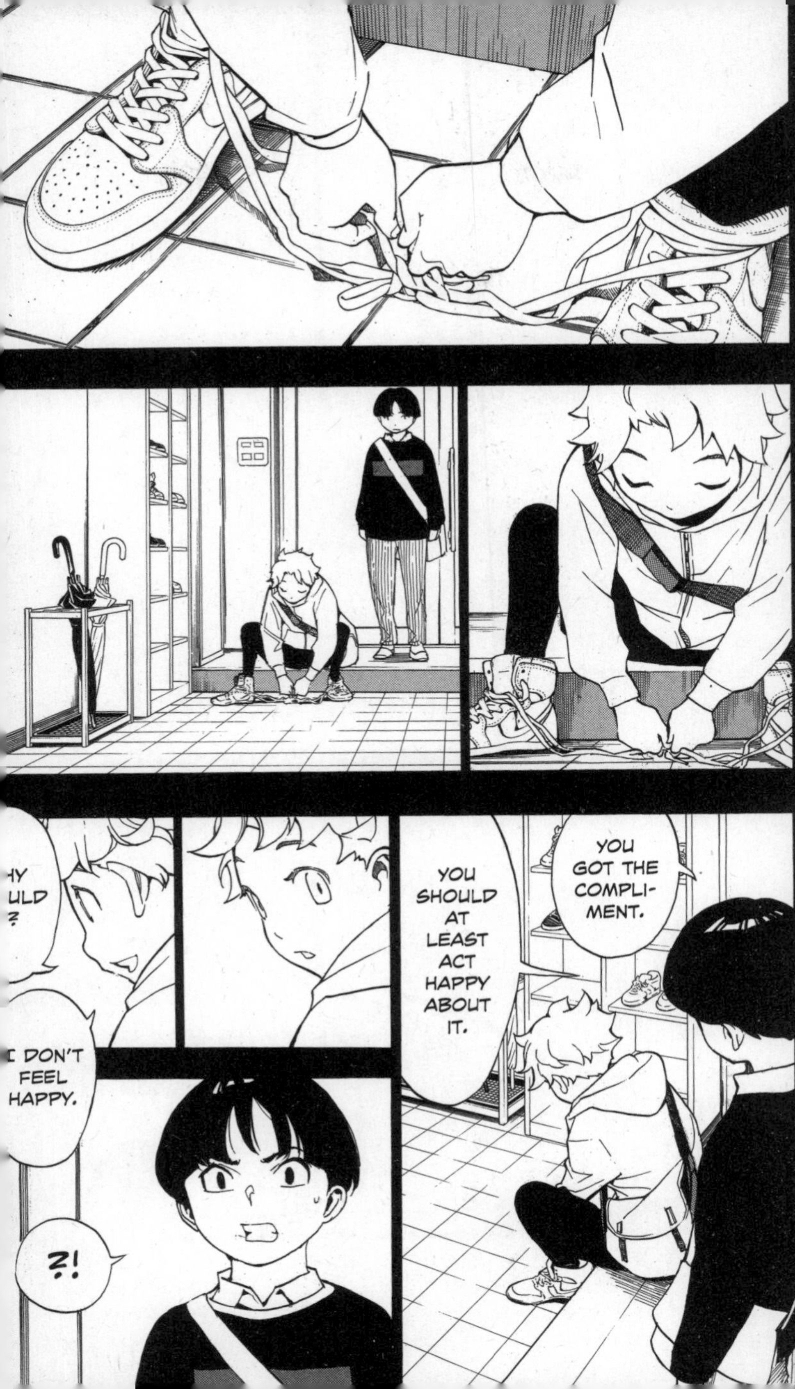
YOU GOT THE COMPLIMENT.
YOU SHOULD AT LEAST ACT HAPPY ABOUT IT.
I DON'T FEEL HAPPY.
?!

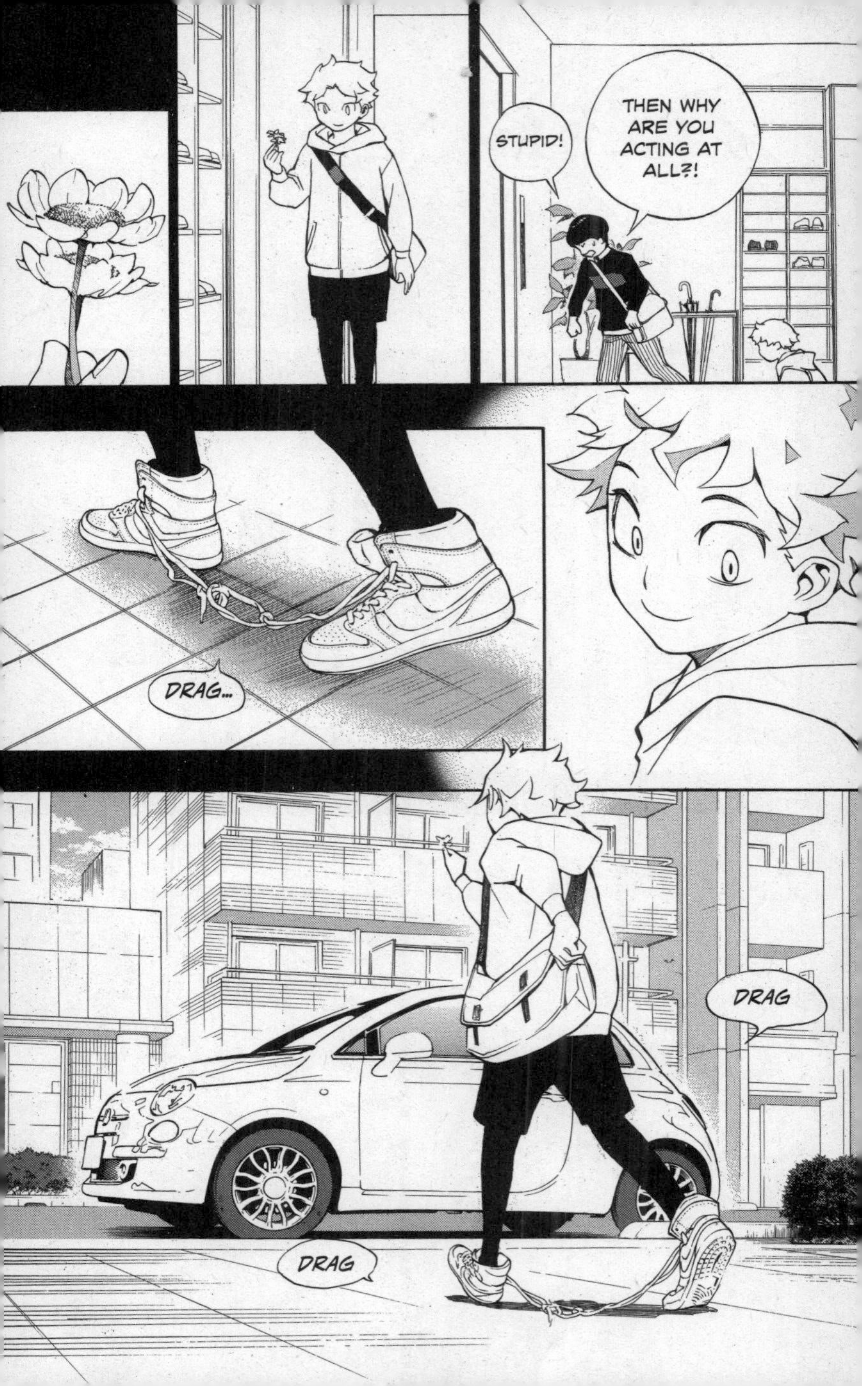
THEN WHY ARE YOU ACTING AT ALL?!
STUPID!
DRAG...
DRAG
DRAG

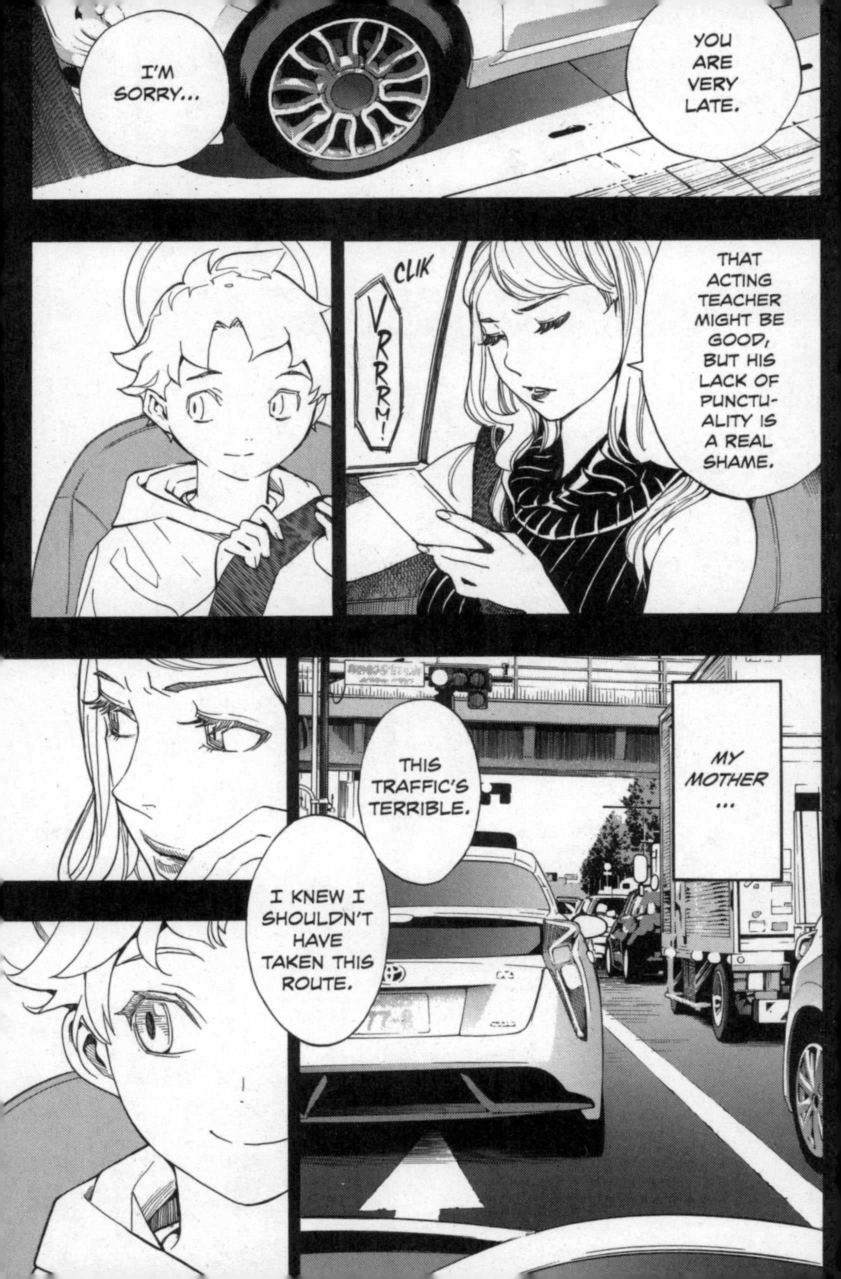
YOU ARE VERY LATE.
I'M SORRY...
THAT ACTING TEACHER MIGHT BE GOOD, BUT HIS LACK OF PUNCTU-ALITY IS A REAL SHAME.
CLIK
VRRRM!
MY MOTHER ...
THIS TRAFFIC'S TERRIBLE.
I KNEW I SHOULDN'T HAVE TAKEN THIS ROUTE.

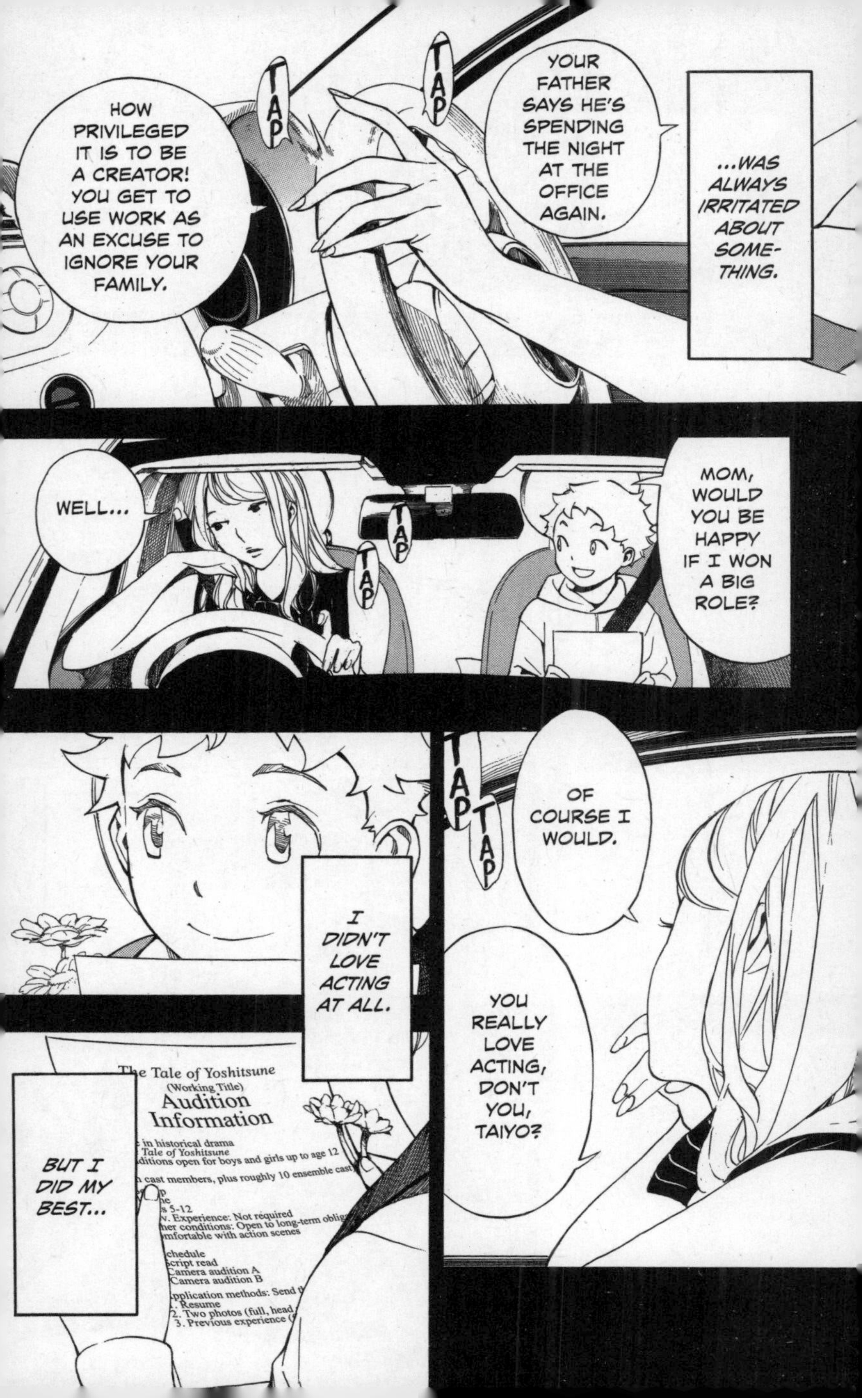
...WAS ALWAYS IRRITATED ABOUT SOMETHING.
YOUR FATHER SAYS HE'S SPENDING THE NIGHT AT THE OFFICE AGAIN.
TAP
TAP
HOW PRIVILEGED IT IS TO BE A CREATOR! YOU GET TO USE WORK AS AN EXCUSE TO IGNORE YOUR FAMILY.
MOM, WOULD YOU BE HAPPY IF I WON A BIG ROLE?
TAP
TAP
WELL...
OF COURSE I WOULD.
TAP
TAP
YOU REALLY LOVE ACTING, DON'T YOU, TAIYO?
I DIDN'T LOVE ACTING AT ALL.
BUT I DID MY BEST...
The Tale of Yoshitsune
(Working Title)
Audition Information
Tale of Yoshitsune
ditions open for boys and girls up to age 12
cast members, plus roughly 10 ensemble cast
s 5-12
v. Experience: Not required
her conditions: Open to long-term oblig
omfortable with action scenes
chedule
cript read
Camera audition A
Camera audition B
Application methods: Send t
. Resume
2. Two photos (full, head
3. Previous experience (

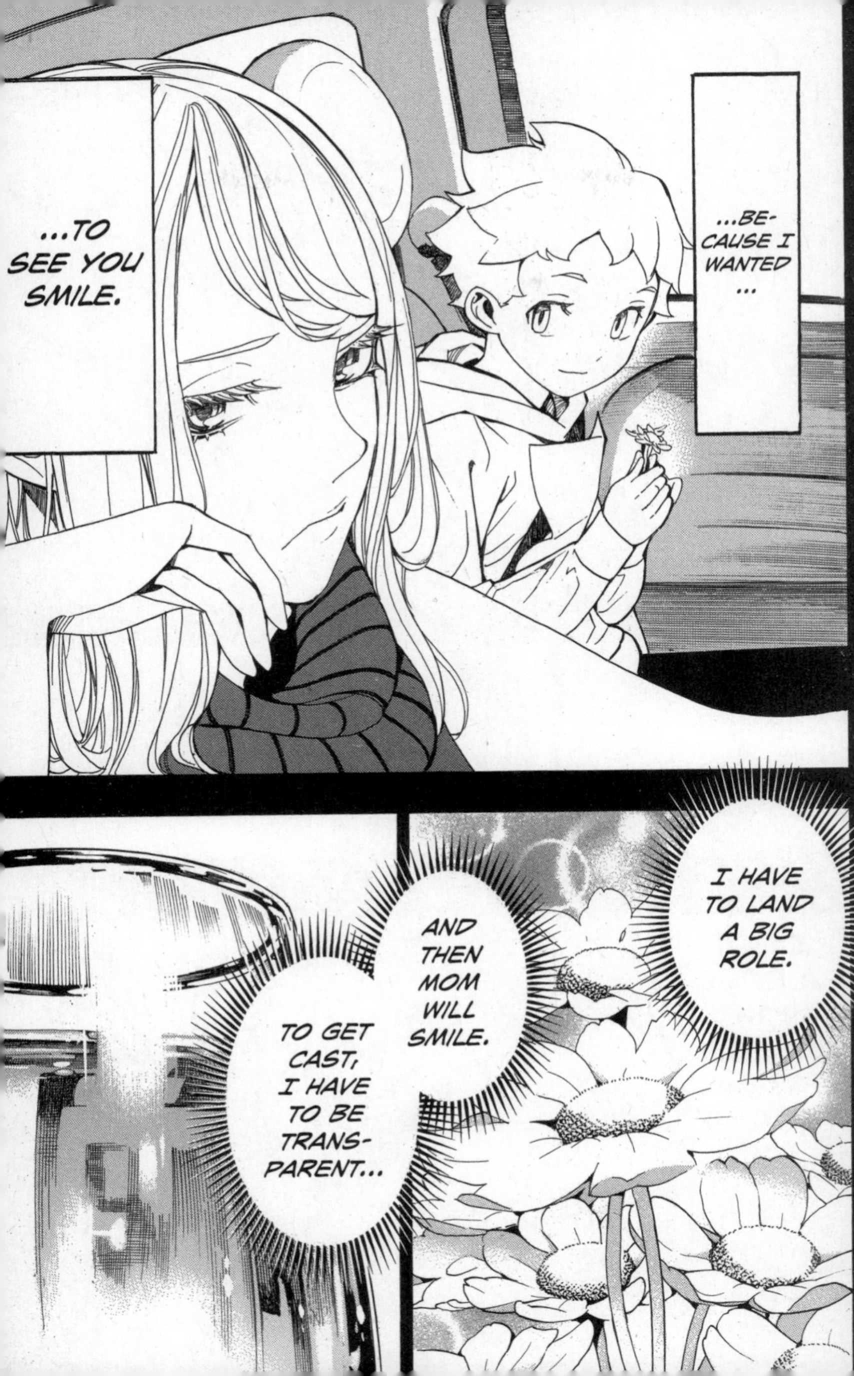
...BE-CAUSE I WANTED ...
...TO SEE YOU SMILE.
I HAVE TO LAND A BIG ROLE.
AND THEN MOM WILL SMILE.
TO GET CAST, I HAVE TO BE TRANS-PARENT...

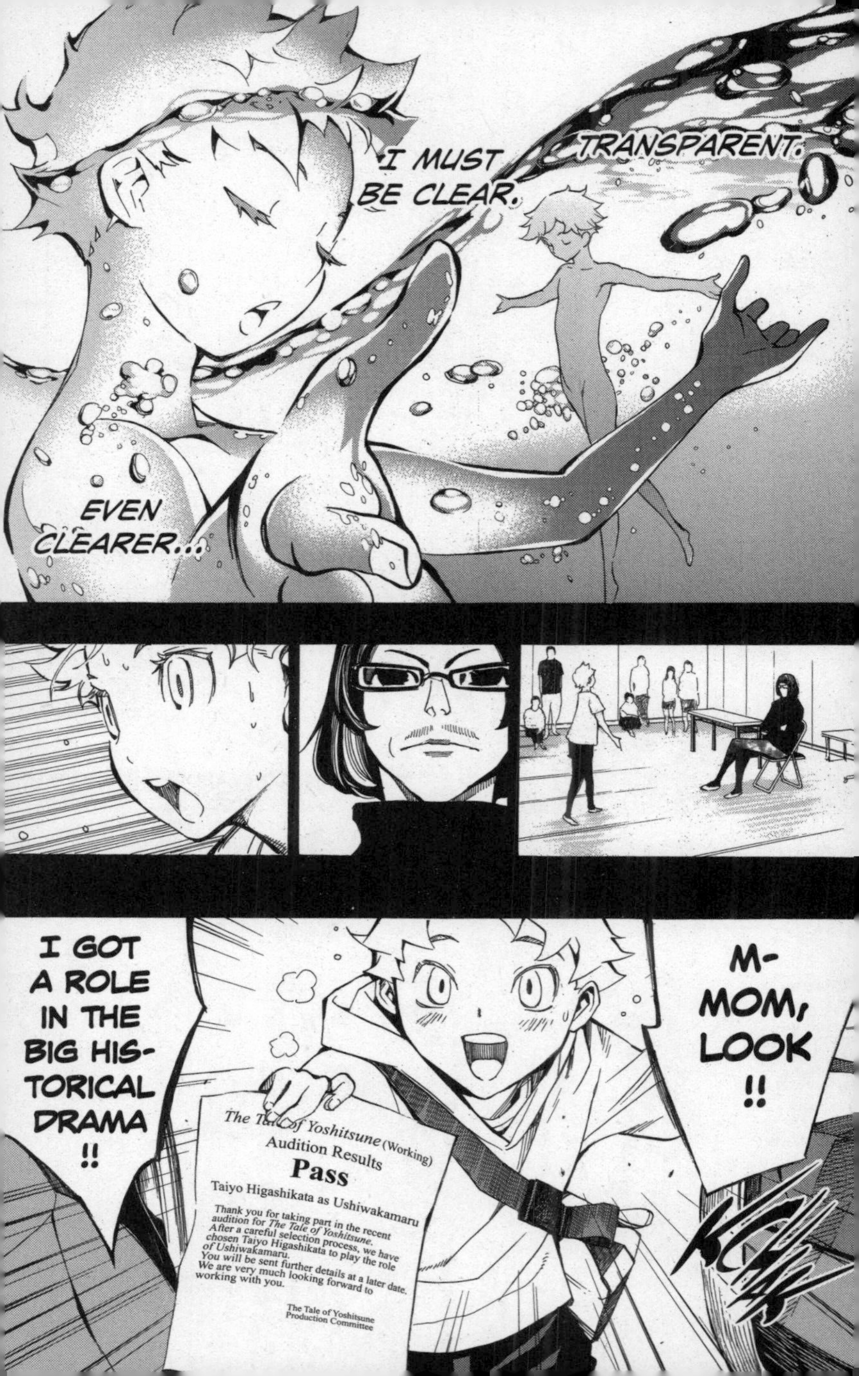
TRANSPARENT.
I MUST BE CLEAR.
EVEN CLEARER...
M-MOM, LOOK!!
I GOT A ROLE IN THE BIG HISTORICAL DRAMA!!
The Tale of Yoshitsune (Working)
Audition Results
Pass
Taiyo Higashikata as Ushiwakamaru
Thank you for taking part in the recent audition for The Tale of Yoshitsune. After a careful selection process, we have chosen Taiyo Higashikata to play the role of Ushiwakamaru.
You will be sent further details at a later date.
We are very much looking forward to working with you.
The Tale of Yoshitsune Production Committee

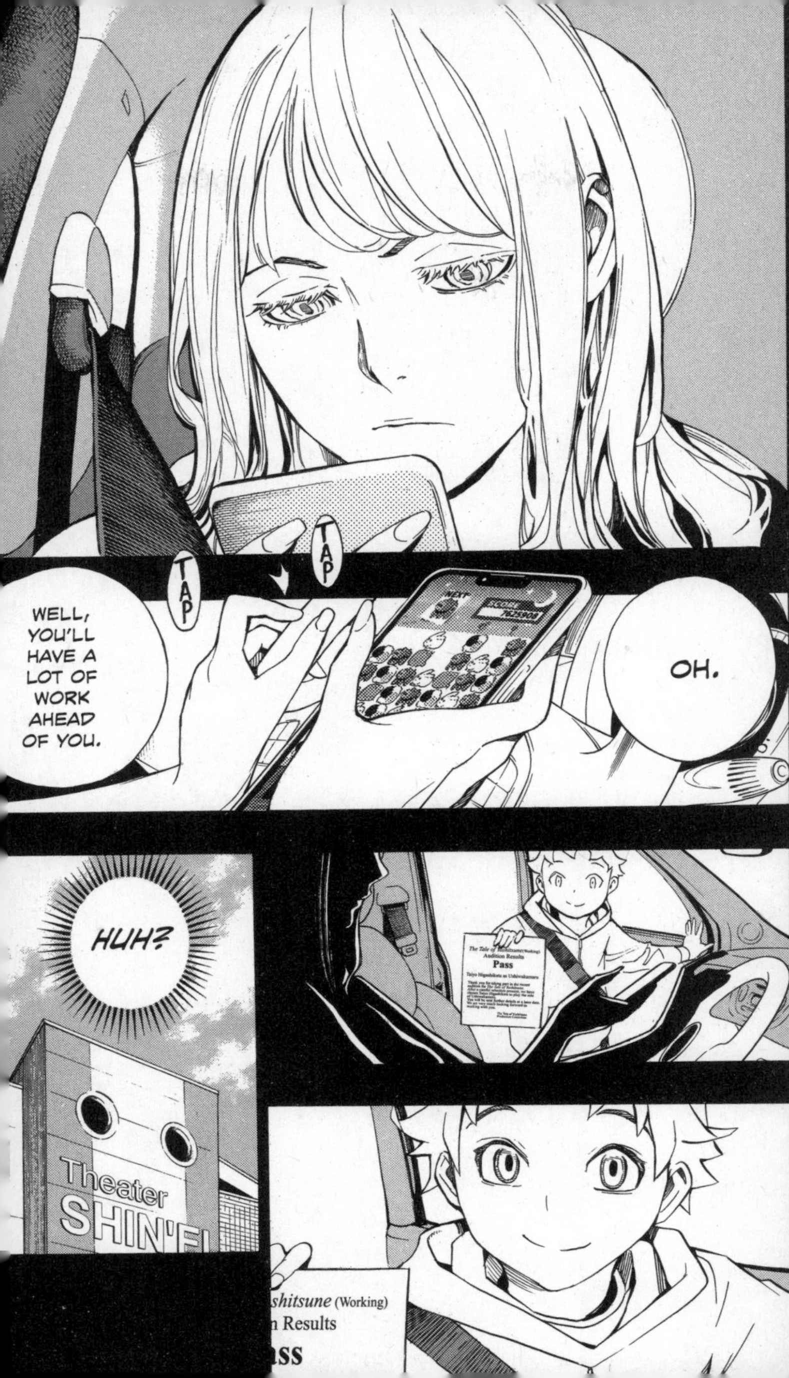
TAP
TAP
OH.
WELL, YOU'LL HAVE A LOT OF WORK AHEAD OF YOU.
The Tale of
Audition Results
Pass
shitsune (Working)
n Results
ass
HUH?
Theater SHIN'EI

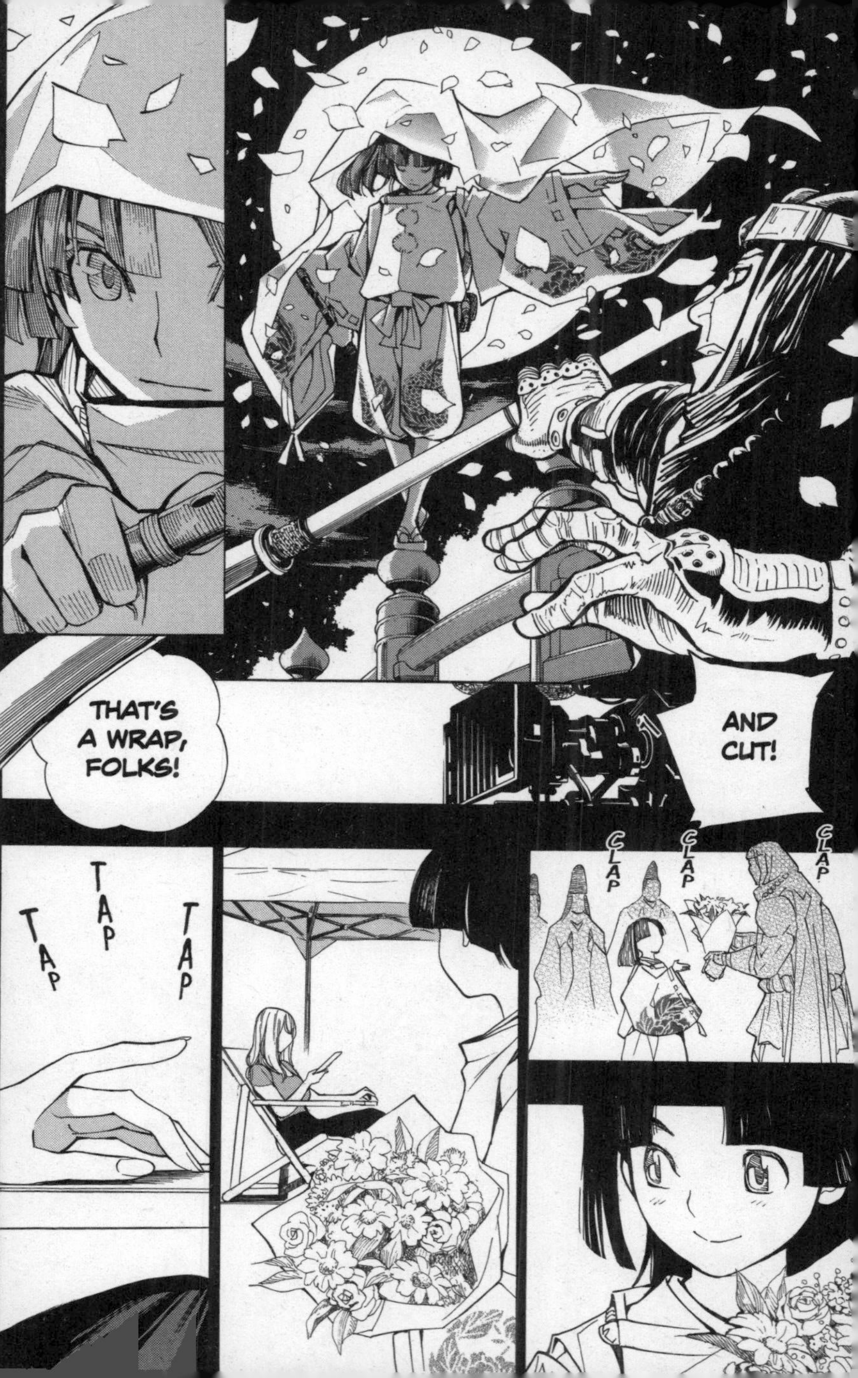
AND CUT!
THAT'S A WRAP, FOLKS!
CLAP
CLAP
CLAP
TAP
TAP
TAP

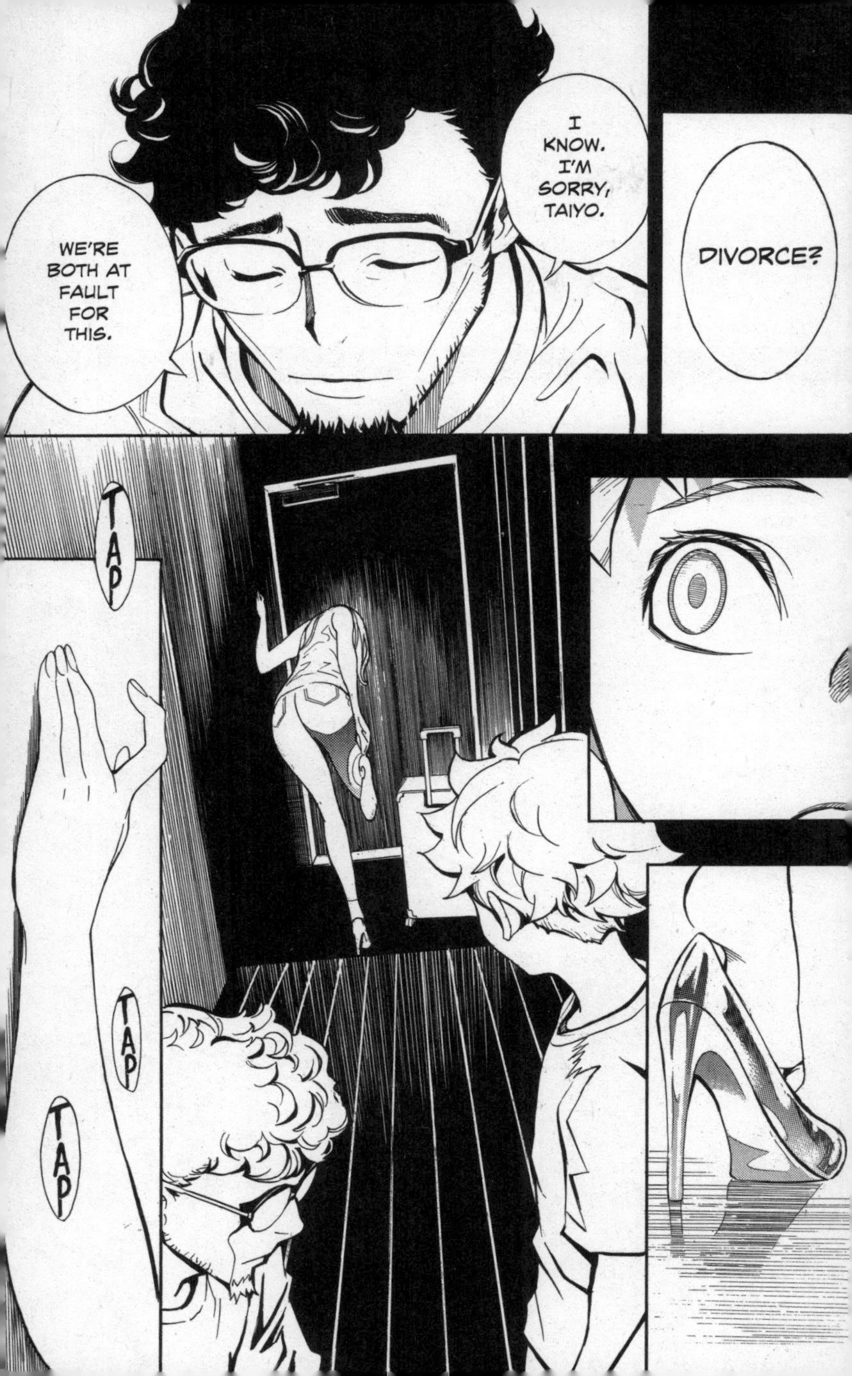
DIVORCE?
I KNOW. I'M SORRY, TAIYO.
WE'RE BOTH AT FAULT FOR THIS.
TAP
TAP
TAP

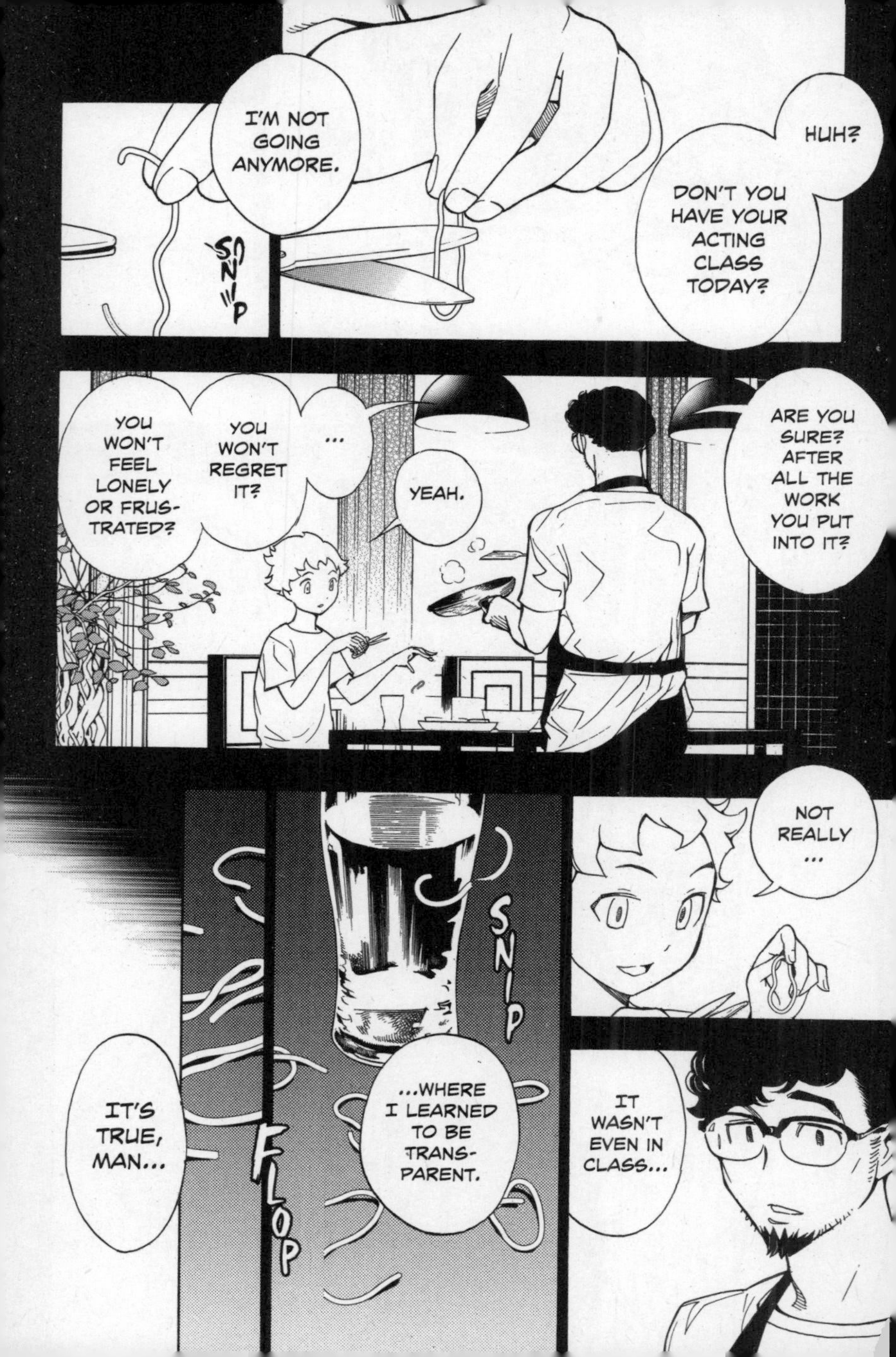
HUH?
DON'T YOU HAVE YOUR ACTING CLASS TODAY?
I'M NOT GOING ANYMORE.
SNIP
ARE YOU SURE? AFTER ALL THE WORK YOU PUT INTO IT?
YEAH.
...
YOU WON'T REGRET IT?
YOU WON'T FEEL LONELY OR FRUS-TRATED?
NOT REALLY ...
IT WASN'T EVEN IN CLASS...
SNIP
...WHERE I LEARNED TO BE TRANS-PARENT.
FLOP
IT'S TRUE, MAN...

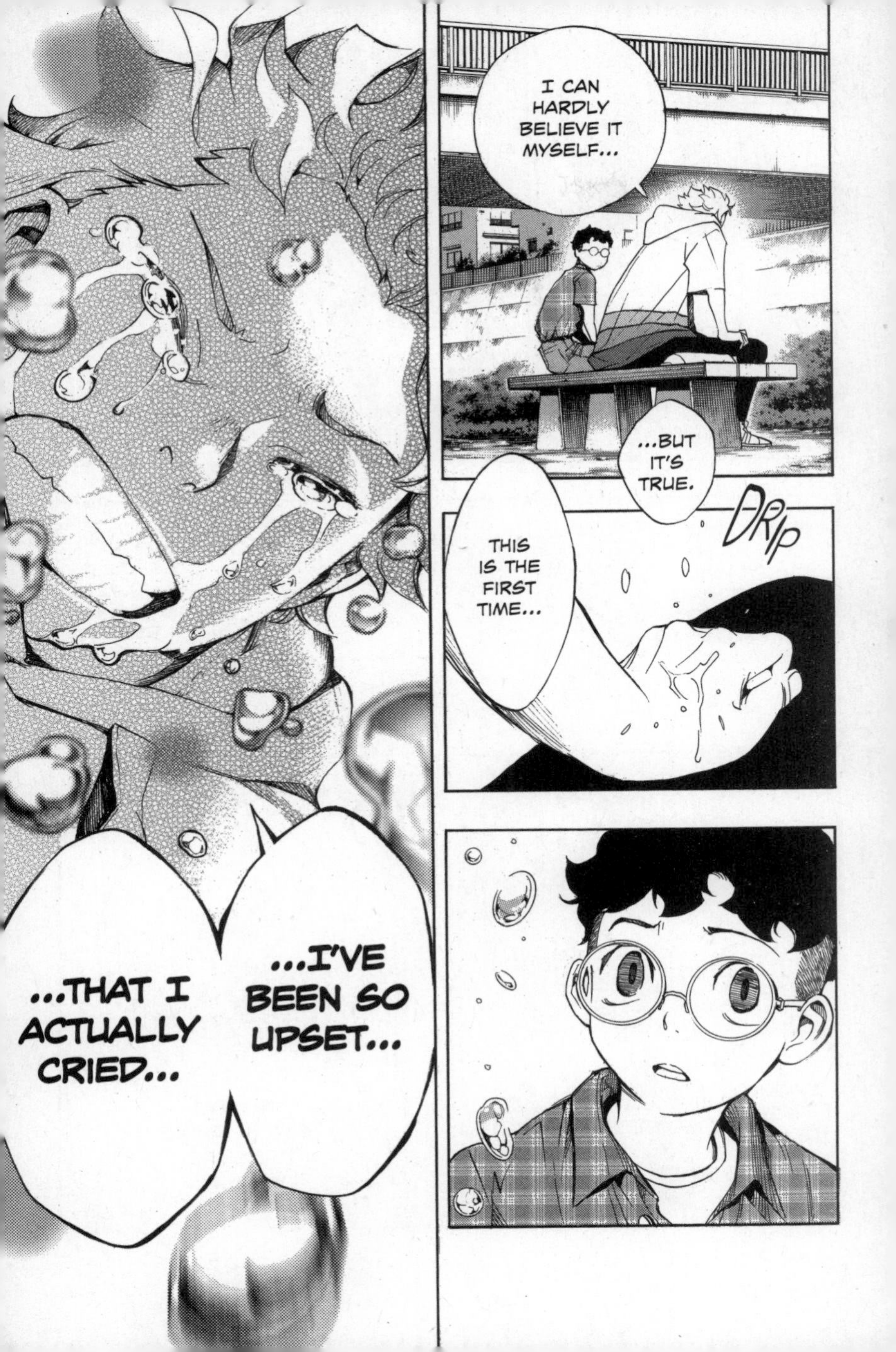
I CAN HARDLY BELIEVE IT MYSELF...
...BUT IT'S TRUE.
THIS IS THE FIRST TIME...
DRIP
...I'VE BEEN SO UPSET...
...THAT I ACTUALLY CRIED...

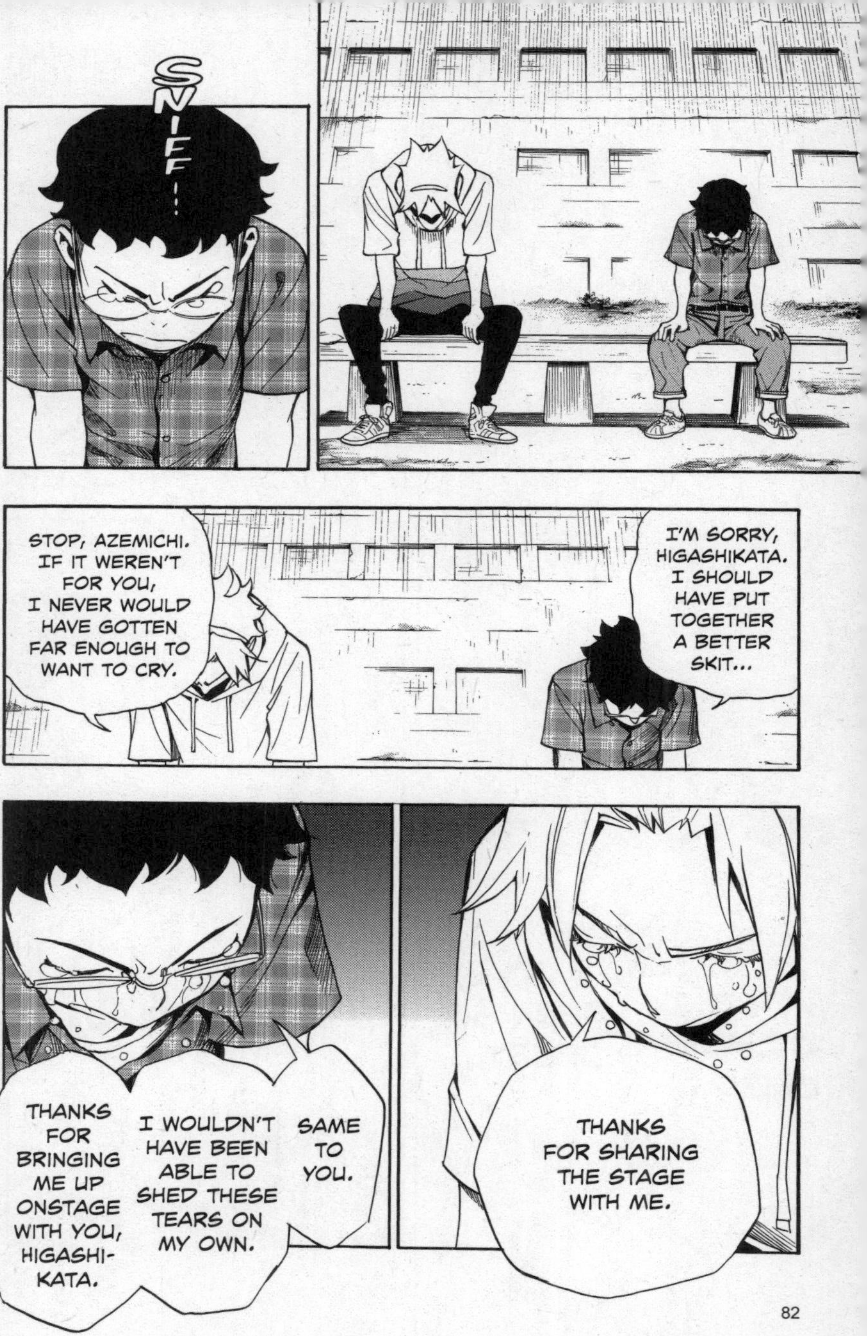
SNIFF!!
I'M SORRY, HIGASHIKATA. I SHOULD HAVE PUT TOGETHER A BETTER SKIT...
STOP, AZEMICHI. IF IT WEREN'T FOR YOU, I NEVER WOULD HAVE GOTTEN FAR ENOUGH TO WANT TO CRY.
THANKS FOR SHARING THE STAGE WITH ME.
SAME TO YOU.
I WOULDN'T HAVE BEEN ABLE TO SHED THESE TEARS ON MY OWN.
THANKS FOR BRINGING ME UP ONSTAGE WITH YOU, HIGASHI-KATA.

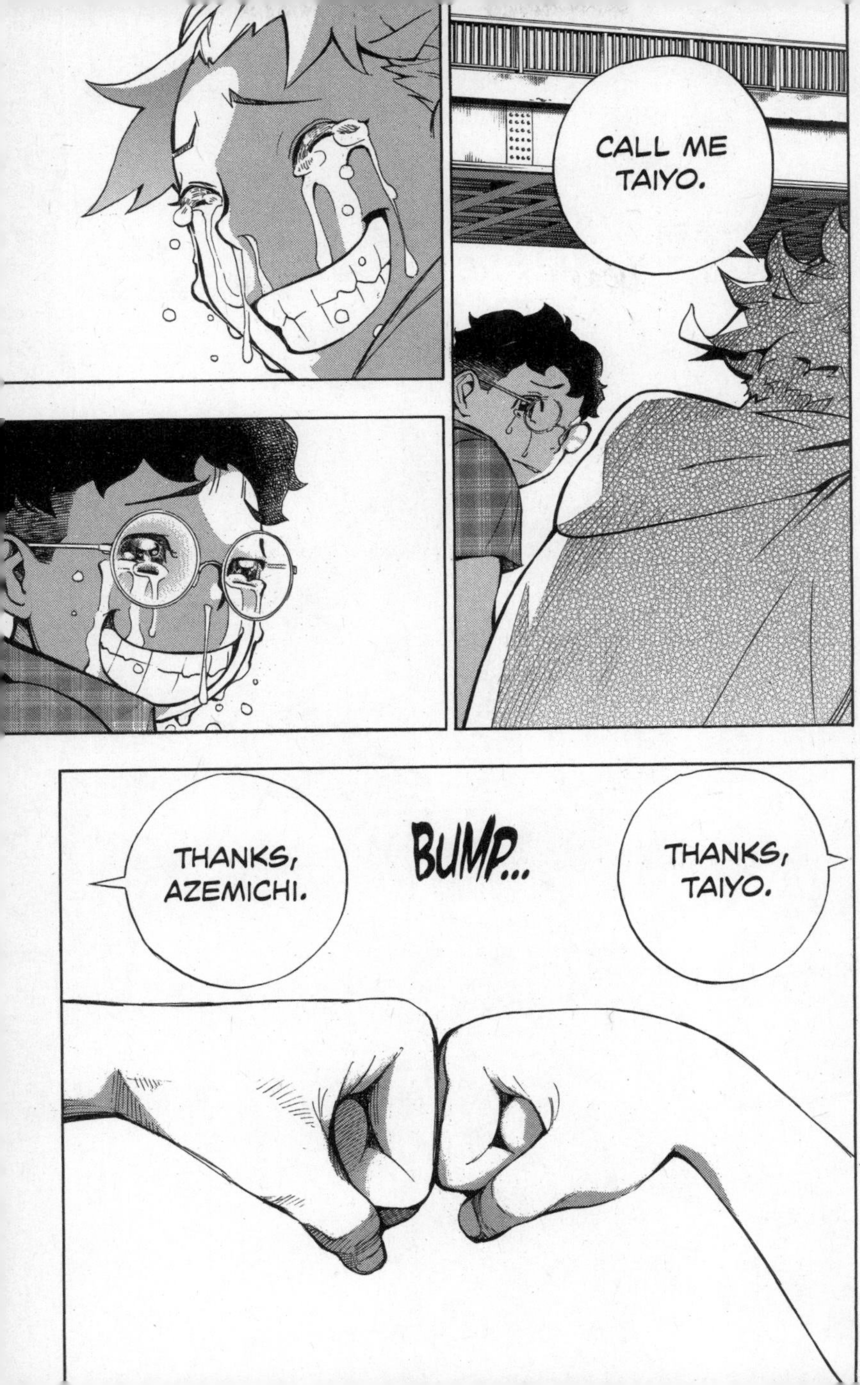
CALL ME TAIYO.
THANKS, TAIYO.
BUMP...
THANKS, AZEMICHI.

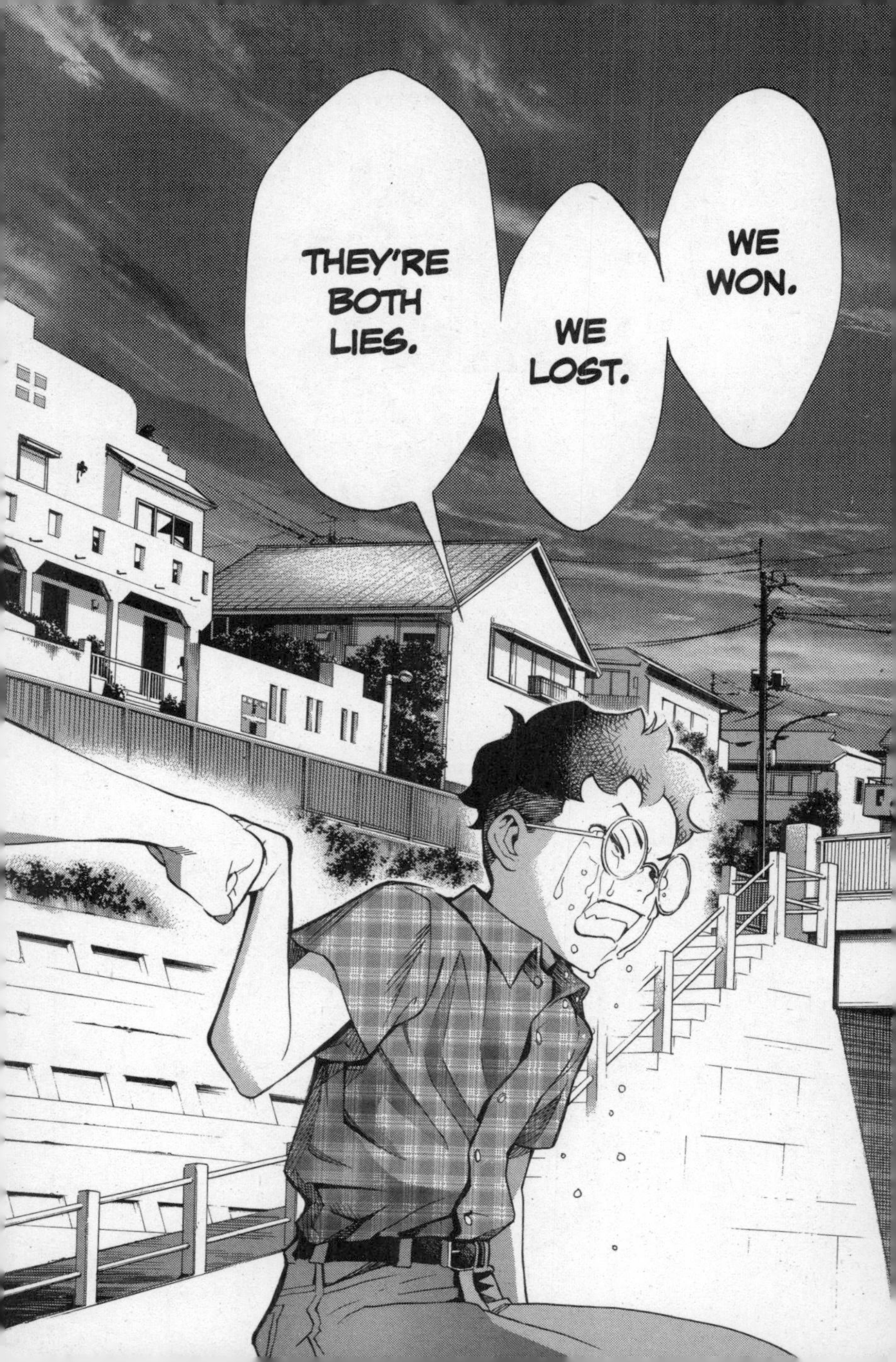
WE WON.
WE LOST.
THEY'RE BOTH LIES.

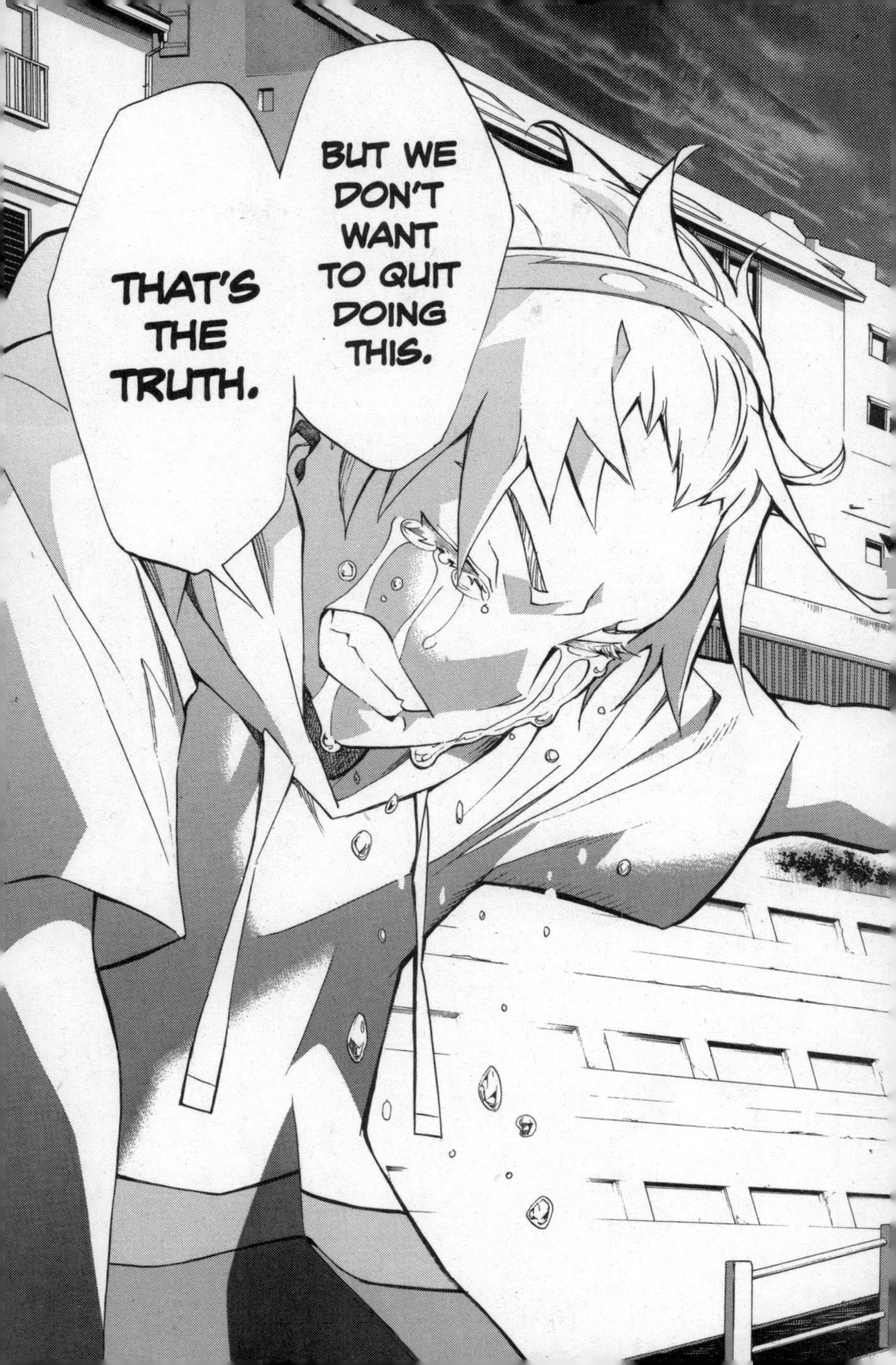
BUT WE DON'T WANT TO QUIT DOING THIS.
THAT'S THE TRUTH.

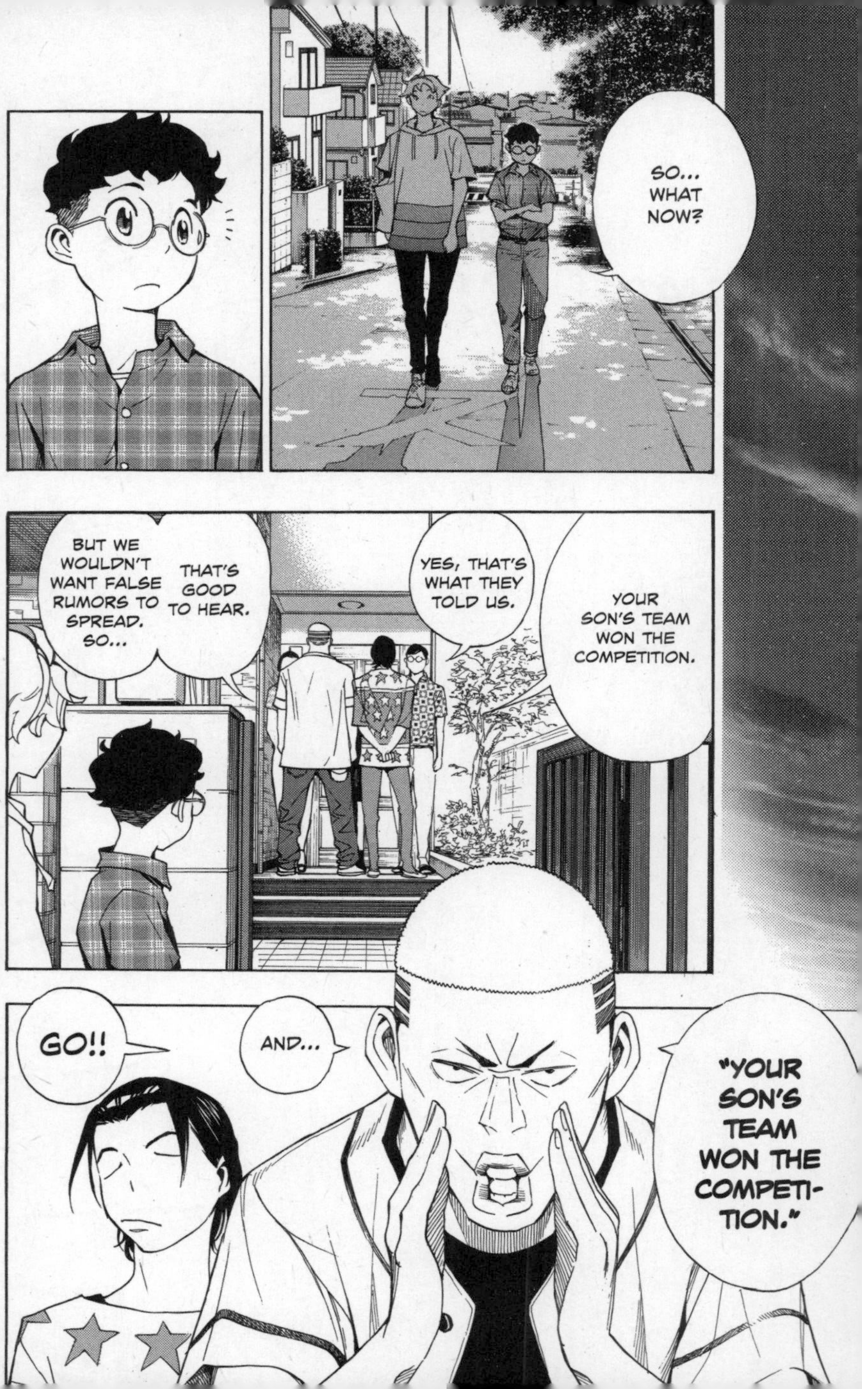
SO... WHAT NOW?
YOUR SON'S TEAM WON THE COMPETITION.
YES, THAT'S WHAT THEY TOLD US.
THAT'S GOOD TO HEAR.
BUT WE WOULDN'T WANT FALSE RUMORS TO SPREAD. SO...
"YOUR SON'S TEAM WON THE COMPETITION."
AND...
GO!!

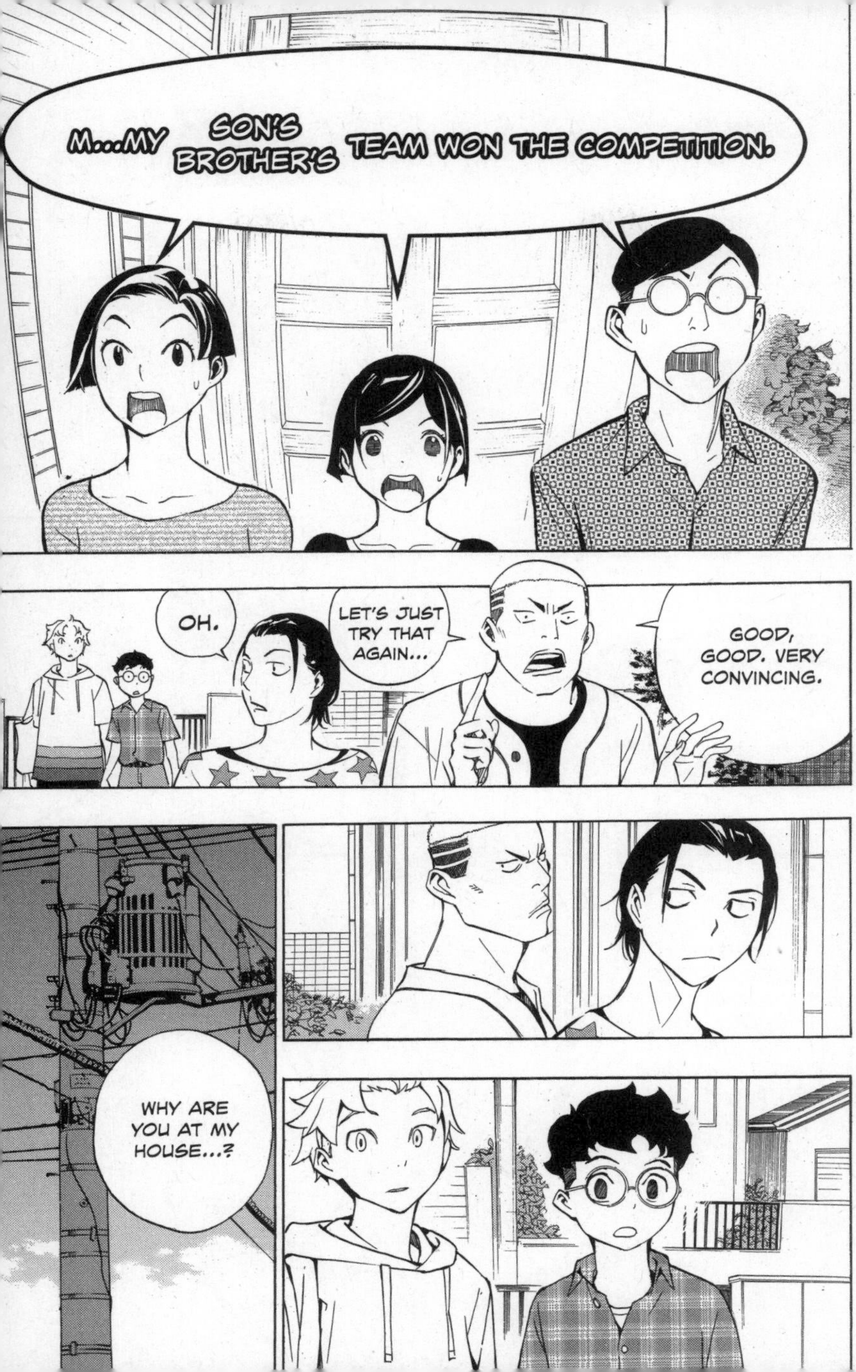
M...MY SON'S BROTHER'S TEAM WON THE COMPETITION.
GOOD, GOOD. VERY CONVINCING.
LET'S JUST TRY THAT AGAIN...
OH.
WHY ARE YOU AT MY HOUSE...?

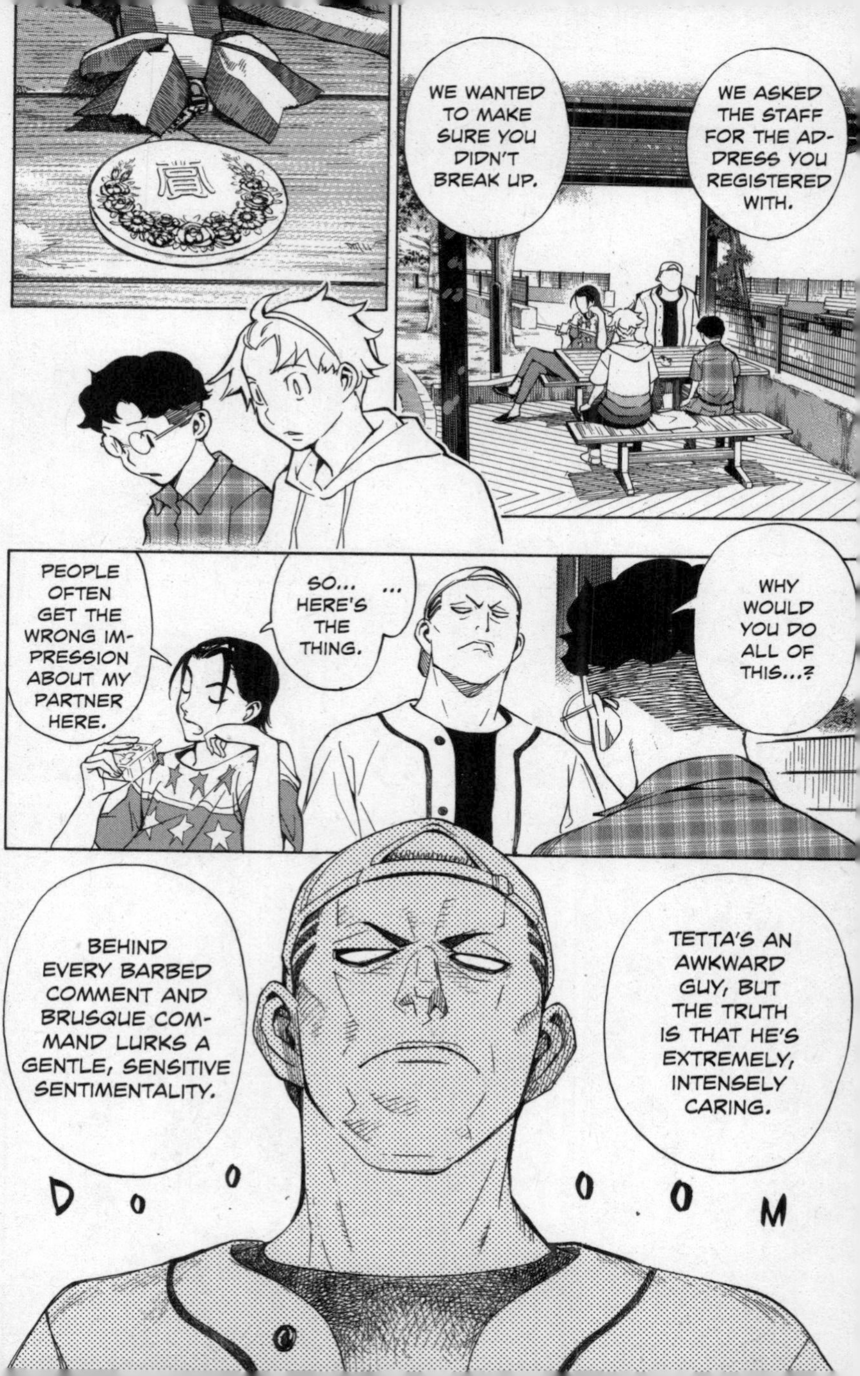
WE ASKED THE STAFF FOR THE AD-DRESS YOU REGISTERED WITH.
WE WANTED TO MAKE SURE YOU DIDN'T BREAK UP.
WHY WOULD YOU DO ALL OF THIS...?
...
SO... HERE'S THE THING.
PEOPLE OFTEN GET THE WRONG IM-PRESSION ABOUT MY PARTNER HERE.
TETTA'S AN AWKWARD GUY, BUT THE TRUTH IS THAT HE'S EXTREMELY, INTENSELY CARING.
BEHIND EVERY BARBED COMMENT AND BRUSQUE COM-MAND LURKS A GENTLE, SENSITIVE SENTIMENTALITY.
DOOOOOM

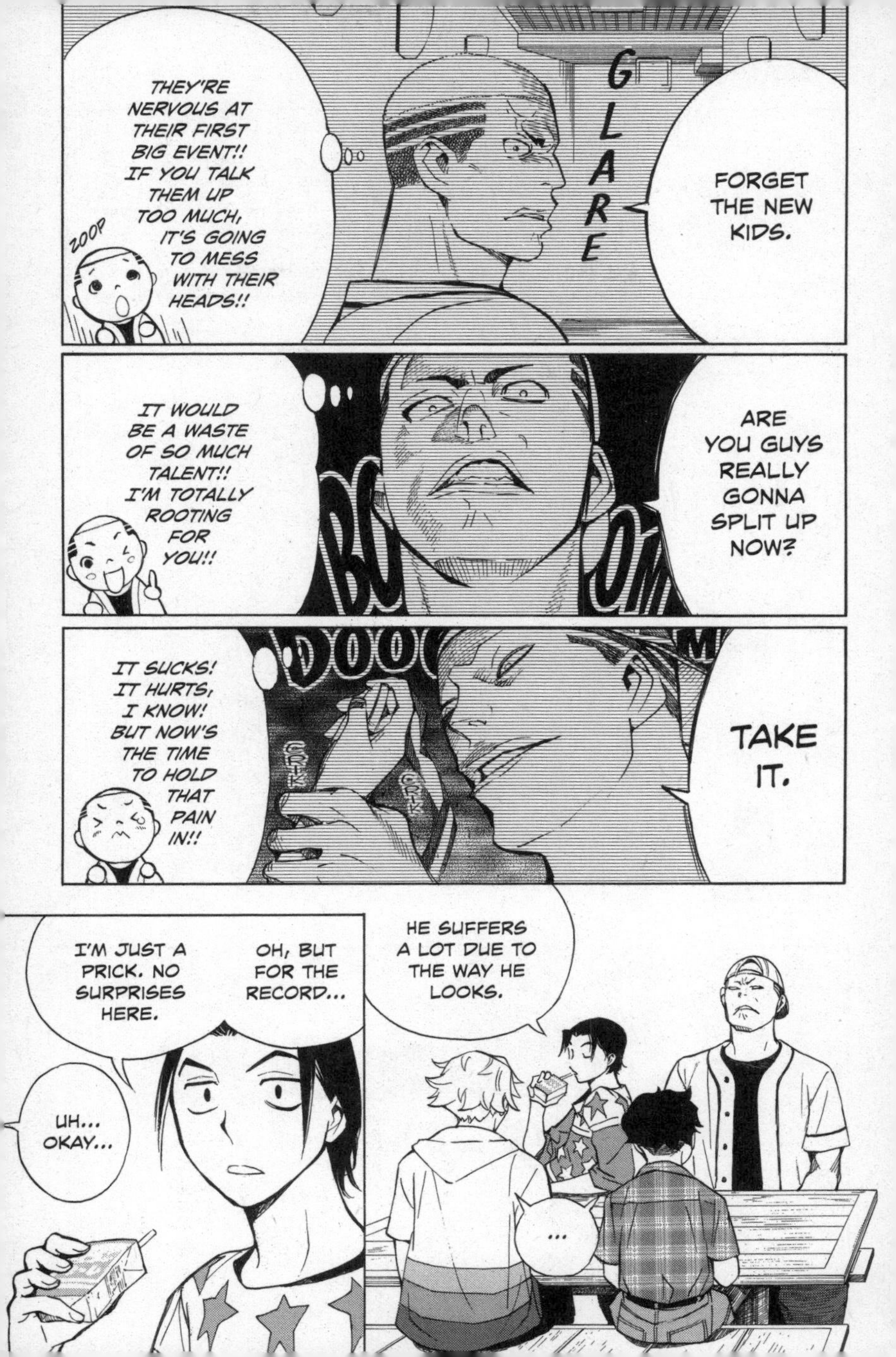
FORGET THE NEW KIDS.
GLARE
THEY'RE NERVOUS AT THEIR FIRST BIG EVENT!! IF YOU TALK THEM UP TOO MUCH, IT'S GOING TO MESS WITH THEIR HEADS!!
ZOOP
ARE YOU GUYS REALLY GONNA SPLIT UP NOW?
IT WOULD BE A WASTE OF SO MUCH TALENT!! I'M TOTALLY ROOTING FOR YOU!!
TAKE IT.
CRIK
CRIK
IT SUCKS! IT HURTS, I KNOW! BUT NOW'S THE TIME TO HOLD THAT PAIN IN!!
HE SUFFERS A LOT DUE TO THE WAY HE LOOKS.
...
OH, BUT FOR THE RECORD...
I'M JUST A PRICK. NO SURPRISES HERE.
UH... OKAY...

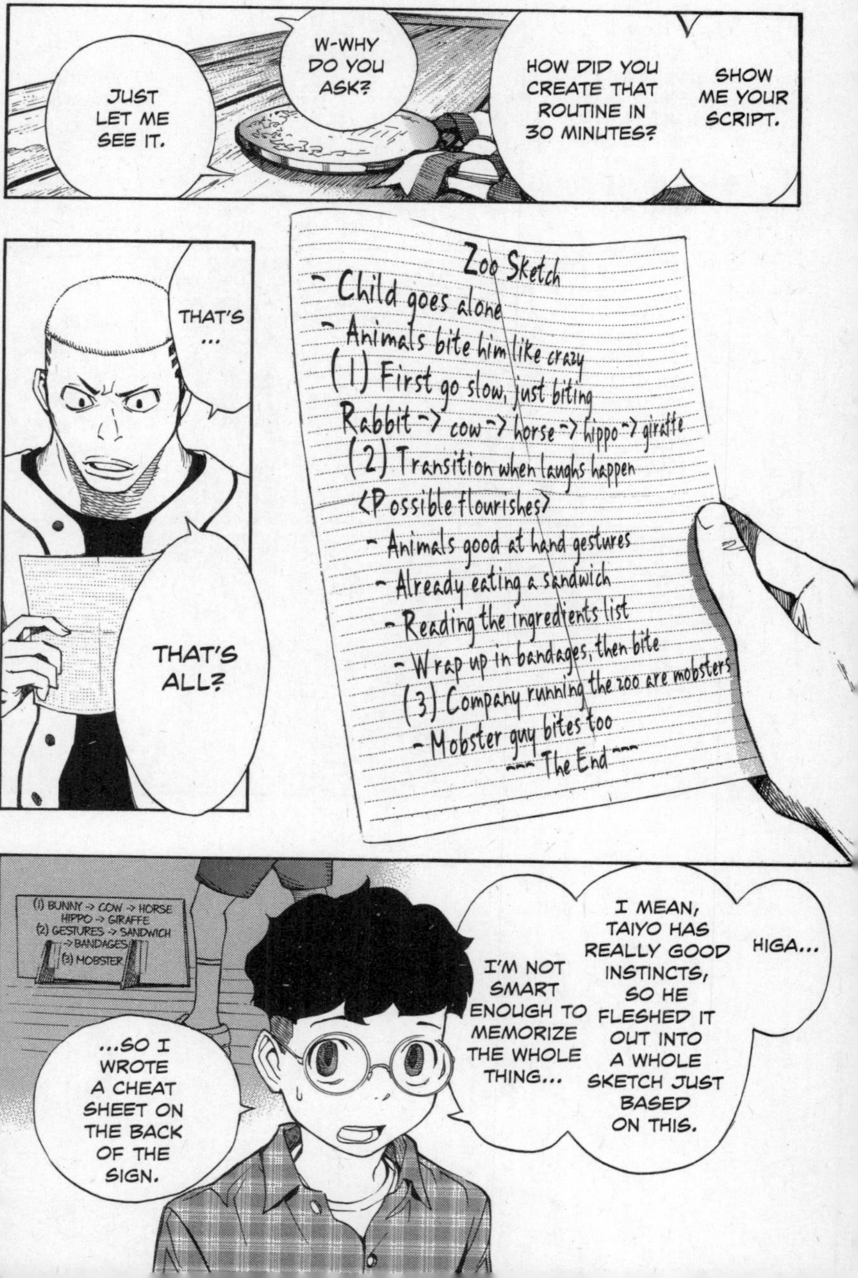
SHOW ME YOUR SCRIPT.
HOW DID YOU CREATE THAT ROUTINE IN 30 MINUTES?
W-WHY DO YOU ASK?
JUST LET ME SEE IT.
Zoo Sketch
- Child goes alone
- Animals bite him like crazy
(1) First go slow, just biting
Rabbit -> cow -> horse -> hippo -> giraffe
(2) Transition when laughs happen
<Possible flourishes>
- Animals good at hand gestures
- Already eating a sandwich
- Reading the ingredients list
- Wrap up in bandages, then bite
(3) Company running the zoo are mobsters
- Mobster guy bites too
--- The End ---
THAT'S...
THAT'S ALL?
HIGA...
I MEAN, TAIYO HAS REALLY GOOD INSTINCTS, SO HE FLESHED IT OUT INTO A WHOLE SKETCH JUST BASED ON THIS.
I'M NOT SMART ENOUGH TO MEMORIZE THE WHOLE THING...
(1) BUNNY -> COW -> HORSE HIPPO -> GIRAFFE (2) GESTURES -> SANDWICH -> BANDAGES (3) MOBSTER
...SO I WROTE A CHEAT SHEET ON THE BACK OF THE SIGN.

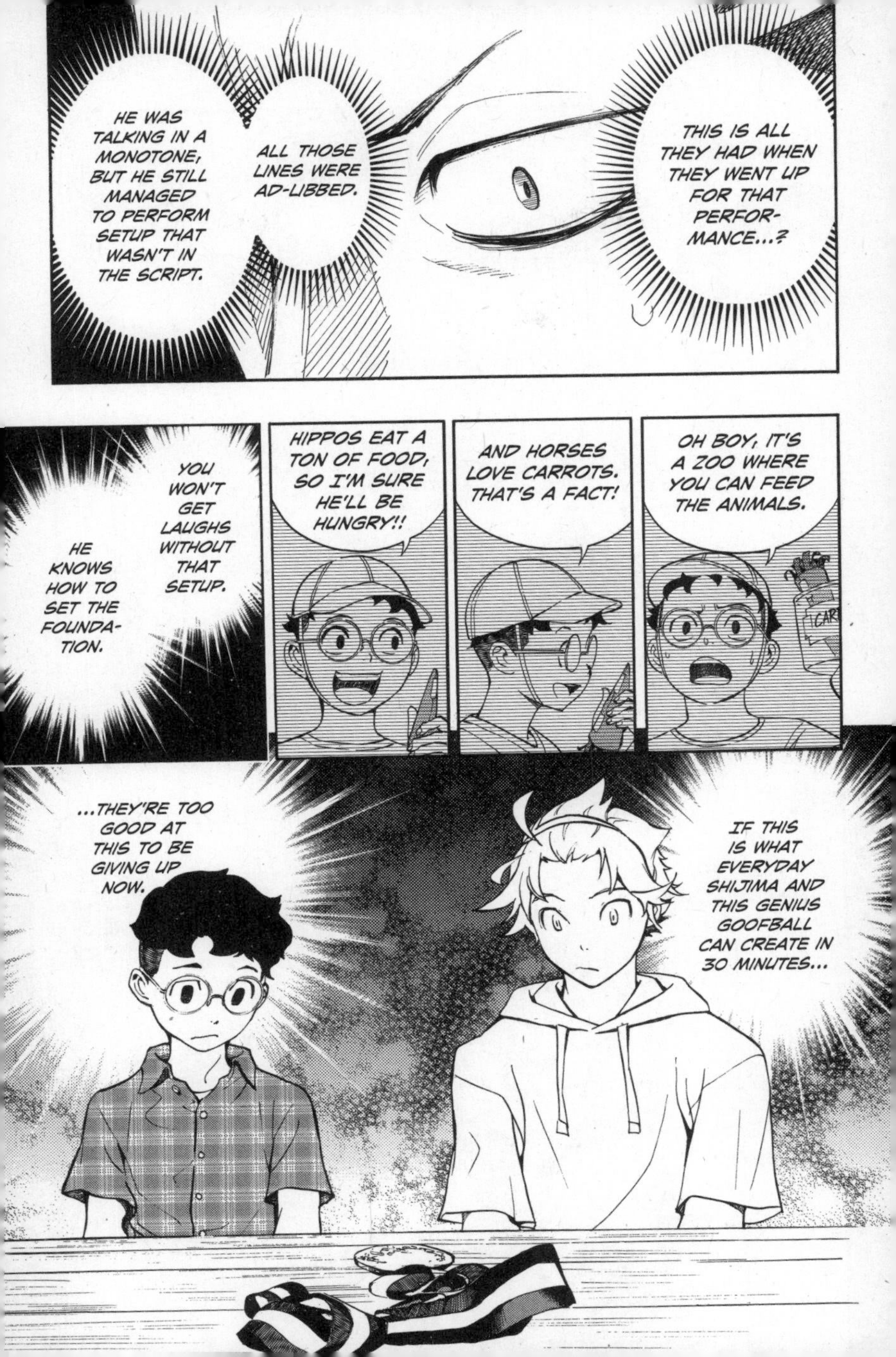
THIS IS ALL THEY HAD WHEN THEY WENT UP FOR THAT PERFORMANCE...?
ALL THOSE LINES WERE AD-LIBBED.
HE WAS TALKING IN A MONOTONE, BUT HE STILL MANAGED TO PERFORM SETUP THAT WASN'T IN THE SCRIPT.
OH BOY, IT'S A ZOO WHERE YOU CAN FEED THE ANIMALS.
AND HORSES LOVE CARROTS. THAT'S A FACT!
HIPPOS EAT A TON OF FOOD, SO I'M SURE HE'LL BE HUNGRY!!
YOU WON'T GET LAUGHS WITHOUT THAT SETUP.
HE KNOWS HOW TO SET THE FOUNDATION.
IF THIS IS WHAT EVERYDAY SHIJIMA AND THIS GENIUS GOOFBALL CAN CREATE IN 30 MINUTES...
...THEY'RE TOO GOOD AT THIS TO BE GIVING UP NOW.

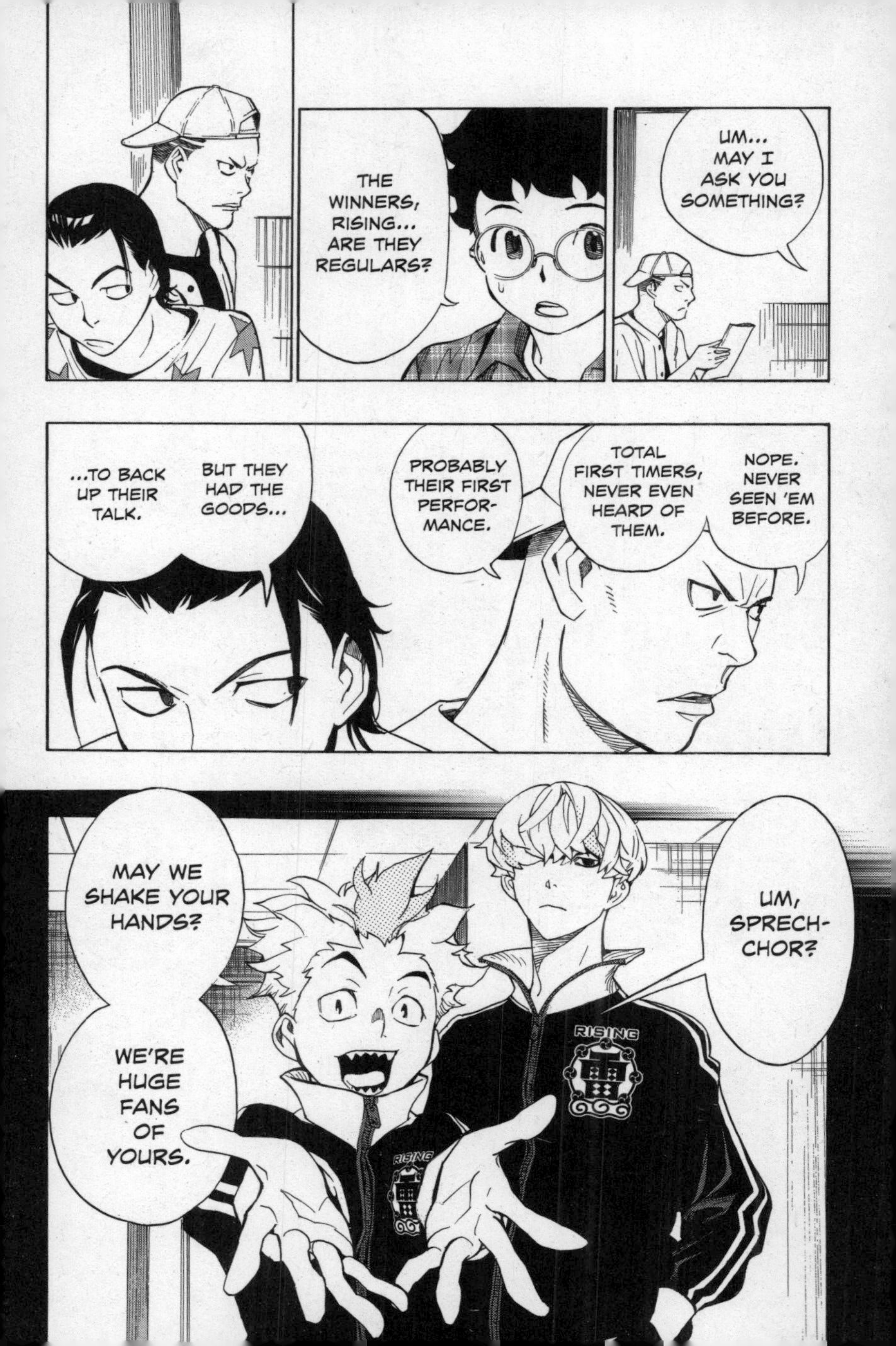
UM... MAY I ASK YOU SOMETHING?
THE WINNERS, RISING... ARE THEY REGULARS?
NOPE. NEVER SEEN 'EM BEFORE.
TOTAL FIRST TIMERS, NEVER EVEN HEARD OF THEM.
PROBABLY THEIR FIRST PERFOR-MANCE.
BUT THEY HAD THE GOODS...
...TO BACK UP THEIR TALK.
UM, SPRECH-CHOR?
RISING
MAY WE SHAKE YOUR HANDS?
WE'RE HUGE FANS OF YOURS.
RISING

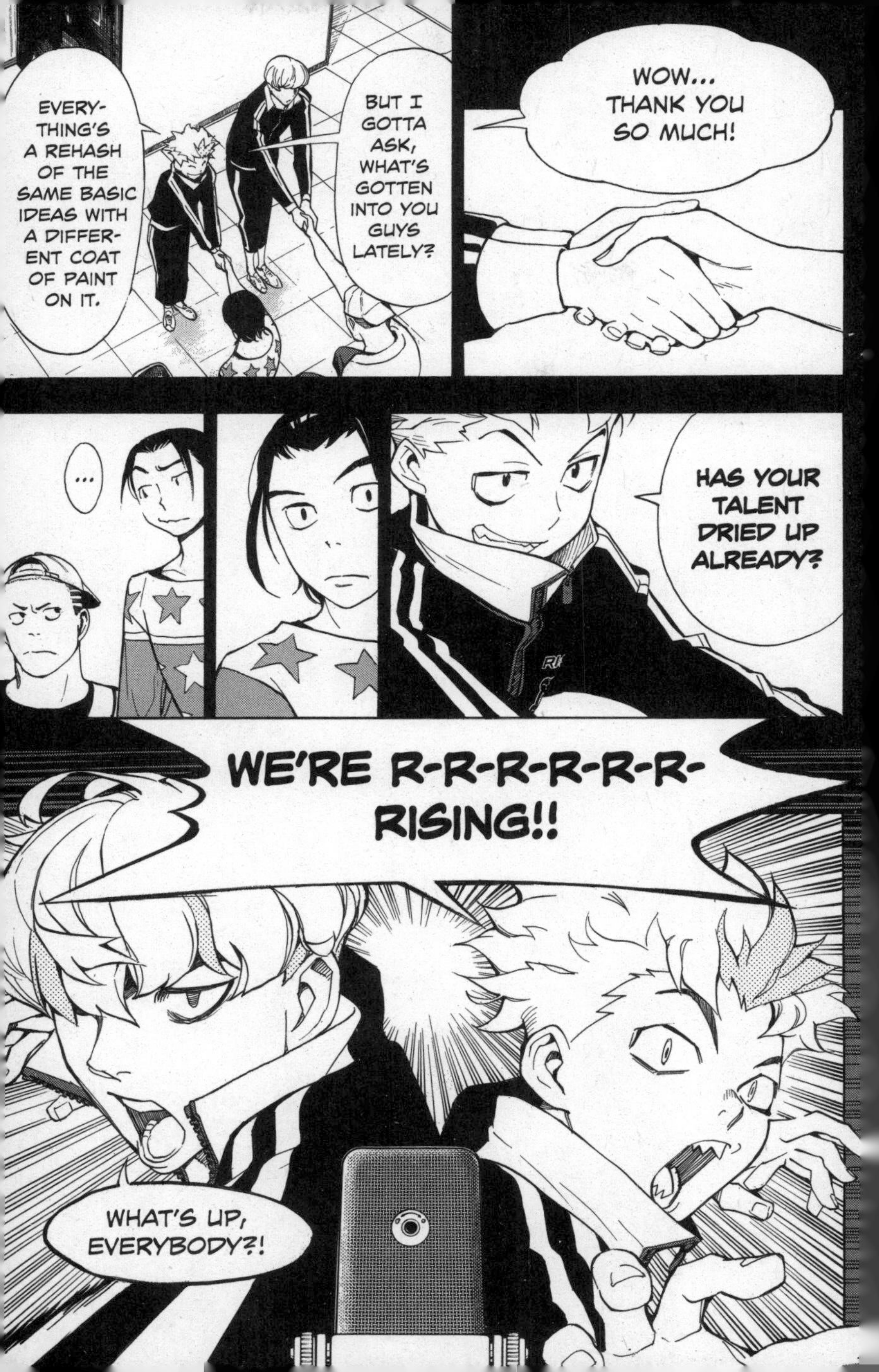
WOW... THANK YOU SO MUCH!
BUT I GOTTA ASK, WHAT'S GOTTEN INTO YOU GUYS LATELY?
EVERY-THING'S A REHASH OF THE SAME BASIC IDEAS WITH A DIFFER-ENT COAT OF PAINT ON IT.
HAS YOUR TALENT DRIED UP ALREADY?
...
WE'RE R-R-R-R-R-R-RISING!!
WHAT'S UP, EVERYBODY?!

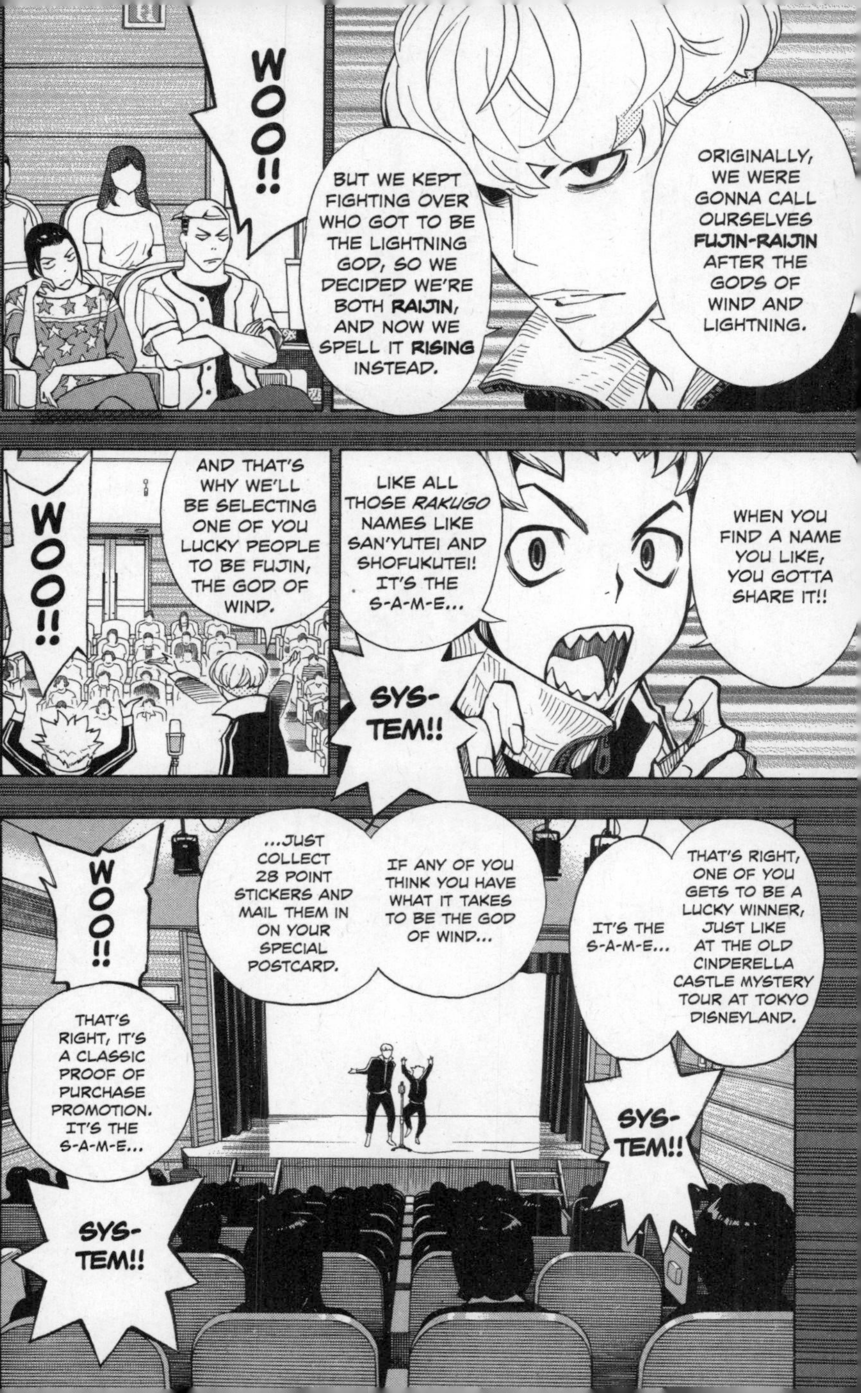
ORIGINALLY, WE WERE GONNA CALL OURSELVES FUJIN-RAIJIN AFTER THE GODS OF WIND AND LIGHTNING.
BUT WE KEPT FIGHTING OVER WHO GOT TO BE THE LIGHTNING GOD, SO WE DECIDED WE'RE BOTH RAIJIN, AND NOW WE SPELL IT RISING INSTEAD.
WOO!!
WHEN YOU FIND A NAME YOU LIKE, YOU GOTTA SHARE IT!!
LIKE ALL THOSE *RAKUGO* NAMES LIKE SAN'YUTEI AND SHOFUKUTEI! IT'S THE S-A-M-E...
SYS-TEM!!
AND THAT'S WHY WE'LL BE SELECTING ONE OF YOU LUCKY PEOPLE TO BE FUJIN, THE GOD OF WIND.
WOO!!
THAT'S RIGHT, ONE OF YOU GETS TO BE A LUCKY WINNER, JUST LIKE AT THE OLD CINDERELLA CASTLE MYSTERY TOUR AT TOKYO DISNEYLAND.
IT'S THE S-A-M-E...
SYS-TEM!!
IF ANY OF YOU THINK YOU HAVE WHAT IT TAKES TO BE THE GOD OF WIND...
...JUST COLLECT 28 POINT STICKERS AND MAIL THEM IN ON YOUR SPECIAL POSTCARD.
WOO!!
THAT'S RIGHT, IT'S A CLASSIC PROOF OF PURCHASE PROMOTION. IT'S THE S-A-M-E...
SYS-TEM!!

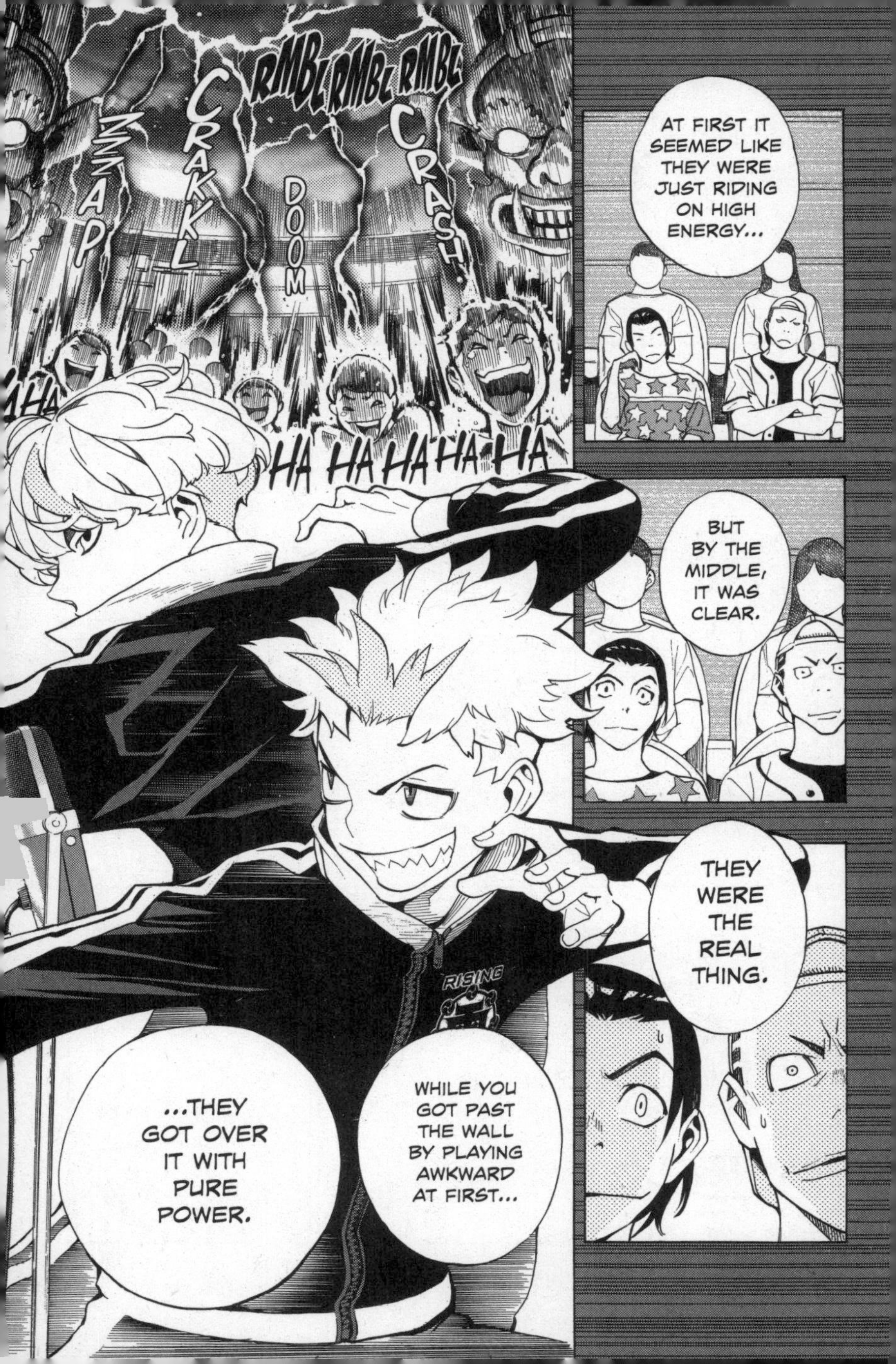
AT FIRST IT SEEMED LIKE THEY WERE JUST RIDING ON HIGH ENERGY...
BUT BY THE MIDDLE, IT WAS CLEAR.
THEY WERE THE REAL THING.
RMBL RMBL RMBL
CRASH
DOOM
CRAKKL
ZZZAP
HA HA HA HA HA
RISING
WHILE YOU GOT PAST THE WALL BY PLAYING AWKWARD AT FIRST...
...THEY GOT OVER IT WITH PURE POWER.

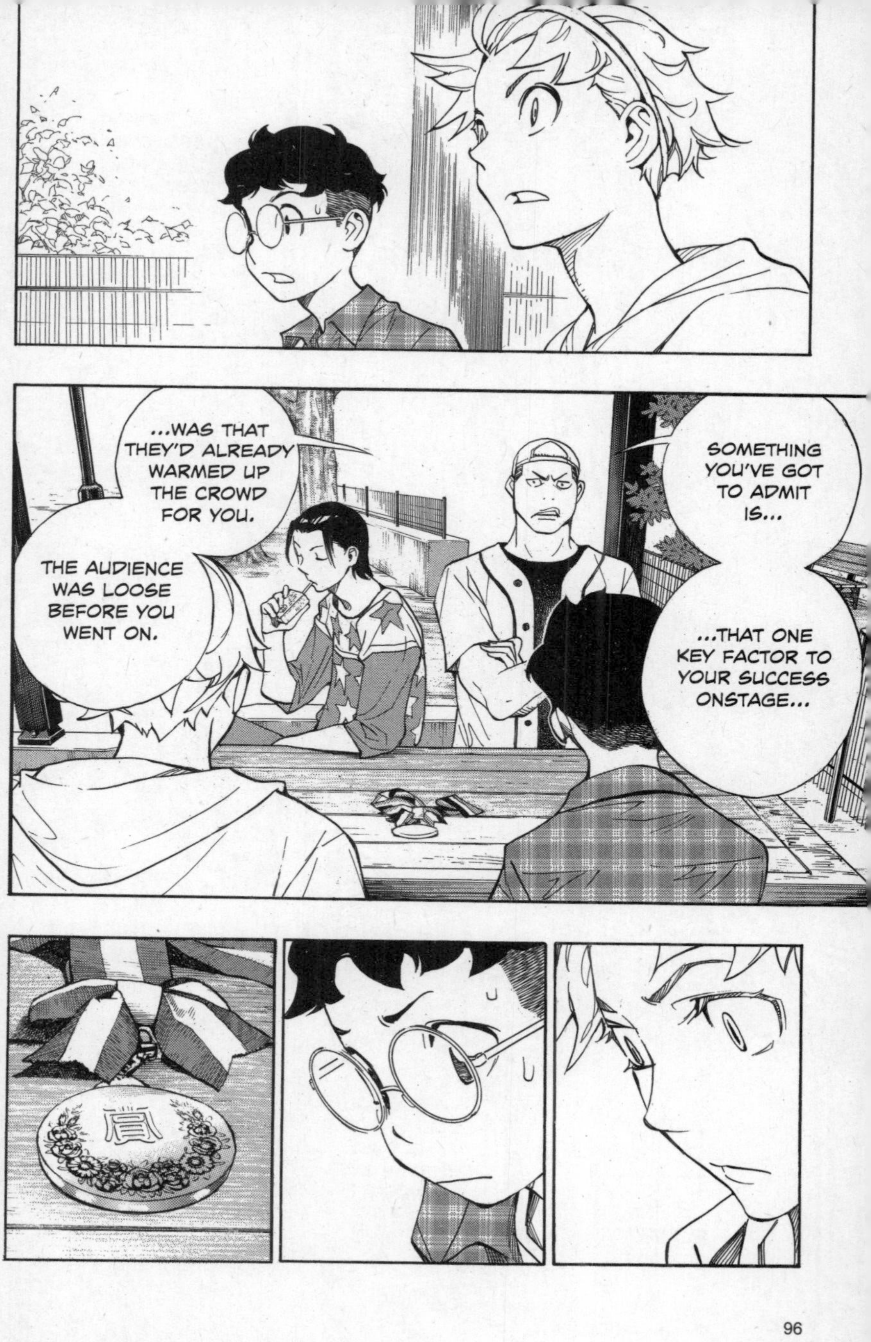
SOMETHING YOU'VE GOT TO ADMIT IS...
...THAT ONE KEY FACTOR TO YOUR SUCCESS ONSTAGE...
...WAS THAT THEY'D ALREADY WARMED UP THE CROWD FOR YOU.
THE AUDIENCE WAS LOOSE BEFORE YOU WENT ON.

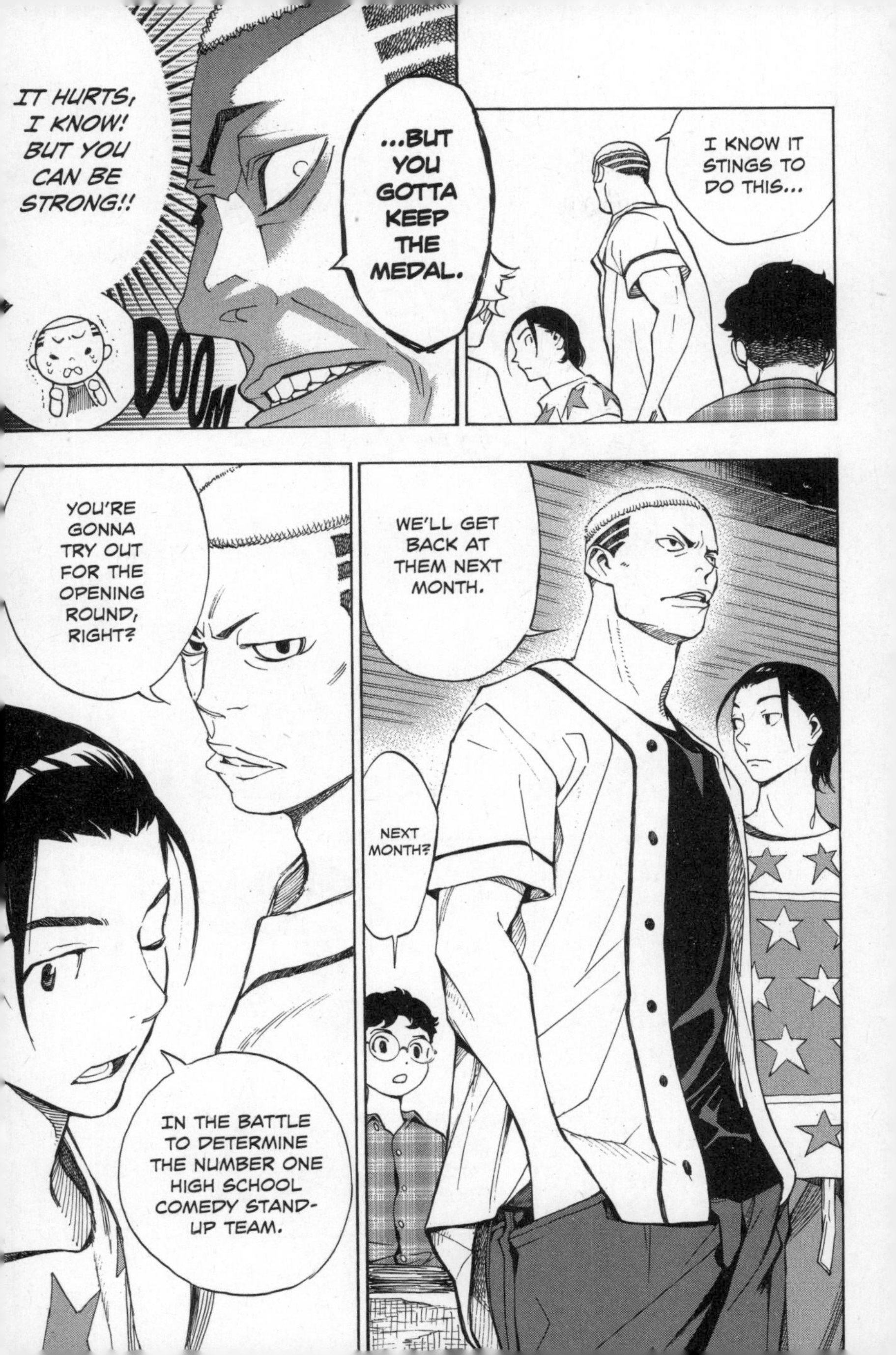
I KNOW IT STINGS TO DO THIS...
...BUT YOU GOTTA KEEP THE MEDAL.
IT HURTS, I KNOW! BUT YOU CAN BE STRONG!!
DOOM
WE'LL GET BACK AT THEM NEXT MONTH.
NEXT MONTH?
YOU'RE GONNA TRY OUT FOR THE OPENING ROUND, RIGHT?
IN THE BATTLE TO DETERMINE THE NUMBER ONE HIGH SCHOOL COMEDY STAND-UP TEAM.

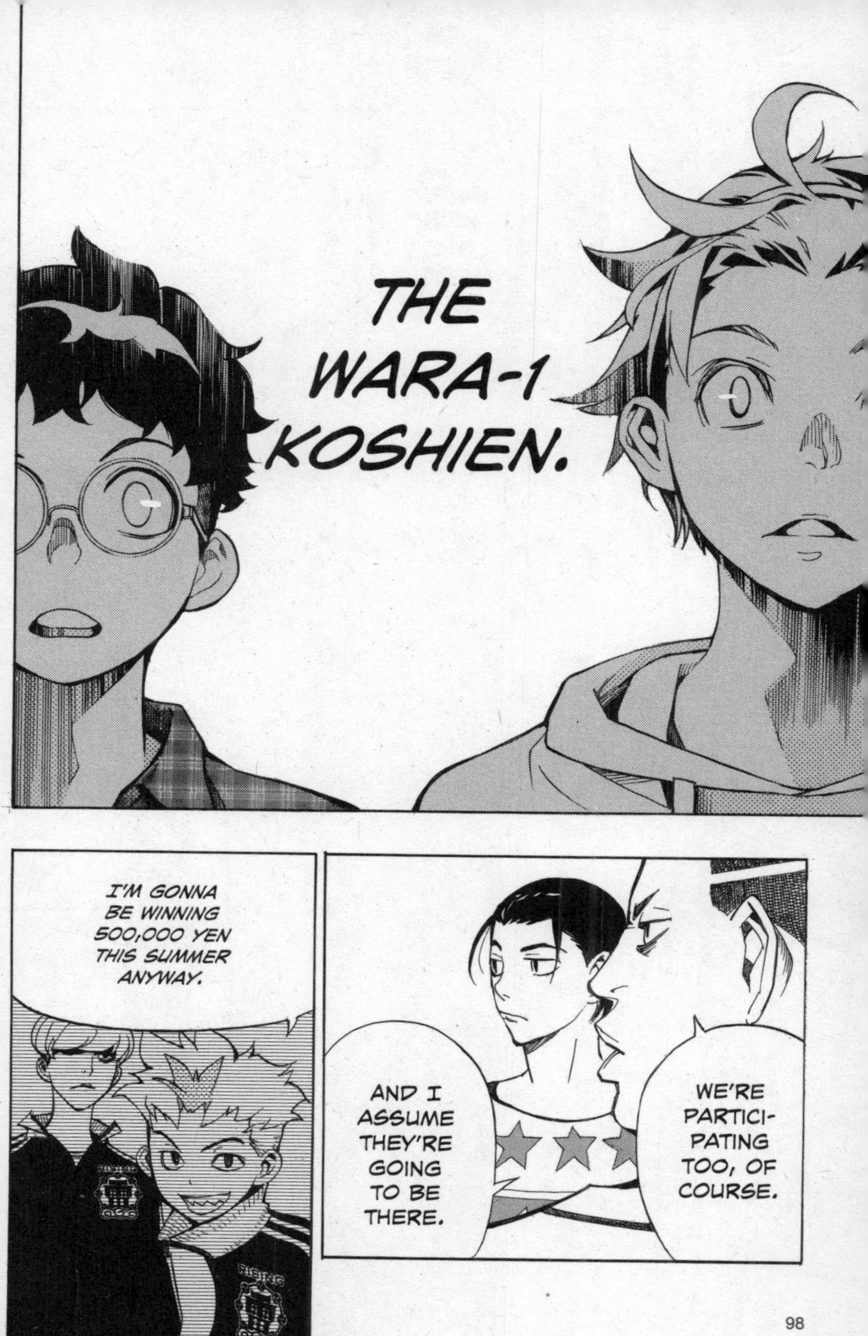
THE WARA-1 KOSHIEN.
WE'RE PARTICI-PATING TOO, OF COURSE.
AND I ASSUME THEY'RE GOING TO BE THERE.
I'M GONNA BE WINNING 500,000 YEN THIS SUMMER ANYWAY.

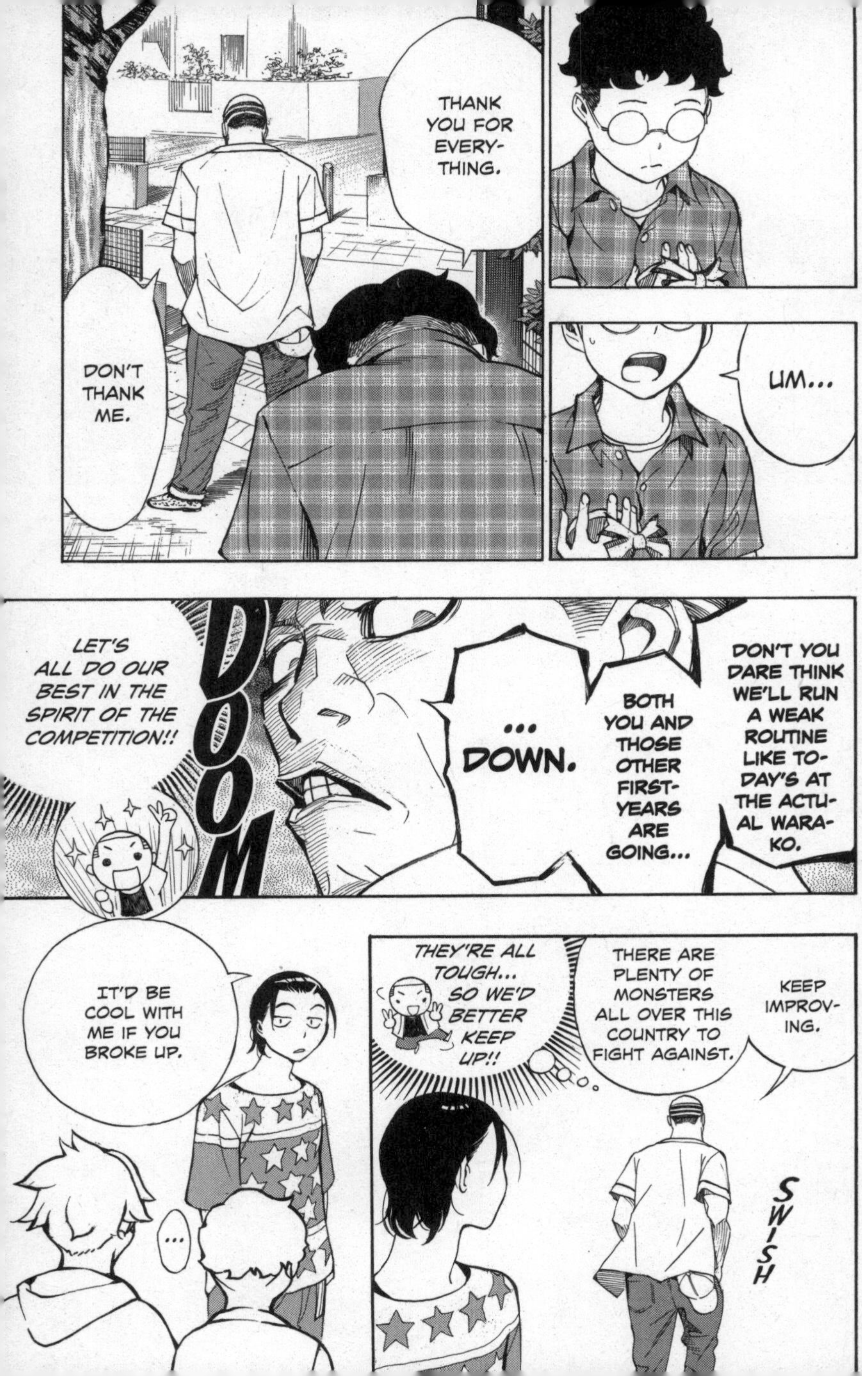
UM...
THANK YOU FOR EVERY-THING.
DON'T THANK ME.
DON'T YOU DARE THINK WE'LL RUN A WEAK ROUTINE LIKE TO-DAY'S AT THE ACTU-AL WARA-KO.
BOTH YOU AND THOSE OTHER FIRST-YEARS ARE GOING...
...DOWN.
DOOM
LET'S ALL DO OUR BEST IN THE SPIRIT OF THE COMPETITION!!
KEEP IMPROV-ING.
THERE ARE PLENTY OF MONSTERS ALL OVER THIS COUNTRY TO FIGHT AGAINST.
THEY'RE ALL TOUGH... SO WE'D BETTER KEEP UP!!
SWISH
IT'D BE COOL WITH ME IF YOU BROKE UP.
...

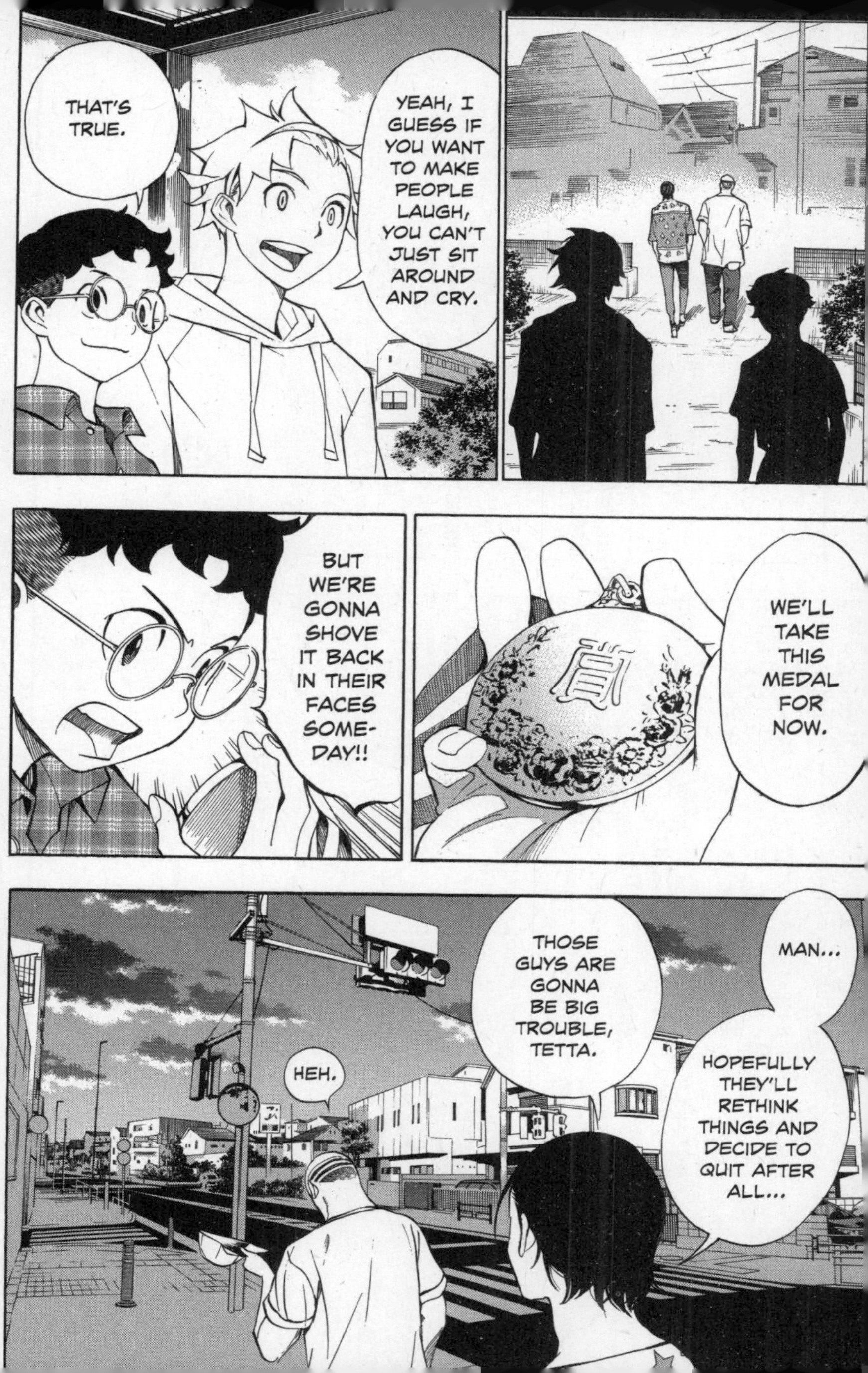
YEAH, I GUESS IF YOU WANT TO MAKE PEOPLE LAUGH, YOU CAN'T JUST SIT AROUND AND CRY.
THAT'S TRUE.
WE'LL TAKE THIS MEDAL FOR NOW.
BUT WE'RE GONNA SHOVE IT BACK IN THEIR FACES SOME-DAY!!
MAN...
HOPEFULLY THEY'LL RETHINK THINGS AND DECIDE TO QUIT AFTER ALL...
THOSE GUYS ARE GONNA BE BIG TROUBLE, TETTA.
HEH.

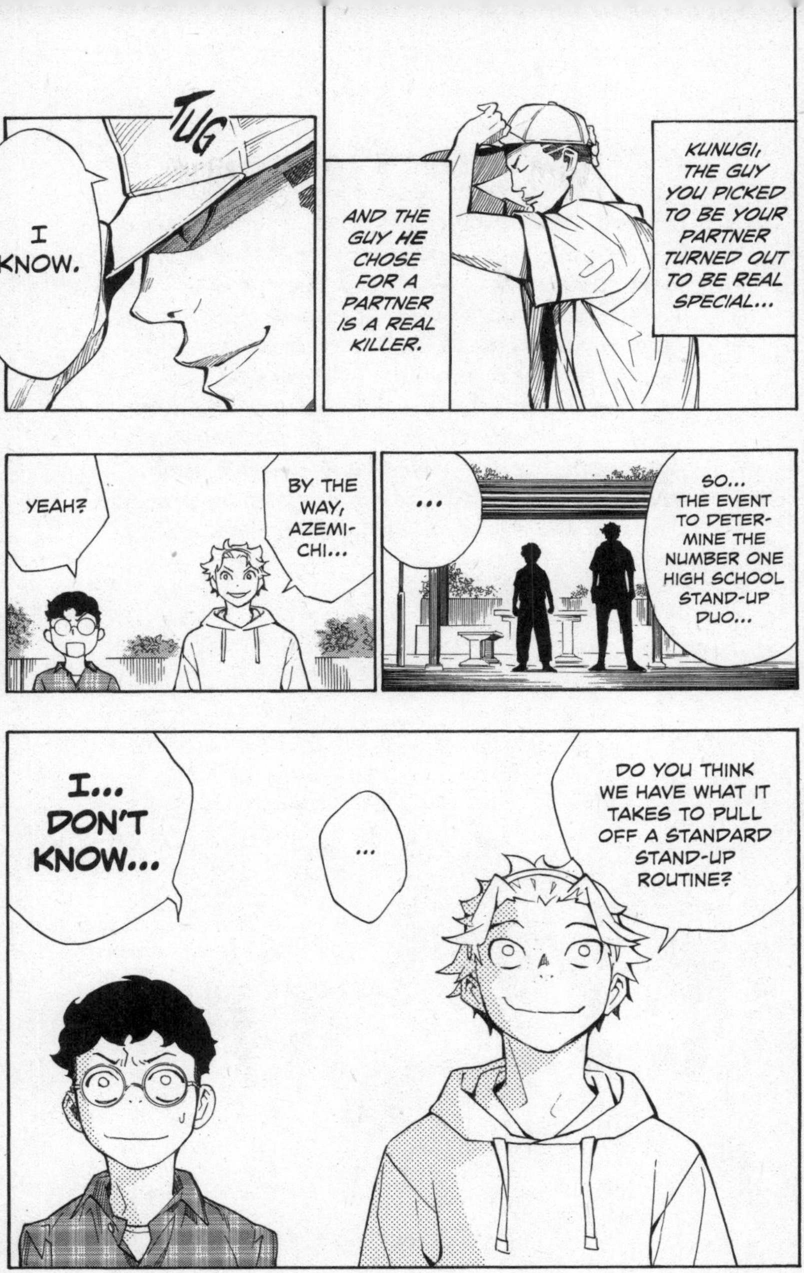
KUNUGI, THE GUY YOU PICKED TO BE YOUR PARTNER TURNED OUT TO BE REAL SPECIAL...
AND THE GUY HE CHOSE FOR A PARTNER IS A REAL KILLER.
TUG
I KNOW.
SO... THE EVENT TO DETERMINE THE NUMBER ONE HIGH SCHOOL STAND-UP DUO...
...
BY THE WAY, AZEMICHI...
YEAH?
DO YOU THINK WE HAVE WHAT IT TAKES TO PULL OFF A STANDARD STAND-UP ROUTINE?
...
I... DON'T KNOW...

Column

So it's the day before we take exams to get into high school. Our homeroom teacher instructed Jicchan, the most popular kid of the class, to "put on some kind of entertainment to cheer up everyone before tomorrow's exams." As the unpopular grub of the class, I just stood there with my dumb mouth hanging open, and thinking, without a care in the world, "I wonder what he's gonna do?" Jicchan said, "I'll perform manzai stand-up with Asakura." We were definitely a hit with the class,but all that I remember was one of the girls giving us an absolute death stare that said, "Stop wasting our precious pre-exam time with this stupid attempt at entertainment!"

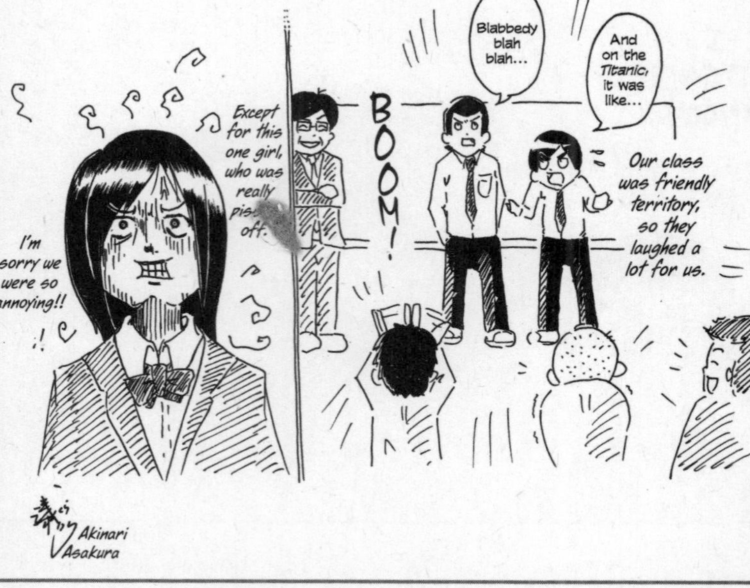

Our class was friendly territory, so they laughed a lot for us.
And on the Titanic, it was like...
Blabbedy blah blah...
BOOM!
Except for this one girl, who was really pis off.
I'm sorry we were so annoying!!
Akinari Asakura

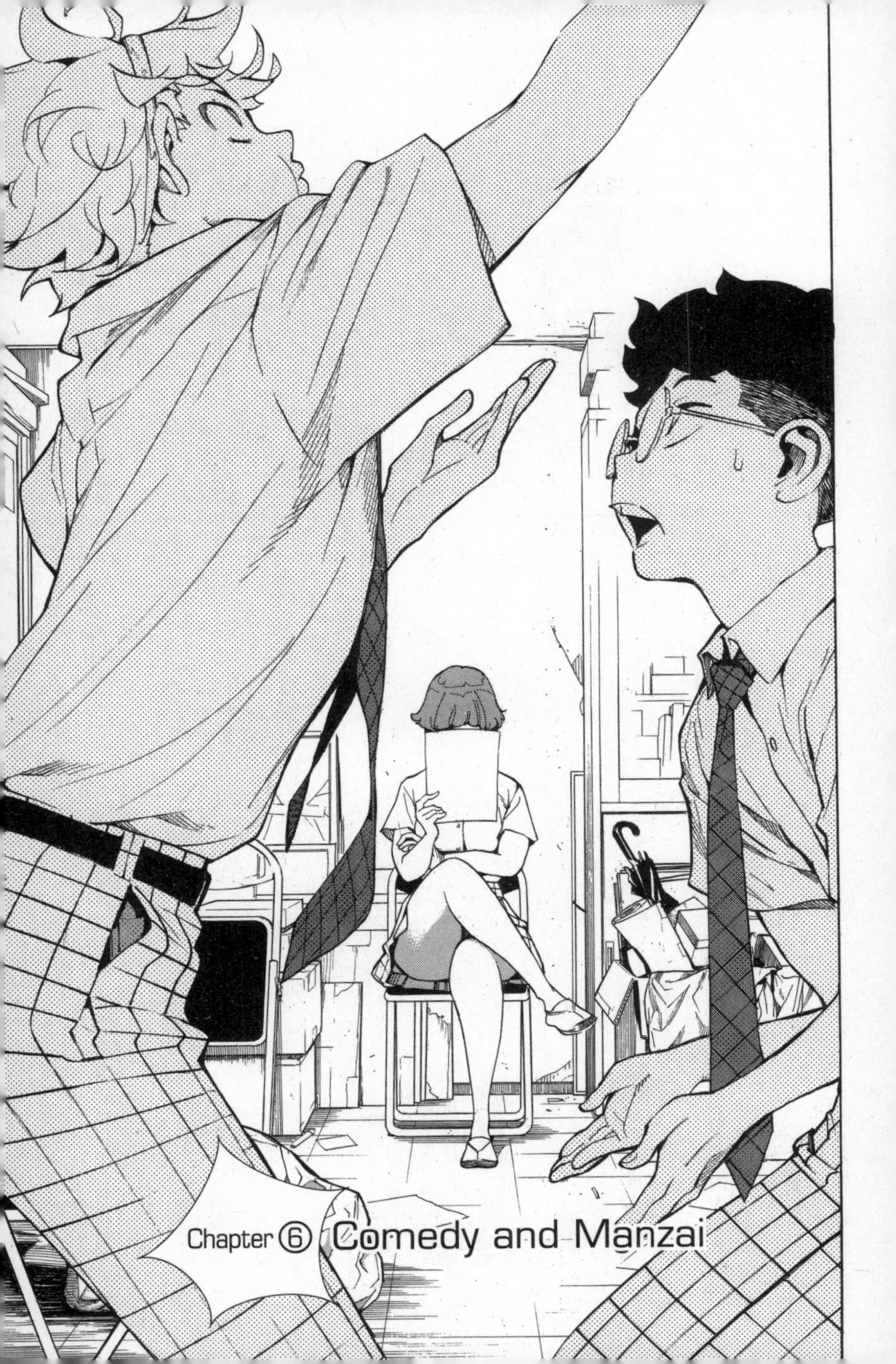
Chapter 6 Comedy and Manzai

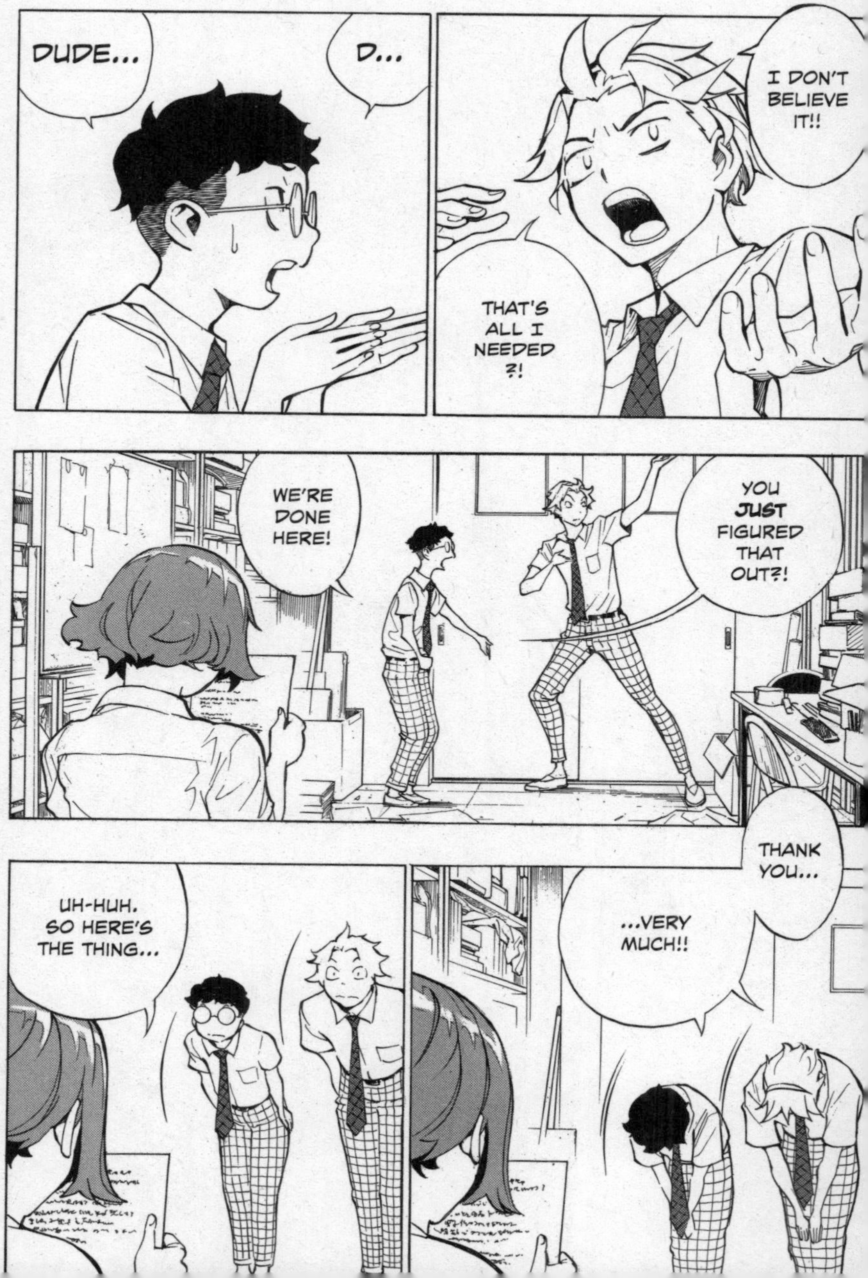
I DON'T BELIEVE IT!!
THAT'S ALL I NEEDED ?!
D...
DUDE...
YOU JUST FIGURED THAT OUT?!
WE'RE DONE HERE!
THANK YOU...
...VERY MUCH!!
UH-HUH. SO HERE'S THE THING...

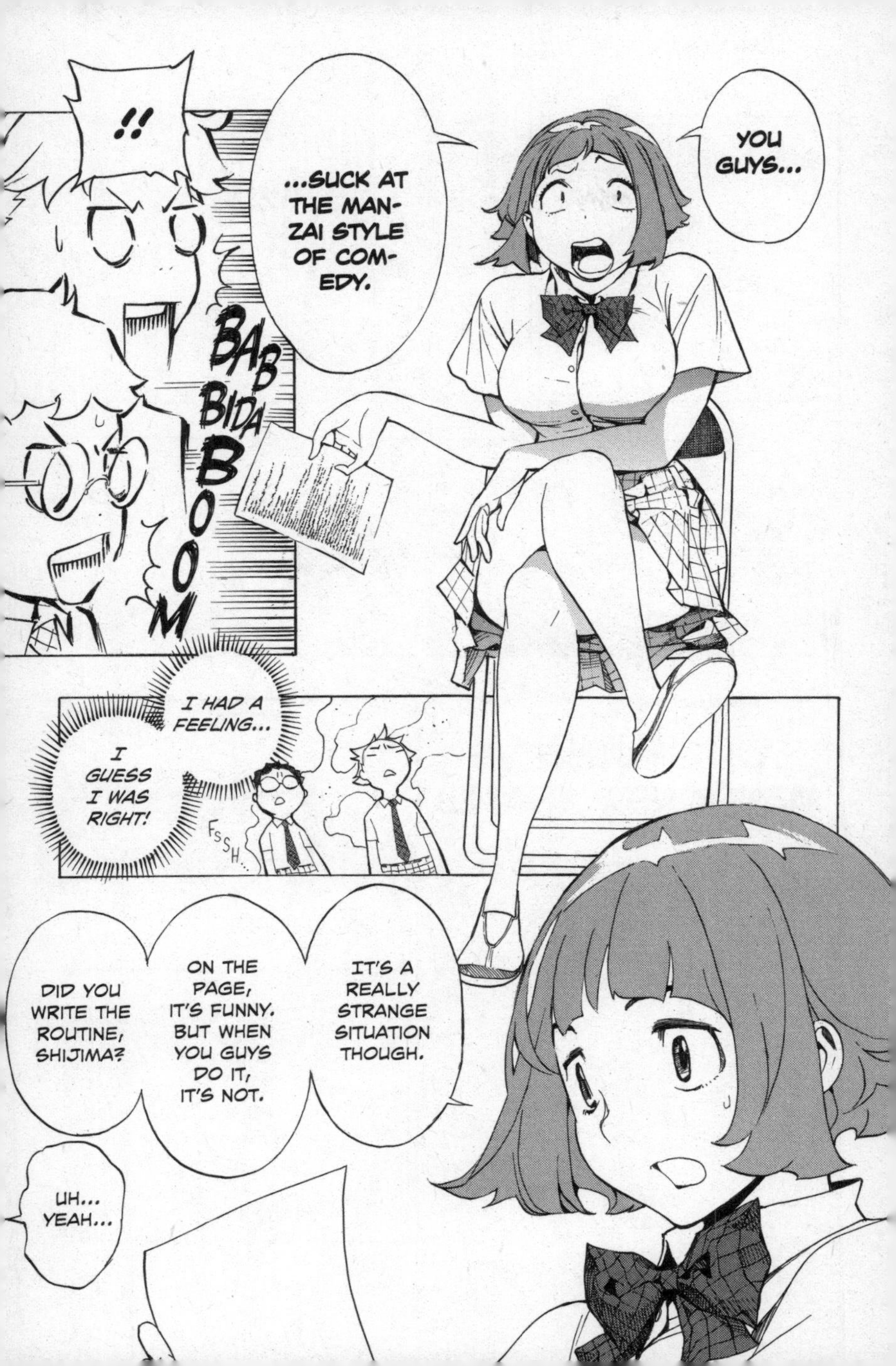
YOU GUYS...
...SUCK AT THE MAN-ZAI STYLE OF COM-EDY.
!!
BAB BIDA BOOOM
I HAD A FEELING...
I GUESS I WAS RIGHT!
FSSH...
IT'S A REALLY STRANGE SITUATION THOUGH.
ON THE PAGE, IT'S FUNNY. BUT WHEN YOU GUYS DO IT, IT'S NOT.
DID YOU WRITE THE ROUTINE, SHIJIMA?
UH... YEAH...

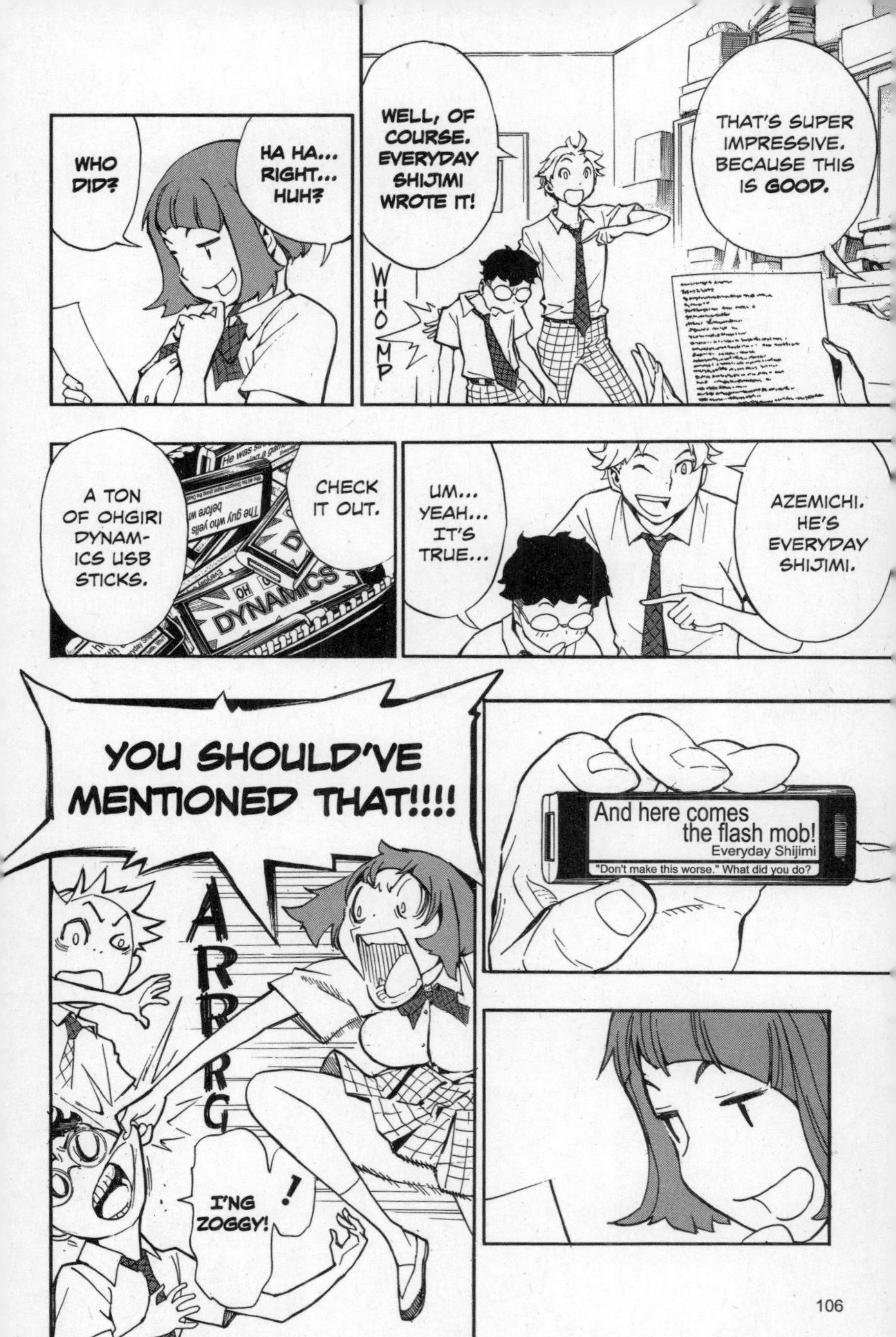

THAT'S SUPER IMPRESSIVE. BECAUSE THIS IS GOOD.
WELL, OF COURSE. EVERYDAY SHIJIMI WROTE IT!
WHOMP
HA HA... RIGHT... HUH?
WHO DID?
AZEMICHI. HE'S EVERYDAY SHIJIMI.
UM... YEAH... IT'S TRUE...
CHECK IT OUT.
A TON OF OHGIRI DYNAMICS USB STICKS.
DYNAMICS
And here comes the flash mob!
Everyday Shijimi
"Don't make this worse." What did you do?
YOU SHOULD'VE MENTIONED THAT!!!!
ARRRG
I'NG ZOGGY!
!

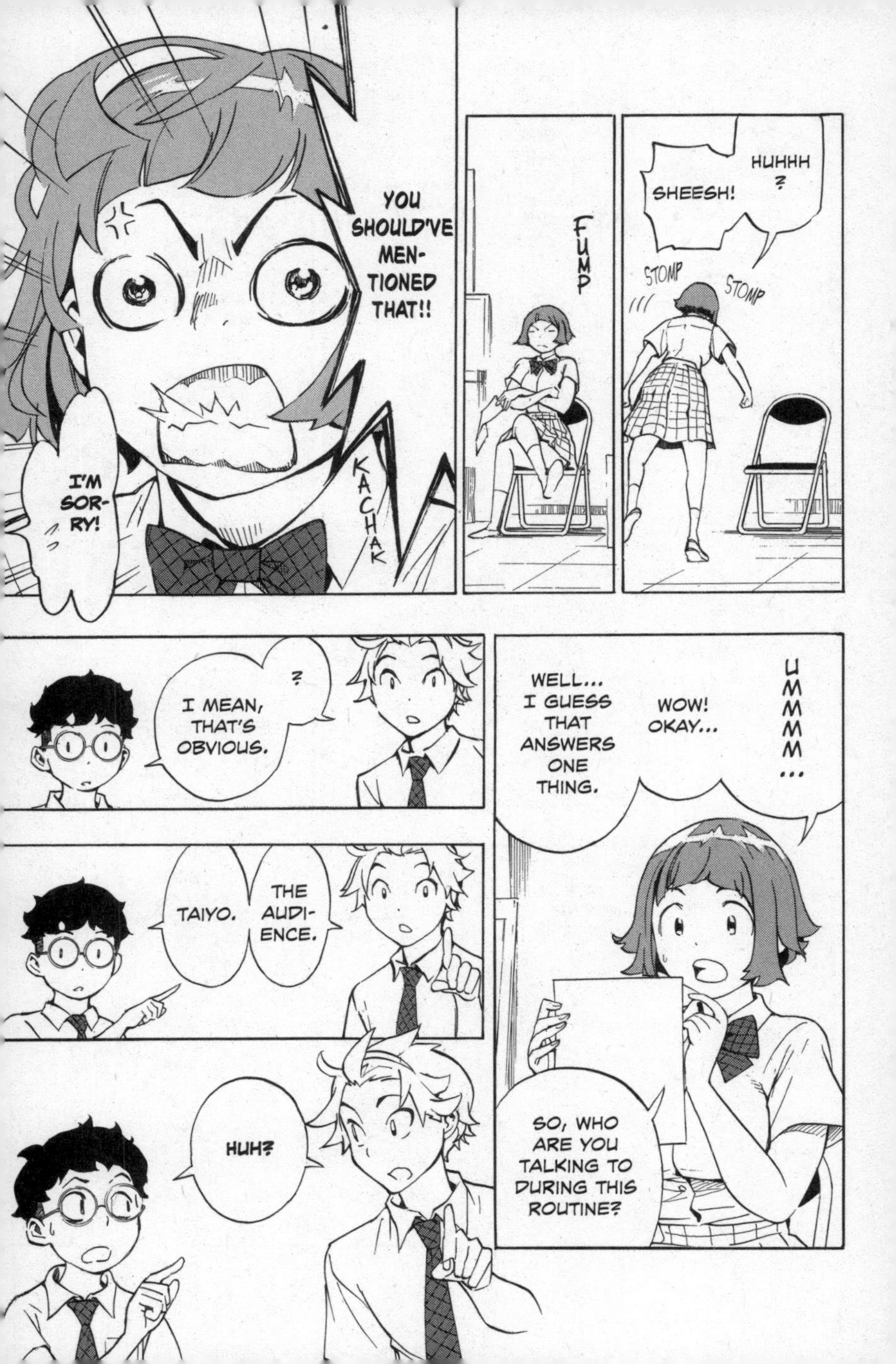
HUHHH?
SHEESH!
STOMP
STOMP
FUMP
YOU SHOULD'VE MENTIONED THAT!!
KACHAK
I'M SORRY!
UMMMM...
WOW! OKAY...
WELL... I GUESS THAT ANSWERS ONE THING.
SO, WHO ARE YOU TALKING TO DURING THIS ROUTINE?
?
I MEAN, THAT'S OBVIOUS.
THE AUDIENCE.
TAIYO.
HUH?

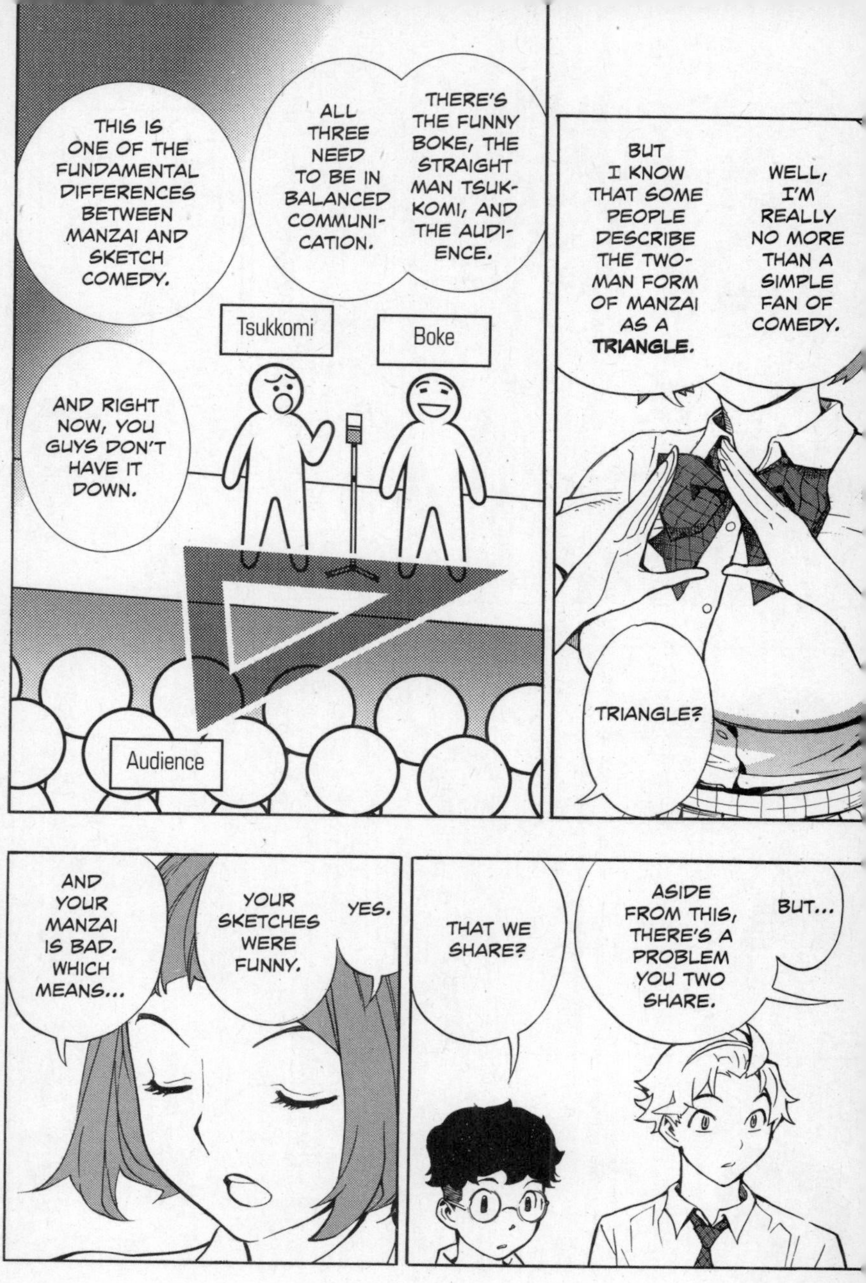
WELL, I'M REALLY NO MORE THAN A SIMPLE FAN OF COMEDY.
BUT I KNOW THAT SOME PEOPLE DESCRIBE THE TWO-MAN FORM OF MANZAI AS A **TRIANGLE.**
TRIANGLE?
THERE'S THE FUNNY BOKE, THE STRAIGHT MAN TSUKKOMI, AND THE AUDIENCE.
ALL THREE NEED TO BE IN BALANCED COMMUNICATION.
THIS IS ONE OF THE FUNDAMENTAL DIFFERENCES BETWEEN MANZAI AND SKETCH COMEDY.
Boke
Tsukkomi
AND RIGHT NOW, YOU GUYS DON'T HAVE IT DOWN.
Audience
BUT...
ASIDE FROM THIS, THERE'S A PROBLEM YOU TWO SHARE.
THAT WE SHARE?
YES.
YOUR SKETCHES WERE FUNNY.
AND YOUR MANZAI IS BAD. WHICH MEANS...

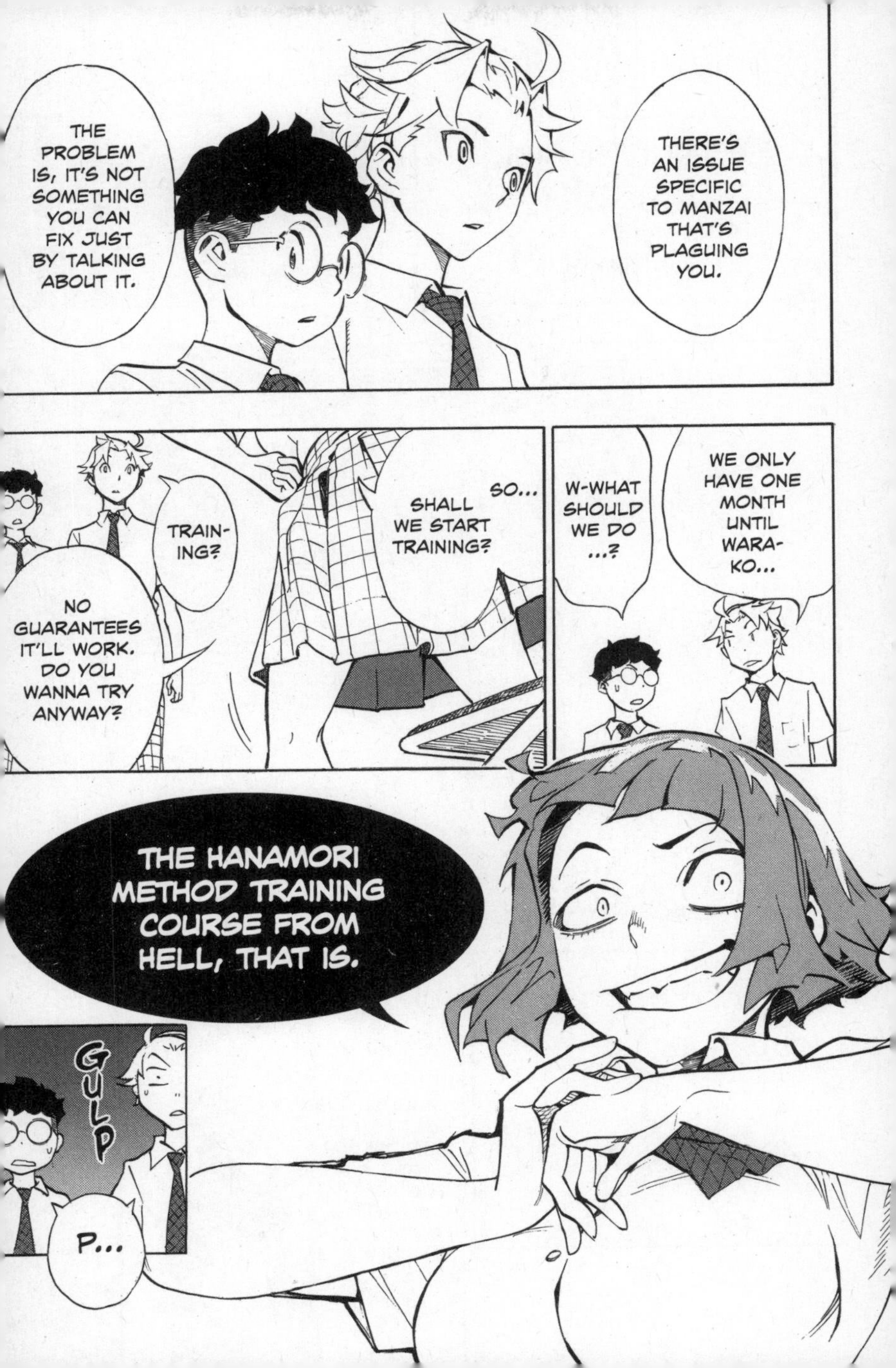
THERE'S AN ISSUE SPECIFIC TO MANZAI THAT'S PLAGUING YOU.
THE PROBLEM IS, IT'S NOT SOMETHING YOU CAN FIX JUST BY TALKING ABOUT IT.
WE ONLY HAVE ONE MONTH UNTIL WARAKO...
W-WHAT SHOULD WE DO ...?
SO... SHALL WE START TRAINING?
TRAINING?
NO GUARANTEES IT'LL WORK. DO YOU WANNA TRY ANYWAY?
THE HANAMORI METHOD TRAINING COURSE FROM HELL, THAT IS.
GULP
P...

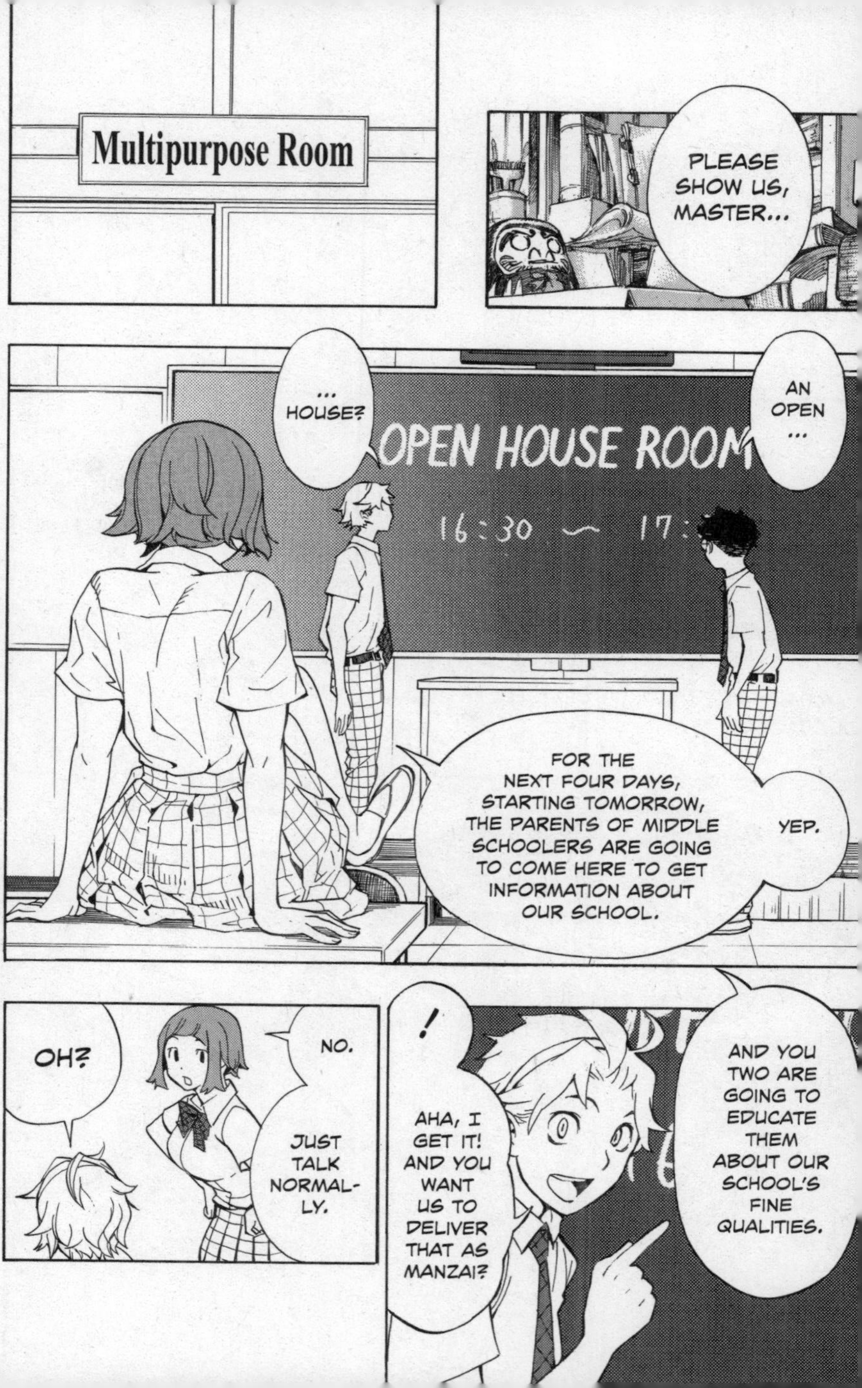
PLEASE SHOW US, MASTER...
Multipurpose Room
AN OPEN ...
OPEN HOUSE ROOM
... HOUSE?
16:30 ~ 17:
YEP.
FOR THE NEXT FOUR DAYS, STARTING TOMORROW, THE PARENTS OF MIDDLE SCHOOLERS ARE GOING TO COME HERE TO GET INFORMATION ABOUT OUR SCHOOL.
AND YOU TWO ARE GOING TO EDUCATE THEM ABOUT OUR SCHOOL'S FINE QUALITIES.
!
AHA, I GET IT! AND YOU WANT US TO DELIVER THAT AS MANZAI?
NO.
OH?
JUST TALK NORMAL-LY.

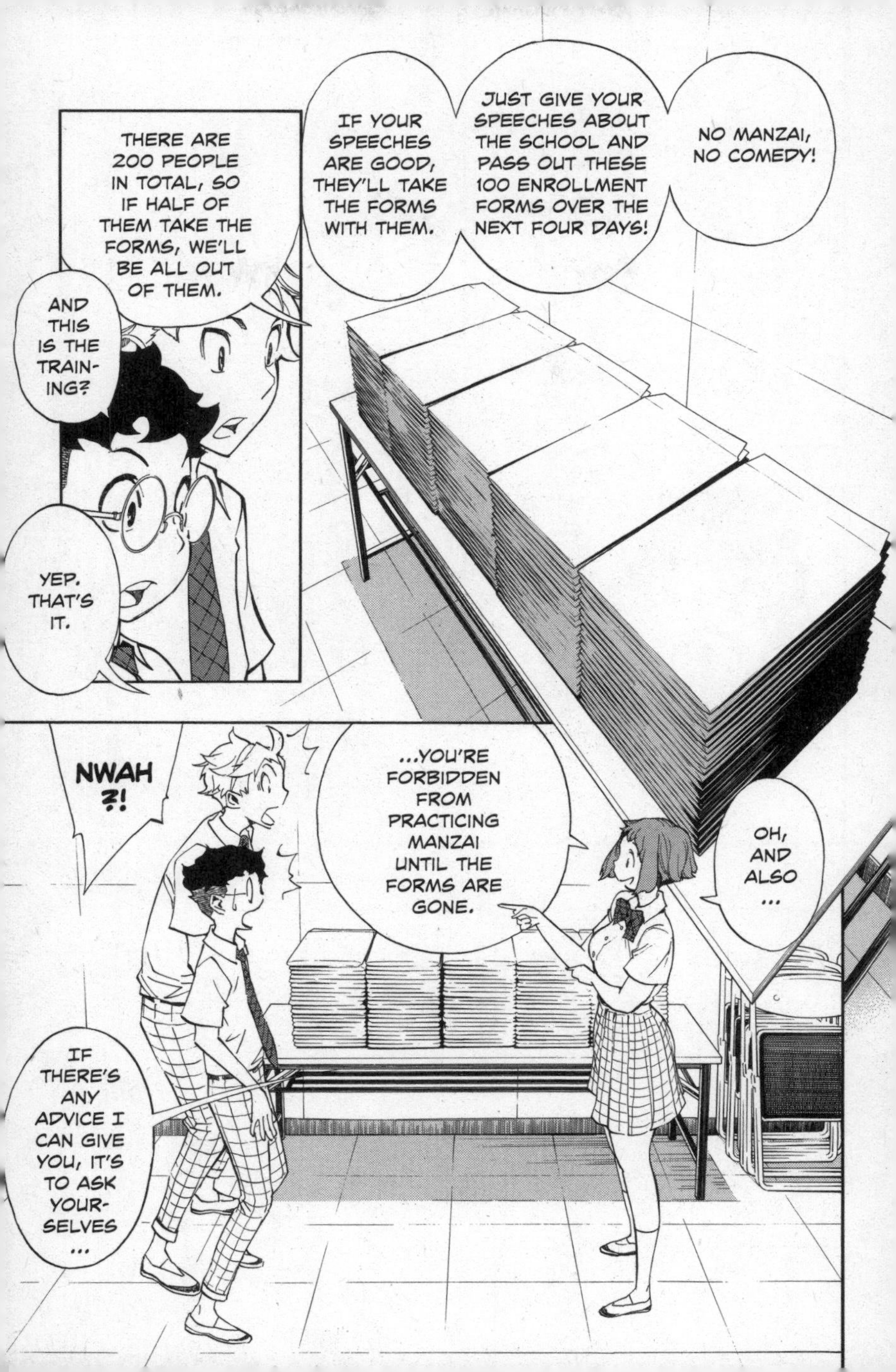
NO MANZAI, NO COMEDY!
JUST GIVE YOUR SPEECHES ABOUT THE SCHOOL AND PASS OUT THESE 100 ENROLLMENT FORMS OVER THE NEXT FOUR DAYS!
IF YOUR SPEECHES ARE GOOD, THEY'LL TAKE THE FORMS WITH THEM.
THERE ARE 200 PEOPLE IN TOTAL, SO IF HALF OF THEM TAKE THE FORMS, WE'LL BE ALL OUT OF THEM.
AND THIS IS THE TRAIN-ING?
YEP. THAT'S IT.
OH, AND ALSO ...
...YOU'RE FORBIDDEN FROM PRACTICING MANZAI UNTIL THE FORMS ARE GONE.
NWAH ?!
IF THERE'S ANY ADVICE I CAN GIVE YOU, IT'S TO ASK YOUR-SELVES ...

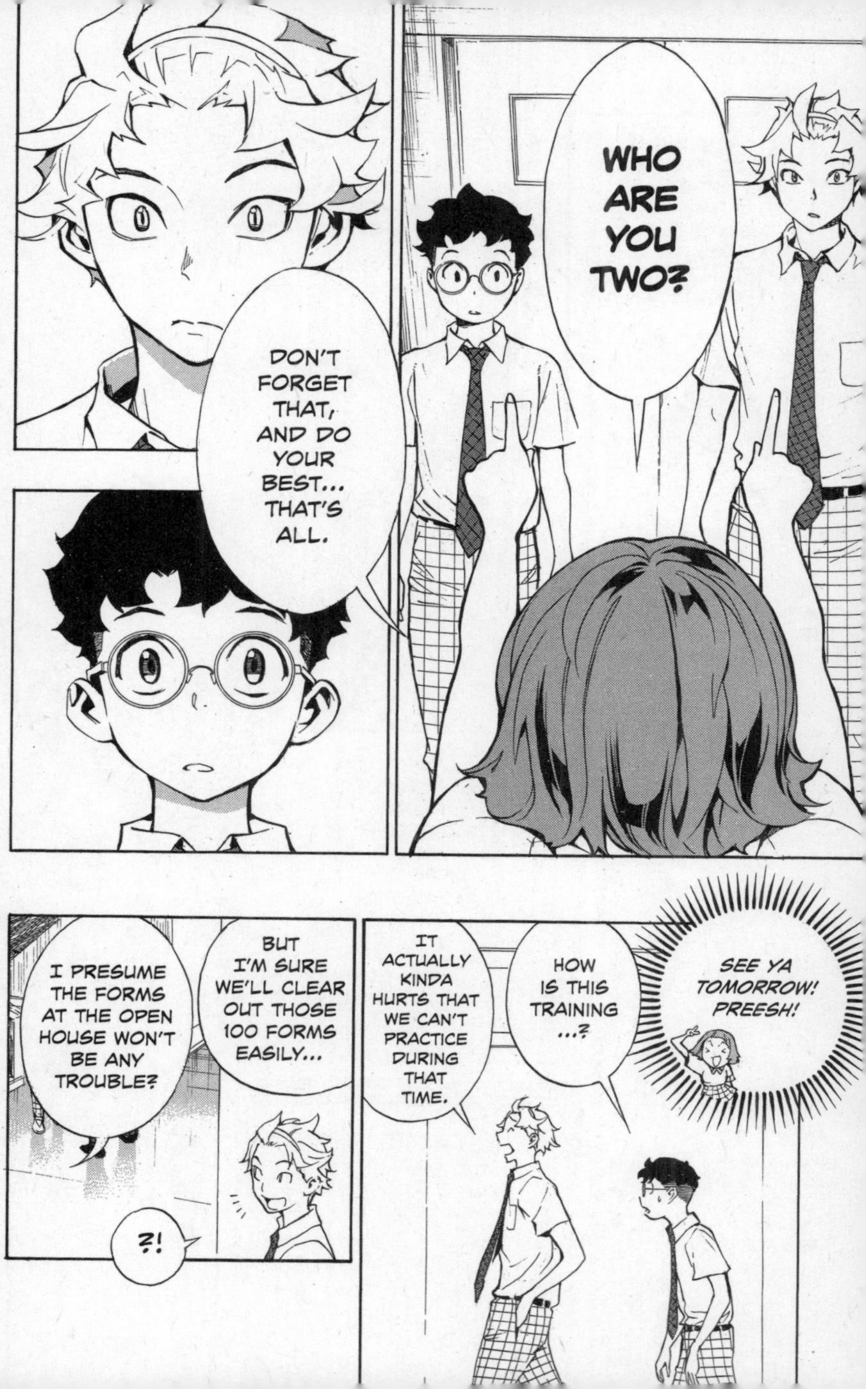
WHO ARE YOU TWO?
DON'T FORGET THAT, AND DO YOUR BEST... THAT'S ALL.
SEE YA TOMORROW! PREESH!
HOW IS THIS TRAINING ...?
IT ACTUALLY KINDA HURTS THAT WE CAN'T PRACTICE DURING THAT TIME.
BUT I'M SURE WE'LL CLEAR OUT THOSE 100 FORMS EASILY...
I PRESUME THE FORMS AT THE OPEN HOUSE WON'T BE ANY TROUBLE?
?!

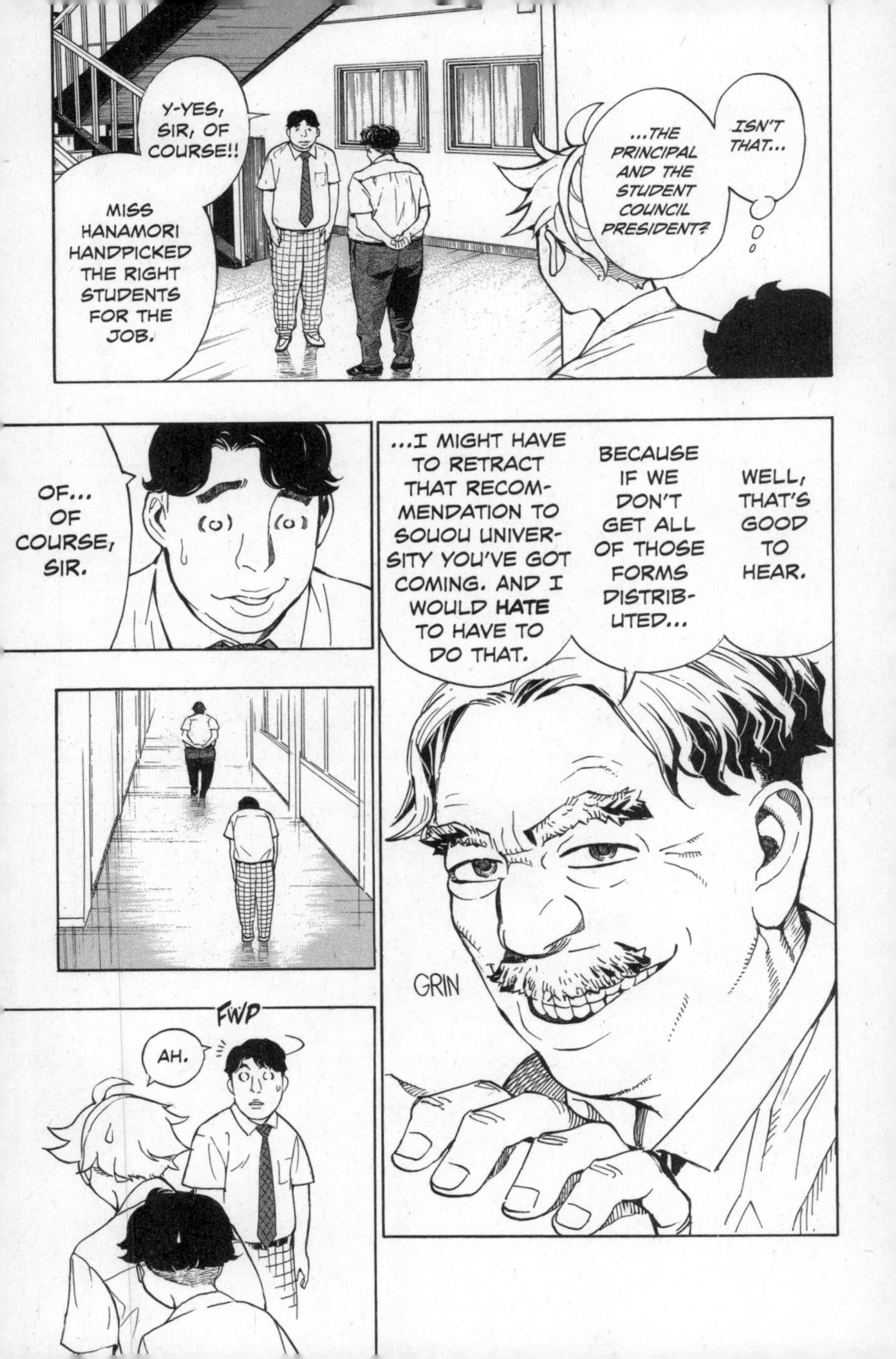
ISN'T THAT...
...THE PRINCIPAL AND THE STUDENT COUNCIL PRESIDENT?
Y-YES, SIR, OF COURSE!!
MISS HANAMORI HANDPICKED THE RIGHT STUDENTS FOR THE JOB.
WELL, THAT'S GOOD TO HEAR.
BECAUSE IF WE DON'T GET ALL OF THOSE FORMS DISTRIBUTED...
...I MIGHT HAVE TO RETRACT THAT RECOMMENDATION TO SOUOU UNIVERSITY YOU'VE GOT COMING. AND I WOULD HATE TO HAVE TO DO THAT.
GRIN
OF... OF COURSE, SIR.
FWP
AH.

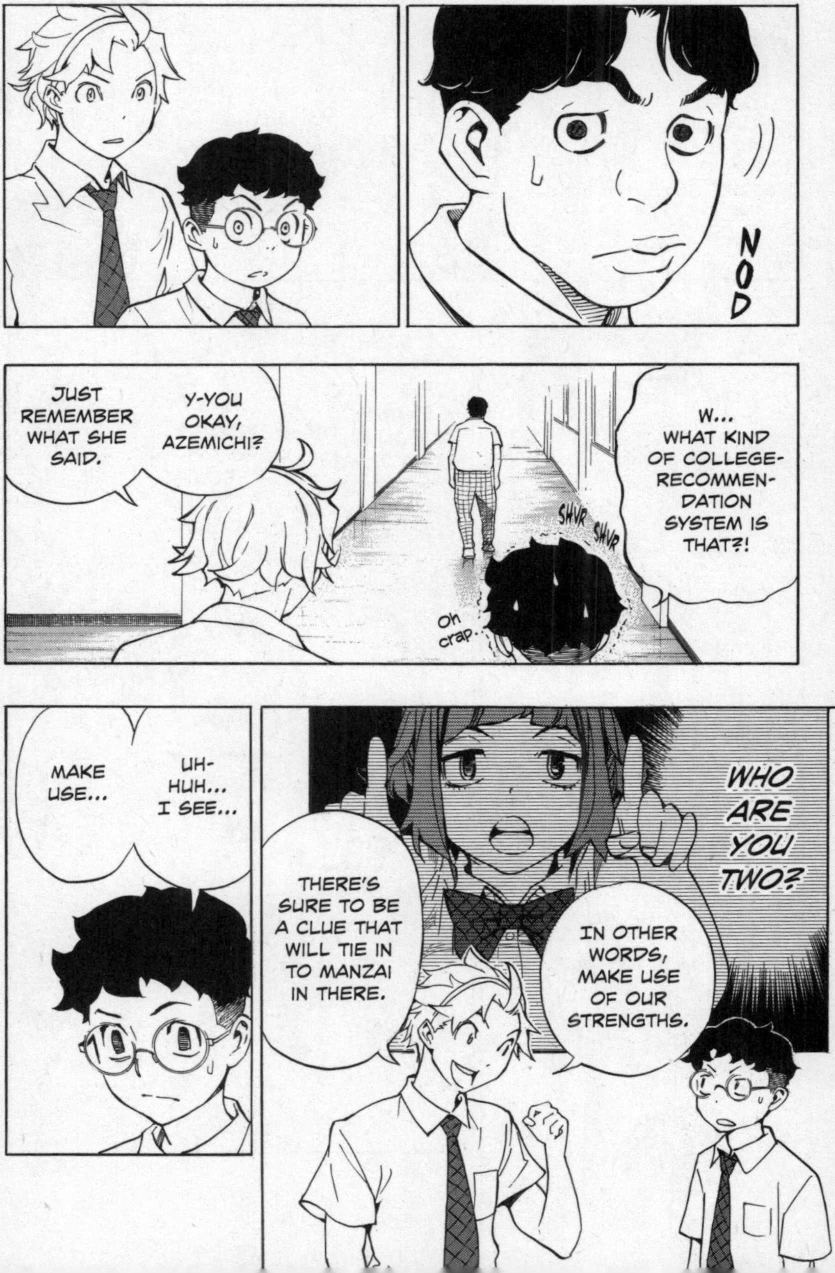
NOD
W... WHAT KIND OF COLLEGE-RECOMMENDATION SYSTEM IS THAT?!
SHVR SHVR
Y-YOU OKAY, AZEMICHI?
JUST REMEMBER WHAT SHE SAID.
Oh crap..
WHO ARE YOU TWO?
THERE'S SURE TO BE A CLUE THAT WILL TIE IN TO MANZAI IN THERE.
IN OTHER WORDS, MAKE USE OF OUR STRENGTHS.
UH-HUH... I SEE...
MAKE USE...

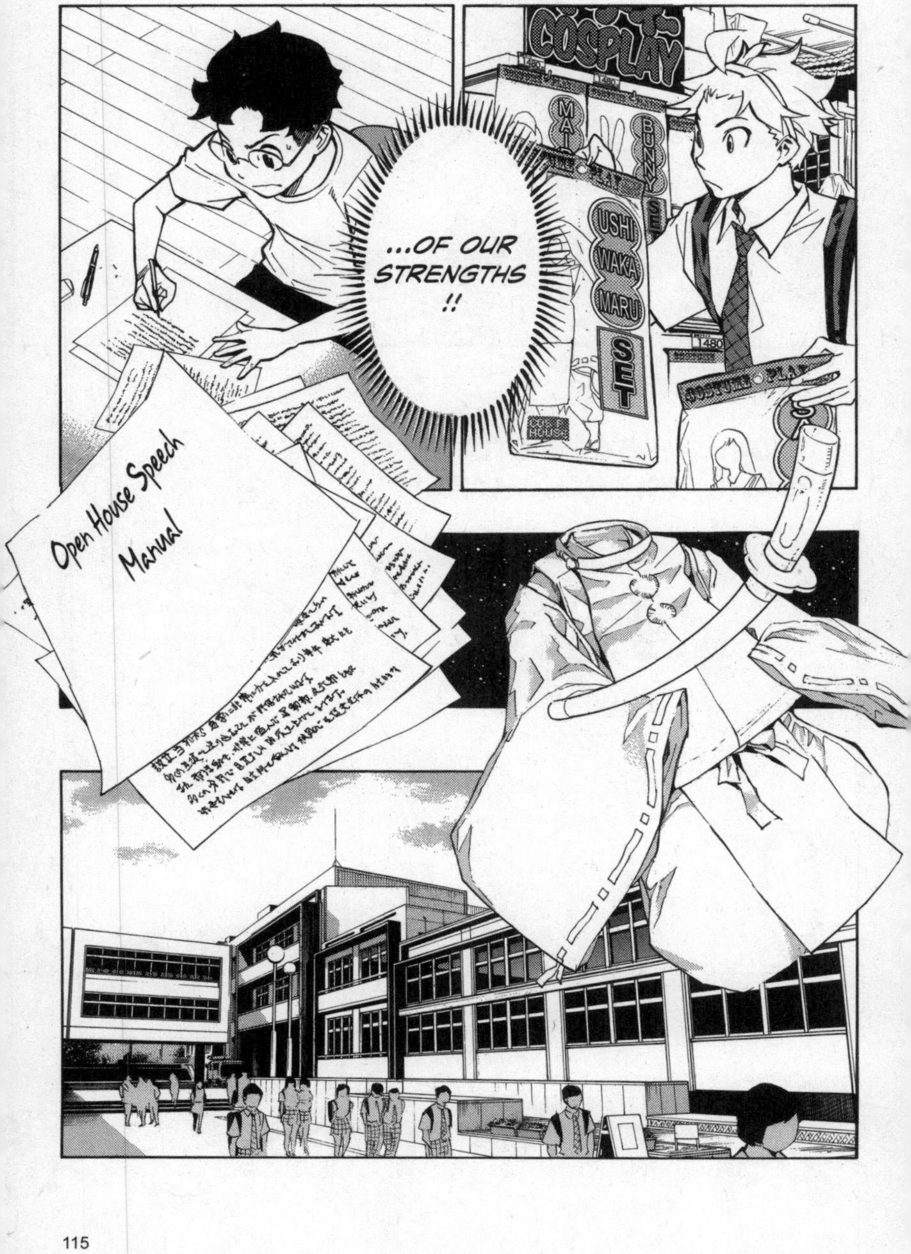
COSPLAY
MAID
BUNNY SET
USHI WAKA MARU SET
COSTUME PLAY
...OF OUR STRENGTHS !!
Open House Speech Manual

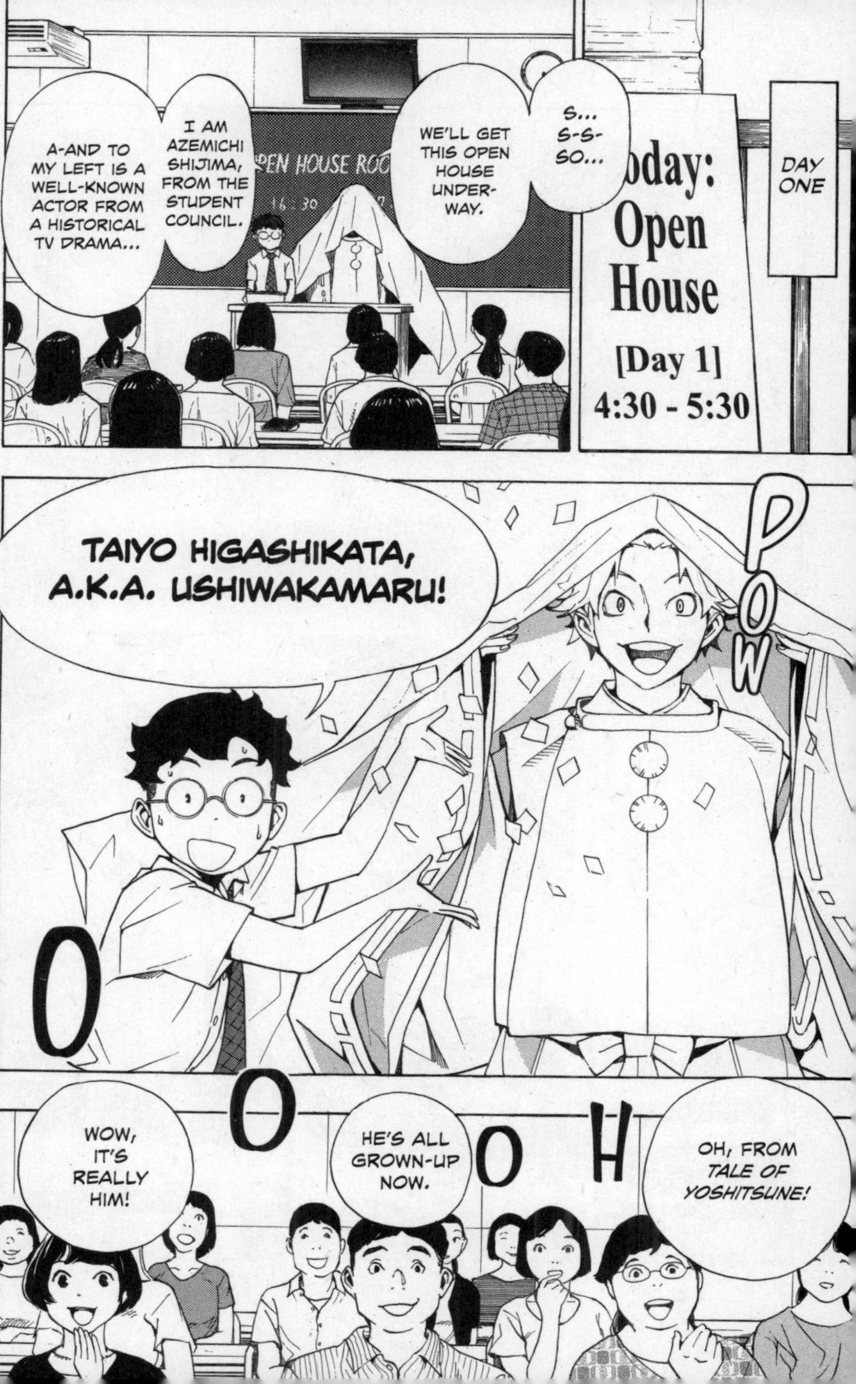
DAY ONE
oday: Open House [Day 1] 4:30 - 5:30
S... S-S-SO...
WE'LL GET THIS OPEN HOUSE UNDER-WAY.
I AM AZEMICHI SHIJIMA, FROM THE STUDENT COUNCIL.
A-AND TO MY LEFT IS A WELL-KNOWN ACTOR FROM A HISTORICAL TV DRAMA...
POW
TAIYO HIGASHIKATA, A.K.A. USHIWAKAMARU!
OOOOH
OH, FROM TALE OF YOSHITSUNE!
HE'S ALL GROWN-UP NOW.
WOW, IT'S REALLY HIM!

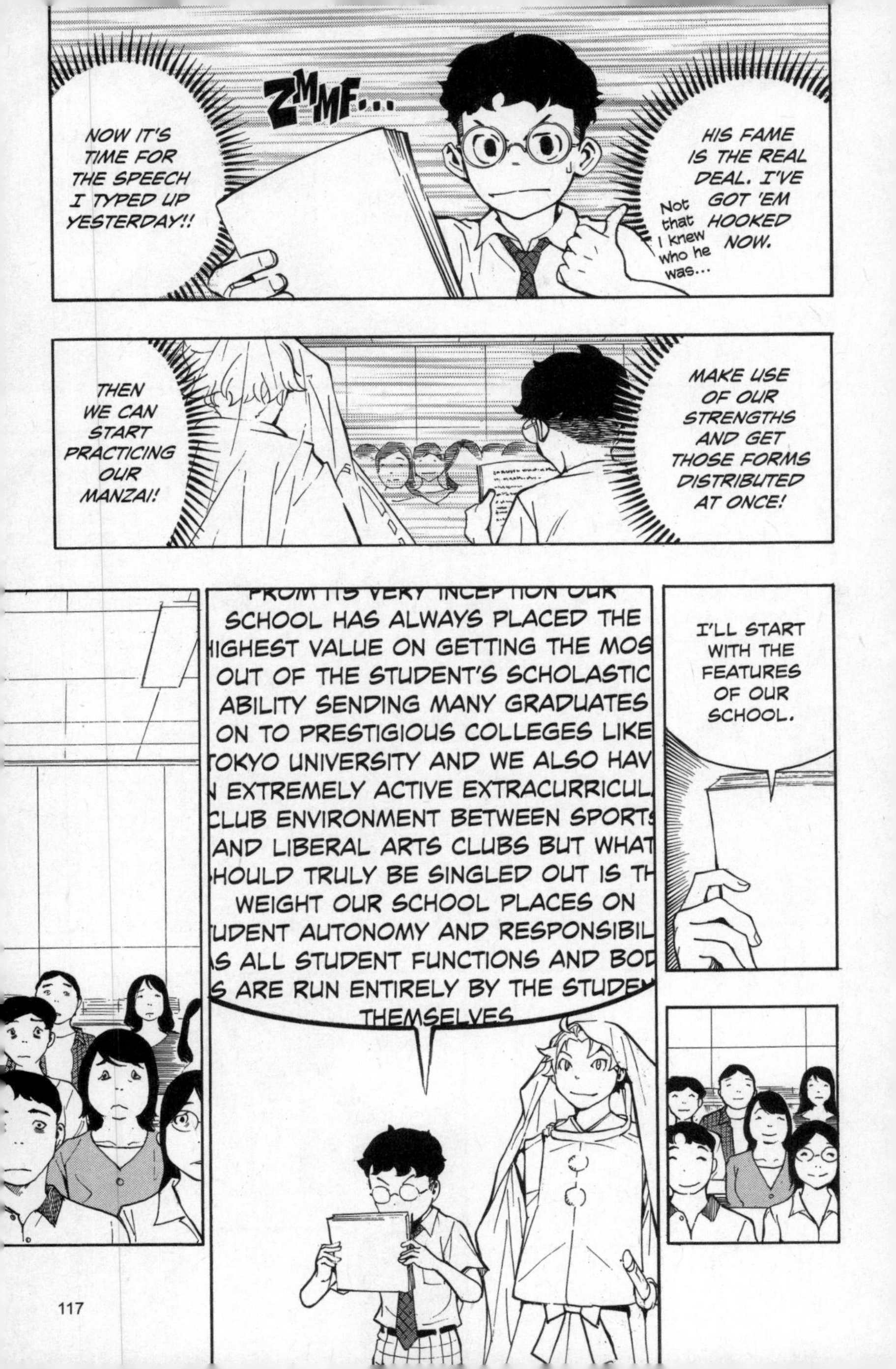
HIS FAME IS THE REAL DEAL. I'VE GOT 'EM HOOKED NOW.
Not that I knew who he was...
ZMMF...
NOW IT'S TIME FOR THE SPEECH I TYPED UP YESTERDAY!!
MAKE USE OF OUR STRENGTHS AND GET THOSE FORMS DISTRIBUTED AT ONCE!
THEN WE CAN START PRACTICING OUR MANZAI!
I'LL START WITH THE FEATURES OF OUR SCHOOL.
FROM ITS VERY INCEPTION OUR SCHOOL HAS ALWAYS PLACED THE HIGHEST VALUE ON GETTING THE MOS OUT OF THE STUDENT'S SCHOLASTIC ABILITY SENDING MANY GRADUATES ON TO PRESTIGIOUS COLLEGES LIKE TOKYO UNIVERSITY AND WE ALSO HAV N EXTREMELY ACTIVE EXTRACURRICUL CLUB ENVIRONMENT BETWEEN SPORTS AND LIBERAL ARTS CLUBS BUT WHAT SHOULD TRULY BE SINGLED OUT IS TH WEIGHT OUR SCHOOL PLACES ON TUDENT AUTONOMY AND RESPONSIBIL S ALL STUDENT FUNCTIONS AND BOD S ARE RUN ENTIRELY BY THE STUDEN THEMSELVES

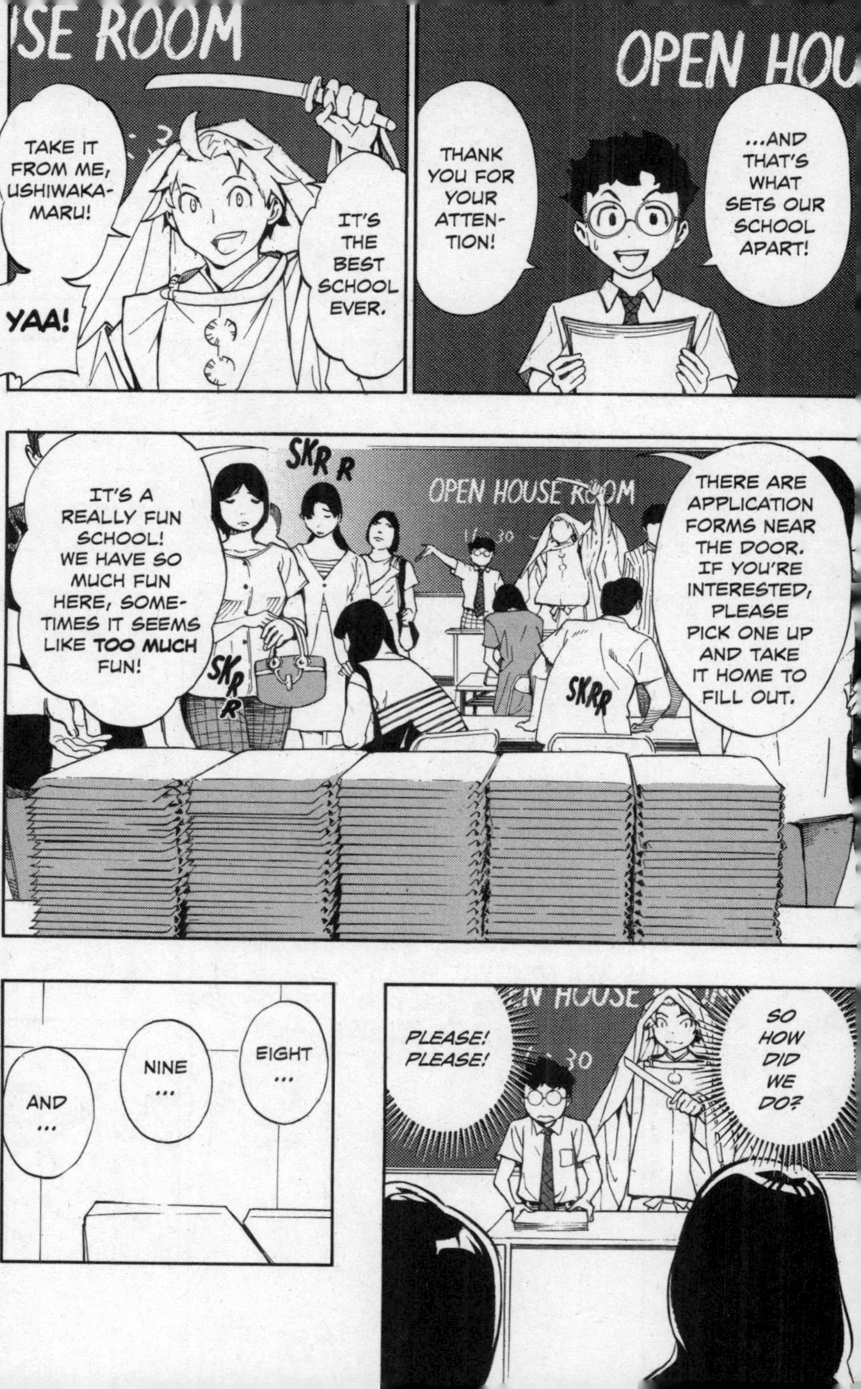
OPEN HOU
...AND THAT'S WHAT SETS OUR SCHOOL APART!
THANK YOU FOR YOUR ATTEN-TION!
SE ROOM
IT'S THE BEST SCHOOL EVER.
TAKE IT FROM ME, USHIWAKA-MARU!
YAA!
THERE ARE APPLICATION FORMS NEAR THE DOOR. IF YOU'RE INTERESTED, PLEASE PICK ONE UP AND TAKE IT HOME TO FILL OUT.
SKRR
OPEN HOUSE ROOM
SKRR
IT'S A REALLY FUN SCHOOL! WE HAVE SO MUCH FUN HERE, SOME-TIMES IT SEEMS LIKE **TOO MUCH** FUN!
SKRR
SO HOW DID WE DO?
PLEASE! PLEASE!
EIGHT ...
NINE ...
AND ...

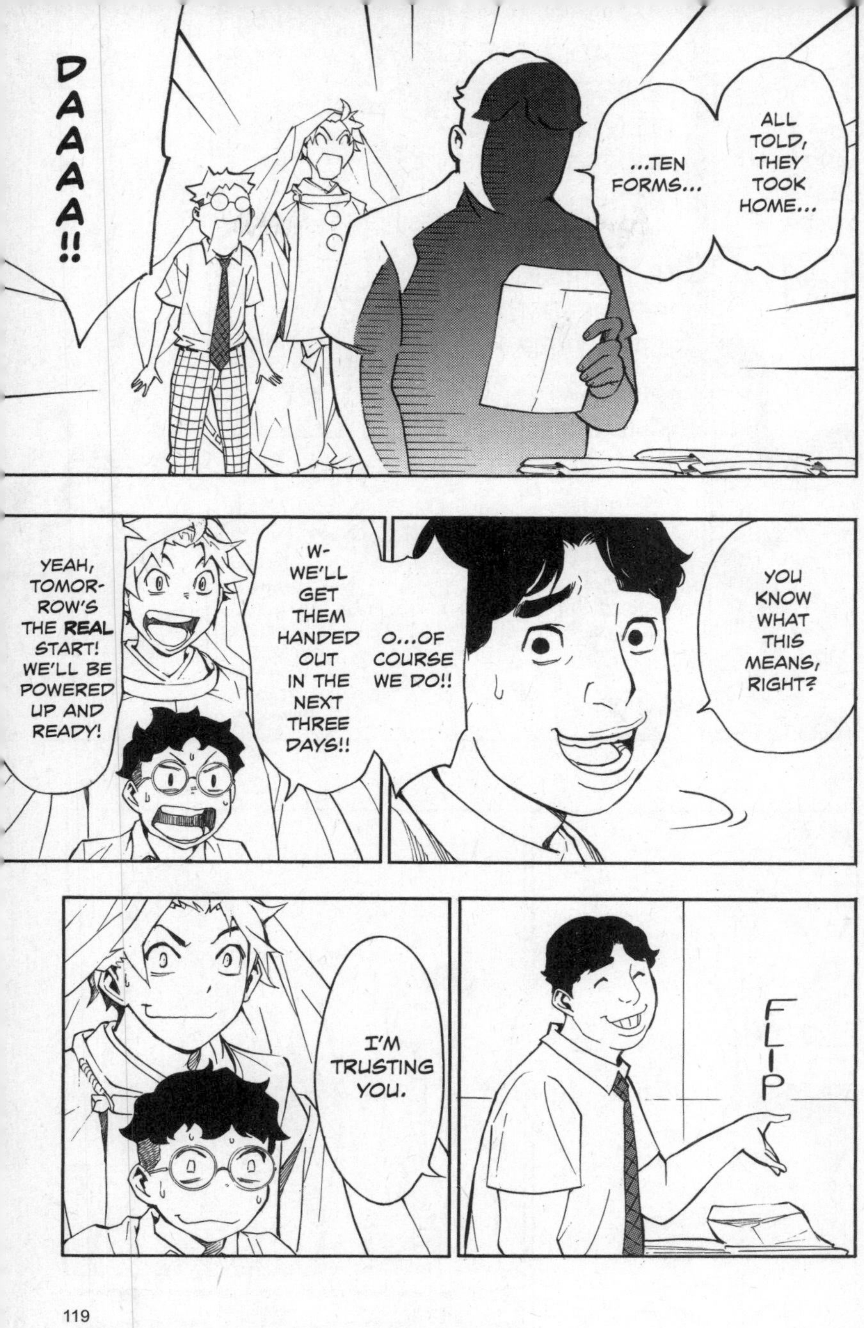
ALL TOLD, THEY TOOK HOME...
...TEN FORMS...
DAAAAA!!
YOU KNOW WHAT THIS MEANS, RIGHT?
O...OF COURSE WE DO!!
W-WE'LL GET THEM HANDED OUT IN THE NEXT THREE DAYS!!
YEAH, TOMORROW'S THE **REAL** START! WE'LL BE POWERED UP AND READY!
FLIP
I'M TRUSTING YOU.

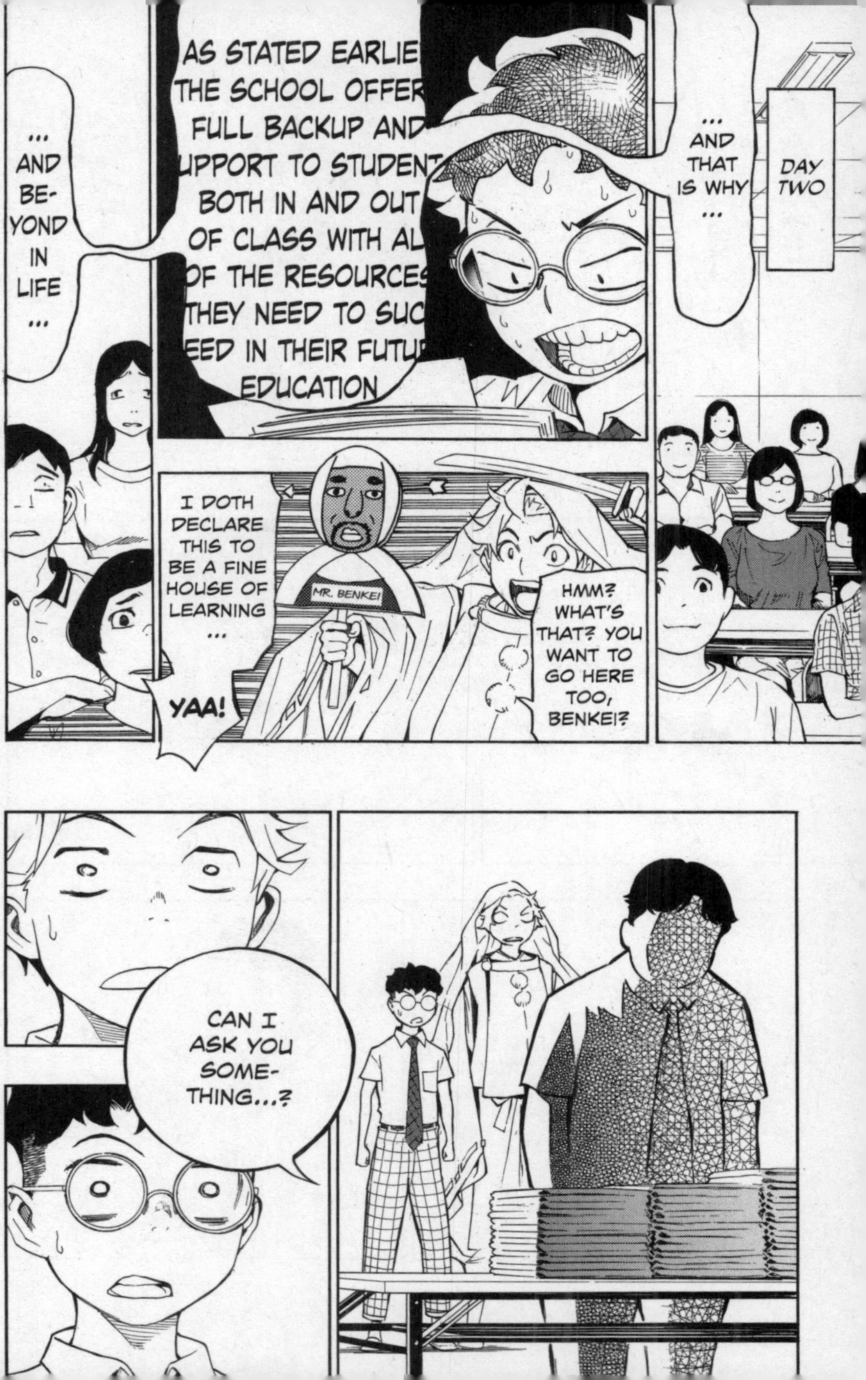
DAY TWO
... AND THAT IS WHY ...
AS STATED EARLIE THE SCHOOL OFFER FULL BACKUP AND UPPORT TO STUDENT BOTH IN AND OUT OF CLASS WITH AL OF THE RESOURCES THEY NEED TO SUC EED IN THEIR FUTU EDUCATION
... AND BE-YOND IN LIFE ...
HMM? WHAT'S THAT? YOU WANT TO GO HERE TOO, BENKEI?
I DOTH DECLARE THIS TO BE A FINE HOUSE OF LEARNING ...
MR. BENKEI
YAA!
CAN I ASK YOU SOME-THING...?

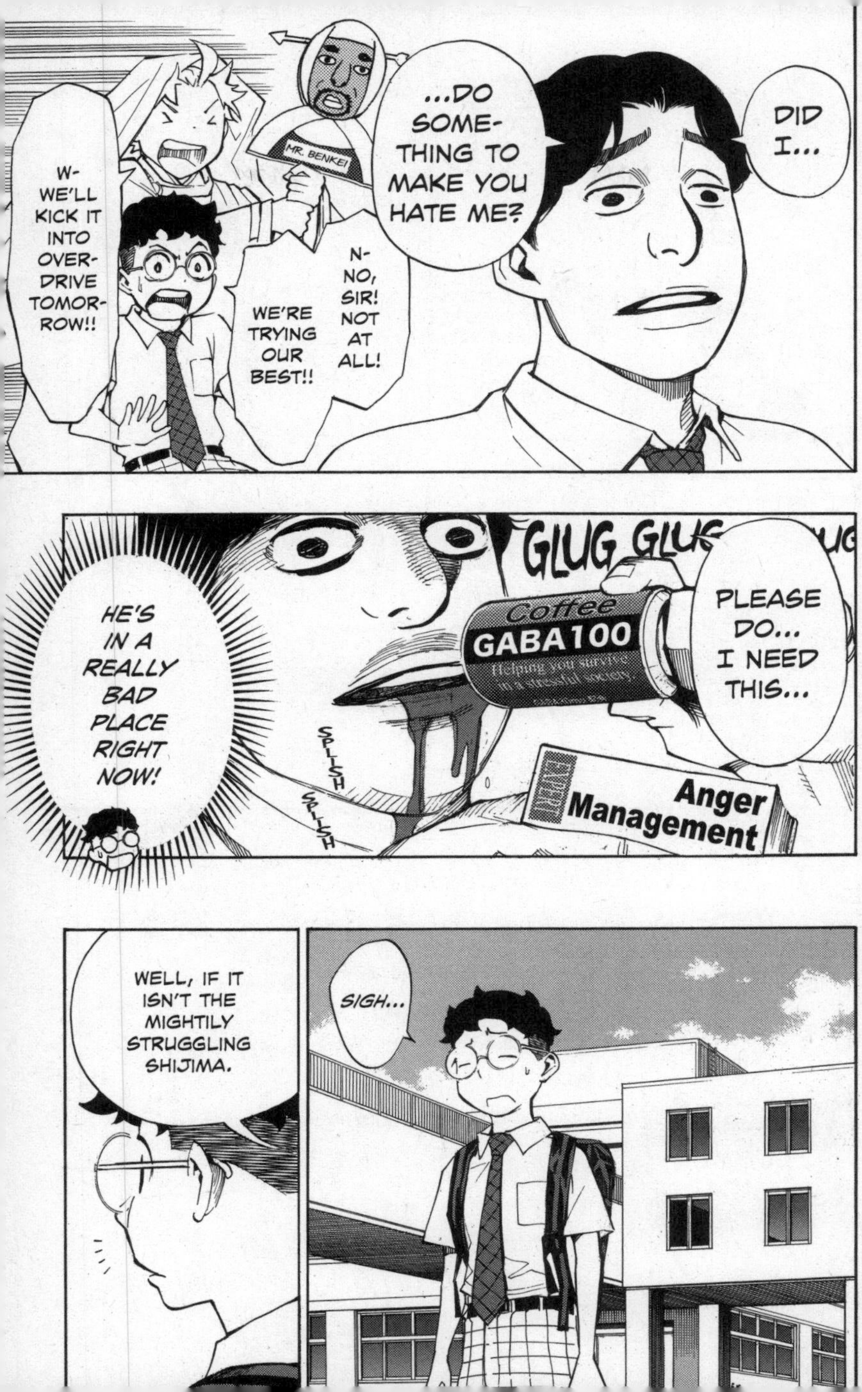
DID I...
...DO SOMETHING TO MAKE YOU HATE ME?
MR. BENKEI
N-NO, SIR! NOT AT ALL!
WE'RE TRYING OUR BEST!!
W-WE'LL KICK IT INTO OVERDRIVE TOMORROW!!
GLUG GLUG
PLEASE DO... I NEED THIS...
Coffee
GABA100
Helping you survive in a stressful society.
Anger Management
SPLISH SPLISH
HE'S IN A REALLY BAD PLACE RIGHT NOW!
SIGH...
WELL, IF IT ISN'T THE MIGHTILY STRUGGLING SHIJIMA.

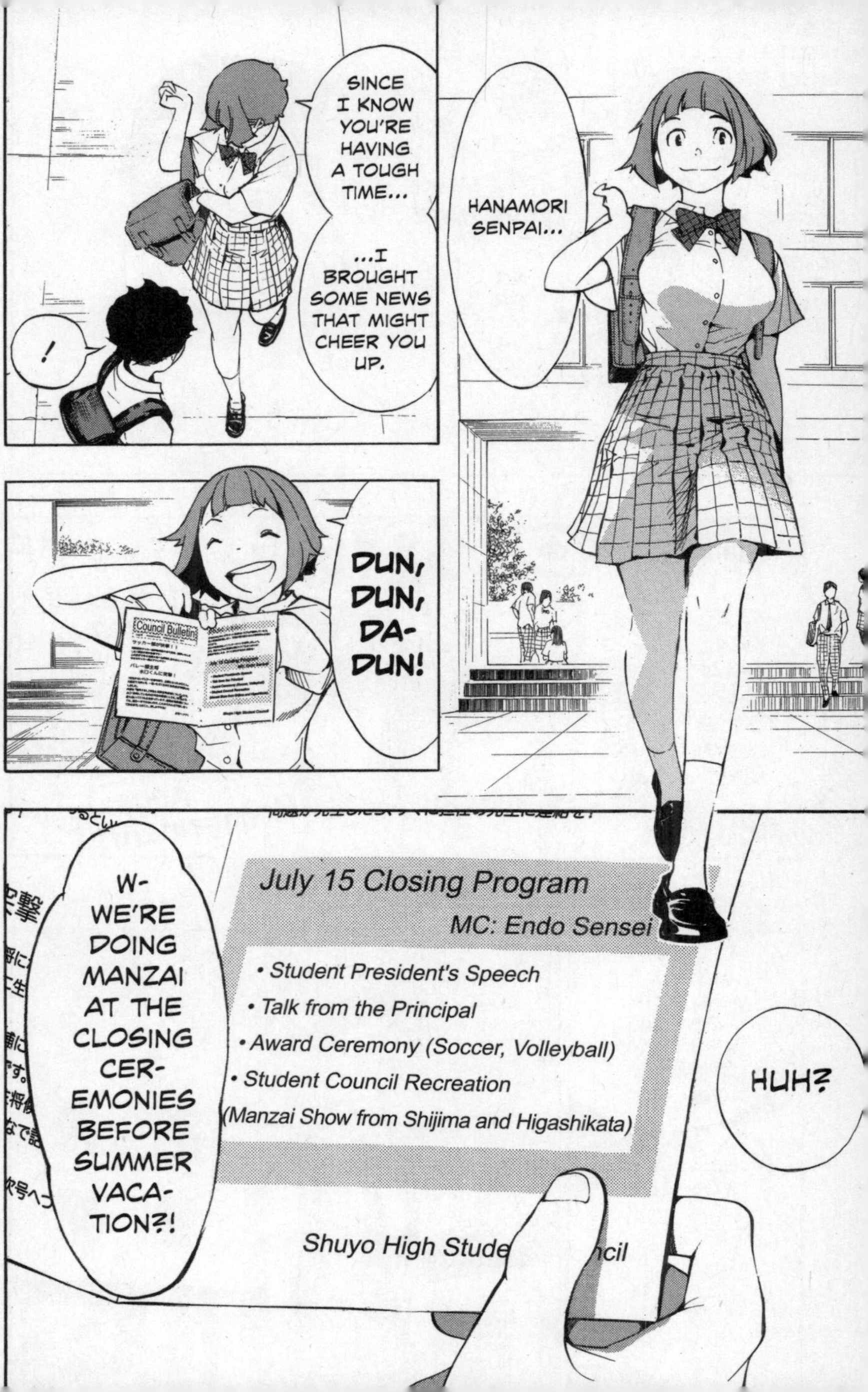

HANAMORI SENPAI...
SINCE I KNOW YOU'RE HAVING A TOUGH TIME... ...I BROUGHT SOME NEWS THAT MIGHT CHEER YOU UP.
!
DUN, DUN, DA-DUN!
Council Bulletin
July 15 Closing Program
MC: Endo Sensei
• Student President's Speech
• Talk from the Principal
• Award Ceremony (Soccer, Volleyball)
• Student Council Recreation
(Manzai Show from Shijima and Higashikata)
Shuyo High Stude ncil
HUH?
W-WE'RE DOING MANZAI AT THE CLOSING CER-EMONIES BEFORE SUMMER VACA-TION?!

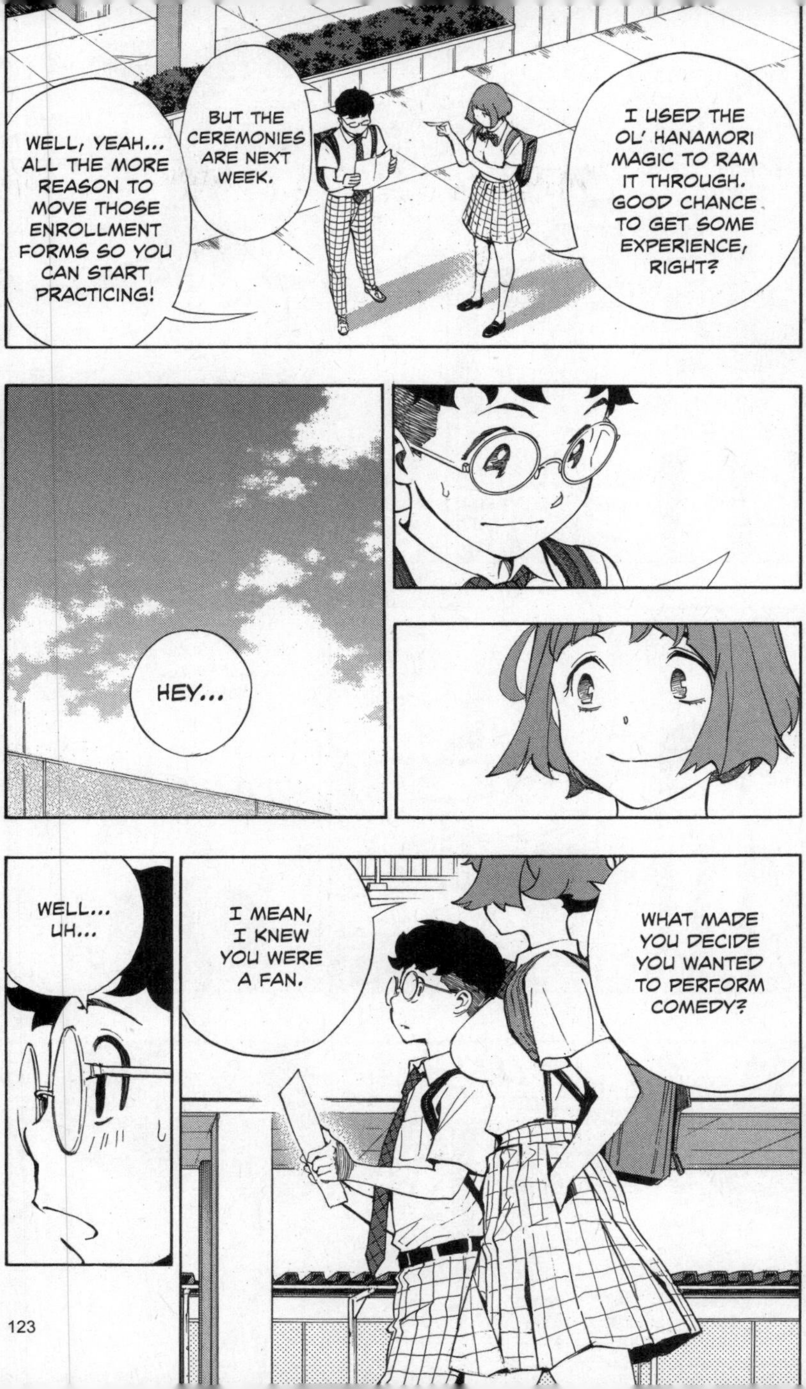
I USED THE OL' HANAMORI MAGIC TO RAM IT THROUGH. GOOD CHANCE TO GET SOME EXPERIENCE, RIGHT?
BUT THE CEREMONIES ARE NEXT WEEK.
WELL, YEAH... ALL THE MORE REASON TO MOVE THOSE ENROLLMENT FORMS SO YOU CAN START PRACTICING!
HEY...
WHAT MADE YOU DECIDE YOU WANTED TO PERFORM COMEDY?
I MEAN, I KNEW YOU WERE A FAN.
WELL... UH...

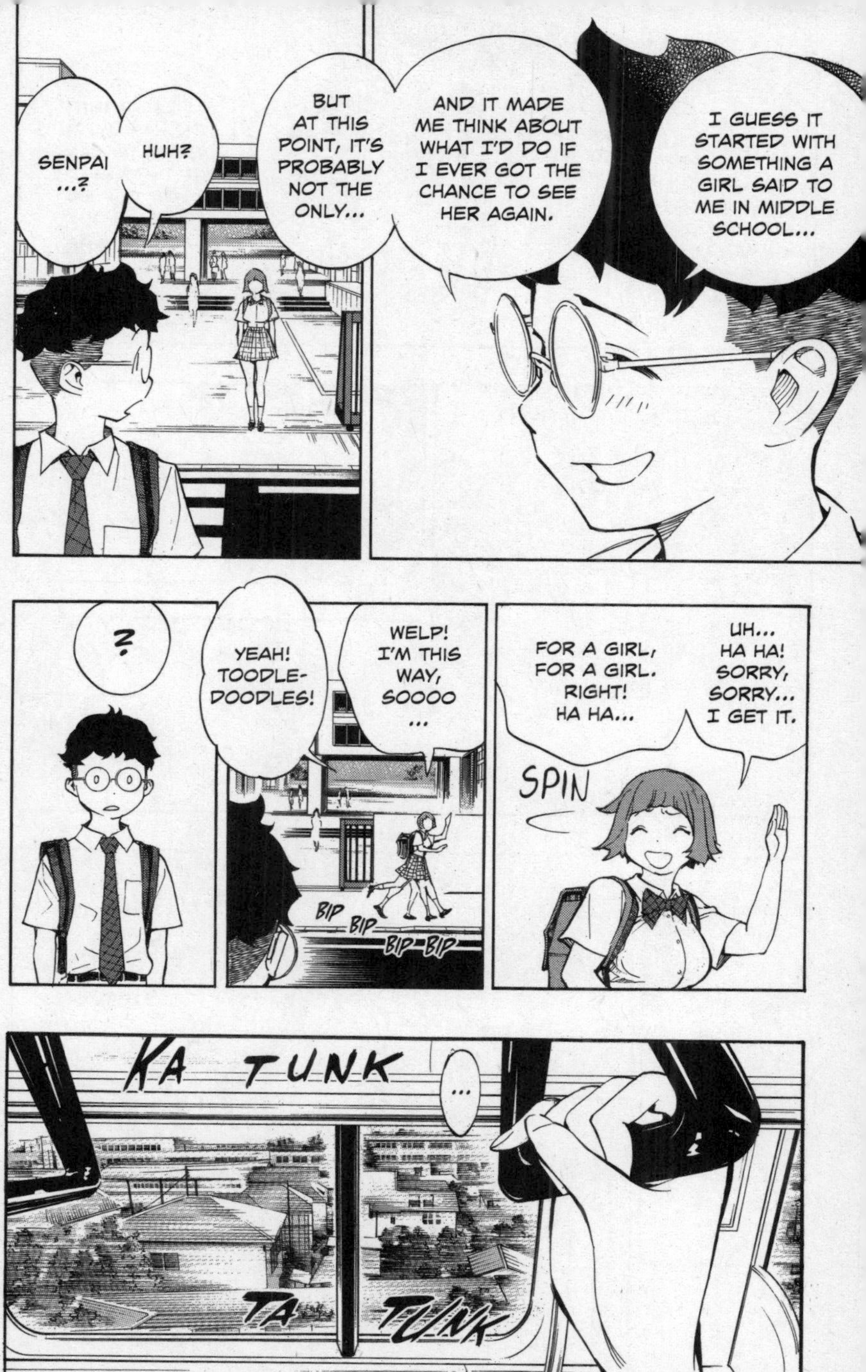
I GUESS IT STARTED WITH SOMETHING A GIRL SAID TO ME IN MIDDLE SCHOOL...
AND IT MADE ME THINK ABOUT WHAT I'D DO IF I EVER GOT THE CHANCE TO SEE HER AGAIN.
BUT AT THIS POINT, IT'S PROBABLY NOT THE ONLY...
HUH?
SENPAI ...?
UH... HA HA! SORRY, SORRY... I GET IT.
FOR A GIRL, FOR A GIRL. RIGHT! HA HA...
SPIN
WELP! I'M THIS WAY, SOOOO ...
YEAH! TOODLE-DOODLES!
BIP BIP BIP BIP
?
KA TUNK
...
TA TUNK

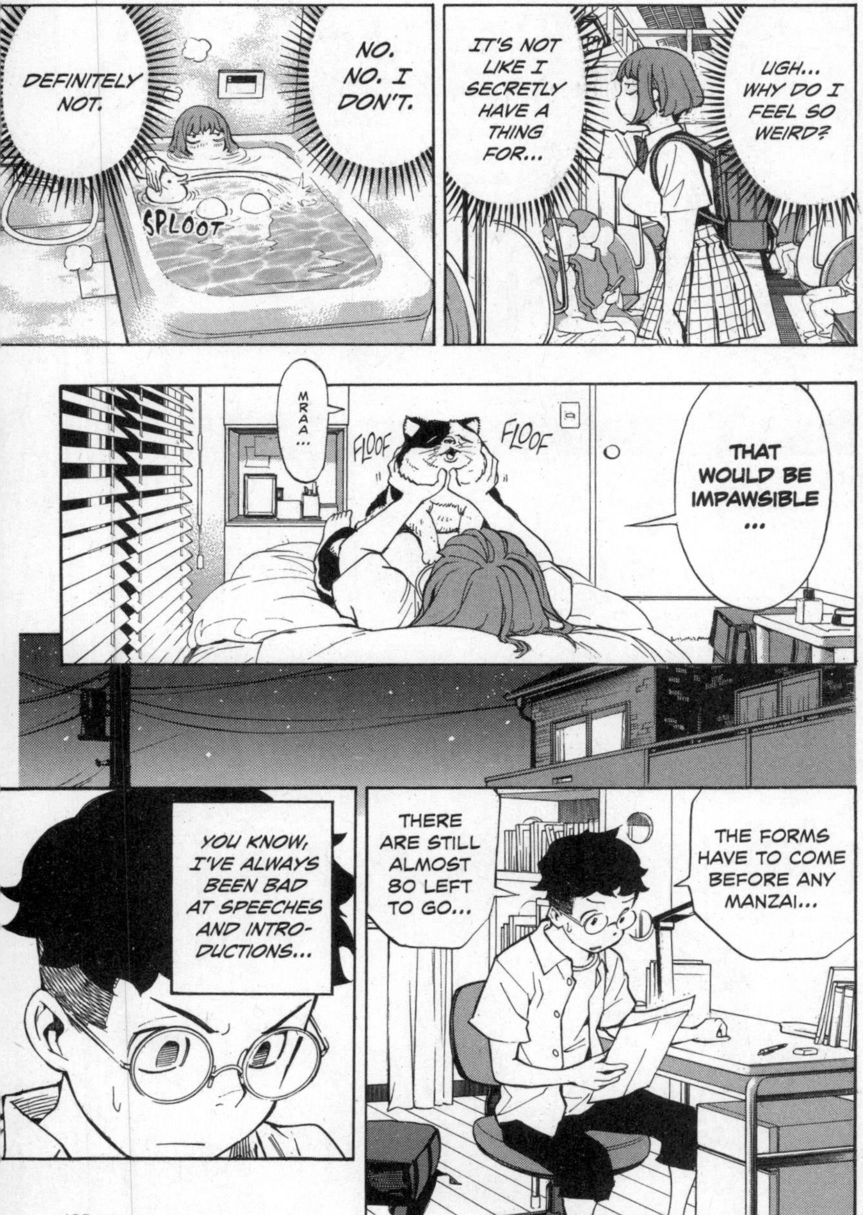
UGH... WHY DO I FEEL SO WEIRD?
IT'S NOT LIKE I SECRETLY HAVE A THING FOR...
NO. NO. I DON'T.
DEFINITELY NOT.
SPLOOT
THAT WOULD BE IMPAWSIBLE...
FLOOF
FLOOF
MRAA...
THE FORMS HAVE TO COME BEFORE ANY MANZAI...
THERE ARE STILL ALMOST 80 LEFT TO GO...
YOU KNOW, I'VE ALWAYS BEEN BAD AT SPEECHES AND INTRO-DUCTIONS...

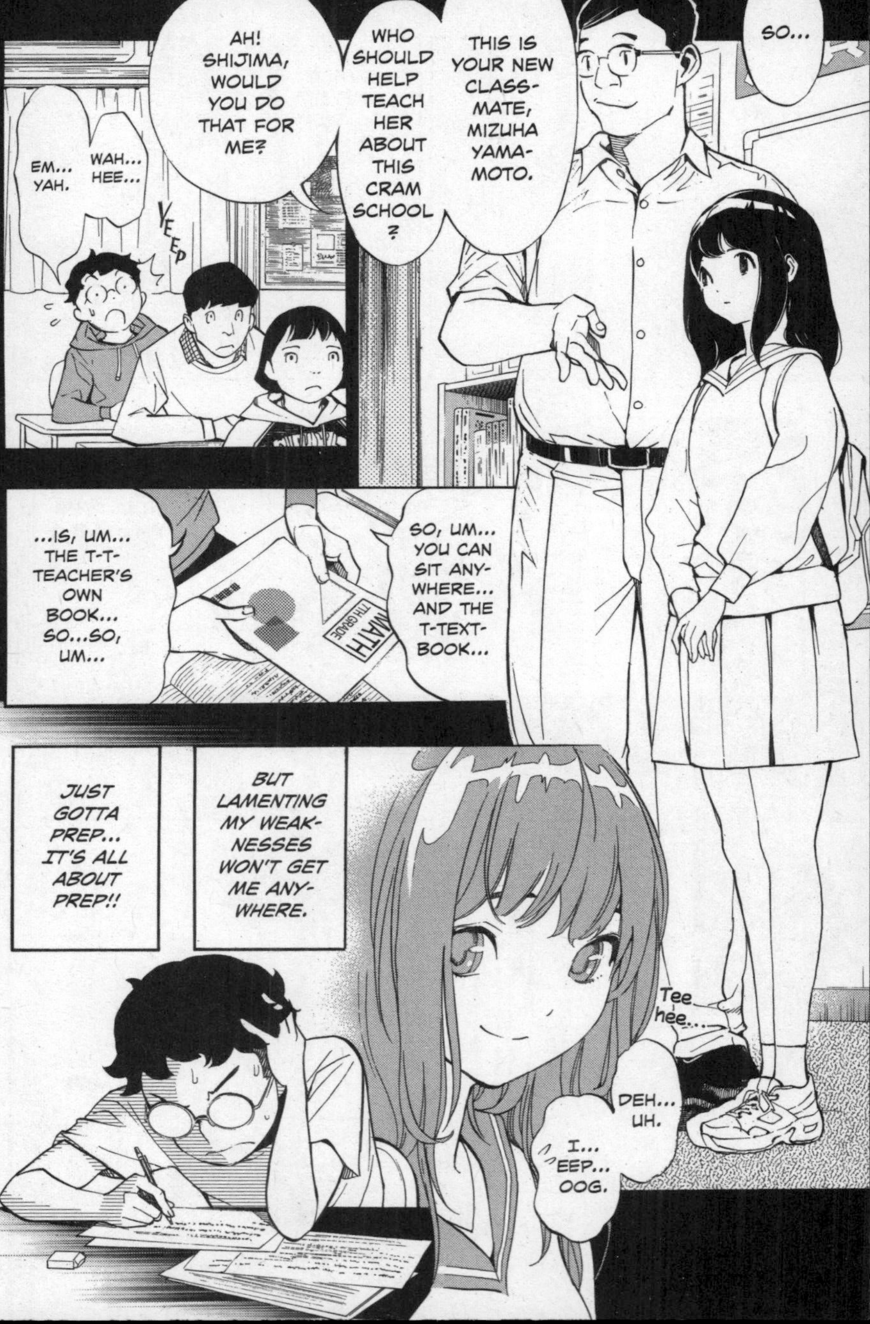
SO...
THIS IS YOUR NEW CLASS-MATE, MIZUHA YAMA-MOTO.
WHO SHOULD HELP TEACH HER ABOUT THIS CRAM SCHOOL?
AH! SHIJIMA, WOULD YOU DO THAT FOR ME?
WAH... HEE...
EM... YAH.
YEEEP
SO, UM... YOU CAN SIT ANY-WHERE... AND THE T-TEXT-BOOK...
...IS, UM... THE T-T-TEACHER'S OWN BOOK... SO...SO, UM...
MATH
7TH GRADE
BUT LAMENTING MY WEAK-NESSES WON'T GET ME ANY-WHERE.
JUST GOTTA PREP... IT'S ALL ABOUT PREP!!
Tee hee...
DEH... UH.
I... EEP... OOG.

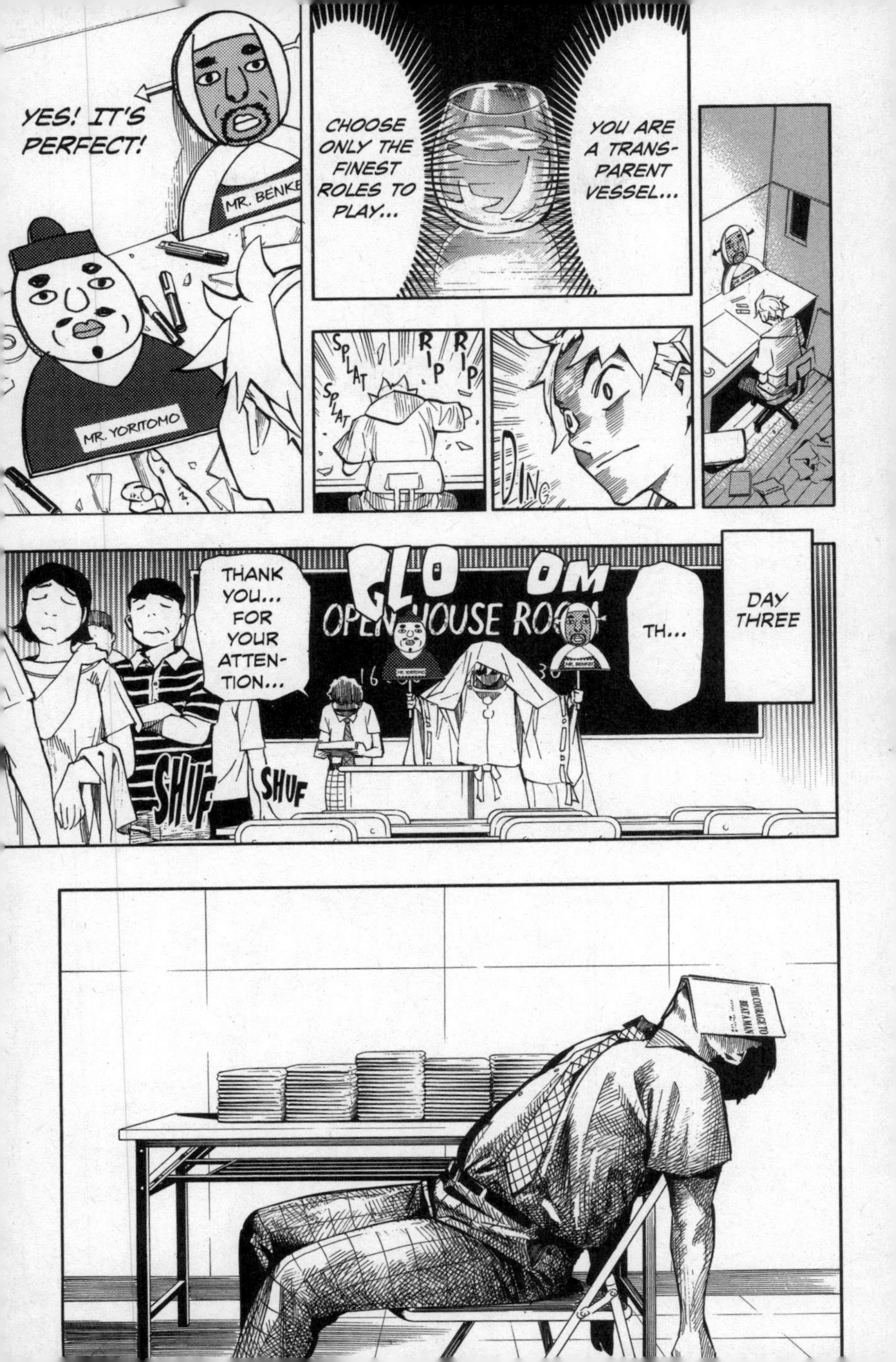
YOU ARE A TRANS-PARENT VESSEL...
CHOOSE ONLY THE FINEST ROLES TO PLAY...
DING
RIP RIP
SPLAT SPLAT
YES! IT'S PERFECT!
MR. BENKE
MR. YORITOMO
DAY THREE
TH...
GLO OM
OPEN HOUSE ROO
THANK YOU... FOR YOUR ATTEN-TION...
SHUF
SHUF
THE COURAGE TO BEAT A MAN

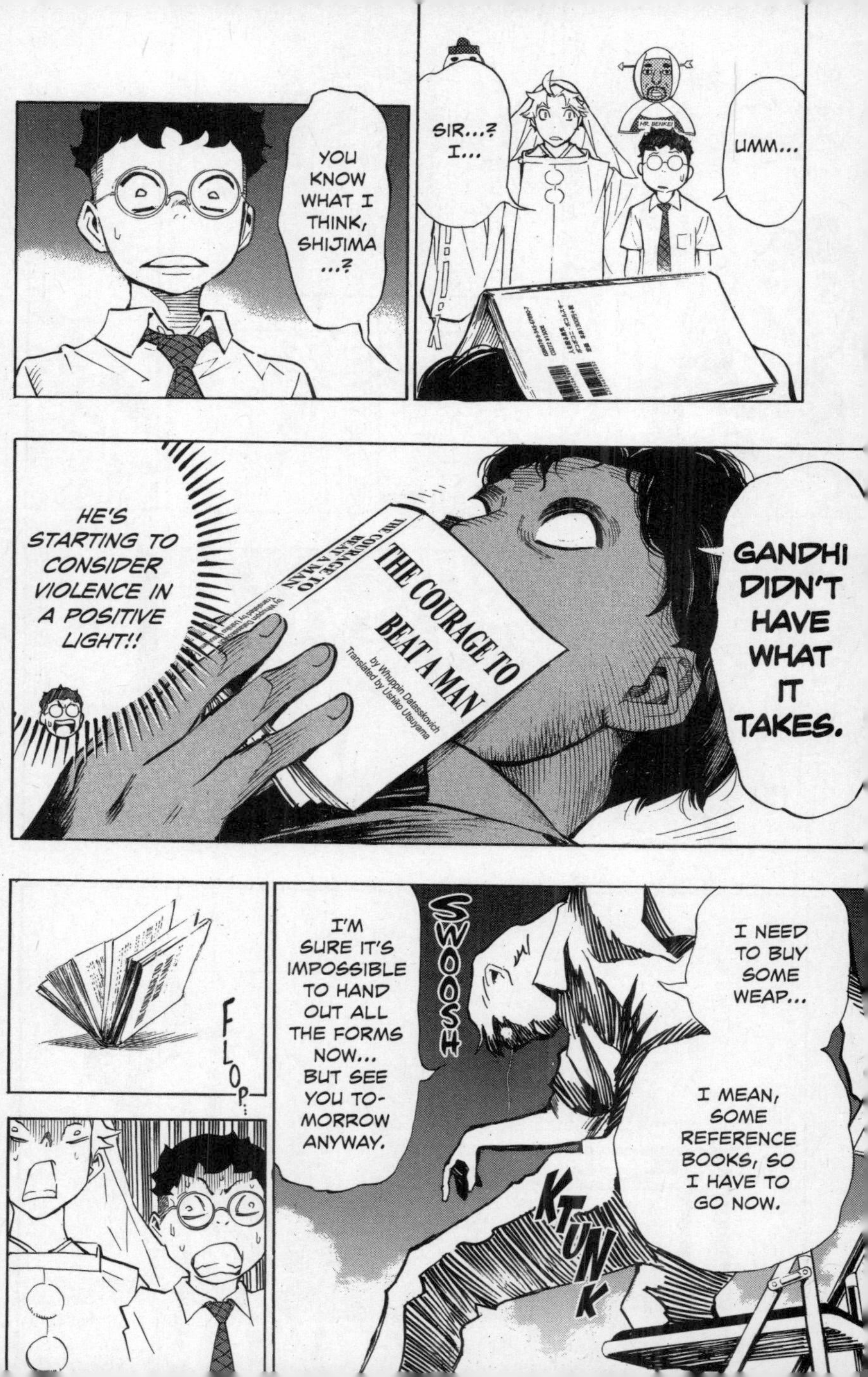
UMM...
MR. BENKEI
SIR...? I...
YOU KNOW WHAT I THINK, SHIJIMA...?
GANDHI DIDN'T HAVE WHAT IT TAKES.
THE COURAGE TO BEAT A MAN
by Whuppin Datasskovich
Translated by Ushiko Utsuyama
HE'S STARTING TO CONSIDER VIOLENCE IN A POSITIVE LIGHT!!
I NEED TO BUY SOME WEAP...
I MEAN, SOME REFERENCE BOOKS, SO I HAVE TO GO NOW.
SWOOSH
I'M SURE IT'S IMPOSSIBLE TO HAND OUT ALL THE FORMS NOW... BUT SEE YOU TO-MORROW ANYWAY.
KTUNK
FLOP

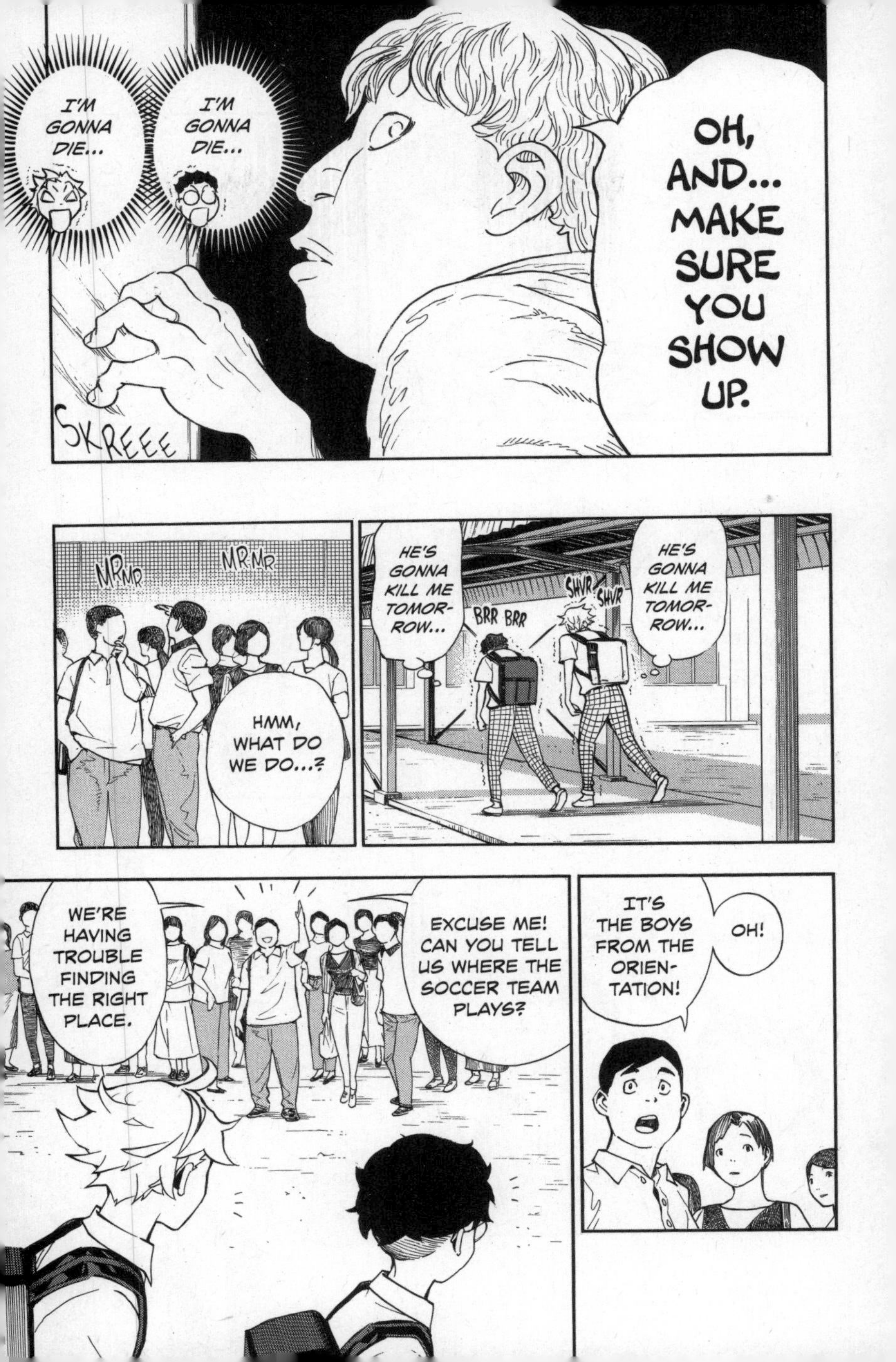
OH, AND... MAKE SURE YOU SHOW UP.
I'M GONNA DIE...
I'M GONNA DIE...
SKREEE
HE'S GONNA KILL ME TOMORROW...
SHVR SHVR
BRR BRR
HE'S GONNA KILL ME TOMORROW...
MRMR
MRMR
HMM, WHAT DO WE DO...?
OH!
IT'S THE BOYS FROM THE ORIENTATION!
EXCUSE ME! CAN YOU TELL US WHERE THE SOCCER TEAM PLAYS?
WE'RE HAVING TROUBLE FINDING THE RIGHT PLACE.

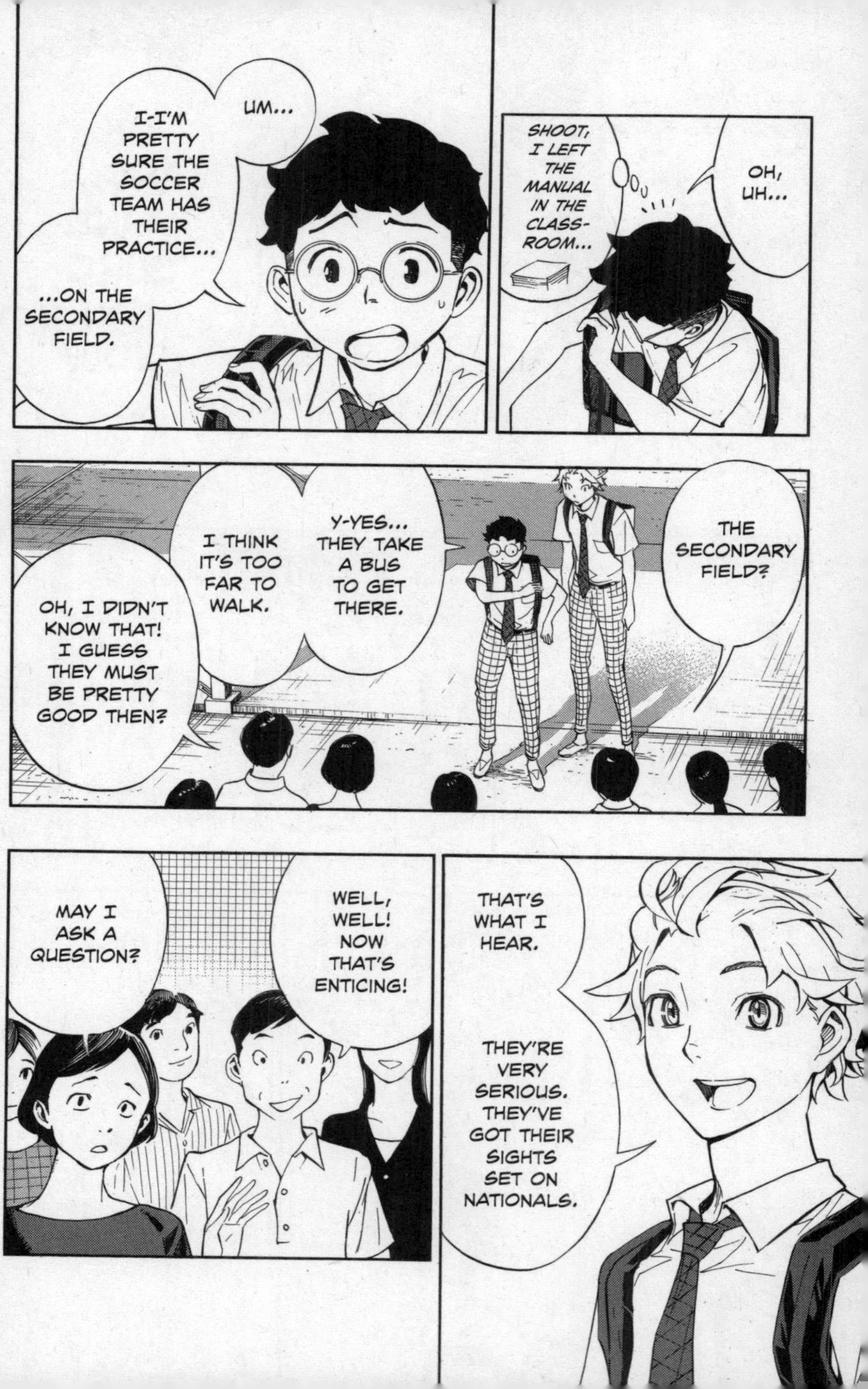
OH, UH...
SHOOT, I LEFT THE MANUAL IN THE CLASSROOM...
UM...
I-I'M PRETTY SURE THE SOCCER TEAM HAS THEIR PRACTICE...
...ON THE SECONDARY FIELD.
THE SECONDARY FIELD?
Y-YES... THEY TAKE A BUS TO GET THERE.
I THINK IT'S TOO FAR TO WALK.
OH, I DIDN'T KNOW THAT! I GUESS THEY MUST BE PRETTY GOOD THEN?
THAT'S WHAT I HEAR.
THEY'RE VERY SERIOUS. THEY'VE GOT THEIR SIGHTS SET ON NATIONALS.
WELL, WELL! NOW THAT'S ENTICING!
MAY I ASK A QUESTION?

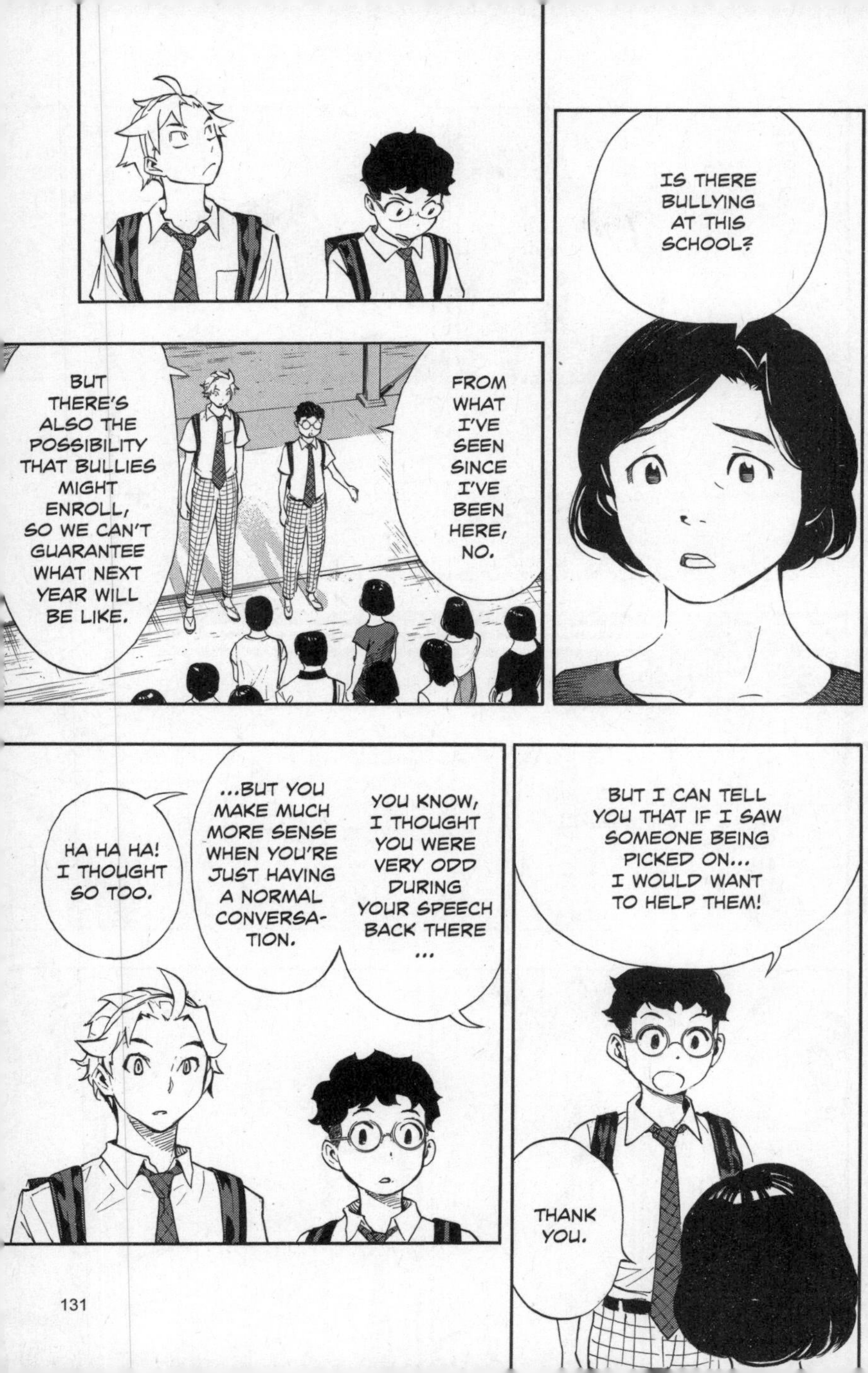
IS THERE BULLYING AT THIS SCHOOL?
FROM WHAT I'VE SEEN SINCE I'VE BEEN HERE, NO.
BUT THERE'S ALSO THE POSSIBILITY THAT BULLIES MIGHT ENROLL, SO WE CAN'T GUARANTEE WHAT NEXT YEAR WILL BE LIKE.
BUT I CAN TELL YOU THAT IF I SAW SOMEONE BEING PICKED ON... I WOULD WANT TO HELP THEM!
THANK YOU.
YOU KNOW, I THOUGHT YOU WERE VERY ODD DURING YOUR SPEECH BACK THERE...
...BUT YOU MAKE MUCH MORE SENSE WHEN YOU'RE JUST HAVING A NORMAL CONVERSATION.
HA HA HA! I THOUGHT SO TOO.

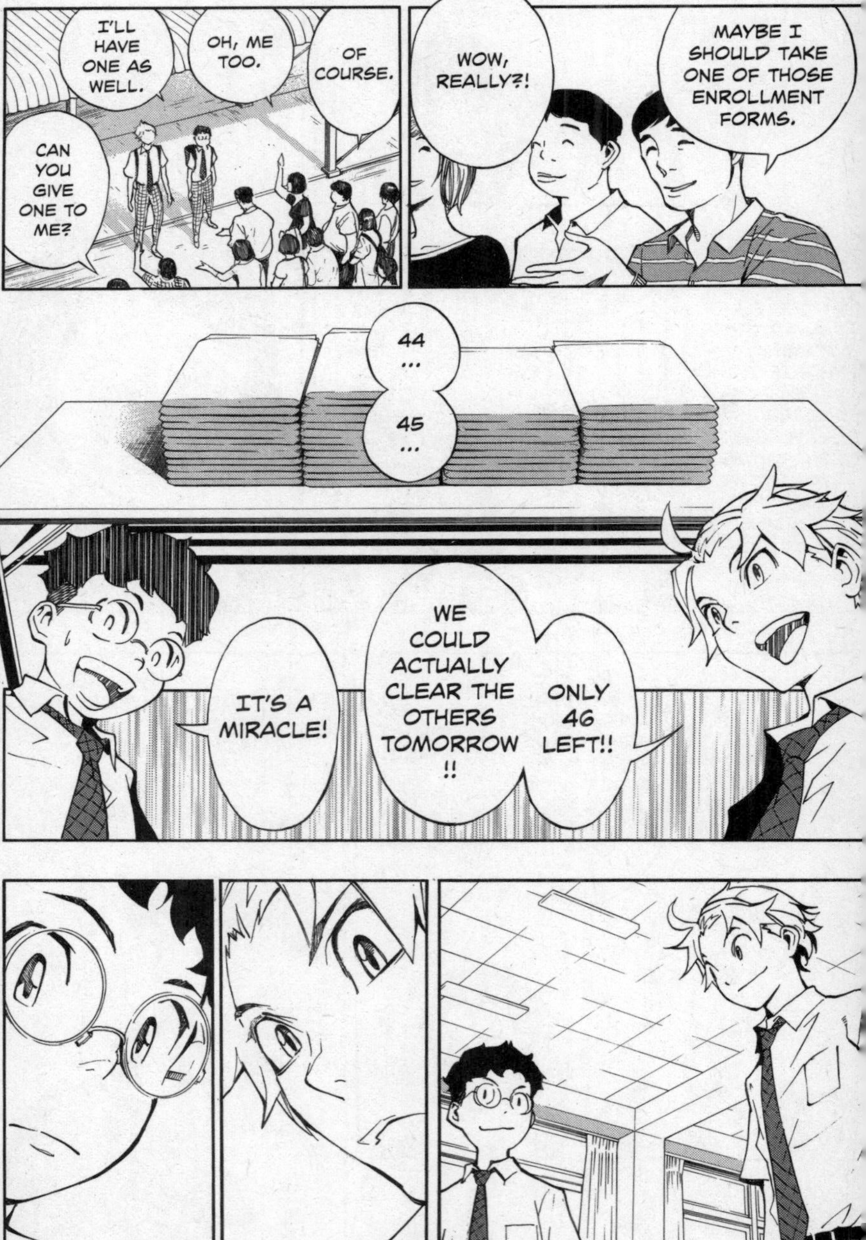
MAYBE I SHOULD TAKE ONE OF THOSE ENROLLMENT FORMS.
WOW, REALLY?!
OF COURSE.
OH, ME TOO.
I'LL HAVE ONE AS WELL.
CAN YOU GIVE ONE TO ME?
44 ...
45 ...
ONLY 46 LEFT!!
WE COULD ACTUALLY CLEAR THE OTHERS TOMORROW !!
IT'S A MIRACLE!

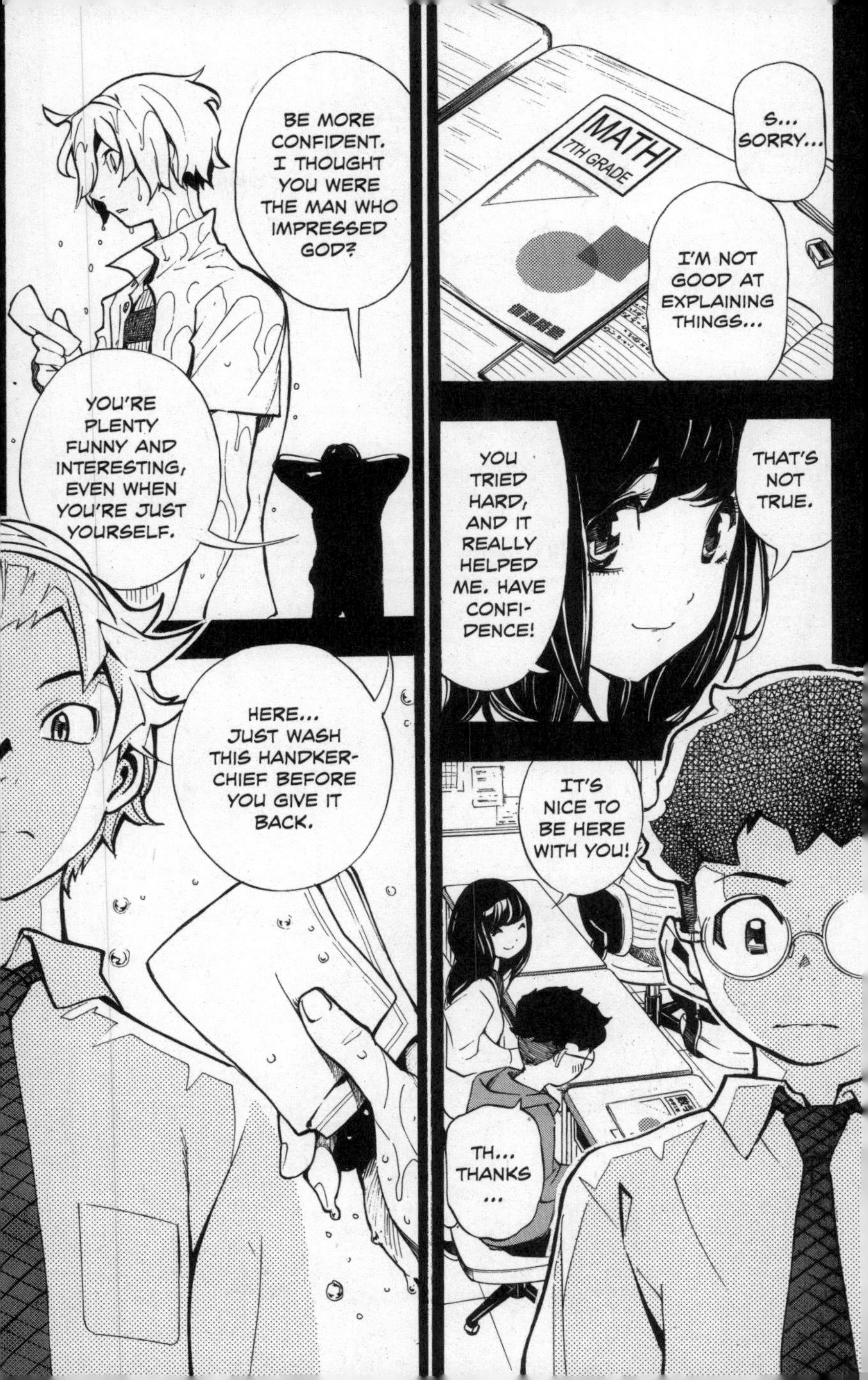
MATH
7TH GRADE
S... SORRY...
I'M NOT GOOD AT EXPLAINING THINGS...
THAT'S NOT TRUE.
YOU TRIED HARD, AND IT REALLY HELPED ME. HAVE CONFI-DENCE!
IT'S NICE TO BE HERE WITH YOU!
TH... THANKS ...
BE MORE CONFIDENT. I THOUGHT YOU WERE THE MAN WHO IMPRESSED GOD?
YOU'RE PLENTY FUNNY AND INTERESTING, EVEN WHEN YOU'RE JUST YOURSELF.
HERE... JUST WASH THIS HANDKER-CHIEF BEFORE YOU GIVE IT BACK.

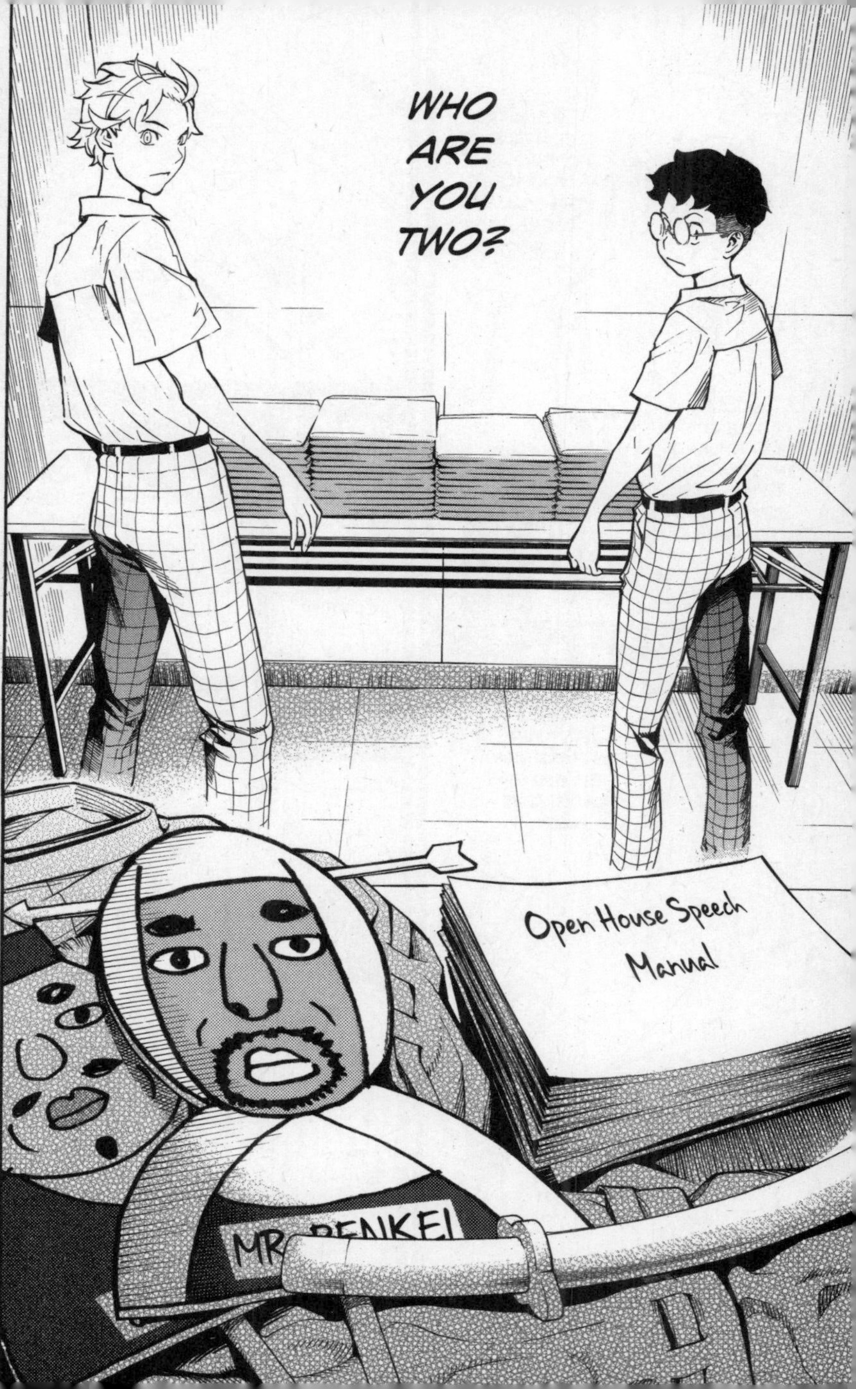
WHO ARE YOU TWO?
Open House Speech Manual
MR BENKEI

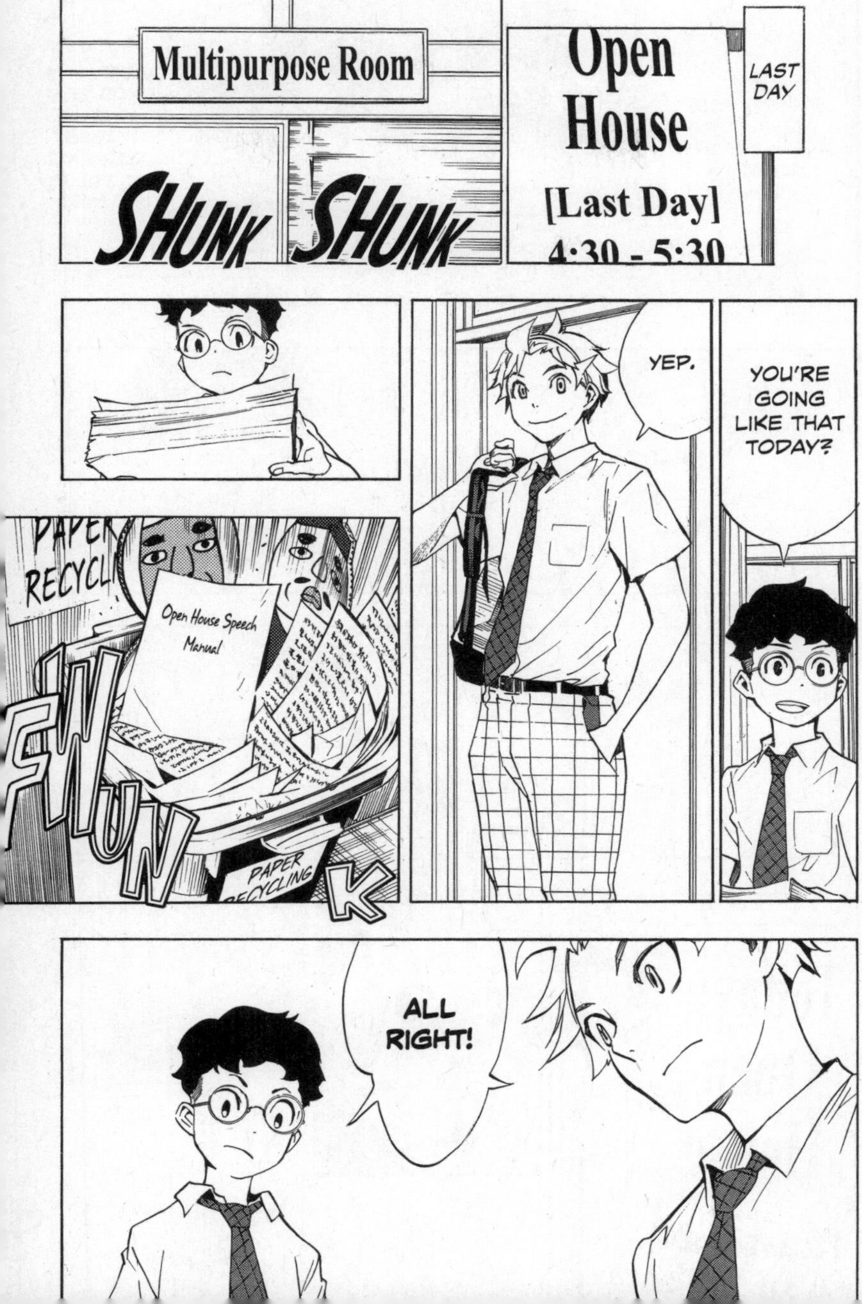
LAST DAY
Open House
[Last Day]
4:30 - 5:30
Multipurpose Room
SHUNK SHUNK
YOU'RE GOING LIKE THAT TODAY?
YEP.
PAPER RECYCLI
Open House Speech Manual
FWUNK
PAPER RECYCLING
ALL RIGHT!

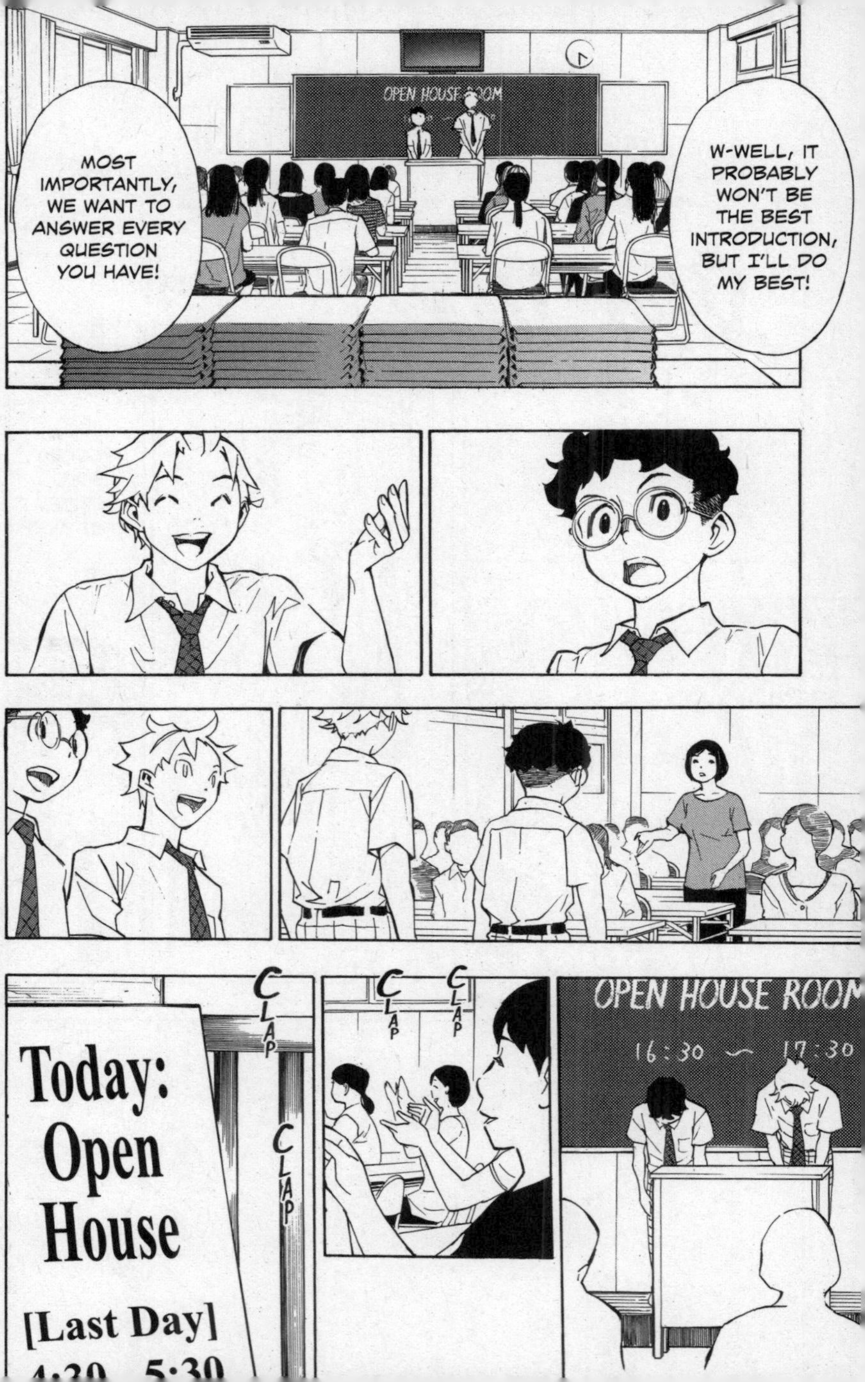
OPEN HOUSE ROOM
W-WELL, IT PROBABLY WON'T BE THE BEST INTRODUCTION, BUT I'LL DO MY BEST!
MOST IMPORTANTLY, WE WANT TO ANSWER EVERY QUESTION YOU HAVE!
OPEN HOUSE ROOM
16:30 ~ 17:30
CLAP
CLAP
CLAP
CLAP
Today: Open House
[Last Day]
4:30 5:30

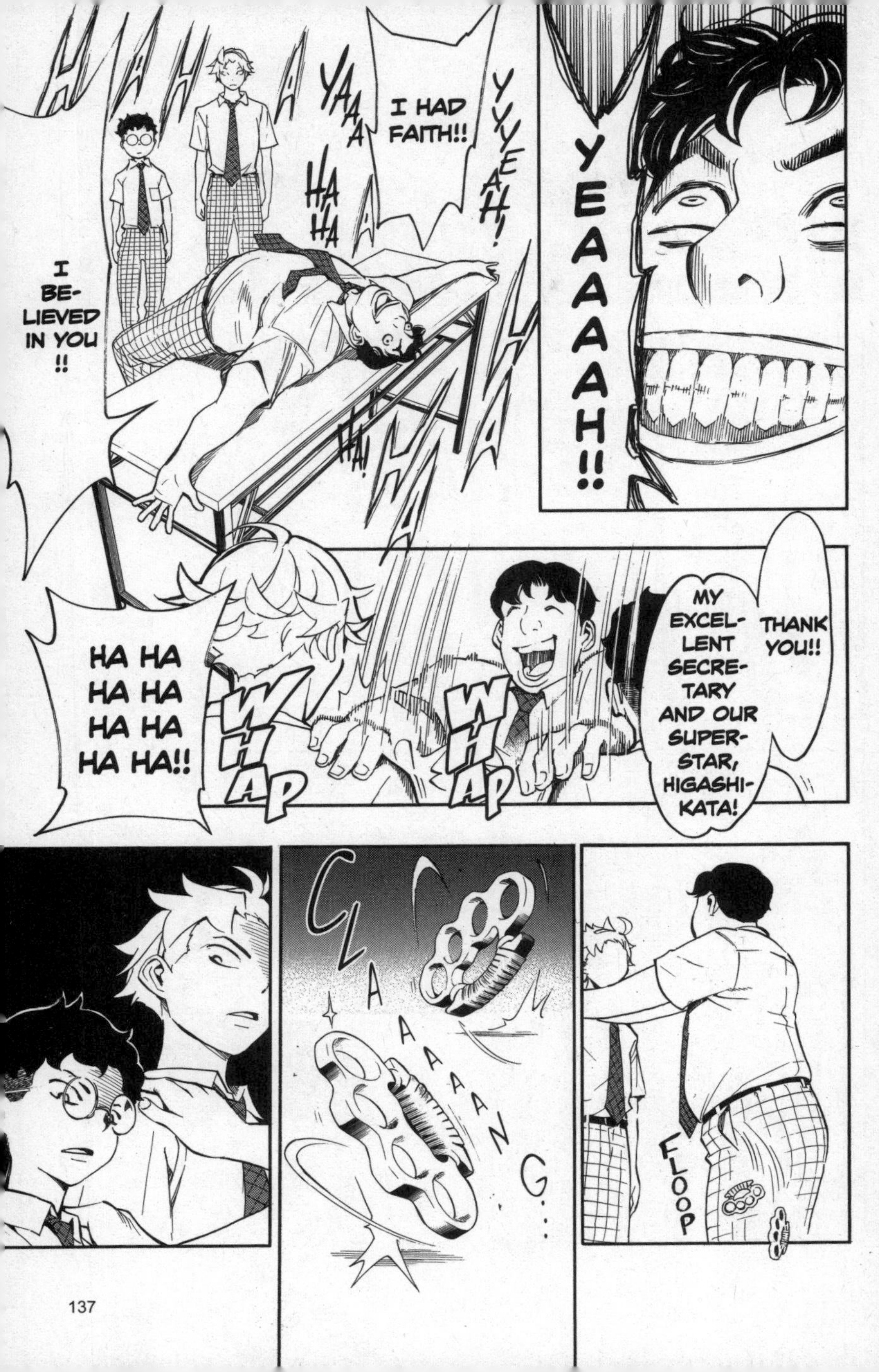
YEAAAAAH!!
YYYEAH!
I HAD FAITH!!
YAAA HA HA HA
HAHAHA HA! HA HA
I BELIEVED IN YOU!!
THANK YOU!!
MY EXCELLENT SECRETARY AND OUR SUPERSTAR, HIGASHIKATA!
HA HA HA HA HA HA HA HA!!
WHAP
WHAP
FLOOP
CLAAAAANG...

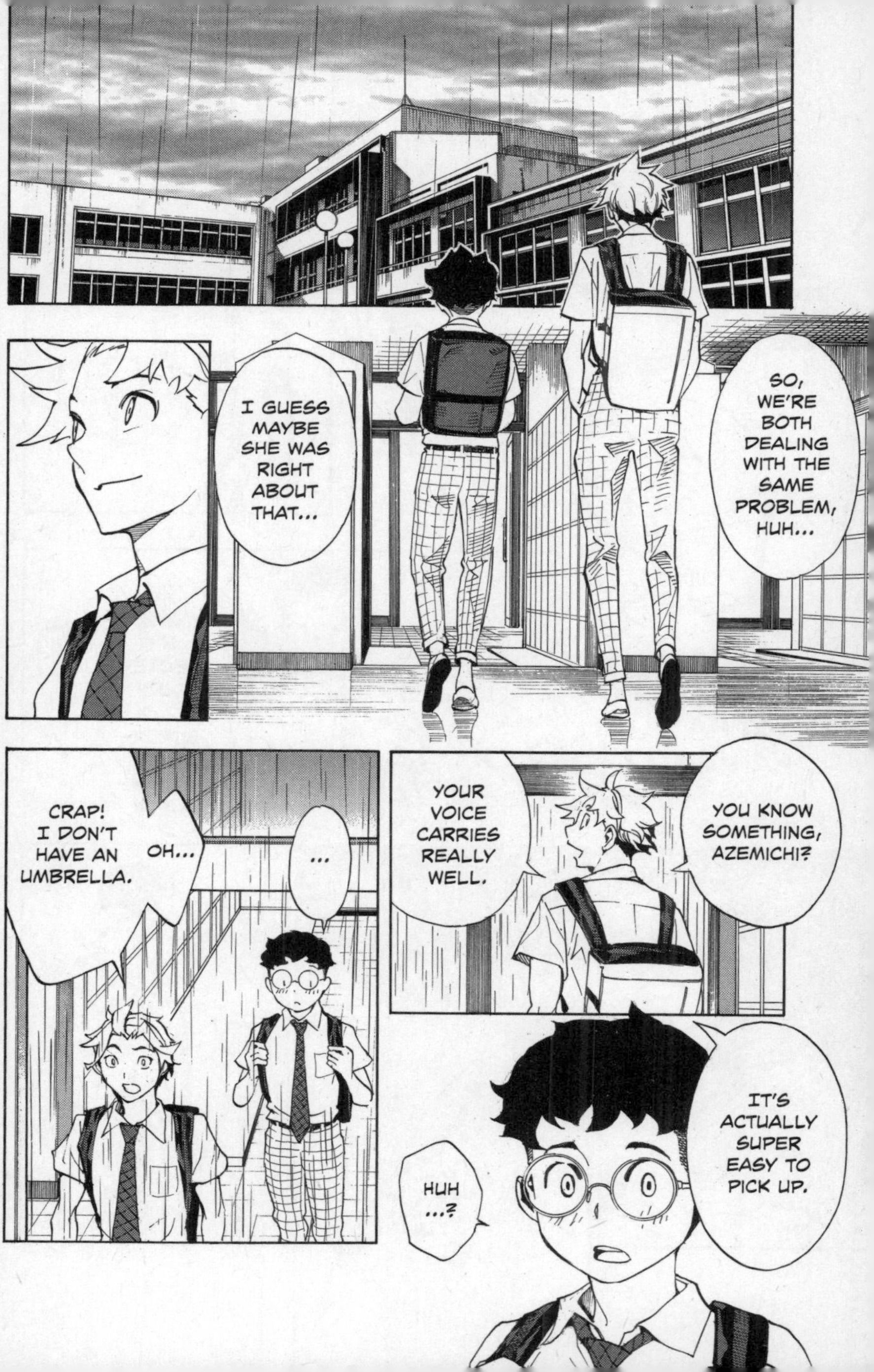
SO, WE'RE BOTH DEALING WITH THE SAME PROBLEM, HUH...
I GUESS MAYBE SHE WAS RIGHT ABOUT THAT...
YOU KNOW SOMETHING, AZEMICHI?
YOUR VOICE CARRIES REALLY WELL.
IT'S ACTUALLY SUPER EASY TO PICK UP.
HUH ...?
...
OH...
CRAP! I DON'T HAVE AN UMBRELLA.

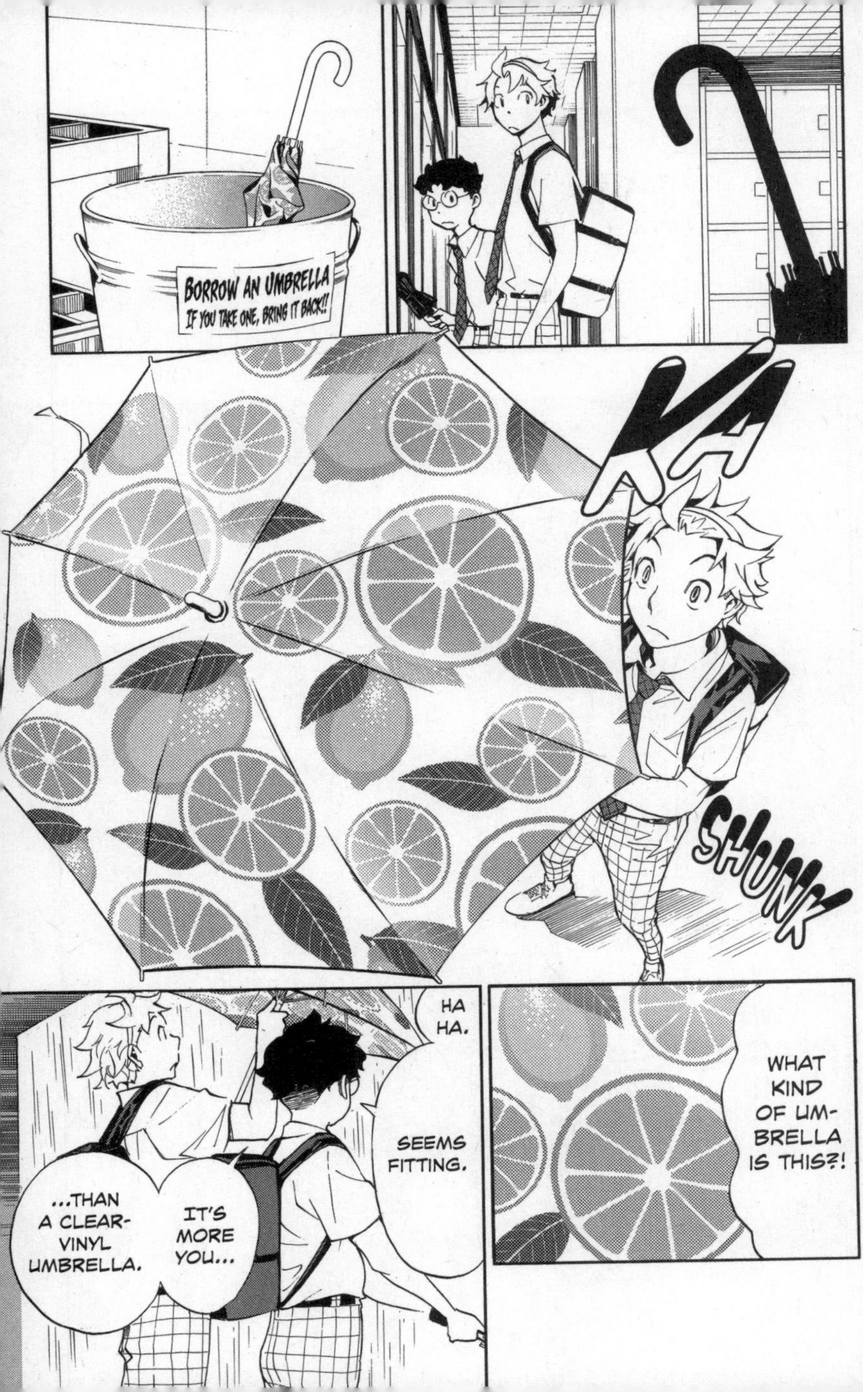
BORROW AN UMBRELLA
IF YOU TAKE ONE, BRING IT BACK!!
VA
SHUNK
WHAT KIND OF UM-BRELLA IS THIS?!
HA HA.
SEEMS FITTING.
IT'S MORE YOU...
...THAN A CLEAR-VINYL UMBRELLA.

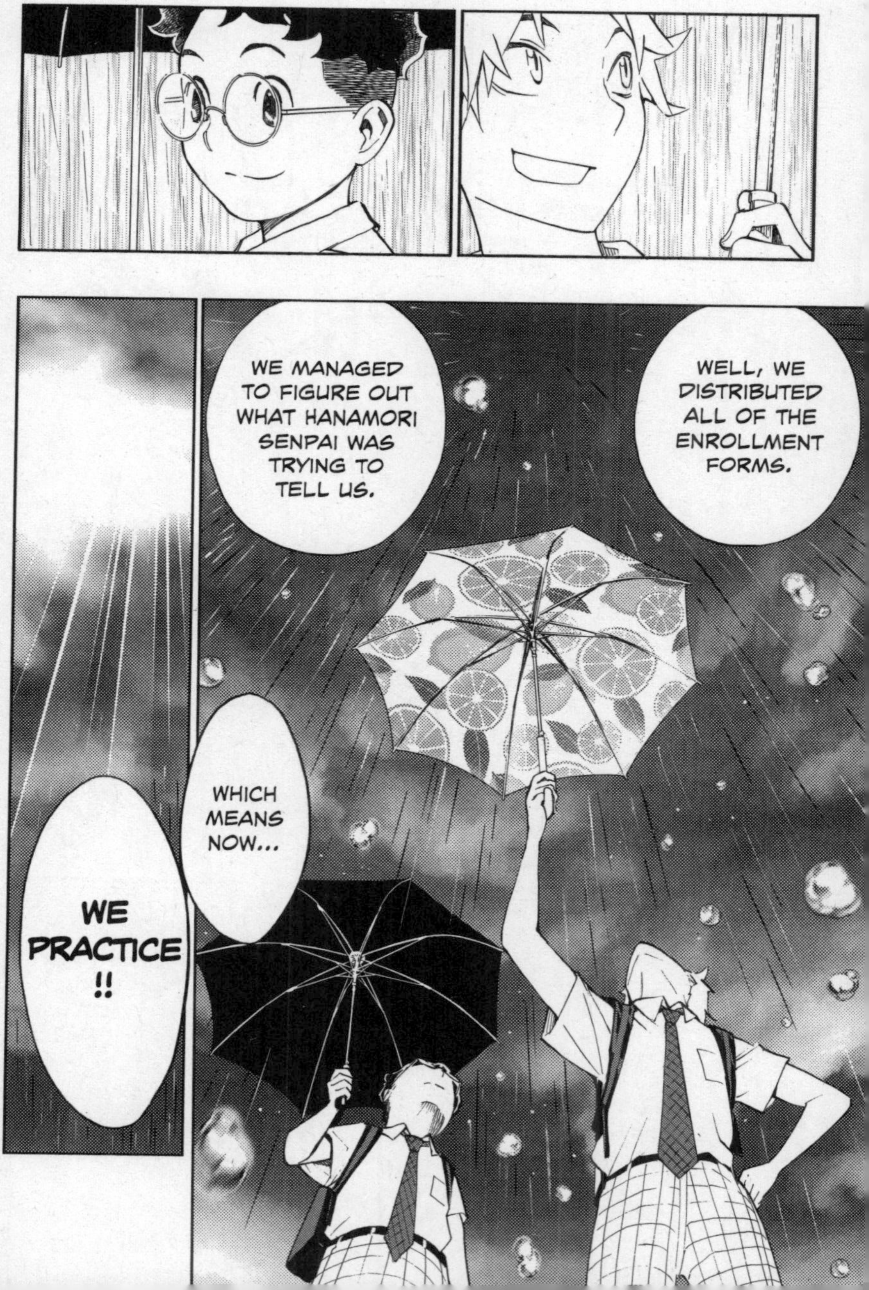
WELL, WE DISTRIBUTED ALL OF THE ENROLLMENT FORMS.
WE MANAGED TO FIGURE OUT WHAT HANAMORI SENPAI WAS TRYING TO TELL US.
WHICH MEANS NOW...
WE PRACTICE!!

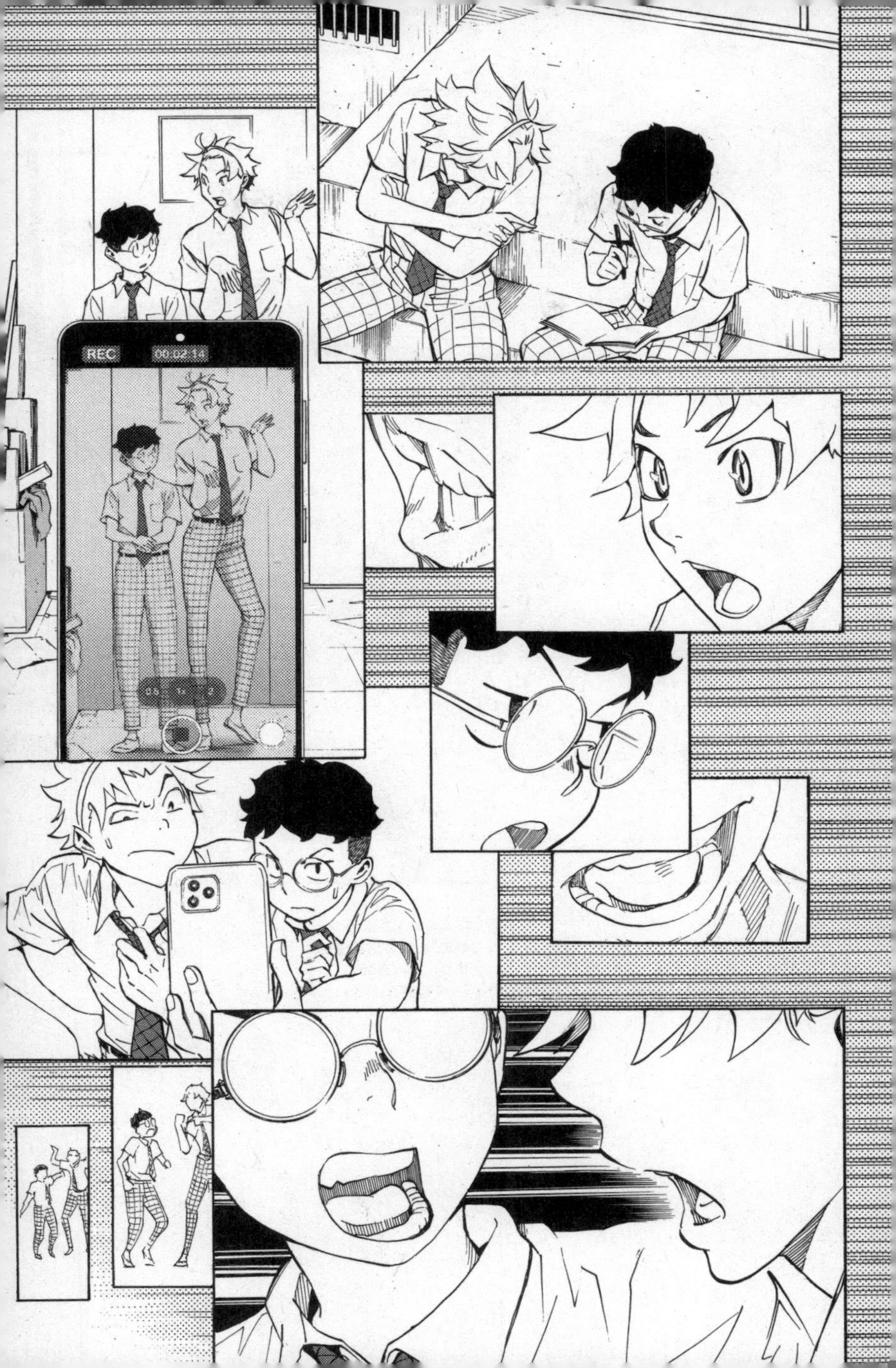
REC
00:02:14

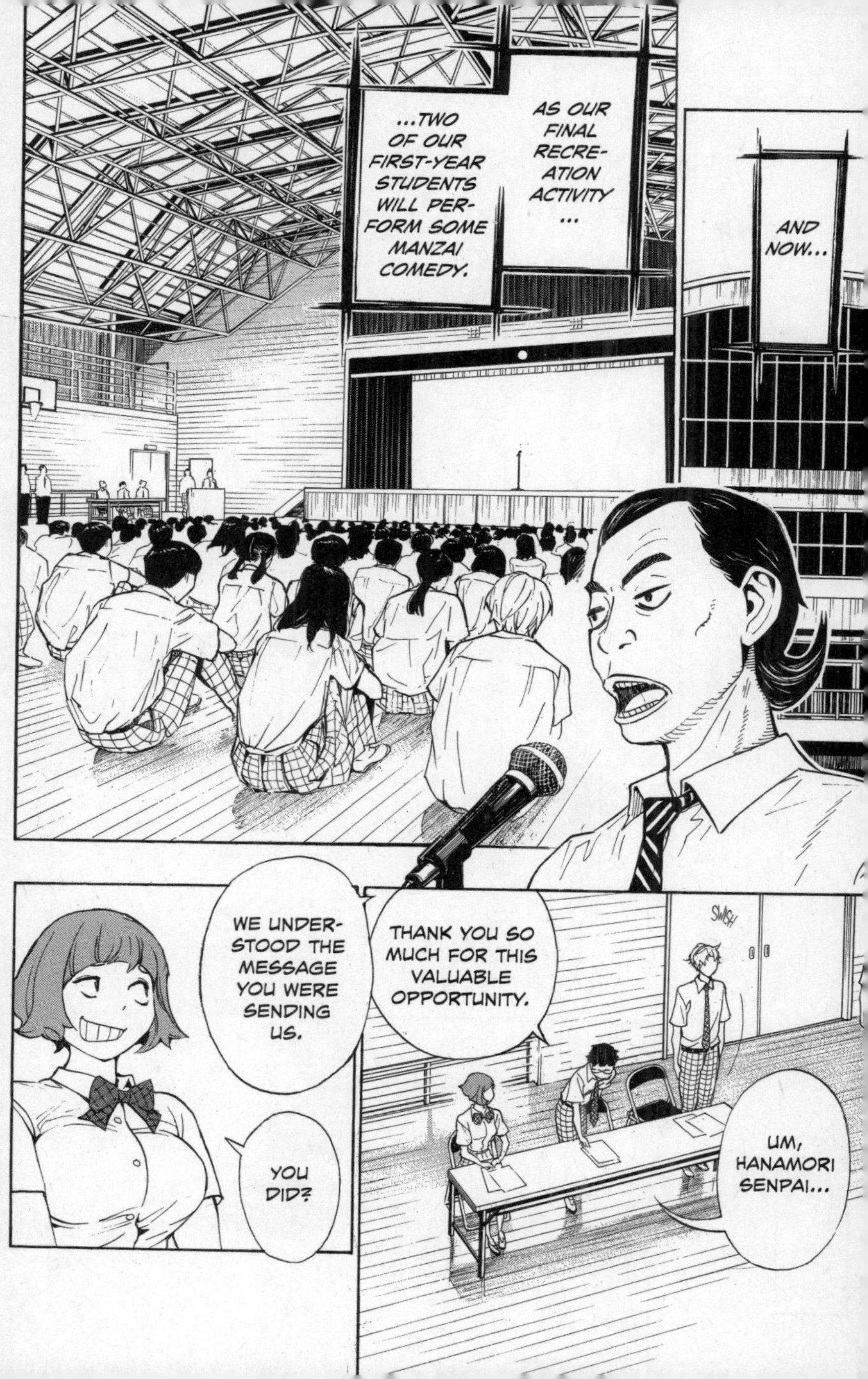
AND NOW...
AS OUR FINAL RECRE-ATION ACTIVITY...
...TWO OF OUR FIRST-YEAR STUDENTS WILL PER-FORM SOME MANZAI COMEDY.
SWISH
THANK YOU SO MUCH FOR THIS VALUABLE OPPORTUNITY.
UM, HANAMORI SENPAI...
WE UNDER-STOOD THE MESSAGE YOU WERE SENDING US.
YOU DID?

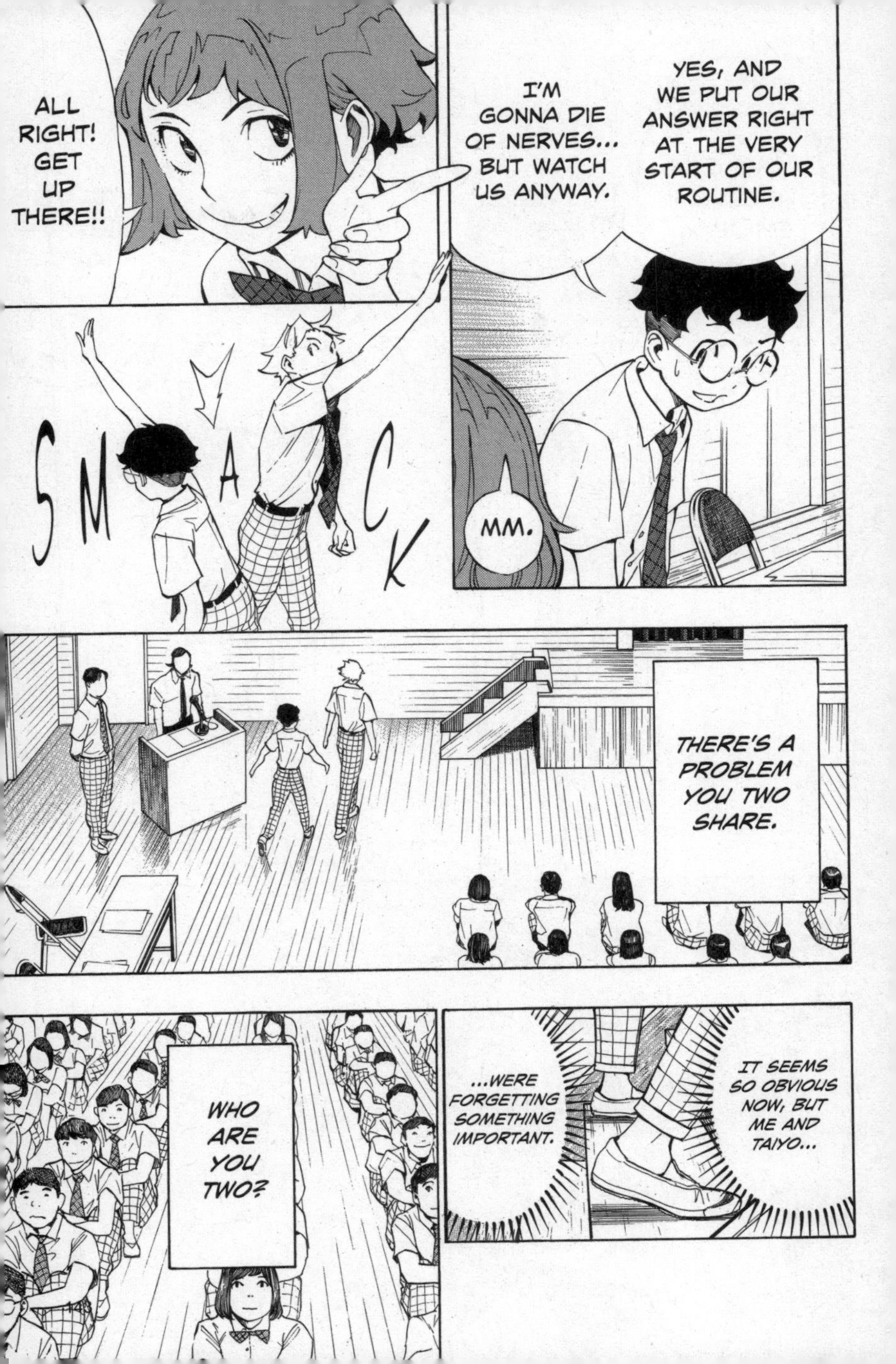
YES, AND WE PUT OUR ANSWER RIGHT AT THE VERY START OF OUR ROUTINE.
I'M GONNA DIE OF NERVES... BUT WATCH US ANYWAY.
MM.
ALL RIGHT! GET UP THERE!!
SMACK
THERE'S A PROBLEM YOU TWO SHARE.
IT SEEMS SO OBVIOUS NOW, BUT ME AND TAIYO...
...WERE FORGETTING SOMETHING IMPORTANT.
WHO ARE YOU TWO?

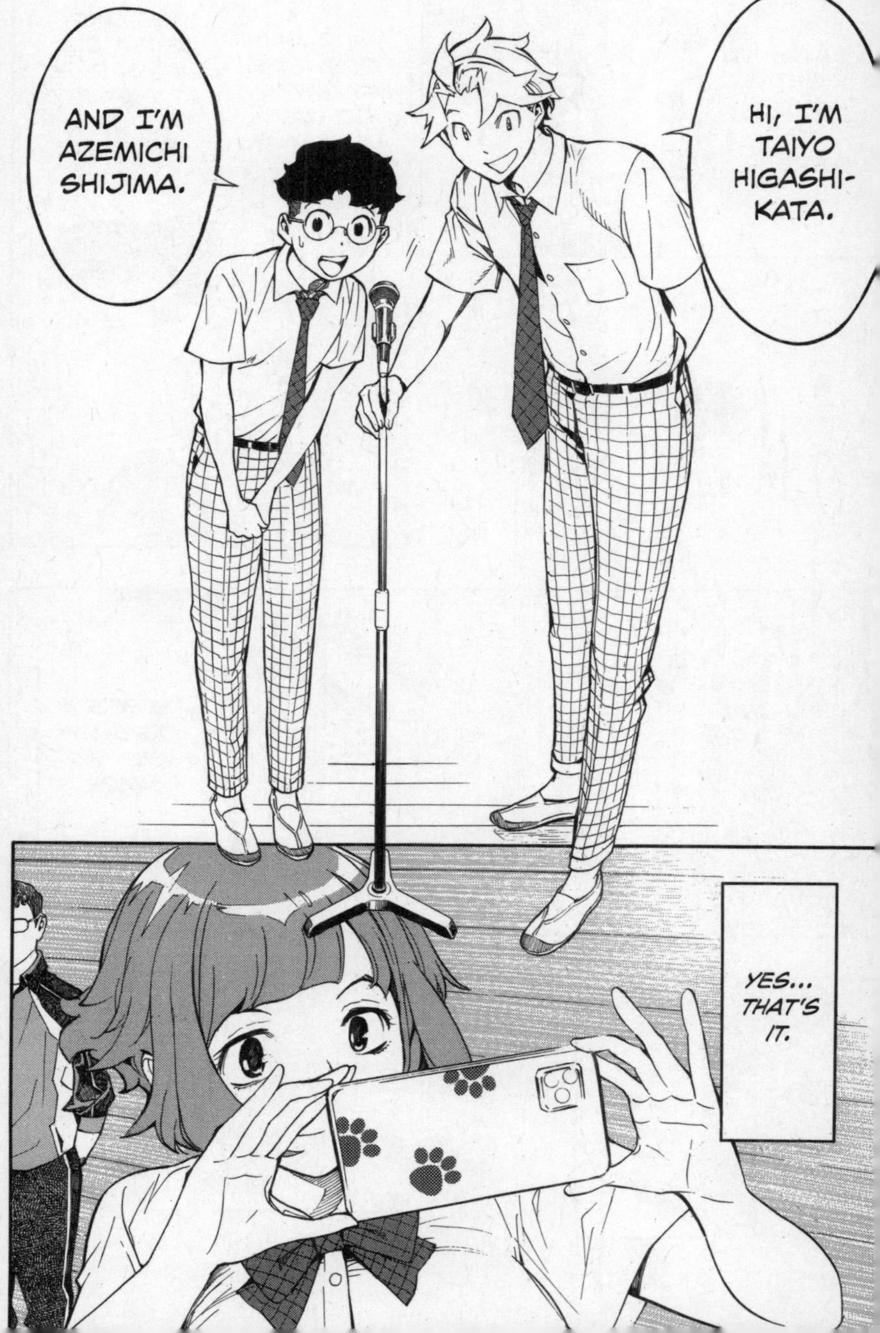
HI, I'M TAIYO HIGASHI-KATA.
AND I'M AZEMICHI SHIJIMA.
YES... THAT'S IT.

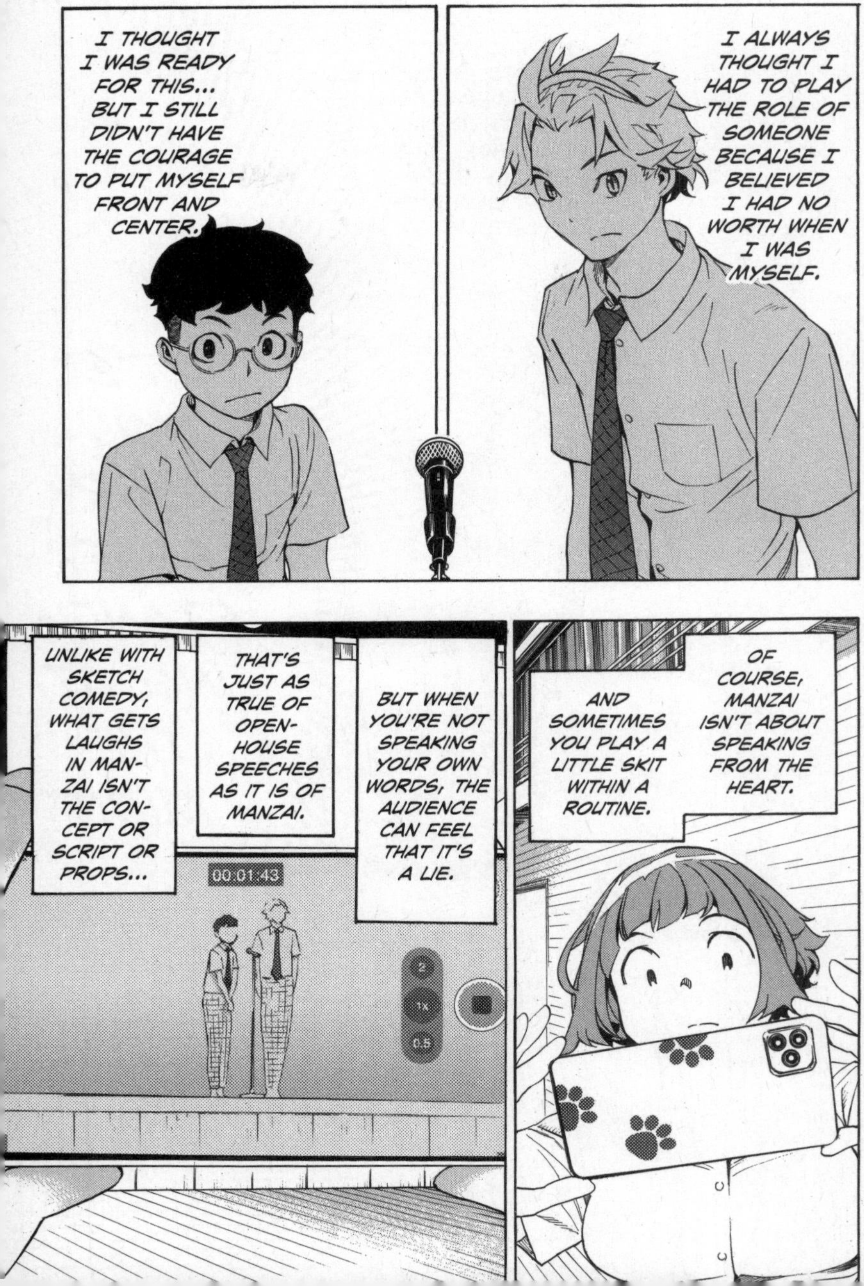
I ALWAYS THOUGHT I HAD TO PLAY THE ROLE OF SOMEONE BECAUSE I BELIEVED I HAD NO WORTH WHEN I WAS MYSELF.
I THOUGHT I WAS READY FOR THIS... BUT I STILL DIDN'T HAVE THE COURAGE TO PUT MYSELF FRONT AND CENTER.
OF COURSE, MANZAI ISN'T ABOUT SPEAKING FROM THE HEART.
AND SOMETIMES YOU PLAY A LITTLE SKIT WITHIN A ROUTINE.
UNLIKE WITH SKETCH COMEDY, WHAT GETS LAUGHS IN MAN-ZAI ISN'T THE CON-CEPT OR SCRIPT OR PROPS...
THAT'S JUST AS TRUE OF OPEN-HOUSE SPEECHES AS IT IS OF MANZAI.
BUT WHEN YOU'RE NOT SPEAKING YOUR OWN WORDS, THE AUDIENCE CAN FEEL THAT IT'S A LIE.
00:01:43
2
1x
0.5

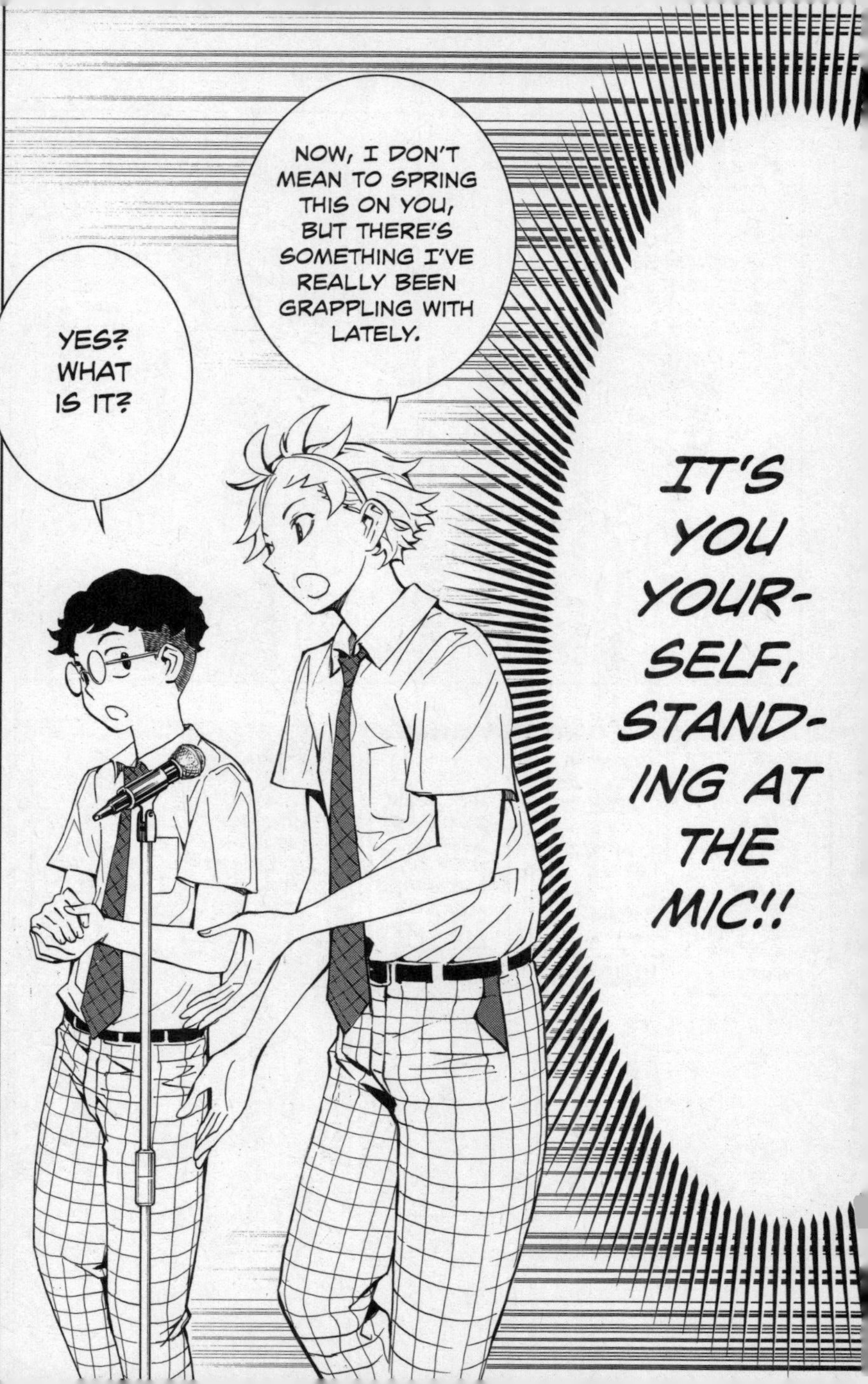
NOW, I DON'T MEAN TO SPRING THIS ON YOU, BUT THERE'S SOMETHING I'VE REALLY BEEN GRAPPLING WITH LATELY.
YES? WHAT IS IT?
IT'S YOU YOURSELF, STANDING AT THE MIC!!

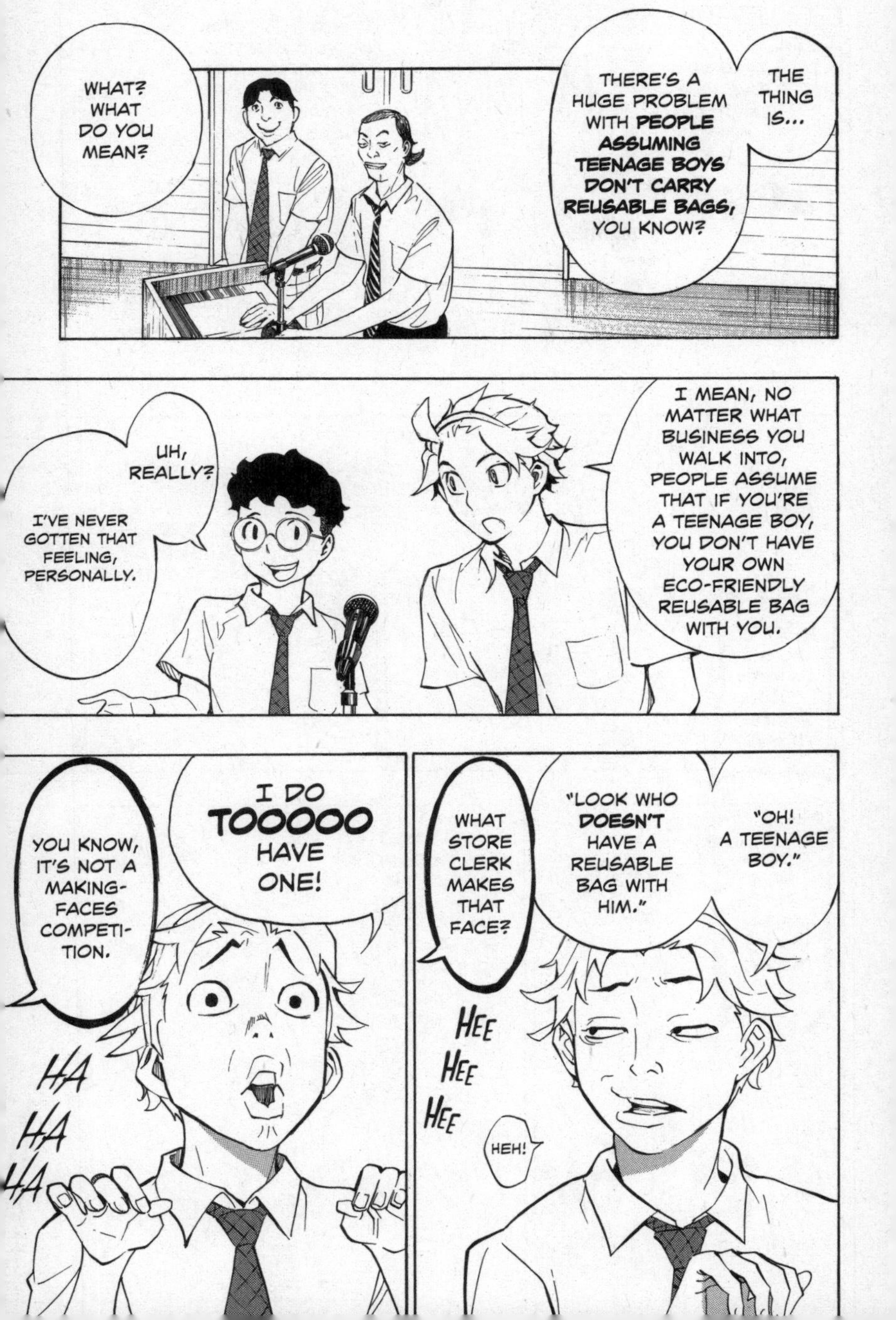
THE THING IS...
THERE'S A HUGE PROBLEM WITH PEOPLE ASSUMING TEENAGE BOYS DON'T CARRY REUSABLE BAGS, YOU KNOW?
WHAT? WHAT DO YOU MEAN?
I MEAN, NO MATTER WHAT BUSINESS YOU WALK INTO, PEOPLE ASSUME THAT IF YOU'RE A TEENAGE BOY, YOU DON'T HAVE YOUR OWN ECO-FRIENDLY REUSABLE BAG WITH YOU.
UH, REALLY?
I'VE NEVER GOTTEN THAT FEELING, PERSONALLY.
"OH! A TEENAGE BOY."
"LOOK WHO DOESN'T HAVE A REUSABLE BAG WITH HIM."
WHAT STORE CLERK MAKES THAT FACE?
HEE HEE HEE
HEH!
I DO TOOOOO HAVE ONE!
YOU KNOW, IT'S NOT A MAKING-FACES COMPETITION.
HA HA HA

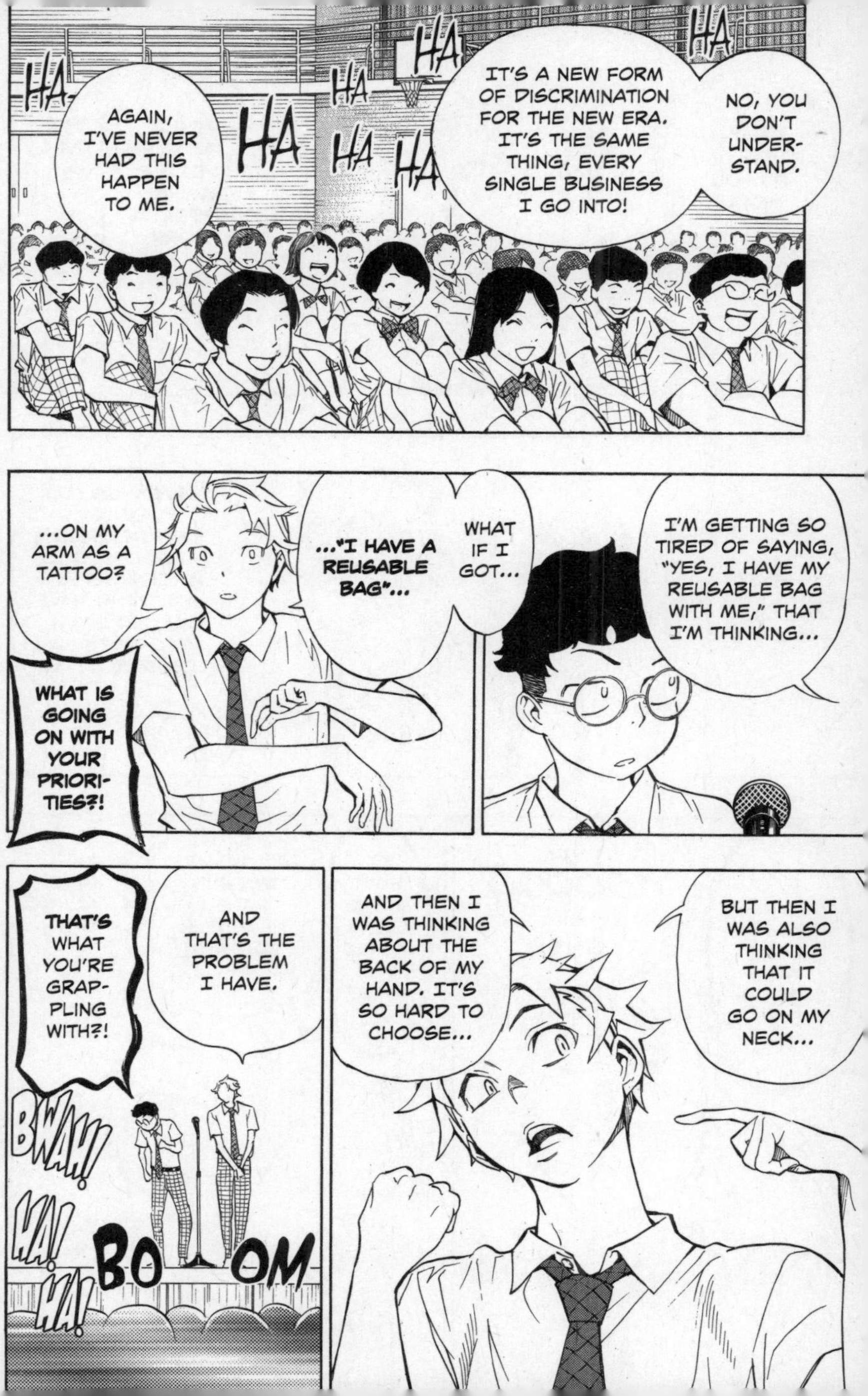
HA HA HA HA HA HA HA
NO, YOU DON'T UNDERSTAND.
IT'S A NEW FORM OF DISCRIMINATION FOR THE NEW ERA. IT'S THE SAME THING, EVERY SINGLE BUSINESS I GO INTO!
AGAIN, I'VE NEVER HAD THIS HAPPEN TO ME.
I'M GETTING SO TIRED OF SAYING, "YES, I HAVE MY REUSABLE BAG WITH ME," THAT I'M THINKING...
WHAT IF I GOT...
..."I HAVE A REUSABLE BAG"...
...ON MY ARM AS A TATTOO?
WHAT IS GOING ON WITH YOUR PRIORITIES?!
BUT THEN I WAS ALSO THINKING THAT IT COULD GO ON MY NECK...
AND THEN I WAS THINKING ABOUT THE BACK OF MY HAND. IT'S SO HARD TO CHOOSE...
AND THAT'S THE PROBLEM I HAVE.
THAT'S WHAT YOU'RE GRAPPLING WITH?!
BWAH!
HA! HA!
BOOM

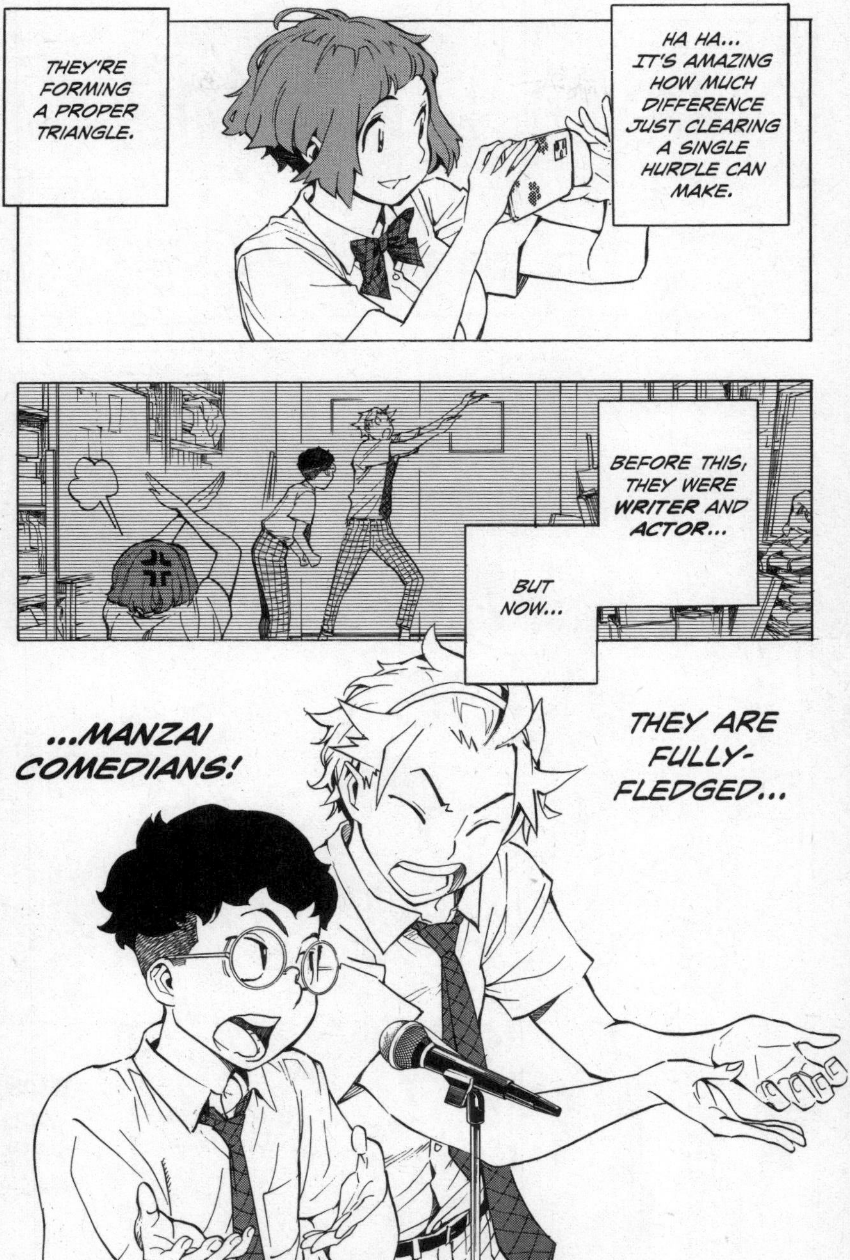
HA HA... IT'S AMAZING HOW MUCH DIFFERENCE JUST CLEARING A SINGLE HURDLE CAN MAKE.
THEY'RE FORMING A PROPER TRIANGLE.
BEFORE THIS, THEY WERE WRITER AND ACTOR...
BUT NOW...
THEY ARE FULLY-FLEDGED...
...MANZAI COMEDIANS!

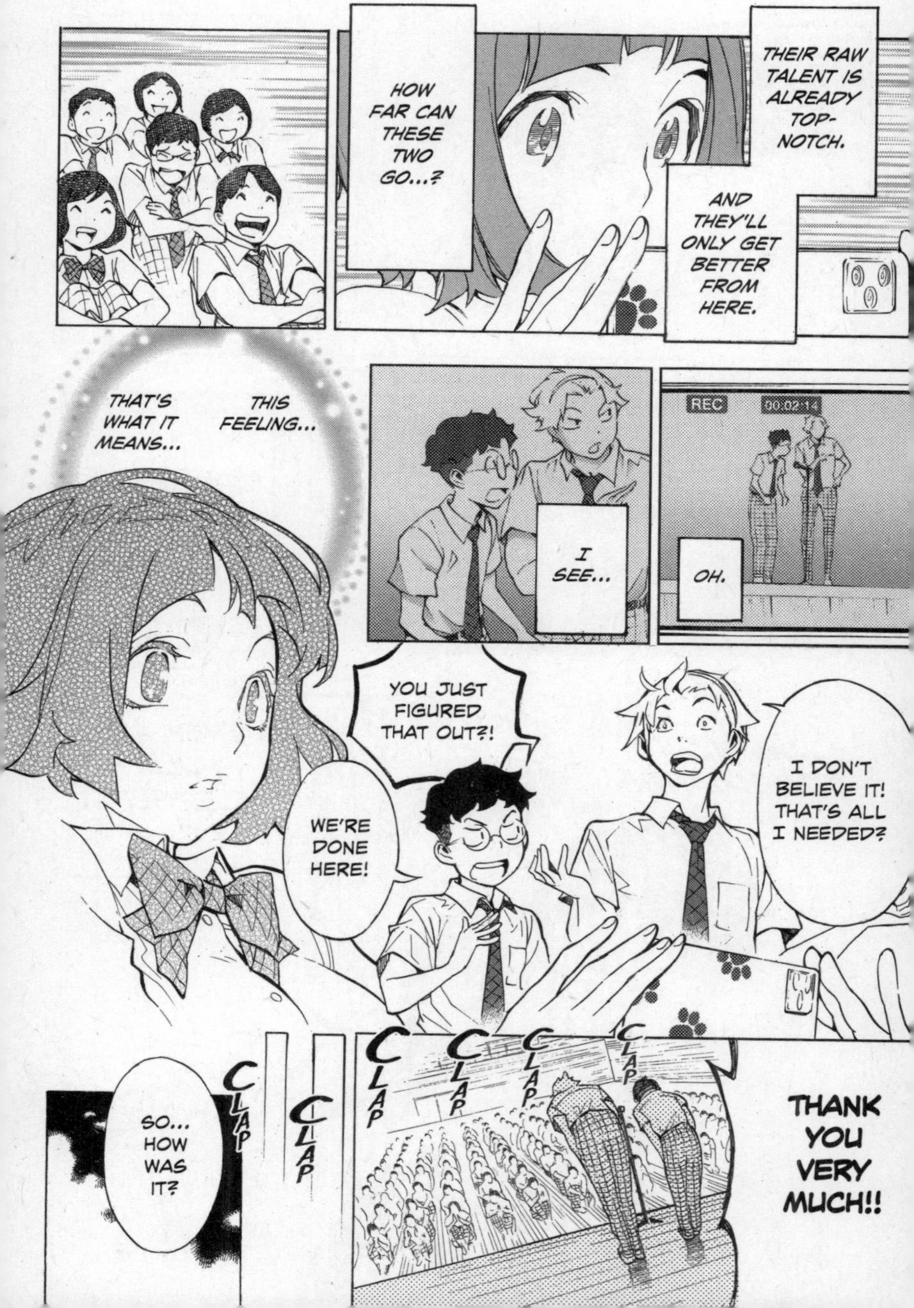
THEIR RAW TALENT IS ALREADY TOP-NOTCH.
AND THEY'LL ONLY GET BETTER FROM HERE.
HOW FAR CAN THESE TWO GO...?
REC
00:02:14
OH.
I SEE...
I DON'T BELIEVE IT! THAT'S ALL I NEEDED?
YOU JUST FIGURED THAT OUT?!
WE'RE DONE HERE!
THIS FEELING...
THAT'S WHAT IT MEANS...
THANK YOU VERY MUCH!!
CLAP
CLAP
CLAP
CLAP
CLAP
CLAP
SO... HOW WAS IT?

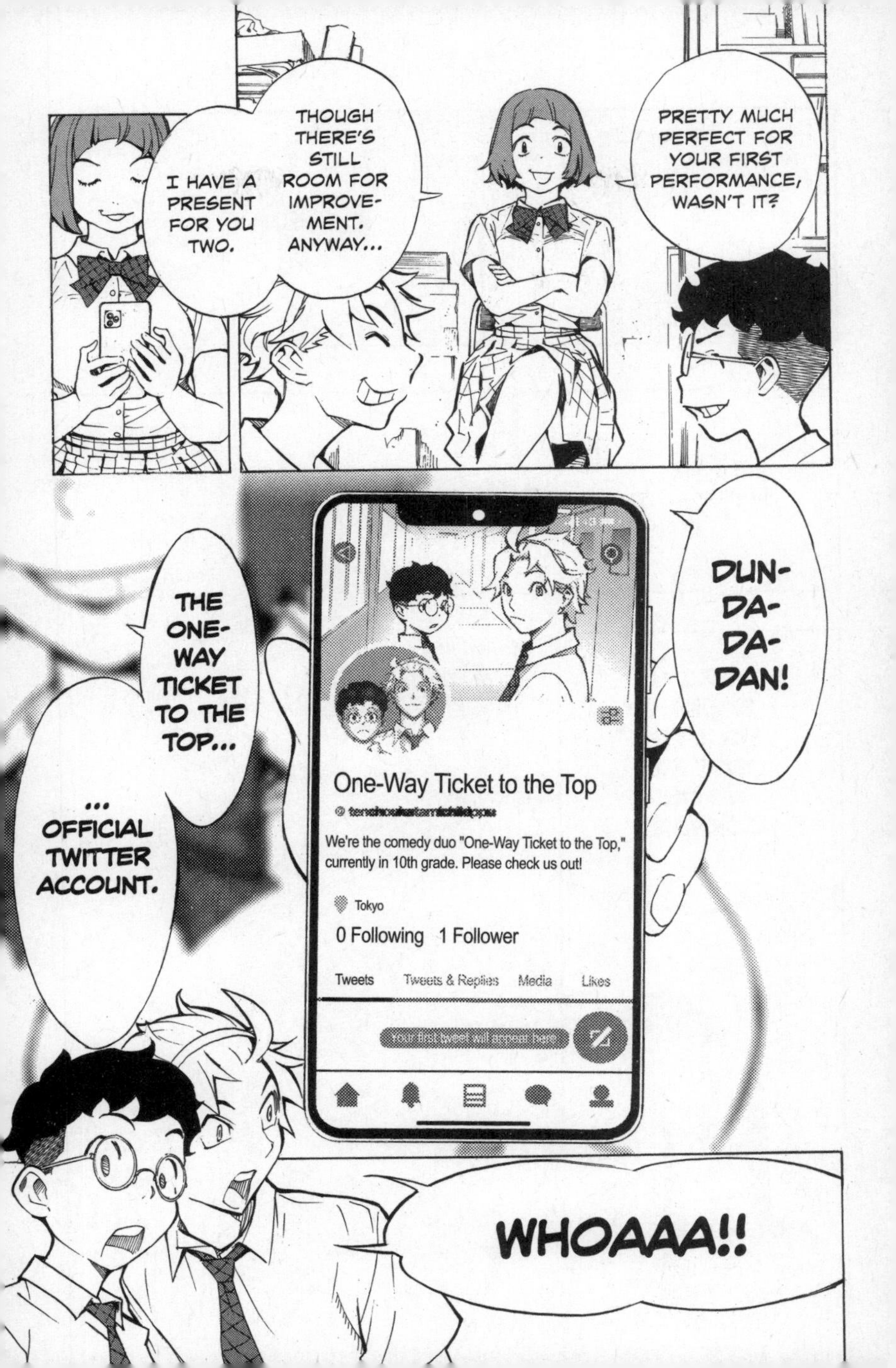
PRETTY MUCH PERFECT FOR YOUR FIRST PERFORMANCE, WASN'T IT?
THOUGH THERE'S STILL ROOM FOR IMPROVEMENT. ANYWAY...
I HAVE A PRESENT FOR YOU TWO.
DUN-DA-DA-DAN!
THE ONE-WAY TICKET TO THE TOP...
One-Way Ticket to the Top
We're the comedy duo "One-Way Ticket to the Top," currently in 10th grade. Please check us out!
Tokyo
0 Following 1 Follower
Tweets
Tweets & Replies
Media
Likes
Your first tweet will appear here
...OFFICIAL TWITTER ACCOUNT.
WHOAAA!!

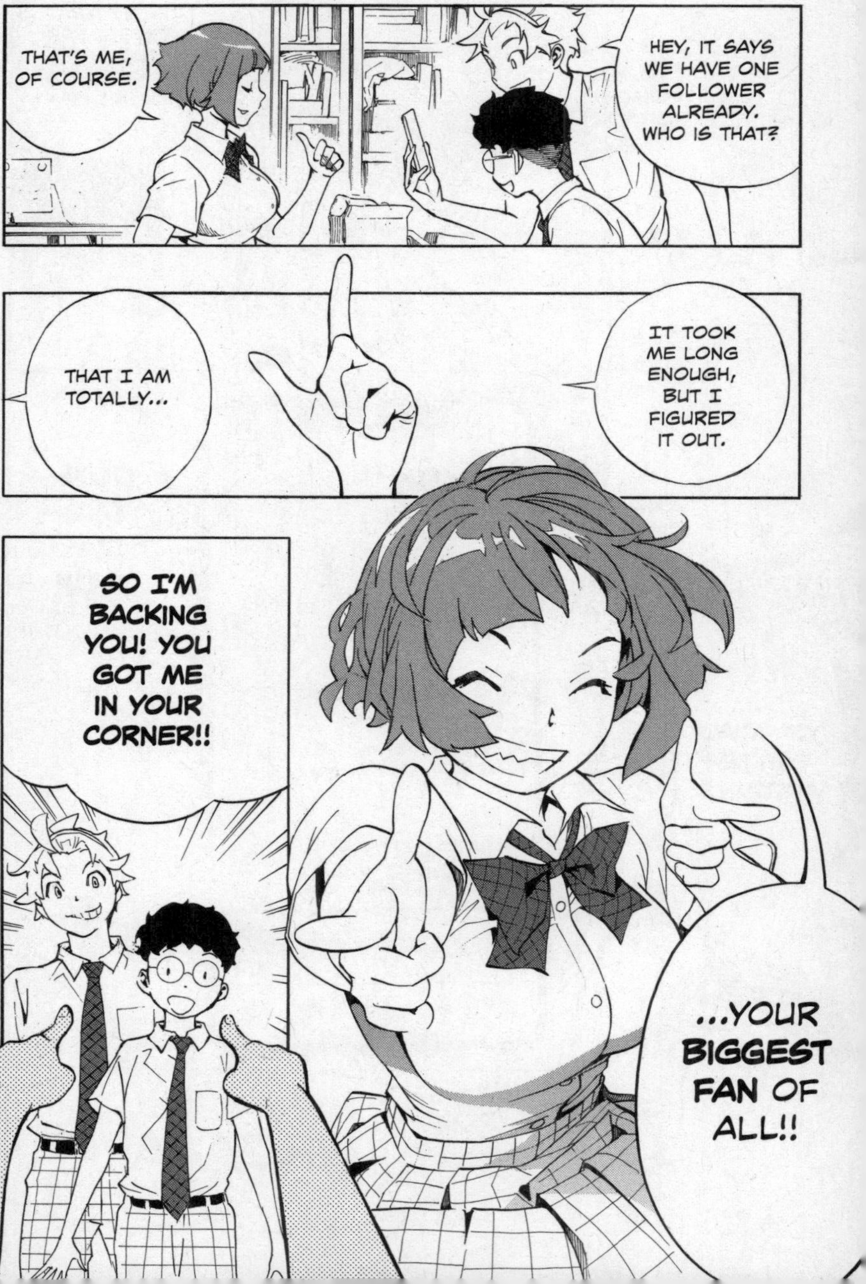
HEY, IT SAYS WE HAVE ONE FOLLOWER ALREADY. WHO IS THAT?
THAT'S ME, OF COURSE.
IT TOOK ME LONG ENOUGH, BUT I FIGURED IT OUT.
THAT I AM TOTALLY...
...YOUR BIGGEST FAN OF ALL!!
SO I'M BACKING YOU! YOU GOT ME IN YOUR CORNER!!

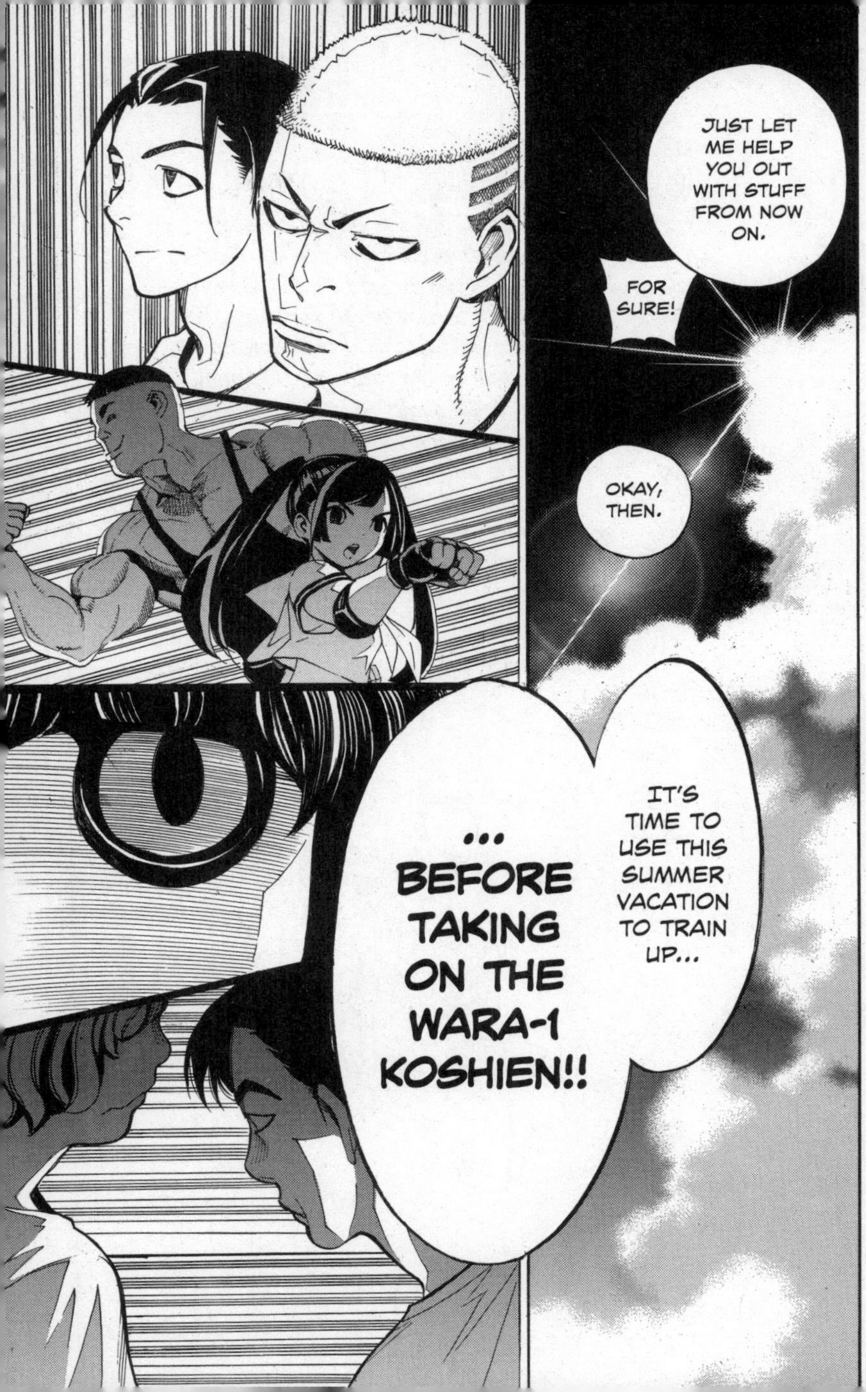
JUST LET ME HELP YOU OUT WITH STUFF FROM NOW ON.
FOR SURE!
OKAY, THEN.
IT'S TIME TO USE THIS SUMMER VACATION TO TRAIN UP...
...BEFORE TAKING ON THE WARA-1 KOSHIEN!!

After middle school, Jicchan and I went to different high schools, but for some reason, we couldn't let go of this strange feeling that we were a duo. Ultimately, we decided that it was time to unveil our skills on a real stage for once. Yes, we decided that, like how Azemichi and Taiyo are attempting to compete in the "Wara-1 Koshien" in this manga, we would compete in the real-life "M-1 Koshien (Current High Schooler Manzai)" event. Would we be a hit or a flop?! What was the fate of our intrepid main characters?! Anyway, thanks for reading these. If there's a desire to know more, I'll continue in the next volume...

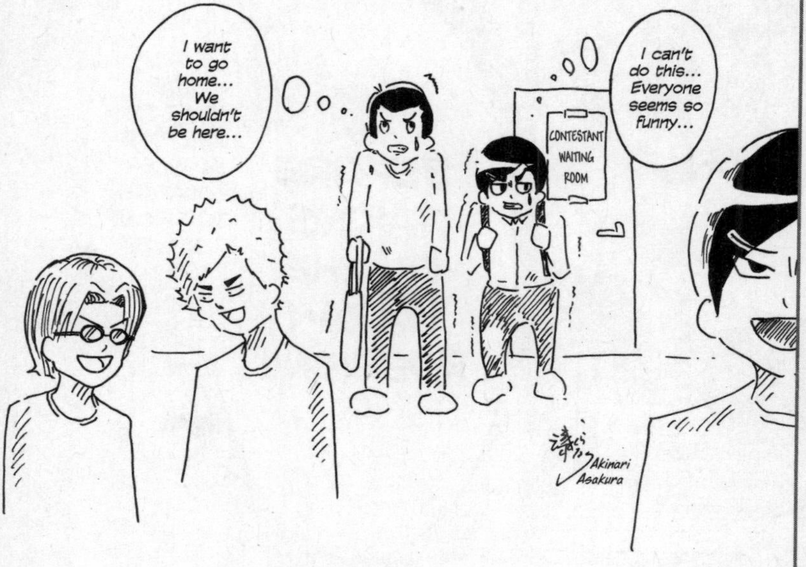
I can't do this... Everyone seems so funny...
CONTESTANT WAITING ROOM
I want to go home... We shouldn't be here...
Akinari Asakura

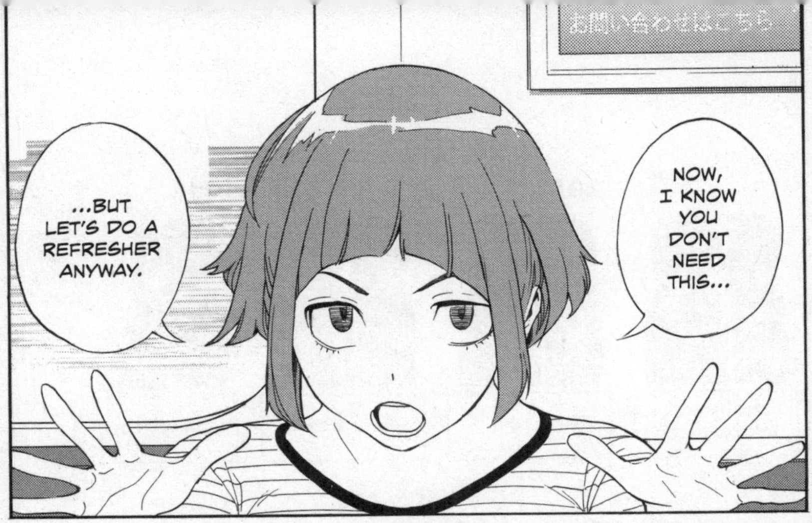
お問い合わせはこちら
NOW, I KNOW YOU DON'T NEED THIS...
...BUT LET'S DO A REFRESHER ANYWAY.

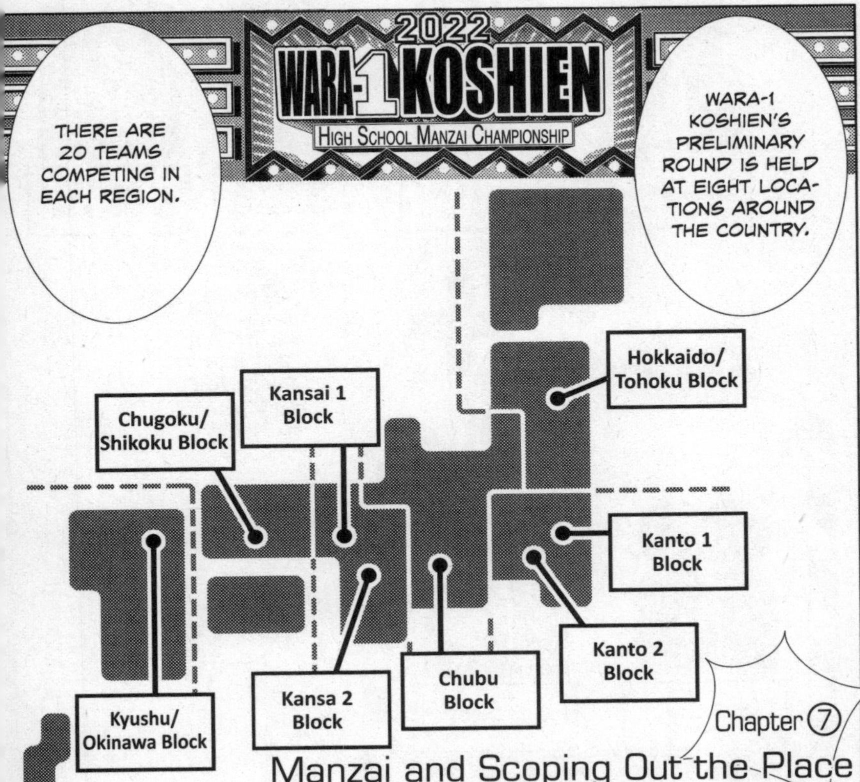
2022
WARA-1 KOSHIEN
HIGH SCHOOL MANZAI CHAMPIONSHIP
WARA-1 KOSHIEN'S PRELIMINARY ROUND IS HELD AT EIGHT LOCATIONS AROUND THE COUNTRY.
THERE ARE 20 TEAMS COMPETING IN EACH REGION.
Hokkaido/ Tohoku Block
Kansai 1 Block
Chugoku/ Shikoku Block
Kanto 1 Block
Kanto 2 Block
Chubu Block
Kansa 2 Block
Kyushu/ Okinawa Block

Chapter 7
Manzai and Scoping Out the Place

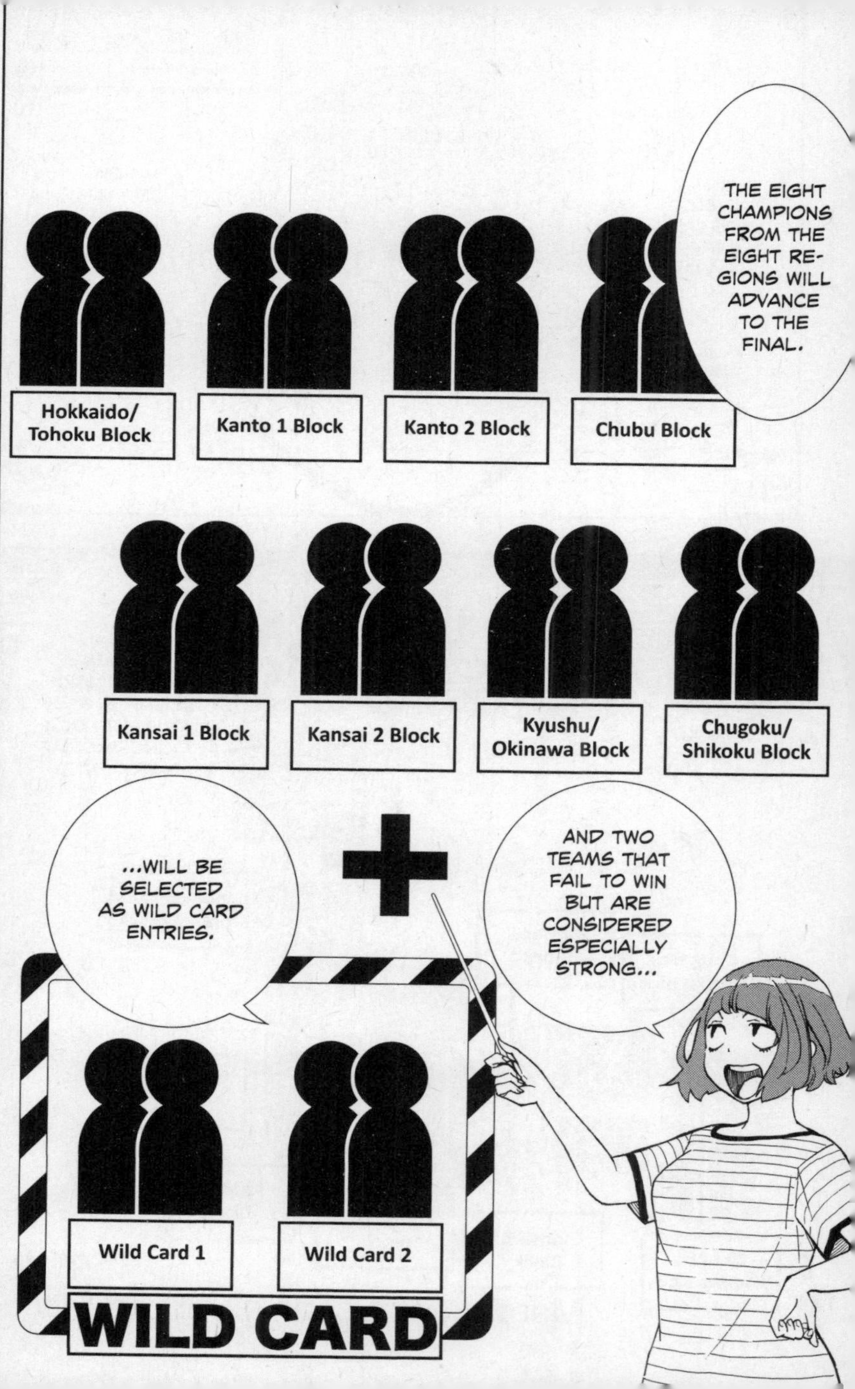
THE EIGHT CHAMPIONS FROM THE EIGHT REGIONS WILL ADVANCE TO THE FINAL.
Hokkaido/ Tohoku Block
Kanto 1 Block
Kanto 2 Block
Chubu Block
Kansai 1 Block
Kansai 2 Block
Kyushu/ Okinawa Block
Chugoku/ Shikoku Block
AND TWO TEAMS THAT FAIL TO WIN BUT ARE CONSIDERED ESPECIALLY STRONG...
...WILL BE SELECTED AS WILD CARD ENTRIES.
Wild Card 1
Wild Card 2
WILD CARD

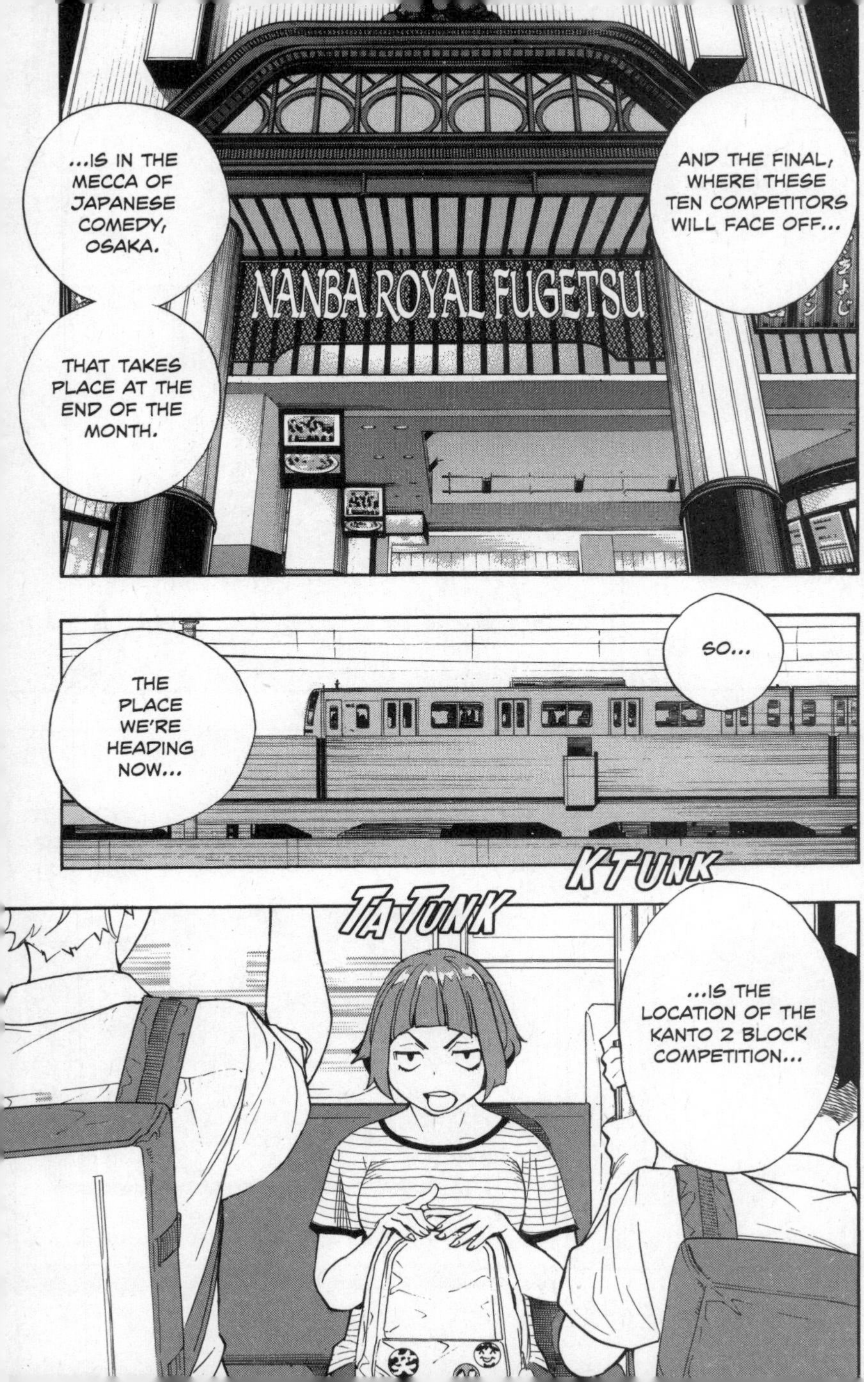
AND THE FINAL, WHERE THESE TEN COMPETITORS WILL FACE OFF...
...IS IN THE MECCA OF JAPANESE COMEDY, OSAKA.
THAT TAKES PLACE AT THE END OF THE MONTH.
NANBA ROYAL FUGETSU
SO...
THE PLACE WE'RE HEADING NOW...
KTUNK
TA TUNK
...IS THE LOCATION OF THE KANTO 2 BLOCK COMPETITION...

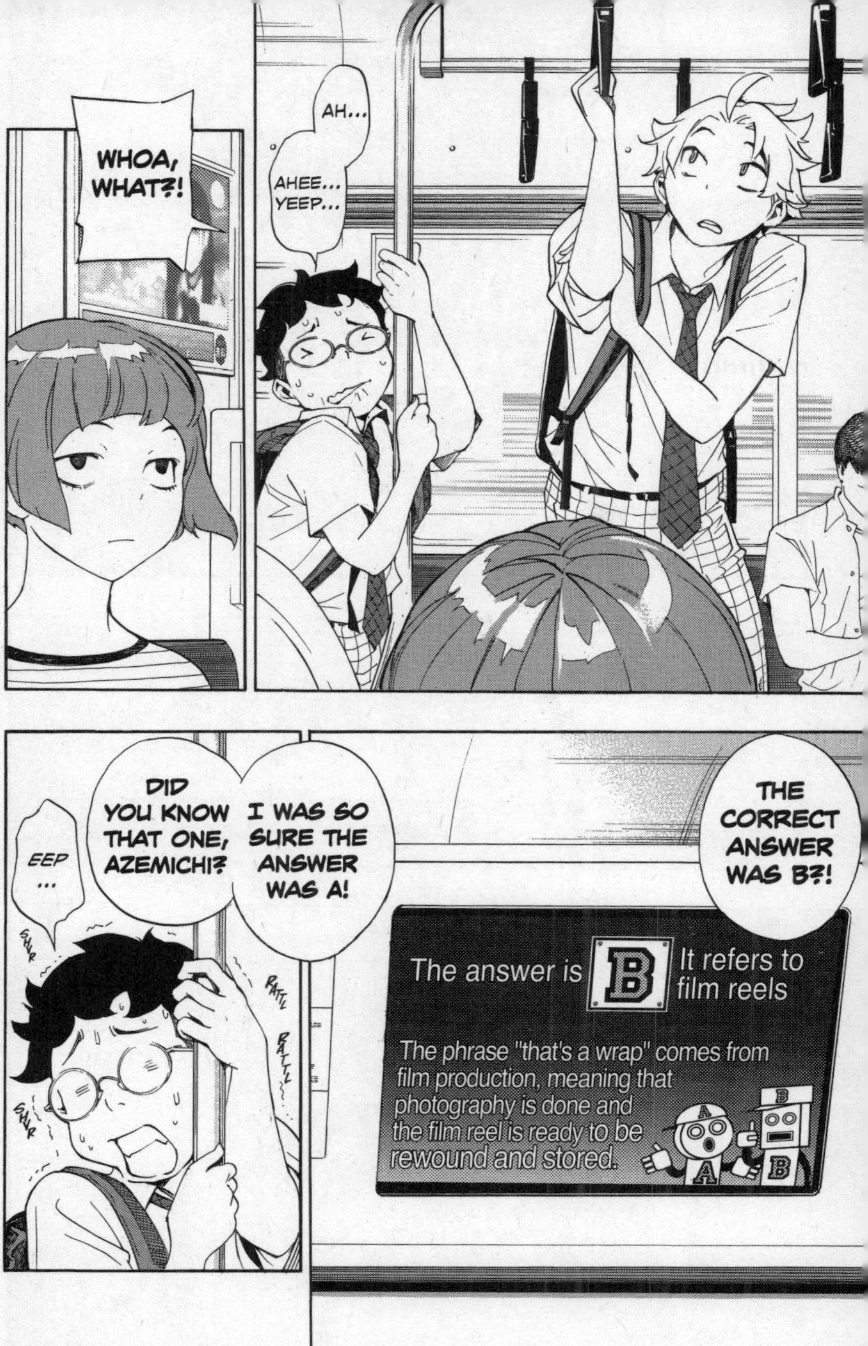
AH...
AHEE... YEEP...
WHOA, WHAT?!
THE CORRECT ANSWER WAS B?!
The answer is B It refers to film reels
The phrase "that's a wrap" comes from film production, meaning that photography is done and the film reel is ready to be rewound and stored.
I WAS SO SURE THE ANSWER WAS A!
DID YOU KNOW THAT ONE, AZEMICHI?
EEP ...
RATTL
RATTL
SHVR
SHVR

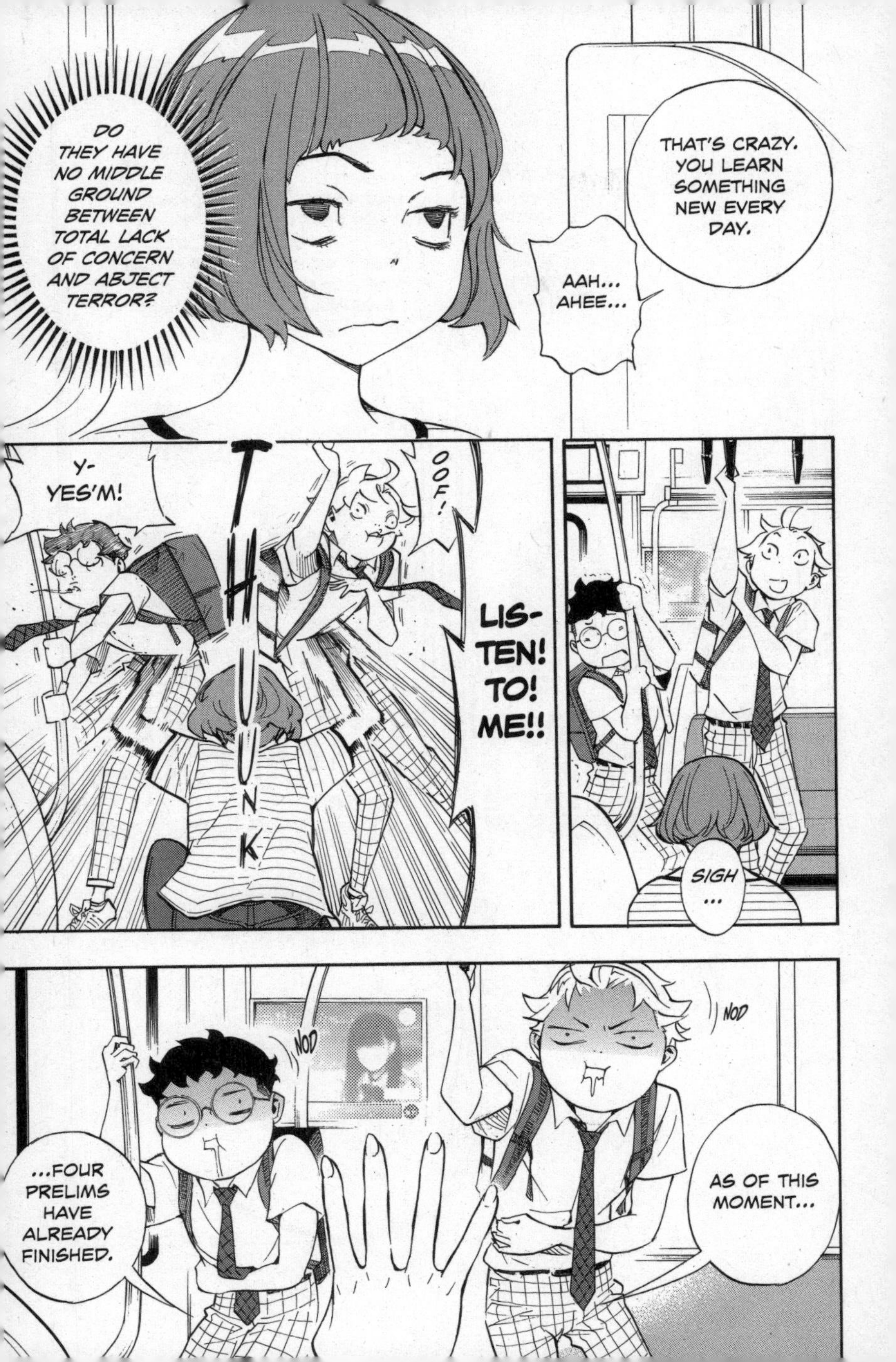
THAT'S CRAZY. YOU LEARN SOMETHING NEW EVERY DAY.
AAH... AHEE...
DO THEY HAVE NO MIDDLE GROUND BETWEEN TOTAL LACK OF CONCERN AND ABJECT TERROR?
SIGH...
LIS-TEN! TO! ME!!
OOF!
THUNK
Y- YES'M!
NOD
AS OF THIS MOMENT...
NOD
...FOUR PRELIMS HAVE ALREADY FINISHED.

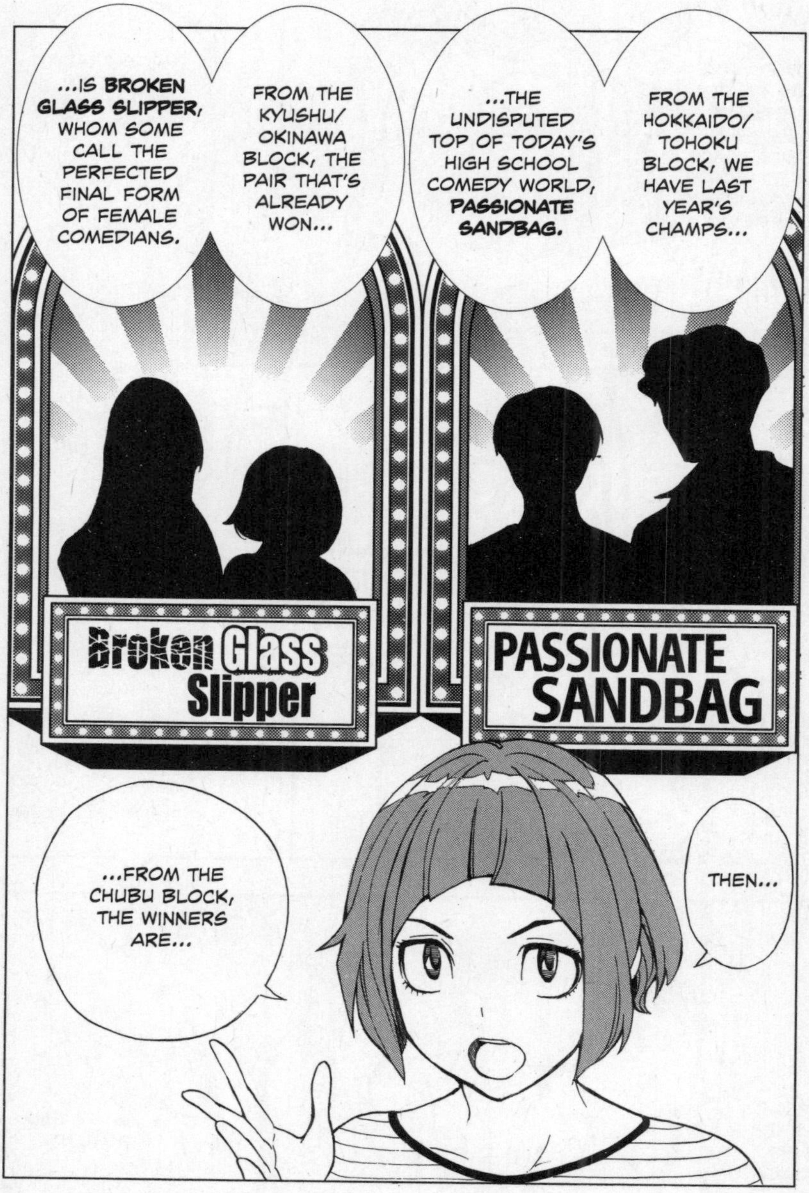
FROM THE HOKKAIDO/ TOHOKU BLOCK, WE HAVE LAST YEAR'S CHAMPS...
...THE UNDISPUTED TOP OF TODAY'S HIGH SCHOOL COMEDY WORLD, PASSIONATE SANDBAG.
FROM THE KYUSHU/ OKINAWA BLOCK, THE PAIR THAT'S ALREADY WON...
...IS BROKEN GLASS SLIPPER, WHOM SOME CALL THE PERFECTED FINAL FORM OF FEMALE COMEDIANS.
PASSIONATE SANDBAG
Broken Glass Slipper
THEN...
...FROM THE CHUBU BLOCK, THE WINNERS ARE...

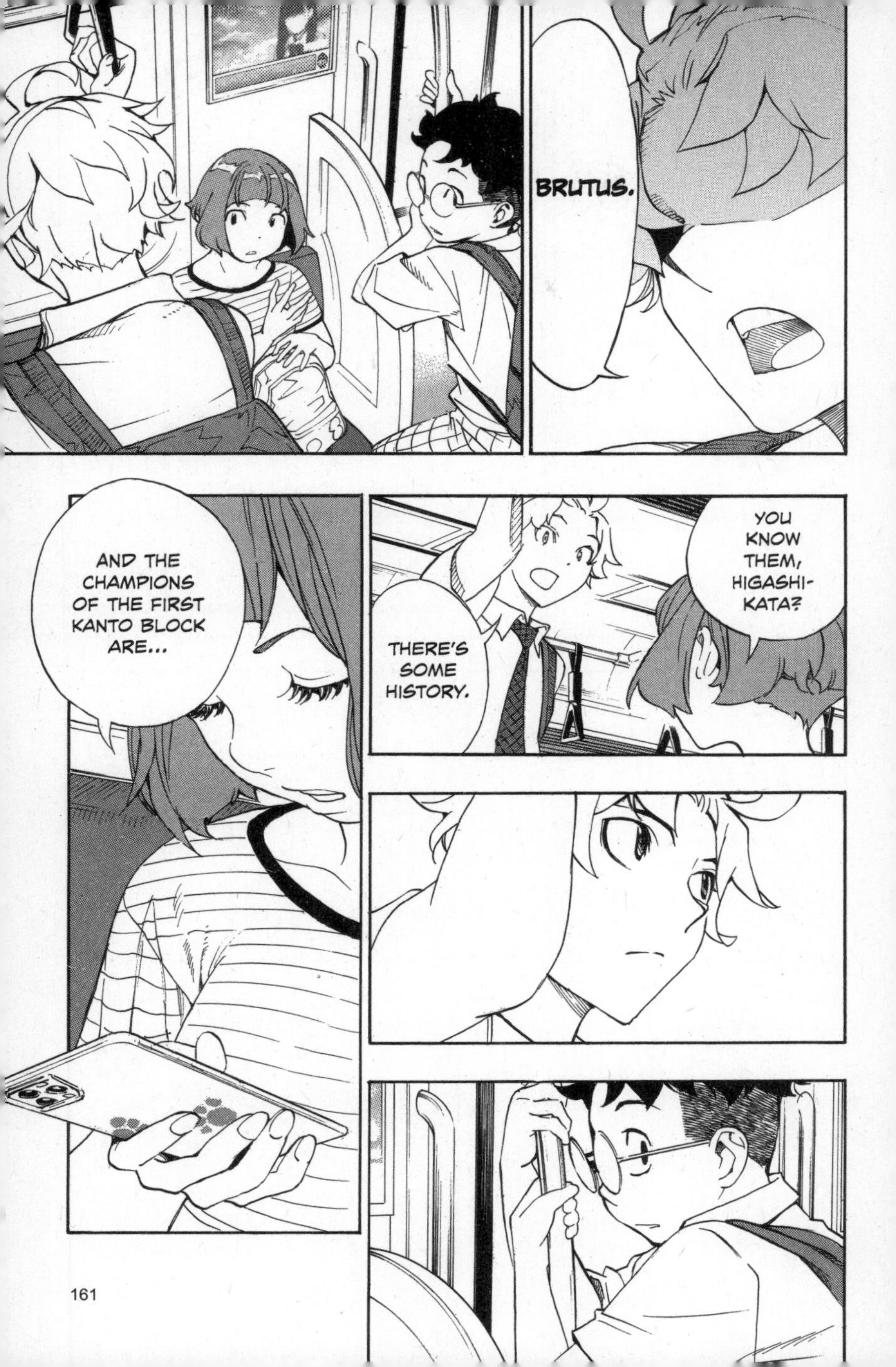
BRUTUS.
YOU KNOW THEM, HIGASHI-KATA?
THERE'S SOME HISTORY.
AND THE CHAMPIONS OF THE FIRST KANTO BLOCK ARE...

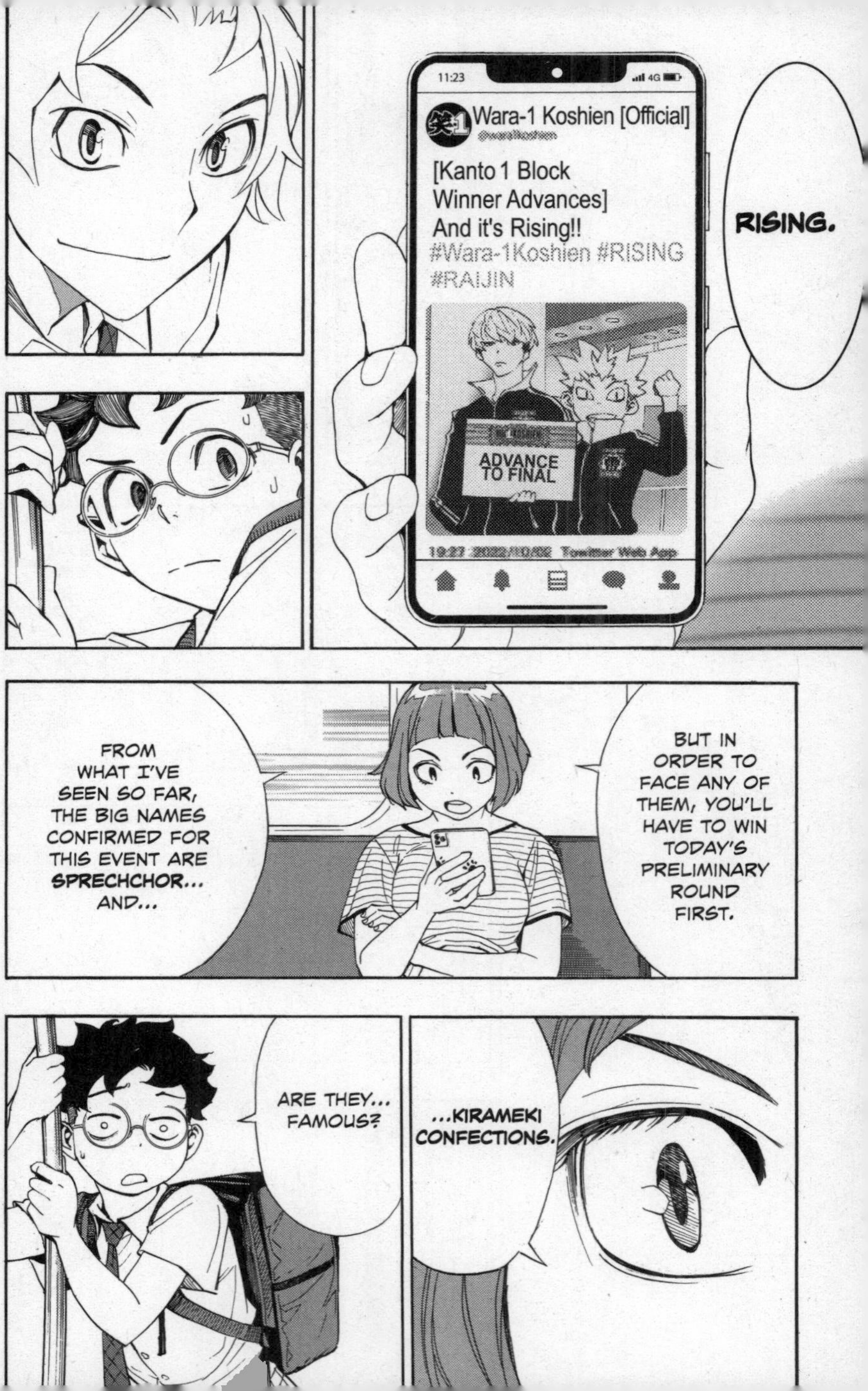
11:23
4G
Wara-1 Koshien [Official]
[Kanto 1 Block Winner Advances] And it's Rising!! #Wara-1Koshien #RISING #RAIJIN
ADVANCE TO FINAL
RISING.
BUT IN ORDER TO FACE ANY OF THEM, YOU'LL HAVE TO WIN TODAY'S PRELIMINARY ROUND FIRST.
FROM WHAT I'VE SEEN SO FAR, THE BIG NAMES CONFIRMED FOR THIS EVENT ARE **SPRECHCHOR...** AND...
...KIRAMEKI CONFECTIONS.
ARE THEY... FAMOUS?

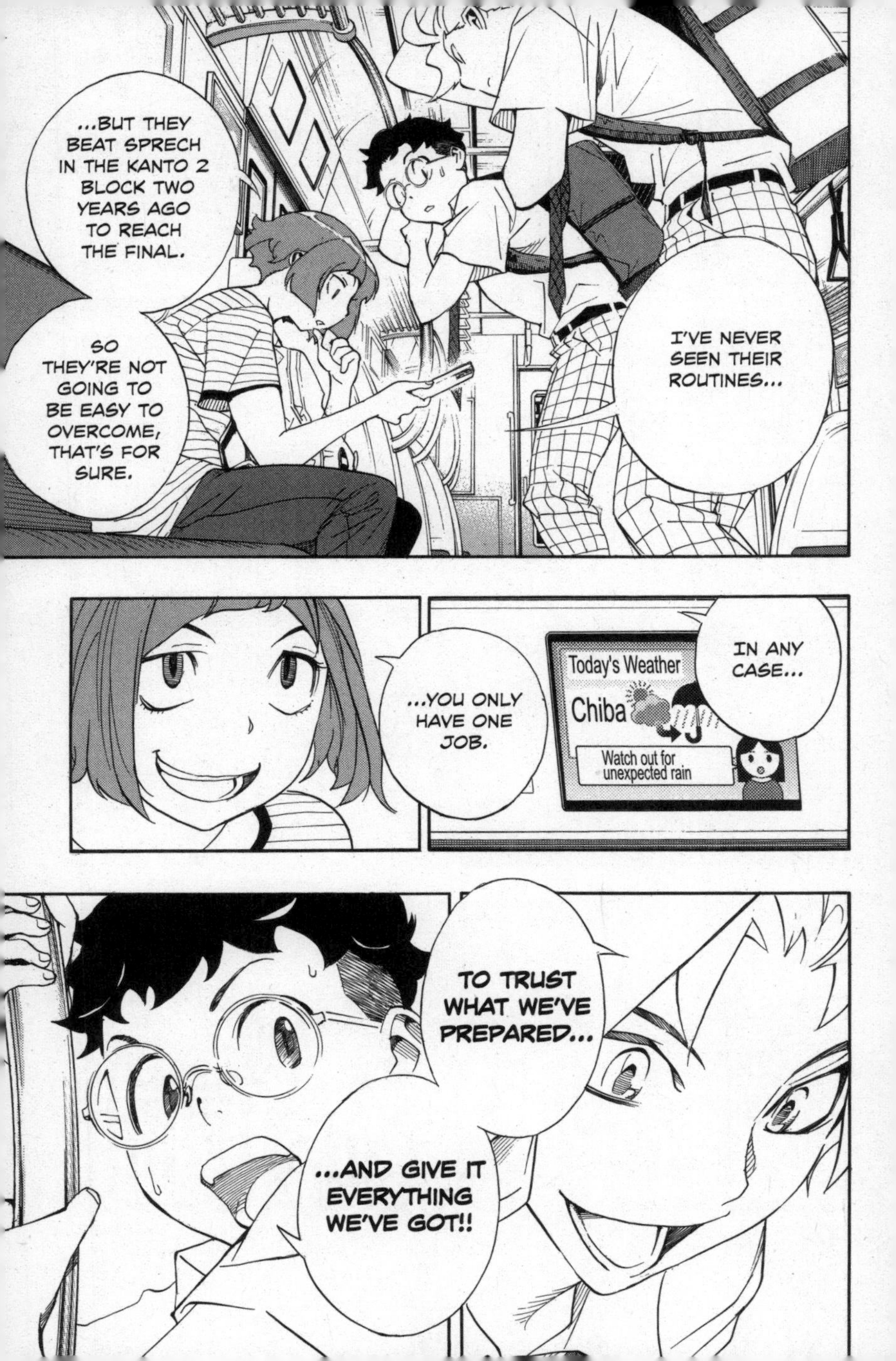
I'VE NEVER SEEN THEIR ROUTINES...
...BUT THEY BEAT SPRECH IN THE KANTO 2 BLOCK TWO YEARS AGO TO REACH THE FINAL.
SO THEY'RE NOT GOING TO BE EASY TO OVERCOME, THAT'S FOR SURE.
IN ANY CASE...
Today's Weather
Chiba
Watch out for unexpected rain
...YOU ONLY HAVE ONE JOB.
TO TRUST WHAT WE'VE PREPARED...
...AND GIVE IT EVERYTHING WE'VE GOT!!

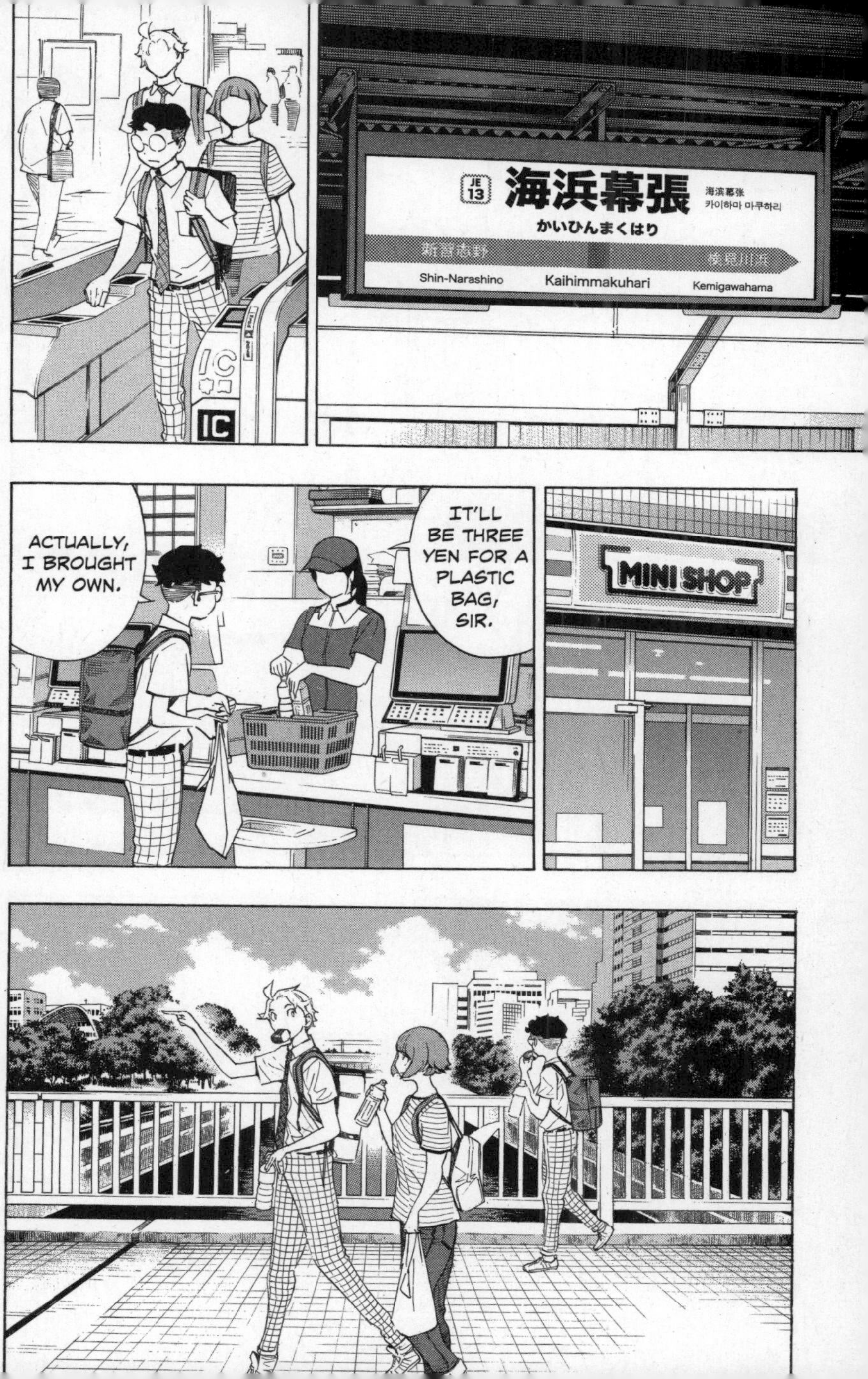
JE 13
海浜幕張
海滨幕张
카이하마 마쿠하리
かいひんまくはり
新習志野
検見川浜
Shin-Narashino
Kaihimmakuhari
Kemigawahama
IC
IC
MINI SHOP
IT'LL BE THREE YEN FOR A PLASTIC BAG, SIR.
ACTUALLY, I BROUGHT MY OWN.

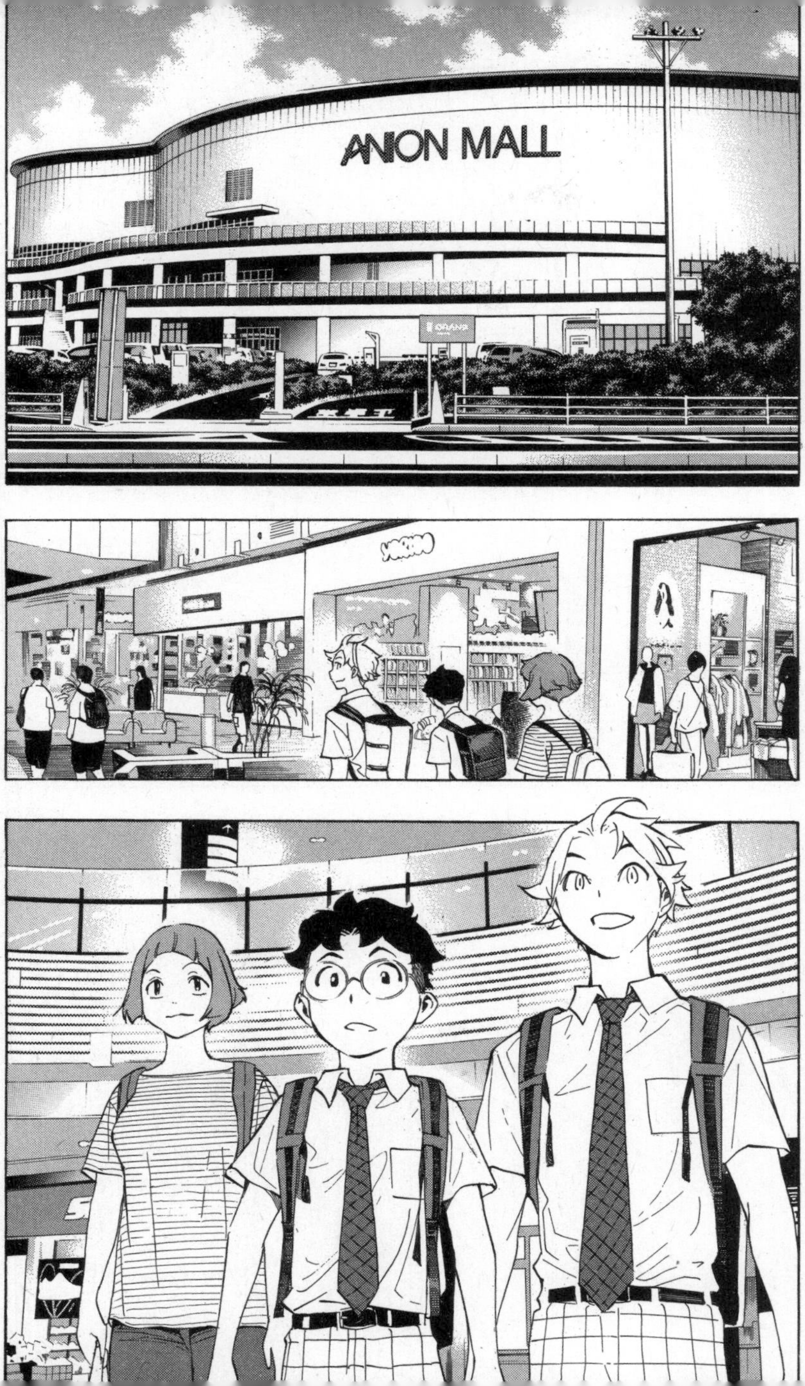
ANION MALL

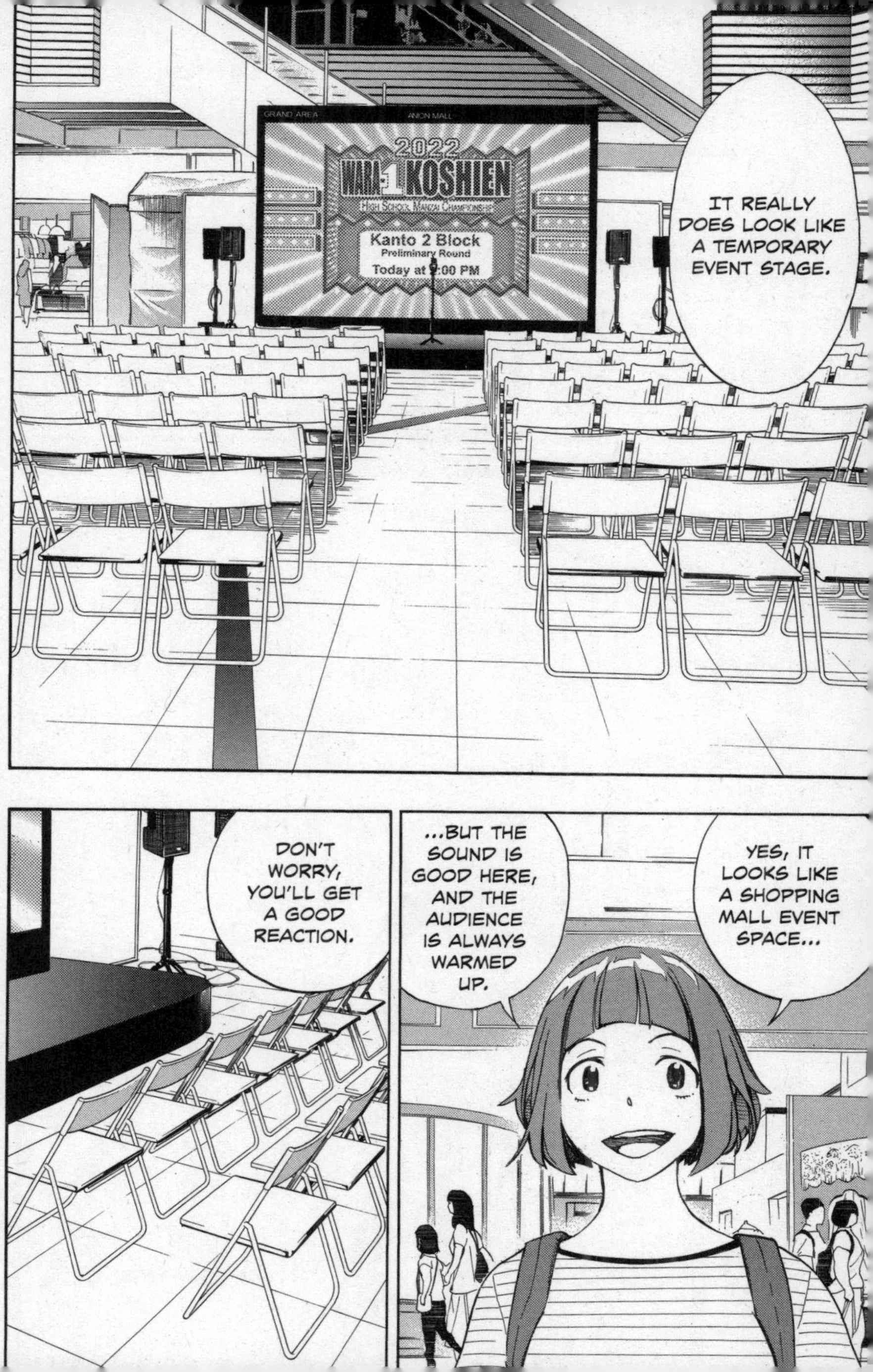
GRAND AREA
ANION MALL
2022 WARA-1 KOSHIEN
High School Manzai Championship
Kanto 2 Block
Preliminary Round
IT REALLY DOES LOOK LIKE A TEMPORARY EVENT STAGE.
YES, IT LOOKS LIKE A SHOPPING MALL EVENT SPACE...
...BUT THE SOUND IS GOOD HERE, AND THE AUDIENCE IS ALWAYS WARMED UP.
DON'T WORRY, YOU'LL GET A GOOD REACTION.

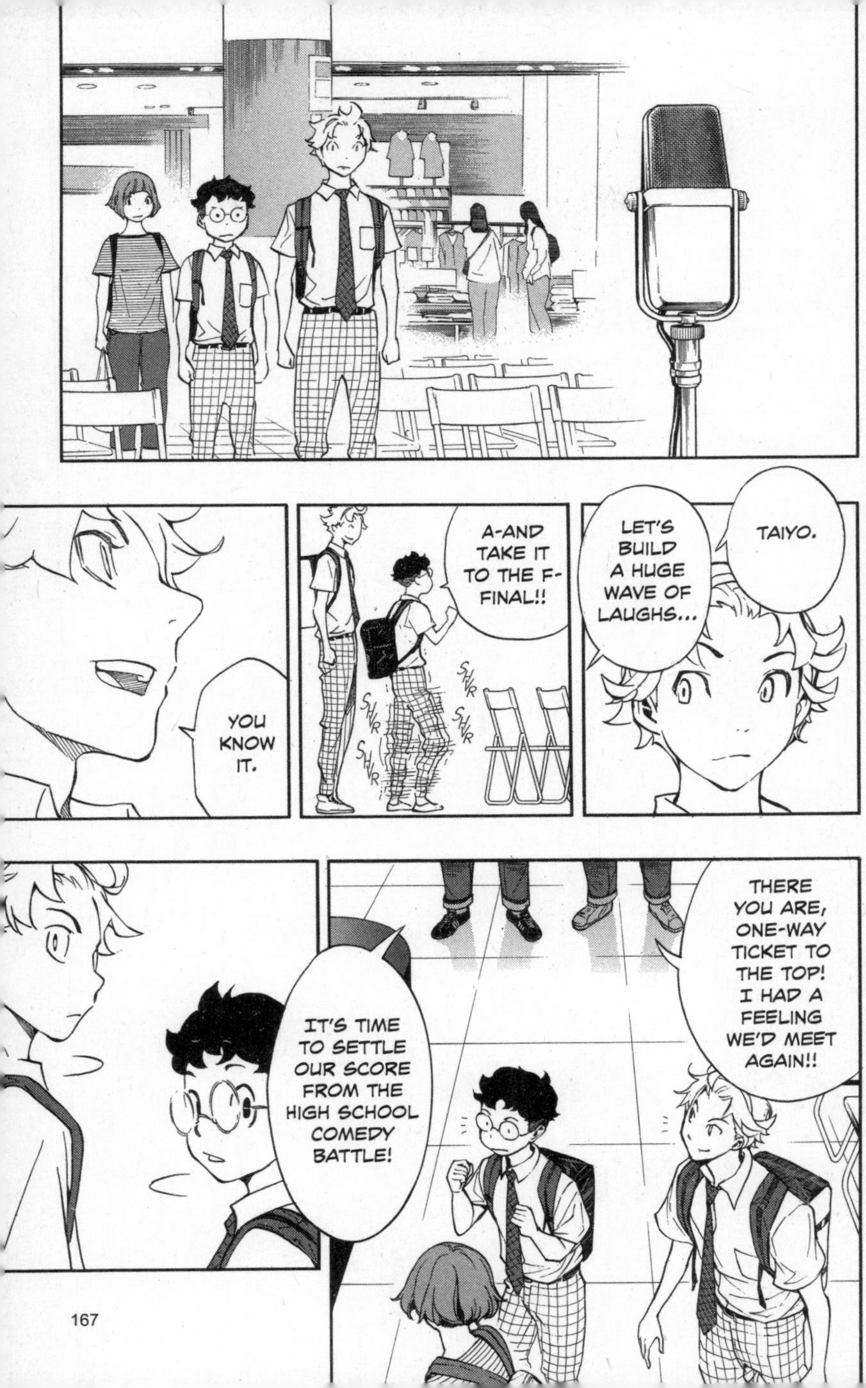
TAIYO.
LET'S BUILD A HUGE WAVE OF LAUGHS...
A-AND TAKE IT TO THE F-FINAL!!
SHVR SHVR SHVR SHVR
YOU KNOW IT.
THERE YOU ARE, ONE-WAY TICKET TO THE TOP! I HAD A FEELING WE'D MEET AGAIN!!
IT'S TIME TO SETTLE OUR SCORE FROM THE HIGH SCHOOL COMEDY BATTLE!

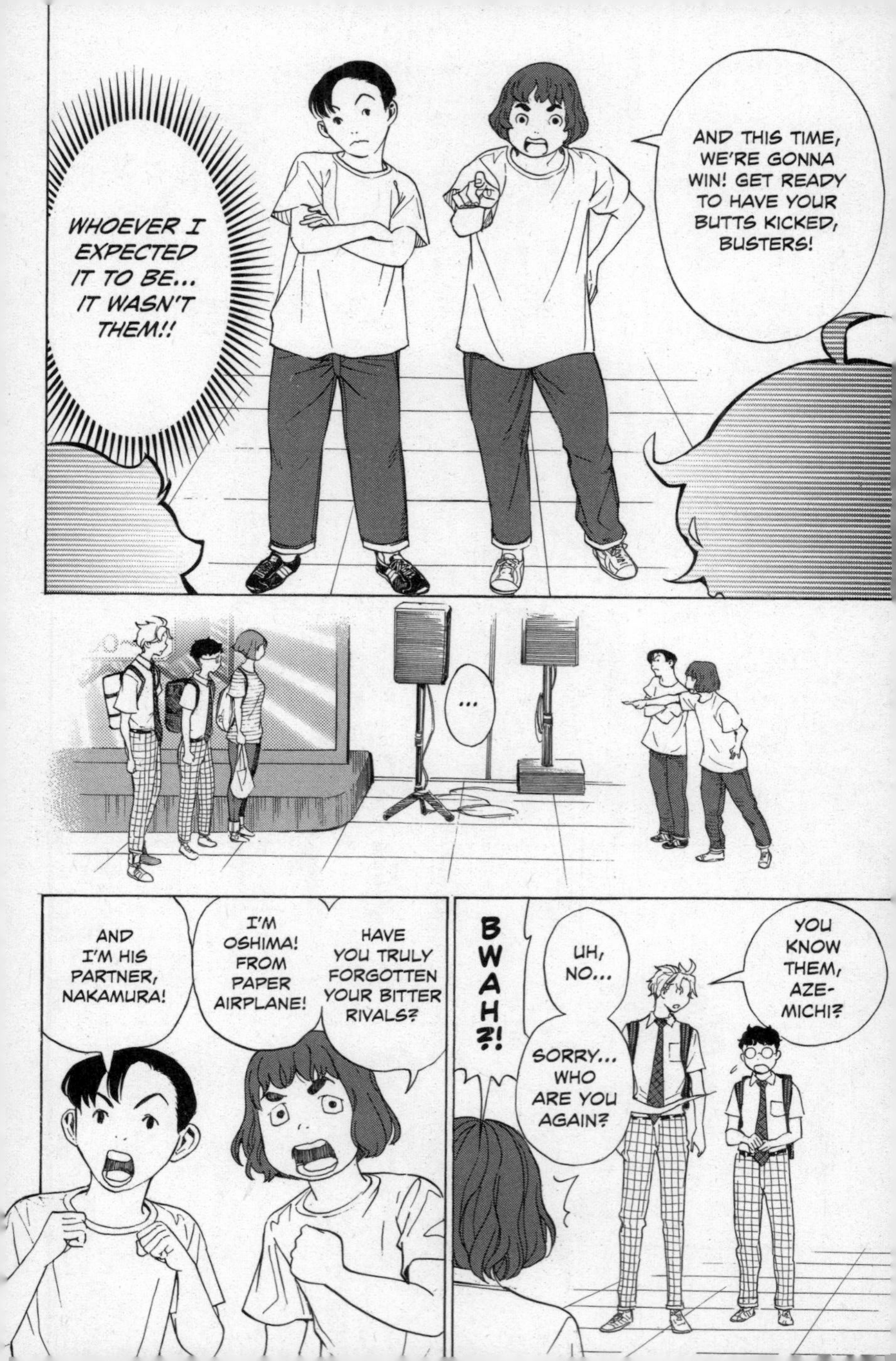
AND THIS TIME, WE'RE GONNA WIN! GET READY TO HAVE YOUR BUTTS KICKED, BUSTERS!
WHOEVER I EXPECTED IT TO BE... IT WASN'T THEM!!
...
YOU KNOW THEM, AZE-MICHI?
UH, NO...
SORRY... WHO ARE YOU AGAIN?
BWAH?!
HAVE YOU TRULY FORGOTTEN YOUR BITTER RIVALS?
I'M OSHIMA! FROM PAPER AIRPLANE!
AND I'M HIS PARTNER, NAKAMURA!

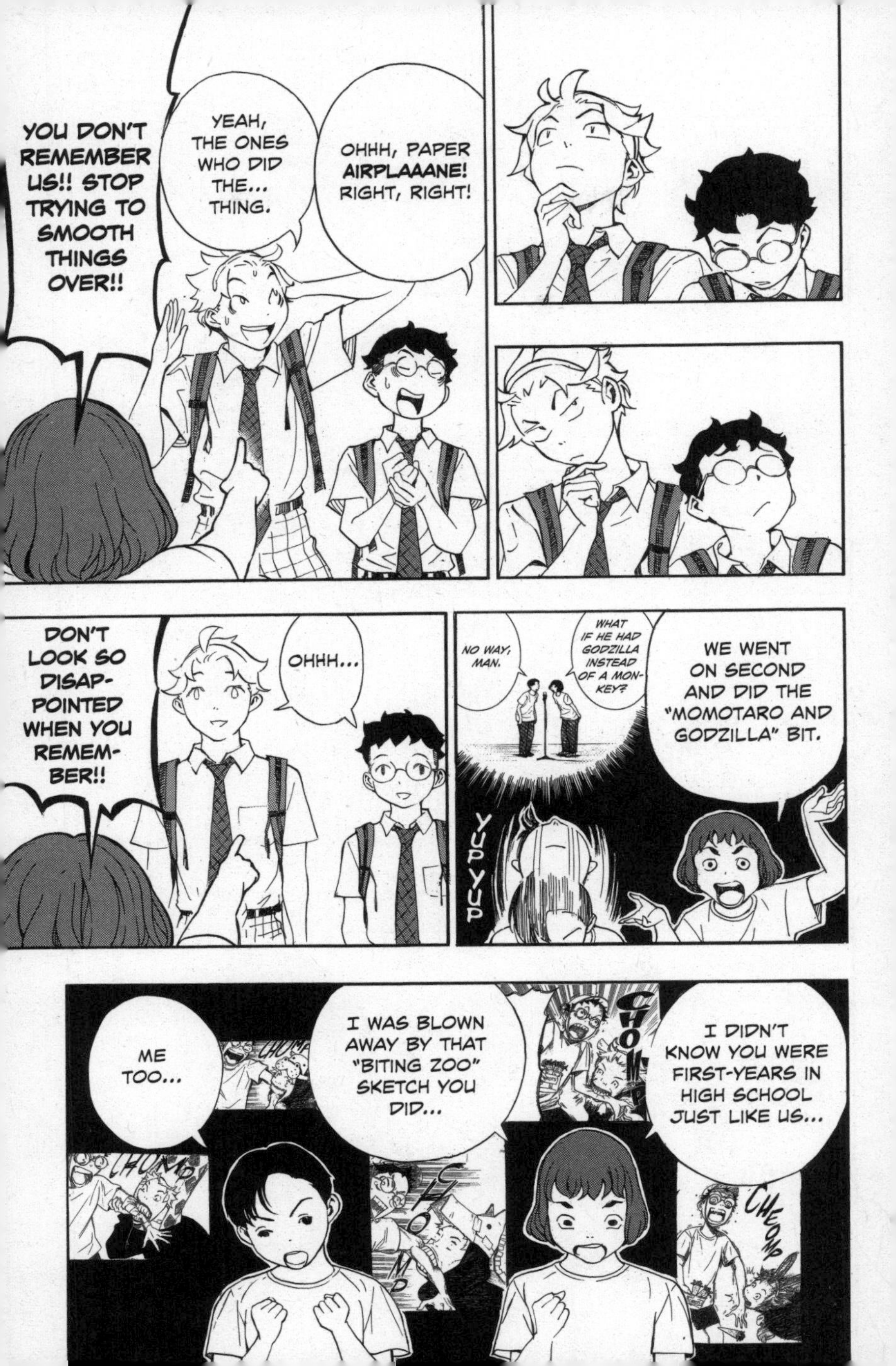
OHHH, PAPER AIRPLAAANE! RIGHT, RIGHT!
YEAH, THE ONES WHO DID THE... THING.
YOU DON'T REMEMBER US!! STOP TRYING TO SMOOTH THINGS OVER!!
WE WENT ON SECOND AND DID THE "MOMOTARO AND GODZILLA" BIT.
WHAT IF HE HAD GODZILLA INSTEAD OF A MONKEY?
NO WAY, MAN.
YUP YUP
OHHH...
DON'T LOOK SO DISAP-POINTED WHEN YOU REMEM-BER!!
I DIDN'T KNOW YOU WERE FIRST-YEARS IN HIGH SCHOOL JUST LIKE US...
CHOMP
CHOMP
I WAS BLOWN AWAY BY THAT "BITING ZOO" SKETCH YOU DID...
ME TOO...

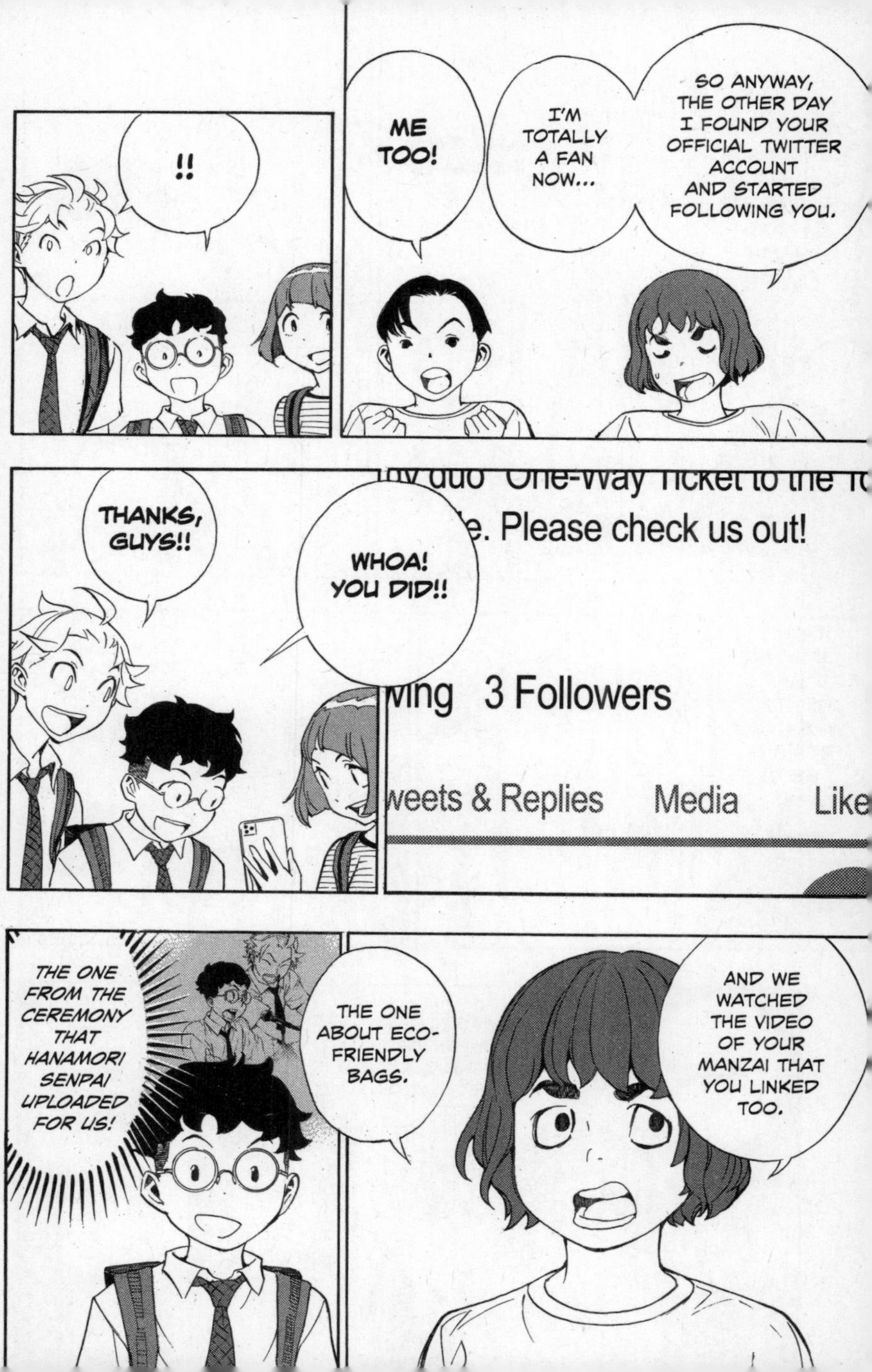
SO ANYWAY, THE OTHER DAY I FOUND YOUR OFFICIAL TWITTER ACCOUNT AND STARTED FOLLOWING YOU.
I'M TOTALLY A FAN NOW...
ME TOO!
!!
e. Please check us out!
wing 3 Followers
weets & Replies
Media
Like
WHOA! YOU DID!!
THANKS, GUYS!!
AND WE WATCHED THE VIDEO OF YOUR MANZAI THAT YOU LINKED TOO.
THE ONE ABOUT ECO-FRIENDLY BAGS.
THE ONE FROM THE CEREMONY THAT HANAMORI SENPAI UPLOADED FOR US!

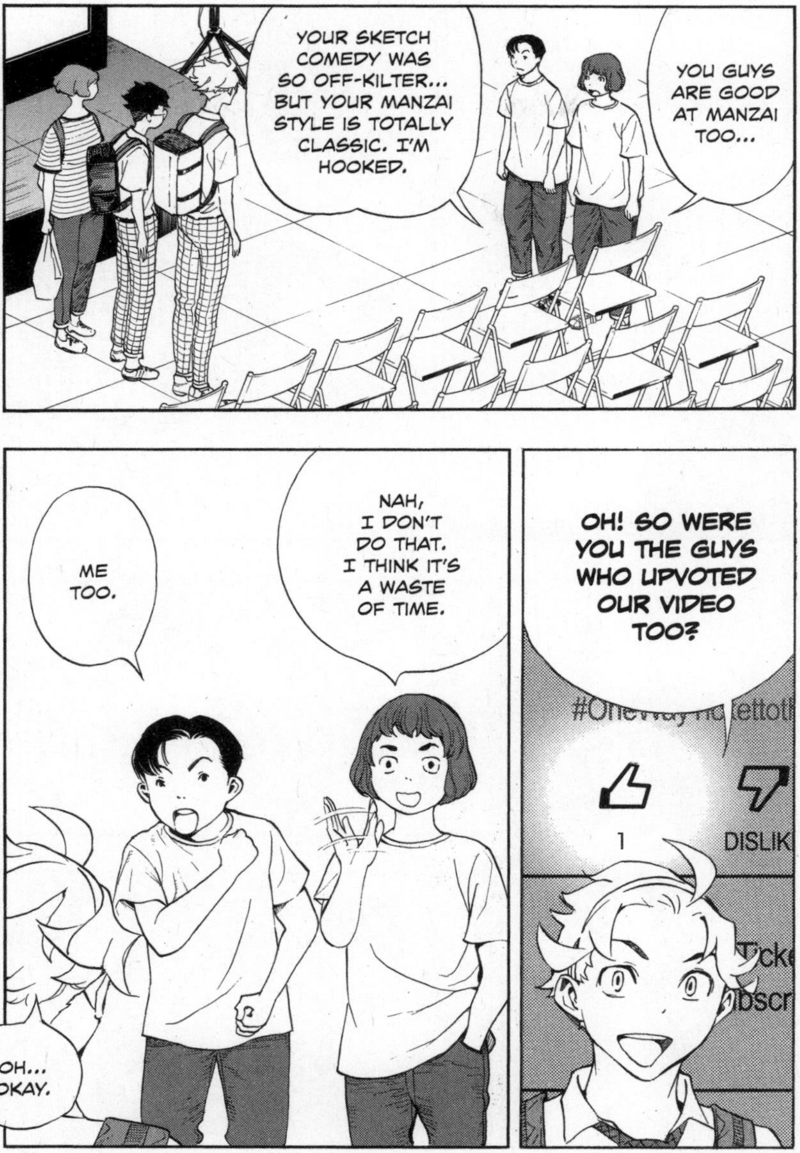
YOU GUYS ARE GOOD AT MANZAI TOO...
YOUR SKETCH COMEDY WAS SO OFF-KILTER... BUT YOUR MANZAI STYLE IS TOTALLY CLASSIC. I'M HOOKED.
OH! SO WERE YOU THE GUYS WHO UPVOTED OUR VIDEO TOO?
1
DISLIK
NAH, I DON'T DO THAT. I THINK IT'S A WASTE OF TIME.
ME TOO.
OH... OKAY.

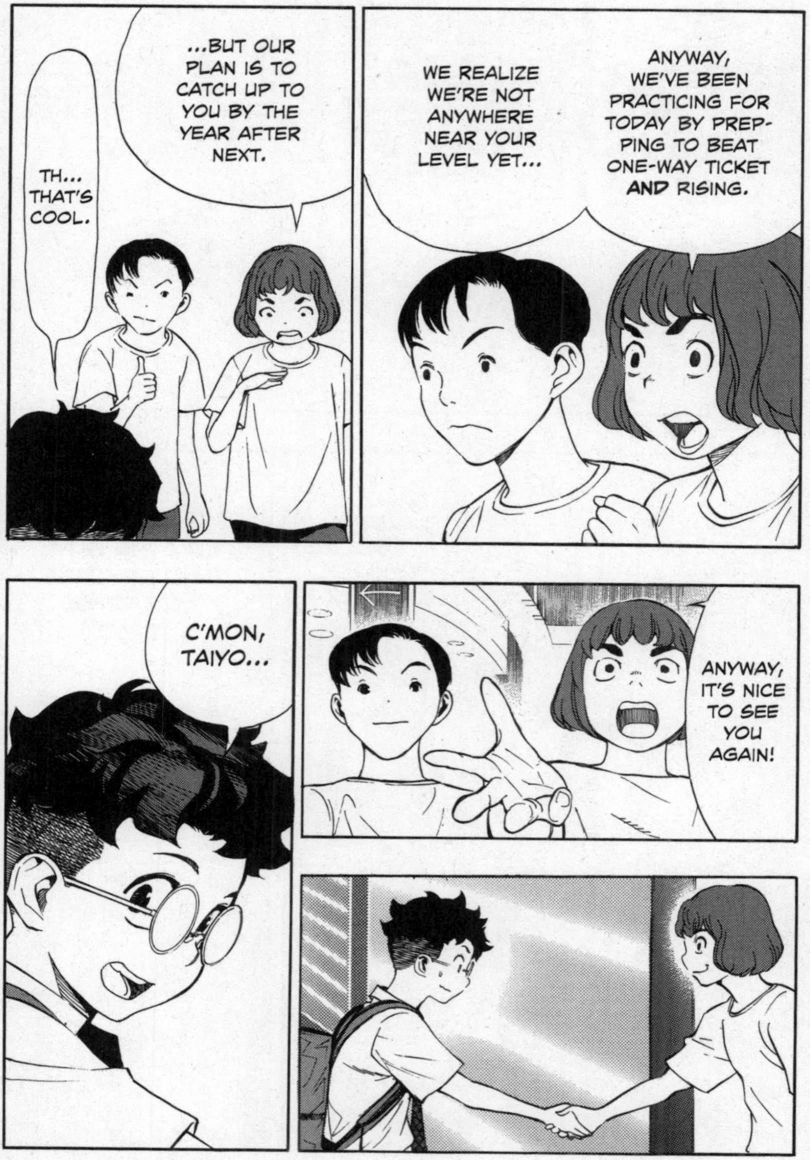
ANYWAY, WE'VE BEEN PRACTICING FOR TODAY BY PREP-PING TO BEAT ONE-WAY TICKET AND RISING.
WE REALIZE WE'RE NOT ANYWHERE NEAR YOUR LEVEL YET...
...BUT OUR PLAN IS TO CATCH UP TO YOU BY THE YEAR AFTER NEXT.
TH... THAT'S COOL.
ANYWAY, IT'S NICE TO SEE YOU AGAIN!
C'MON, TAIYO...

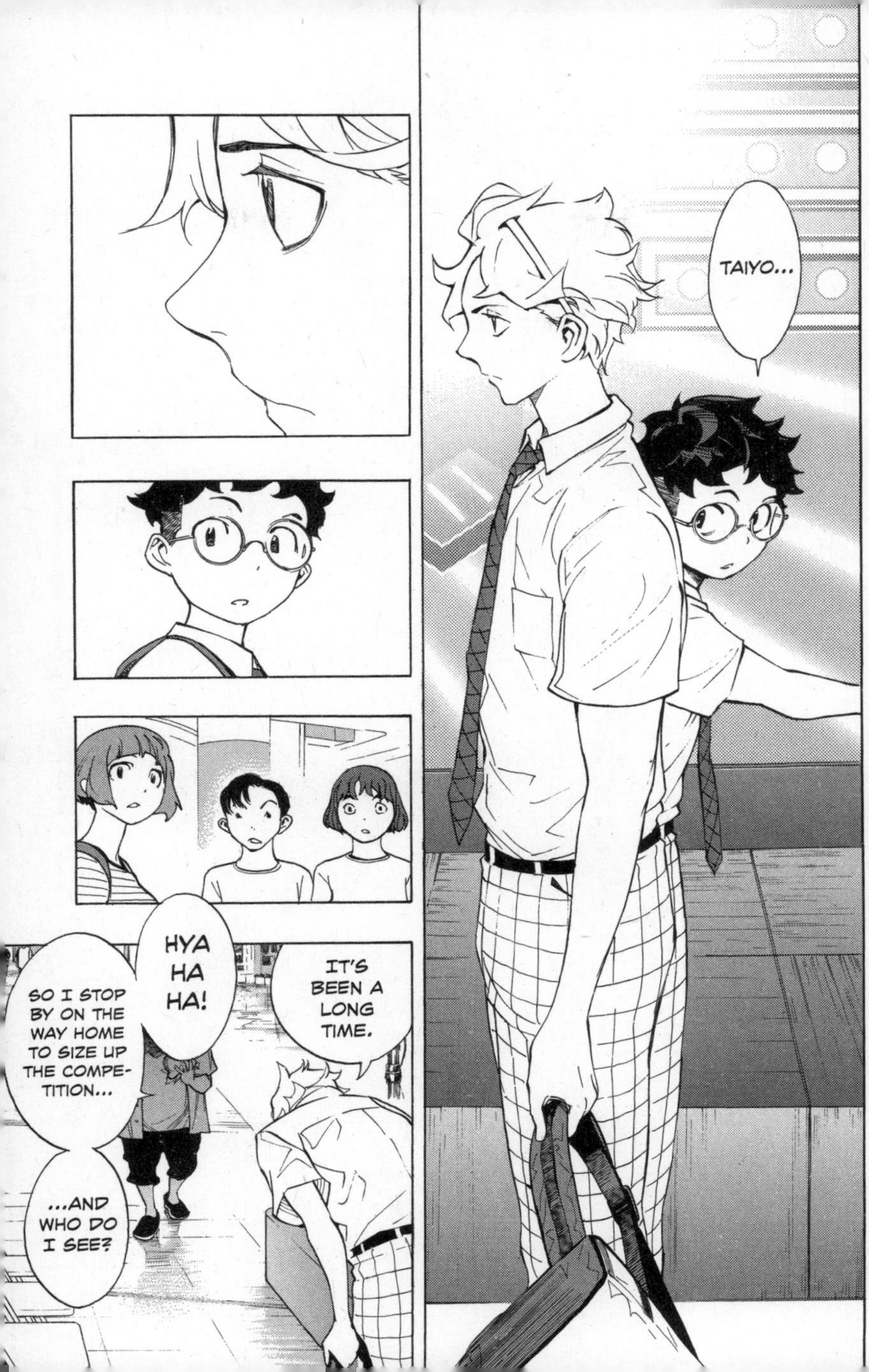
TAIYO...
IT'S BEEN A LONG TIME.
HYA HA HA!
SO I STOP BY ON THE WAY HOME TO SIZE UP THE COMPETITION...
...AND WHO DO I SEE?

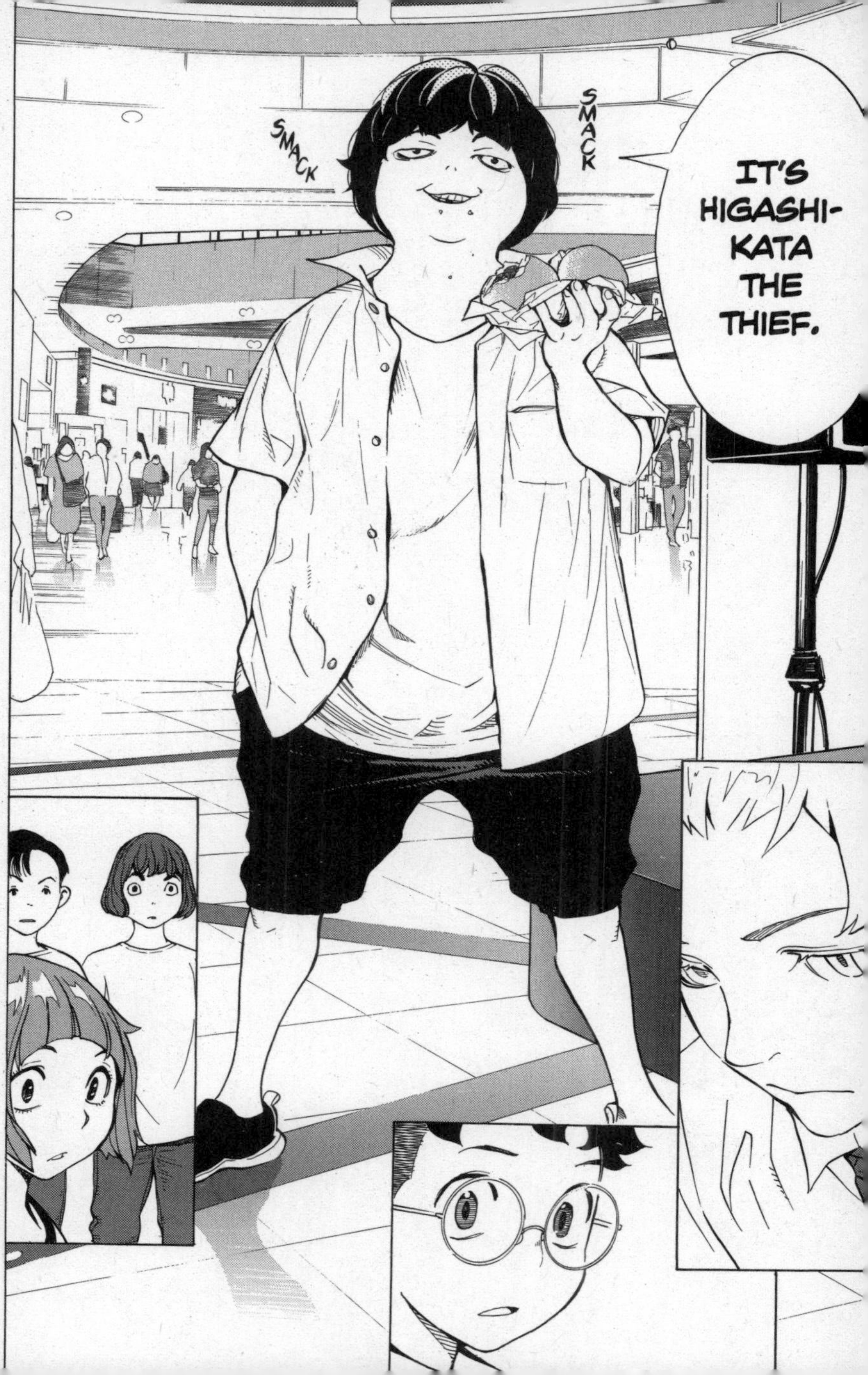
IT'S HIGASHI-KATA THE THIEF.
SMACK
SMACK

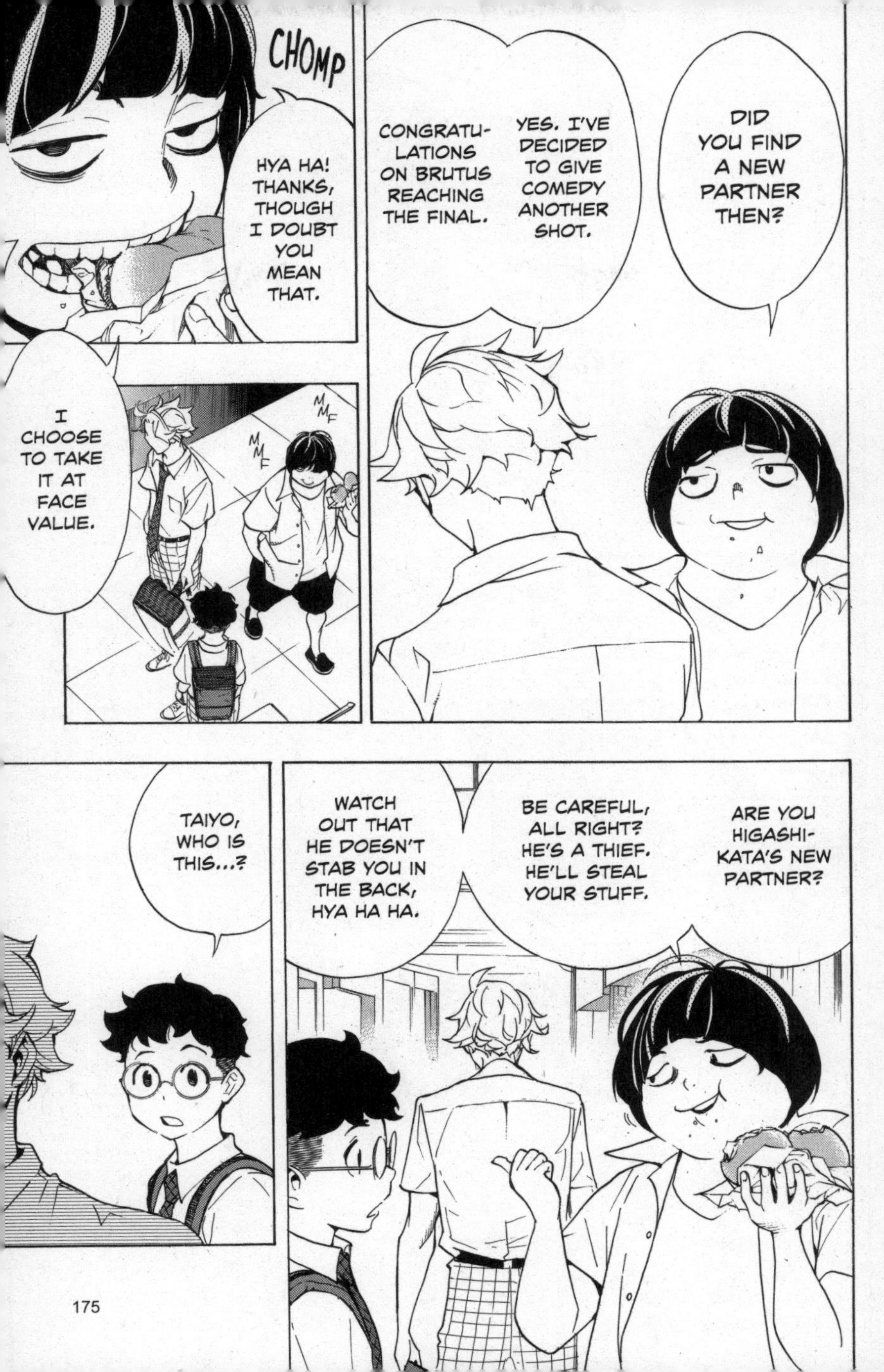
DID YOU FIND A NEW PARTNER THEN?
YES. I'VE DECIDED TO GIVE COMEDY ANOTHER SHOT.
CONGRATULATIONS ON BRUTUS REACHING THE FINAL.
CHOMP
HYA HA! THANKS, THOUGH I DOUBT YOU MEAN THAT.
MMF
MMF
I CHOOSE TO TAKE IT AT FACE VALUE.
ARE YOU HIGASHIKATA'S NEW PARTNER?
BE CAREFUL, ALL RIGHT? HE'S A THIEF. HE'LL STEAL YOUR STUFF.
WATCH OUT THAT HE DOESN'T STAB YOU IN THE BACK, HYA HA HA.
TAIYO, WHO IS THIS...?

I...IS THAT RYUKI NAZUTANI?!

UP UNTIL LAST YEAR, HE WAS IN A DUO CALLED SELINENTIUS.

RUSTLE

HE'S RYUKI NAZUTANI, FROM BRUTUS.

MUNCH

MUNCH

BUT THEN KUNUGI...

RANKING
WARA KOSHIEN

1	Passionate Sandbag
2	Broken Glass Slipper
3	Selinentius
4	Pascal 800
5	Sprechchor
6	Morning Steak
7	Pangolin
8	Sweet Potato Combo
9	REAL DRIVE
10	Applause A Pause

THEY WERE REALLY GOOD. THEY RANKED HIGH IN THE WARA-KO FINAL LAST YEAR.

SELINENTIUS WAS NAZUTANI AND SOMEONE NAMED SAKUTARO KUNUGI.

THAT SUCKS, RIGHT? BASICALLY, HIGASHI-KATA'S A THIEF.

...AND LEFT ME BLOWING IN THE WIND! HYA HA!

...SUDDENLY DECIDED HE WANTED TO PARTNER UP WITH **THIS GUY** INSTEAD...

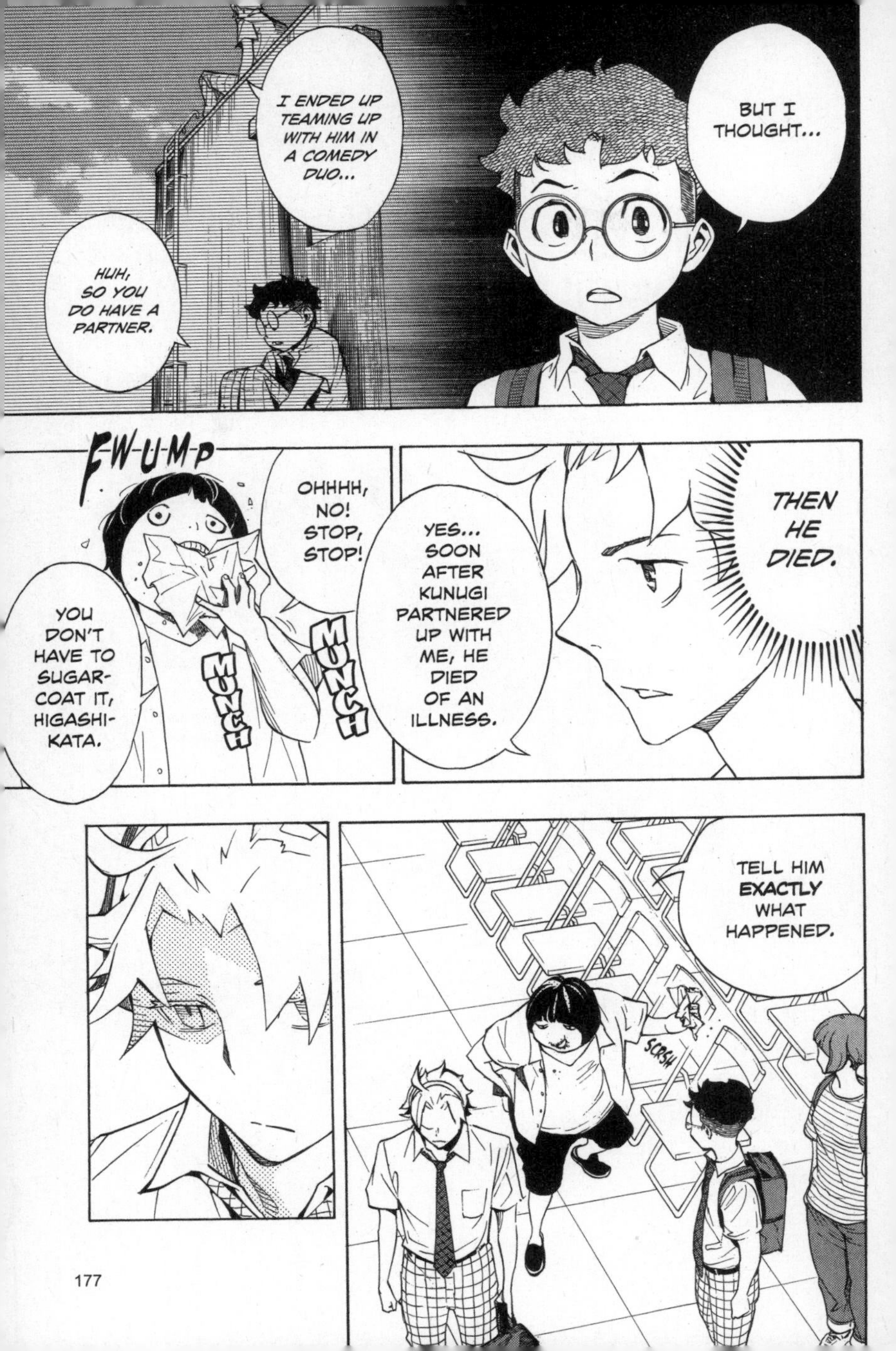
BUT I THOUGHT...
I ENDED UP TEAMING UP WITH HIM IN A COMEDY DUO...
HUH, SO YOU DO HAVE A PARTNER.
THEN HE DIED.
YES... SOON AFTER KUNUGI PARTNERED UP WITH ME, HE DIED OF AN ILLNESS.
F-W-U-M-P
OHHHH, NO! STOP, STOP!
MUNCH
MUNCH
YOU DON'T HAVE TO SUGAR-COAT IT, HIGASHI-KATA.
TELL HIM EXACTLY WHAT HAPPENED.
SCRSH

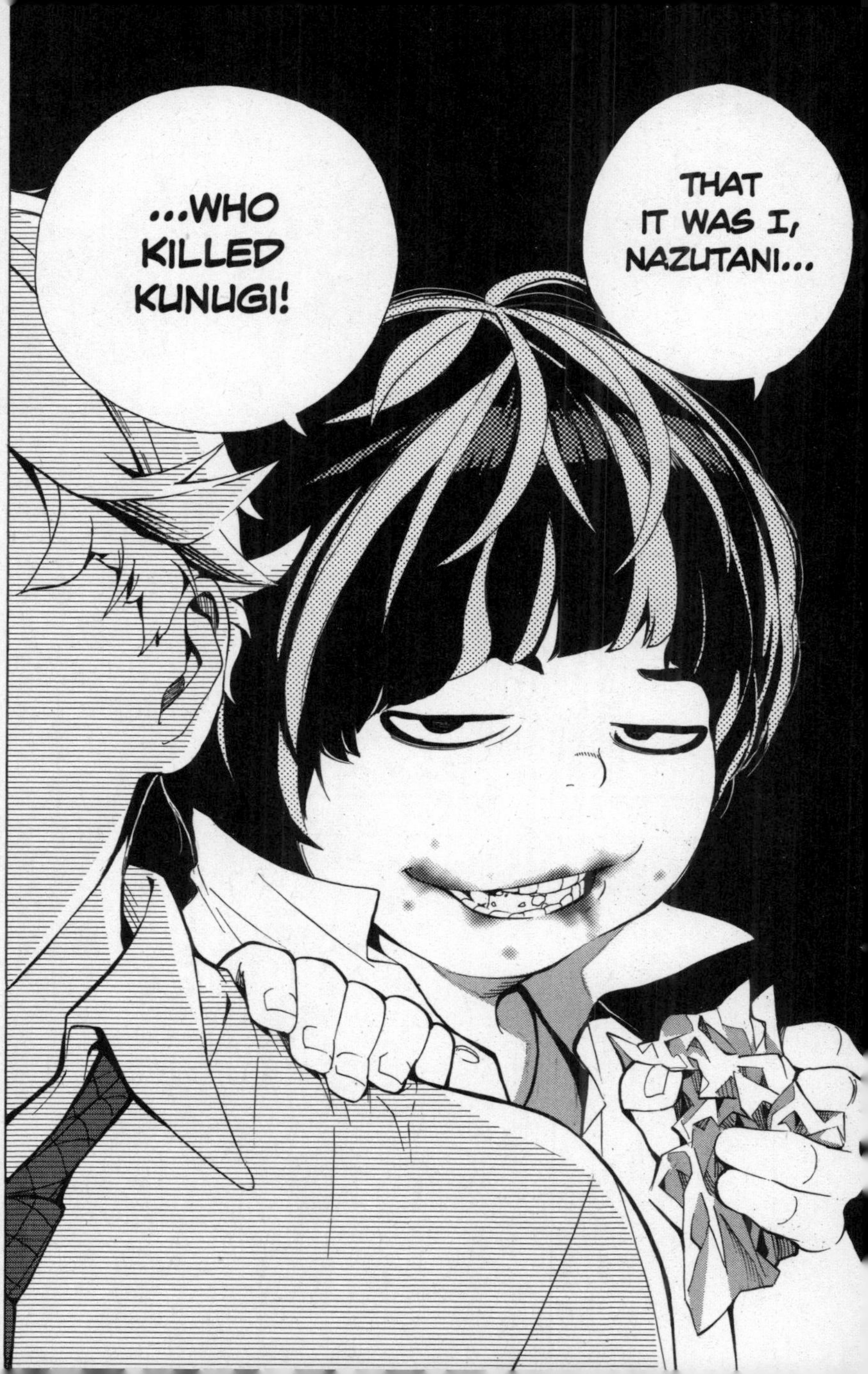
THAT IT WAS I, NAZUTANI...
...WHO KILLED KUNUGI!

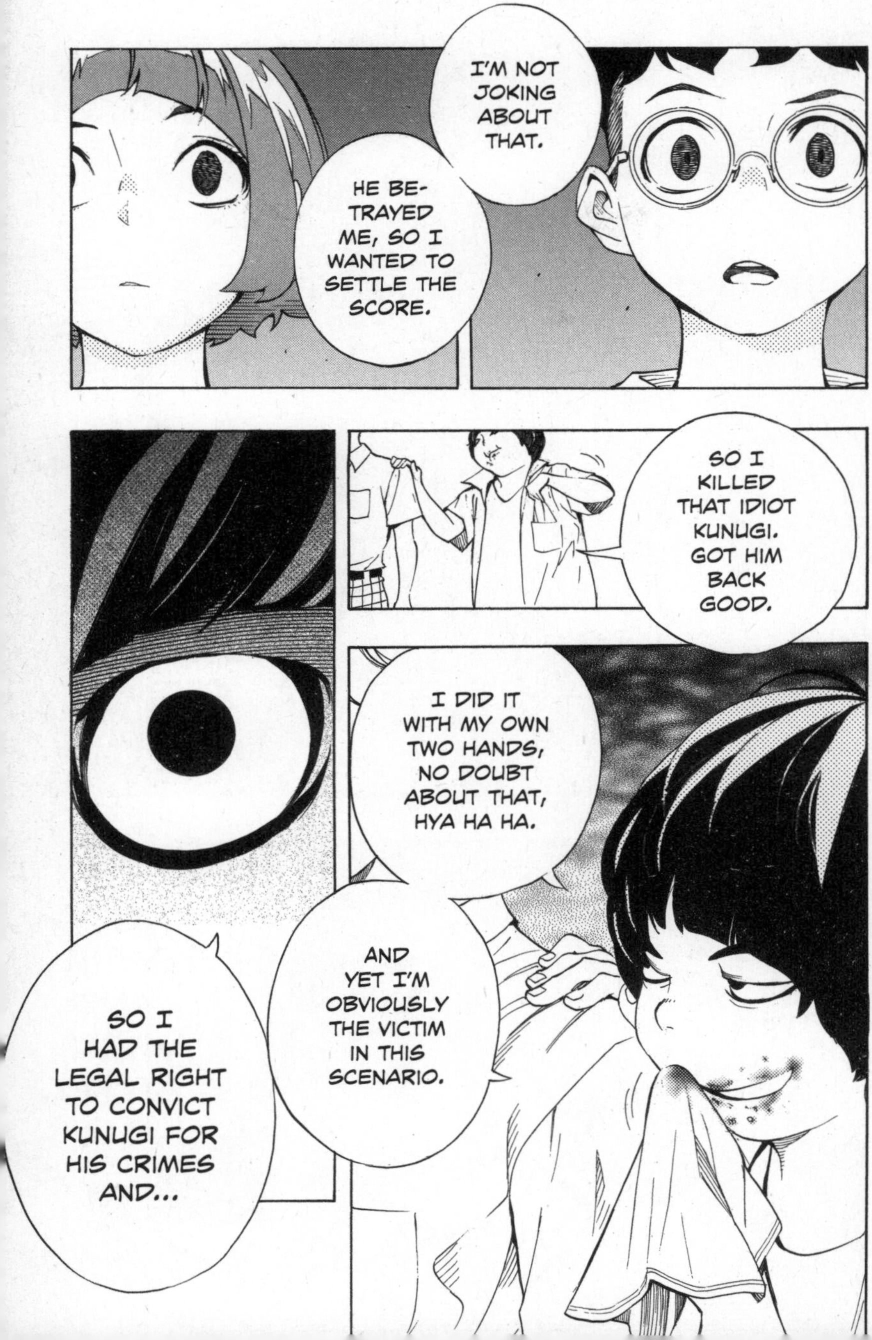
I'M NOT JOKING ABOUT THAT.
HE BE-TRAYED ME, SO I WANTED TO SETTLE THE SCORE.
SO I KILLED THAT IDIOT KUNUGI. GOT HIM BACK GOOD.
I DID IT WITH MY OWN TWO HANDS, NO DOUBT ABOUT THAT, HYA HA HA.
AND YET I'M OBVIOUSLY THE VICTIM IN THIS SCENARIO.
SO I HAD THE LEGAL RIGHT TO CONVICT KUNUGI FOR HIS CRIMES AND...

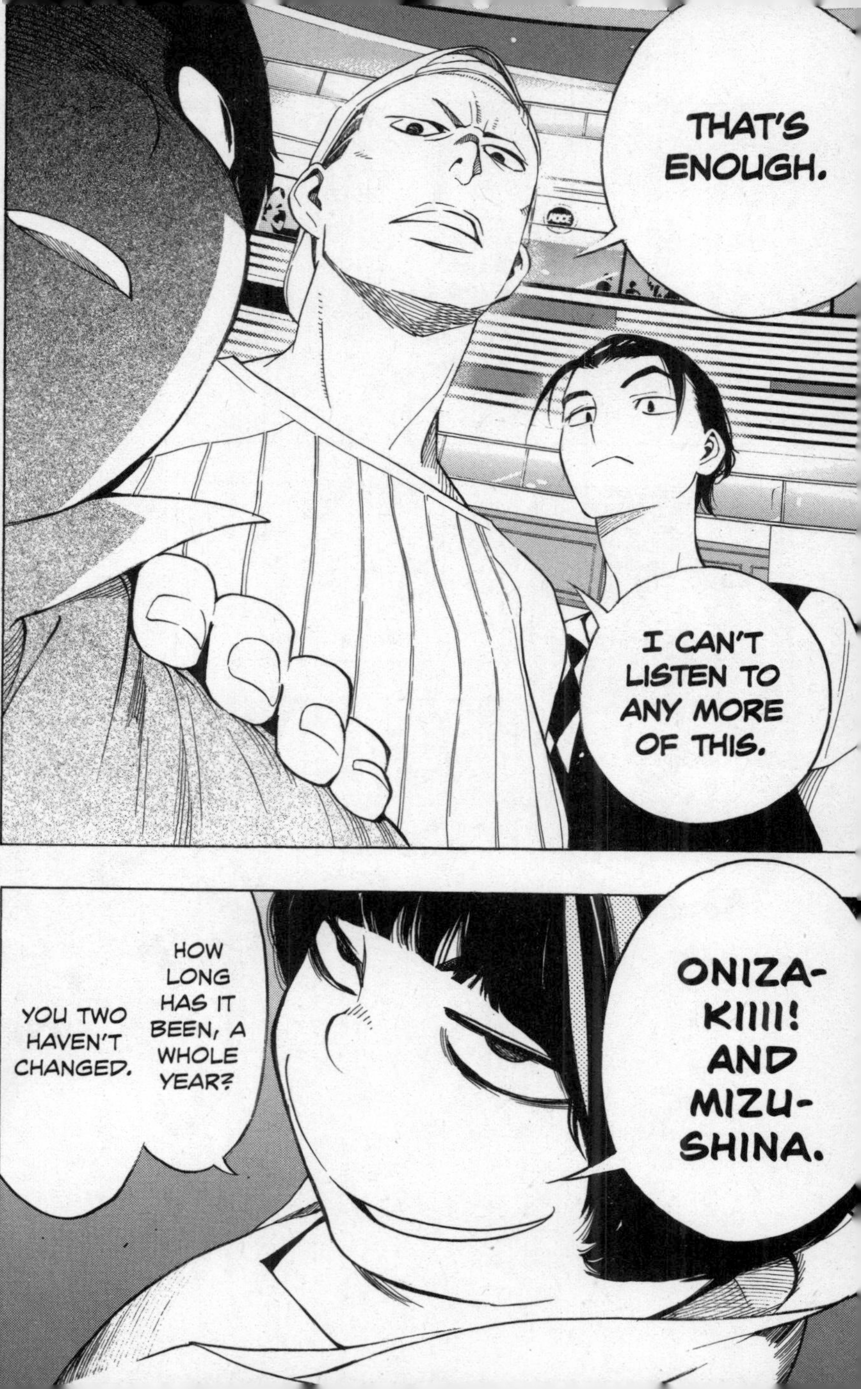
THAT'S ENOUGH.
I CAN'T LISTEN TO ANY MORE OF THIS.
ONIZA-KIIII! AND MIZU-SHINA.
HOW LONG HAS IT BEEN, A WHOLE YEAR?
YOU TWO HAVEN'T CHANGED.

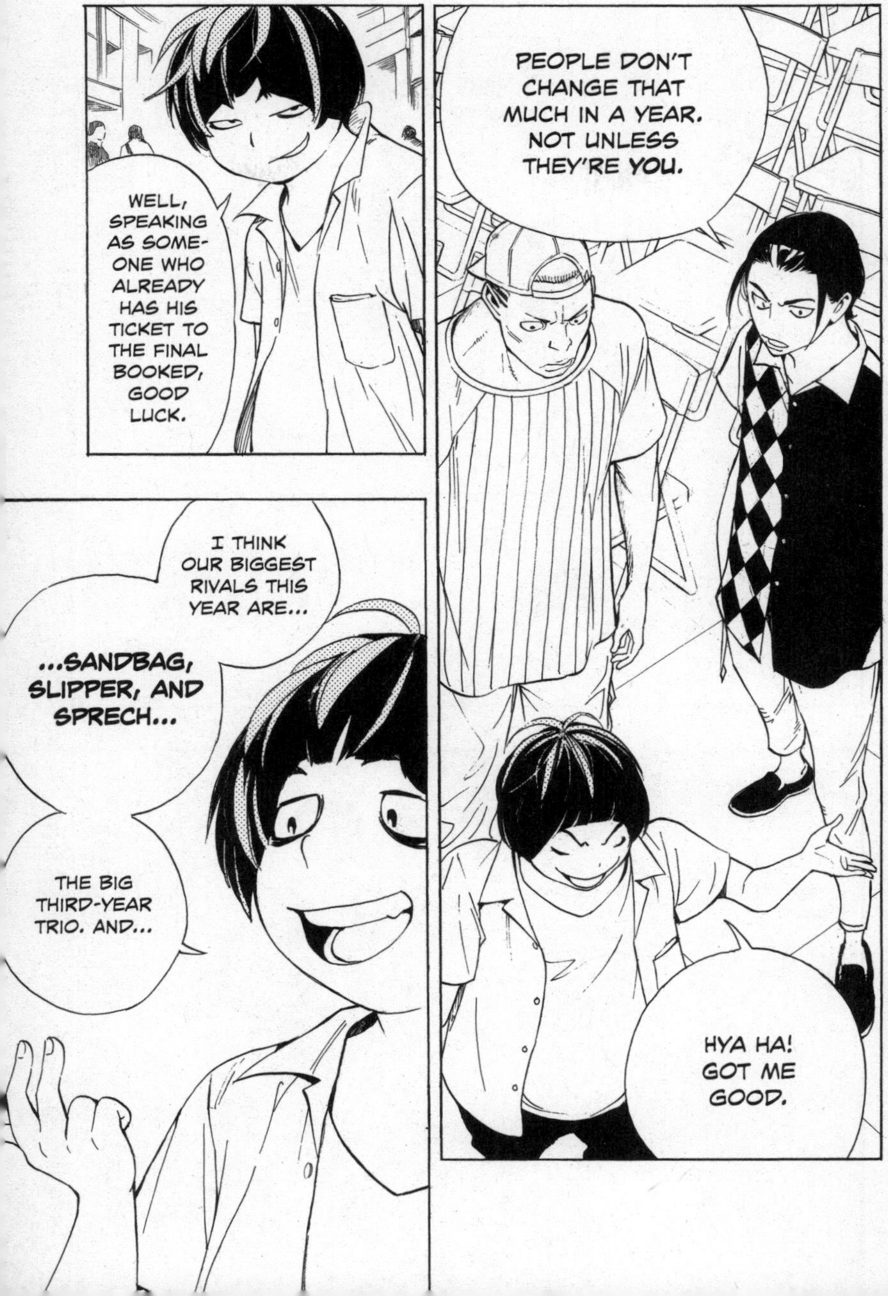
PEOPLE DON'T CHANGE THAT MUCH IN A YEAR. NOT UNLESS THEY'RE **YOU.**
HYA HA! GOT ME GOOD.
WELL, SPEAKING AS SOME-ONE WHO ALREADY HAS HIS TICKET TO THE FINAL BOOKED, GOOD LUCK.
I THINK OUR BIGGEST RIVALS THIS YEAR ARE...
...SANDBAG, SLIPPER, AND SPRECH...
THE BIG THIRD-YEAR TRIO. AND...

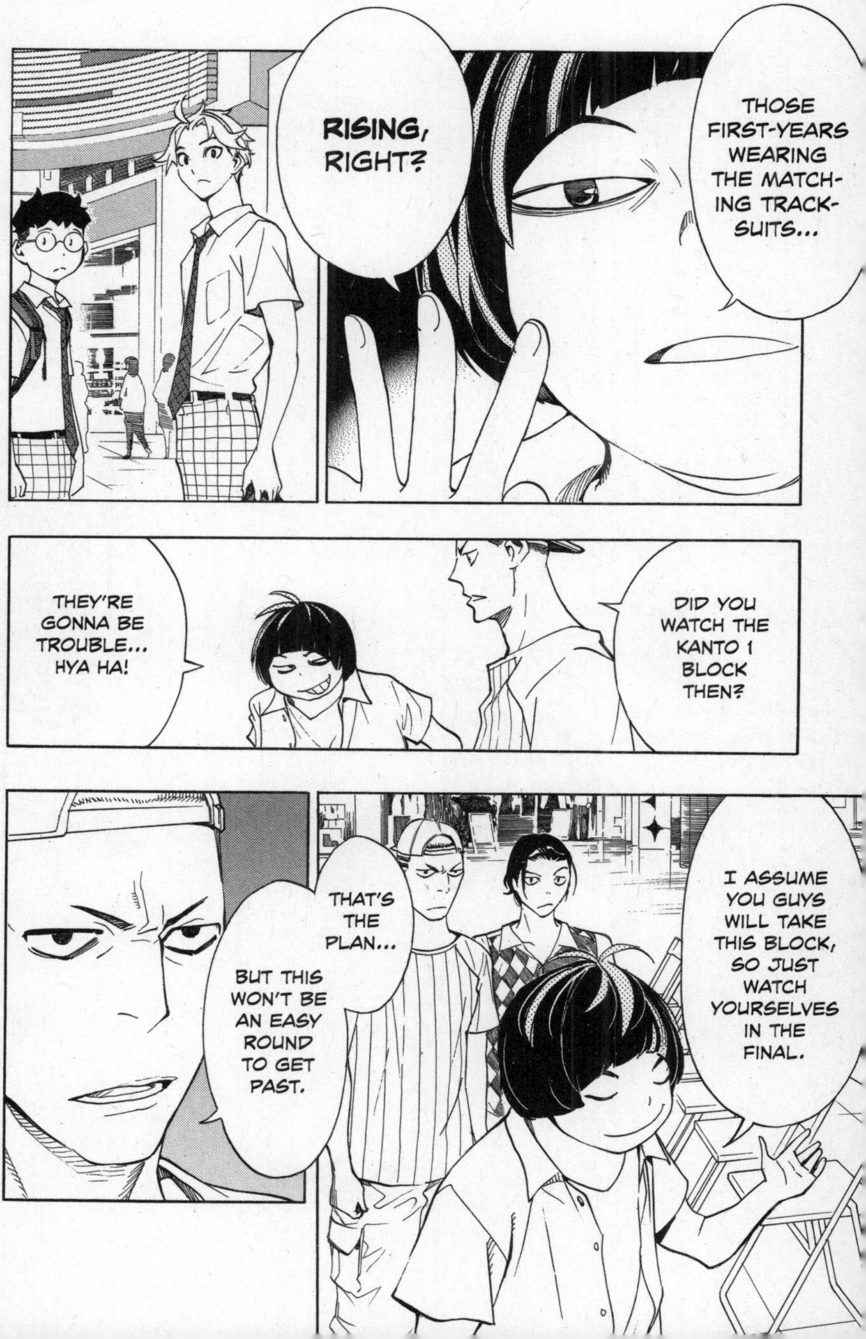
THOSE FIRST-YEARS WEARING THE MATCHING TRACKSUITS...
RISING, RIGHT?
DID YOU WATCH THE KANTO 1 BLOCK THEN?
THEY'RE GONNA BE TROUBLE... HYA HA!
I ASSUME YOU GUYS WILL TAKE THIS BLOCK, SO JUST WATCH YOURSELVES IN THE FINAL.
THAT'S THE PLAN...
BUT THIS WON'T BE AN EASY ROUND TO GET PAST.

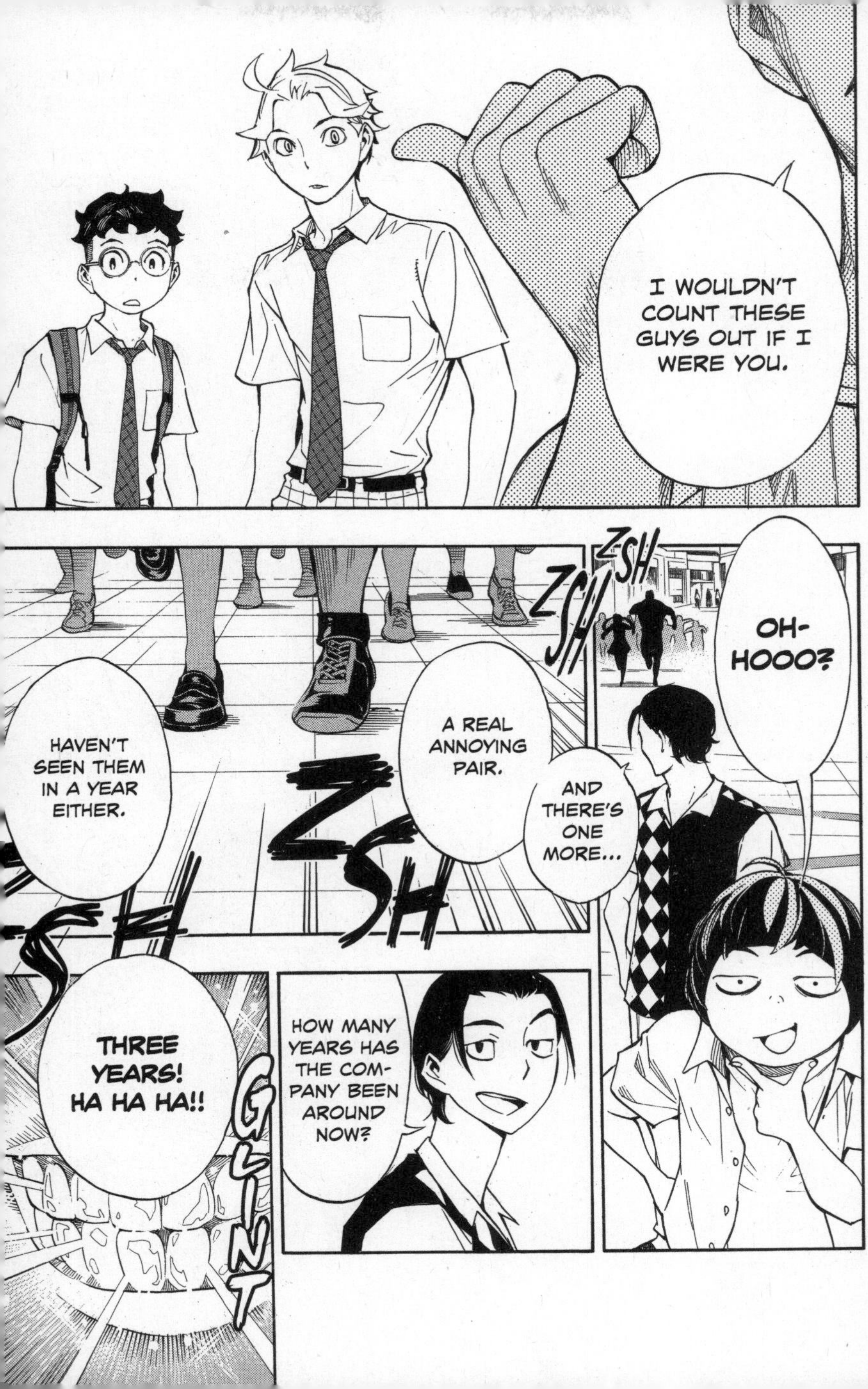
I WOULDN'T COUNT THESE GUYS OUT IF I WERE YOU.
OH-HOOO?
AND THERE'S ONE MORE...
ZSH ZSH
A REAL ANNOYING PAIR.
ZSH
HAVEN'T SEEN THEM IN A YEAR EITHER.
HOW MANY YEARS HAS THE COM-PANY BEEN AROUND NOW?
THREE YEARS! HA HA HA!!
GLINT

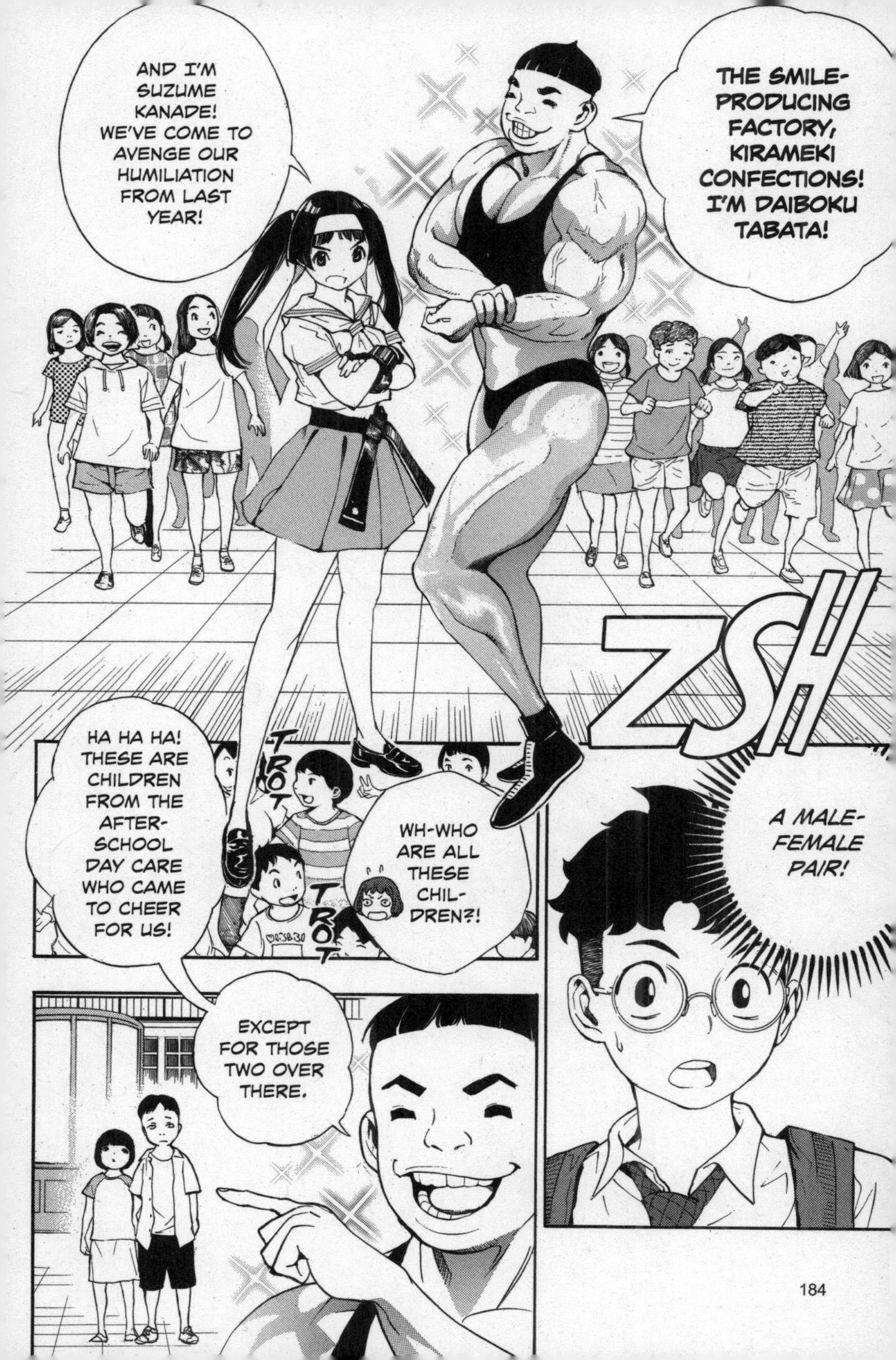
THE SMILE-PRODUCING FACTORY, KIRAMEKI CONFECTIONS! I'M DAIBOKU TABATA!
AND I'M SUZUME KANADE! WE'VE COME TO AVENGE OUR HUMILIATION FROM LAST YEAR!
ZSH
A MALE-FEMALE PAIR!
WH-WHO ARE ALL THESE CHIL-DREN?!
HA HA HA! THESE ARE CHILDREN FROM THE AFTER-SCHOOL DAY CARE WHO CAME TO CHEER FOR US!
TROT
TROT
EXCEPT FOR THOSE TWO OVER THERE.

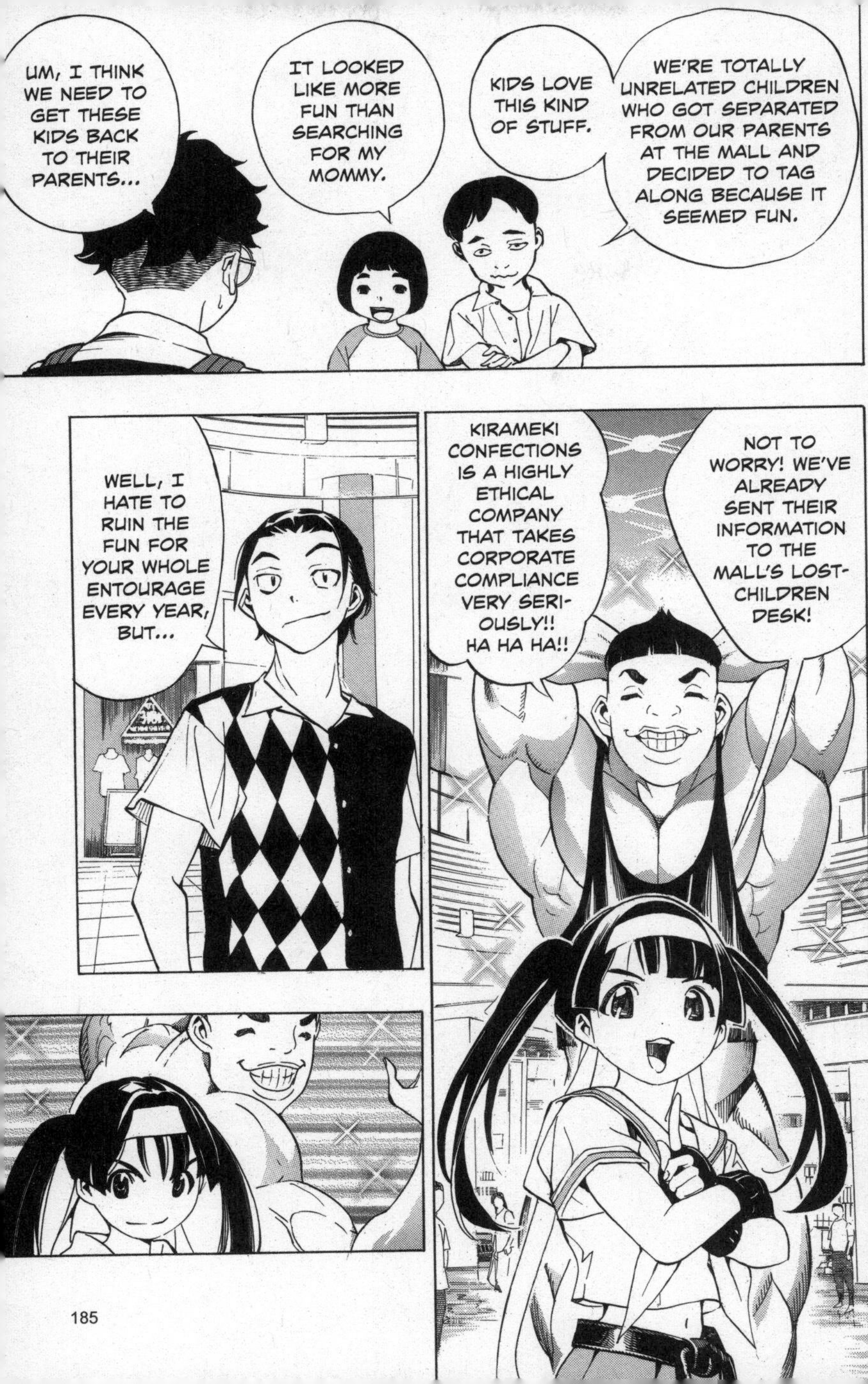
WE'RE TOTALLY UNRELATED CHILDREN WHO GOT SEPARATED FROM OUR PARENTS AT THE MALL AND DECIDED TO TAG ALONG BECAUSE IT SEEMED FUN.
KIDS LOVE THIS KIND OF STUFF.
IT LOOKED LIKE MORE FUN THAN SEARCHING FOR MY MOMMY.
UM, I THINK WE NEED TO GET THESE KIDS BACK TO THEIR PARENTS...
NOT TO WORRY! WE'VE ALREADY SENT THEIR INFORMATION TO THE MALL'S LOST-CHILDREN DESK!
KIRAMEKI CONFECTIONS IS A HIGHLY ETHICAL COMPANY THAT TAKES CORPORATE COMPLIANCE VERY SERIOUSLY!! HA HA HA!!
WELL, I HATE TO RUIN THE FUN FOR YOUR WHOLE ENTOURAGE EVERY YEAR, BUT...

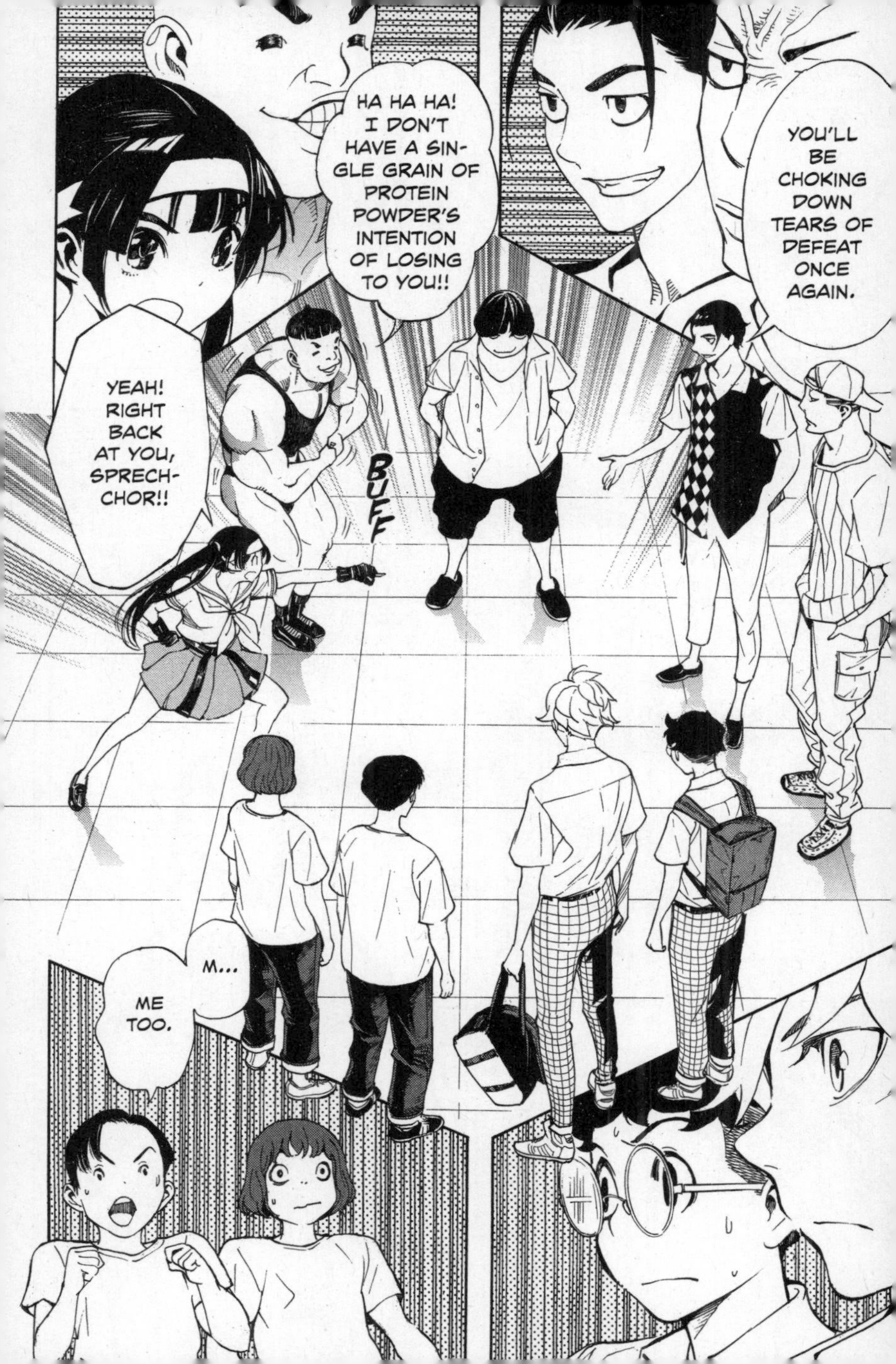
YOU'LL BE CHOKING DOWN TEARS OF DEFEAT ONCE AGAIN.
HA HA HA! I DON'T HAVE A SIN-GLE GRAIN OF PROTEIN POWDER'S INTENTION OF LOSING TO YOU!!
YEAH! RIGHT BACK AT YOU, SPRECH-CHOR!!
BUFF
M...
ME TOO.

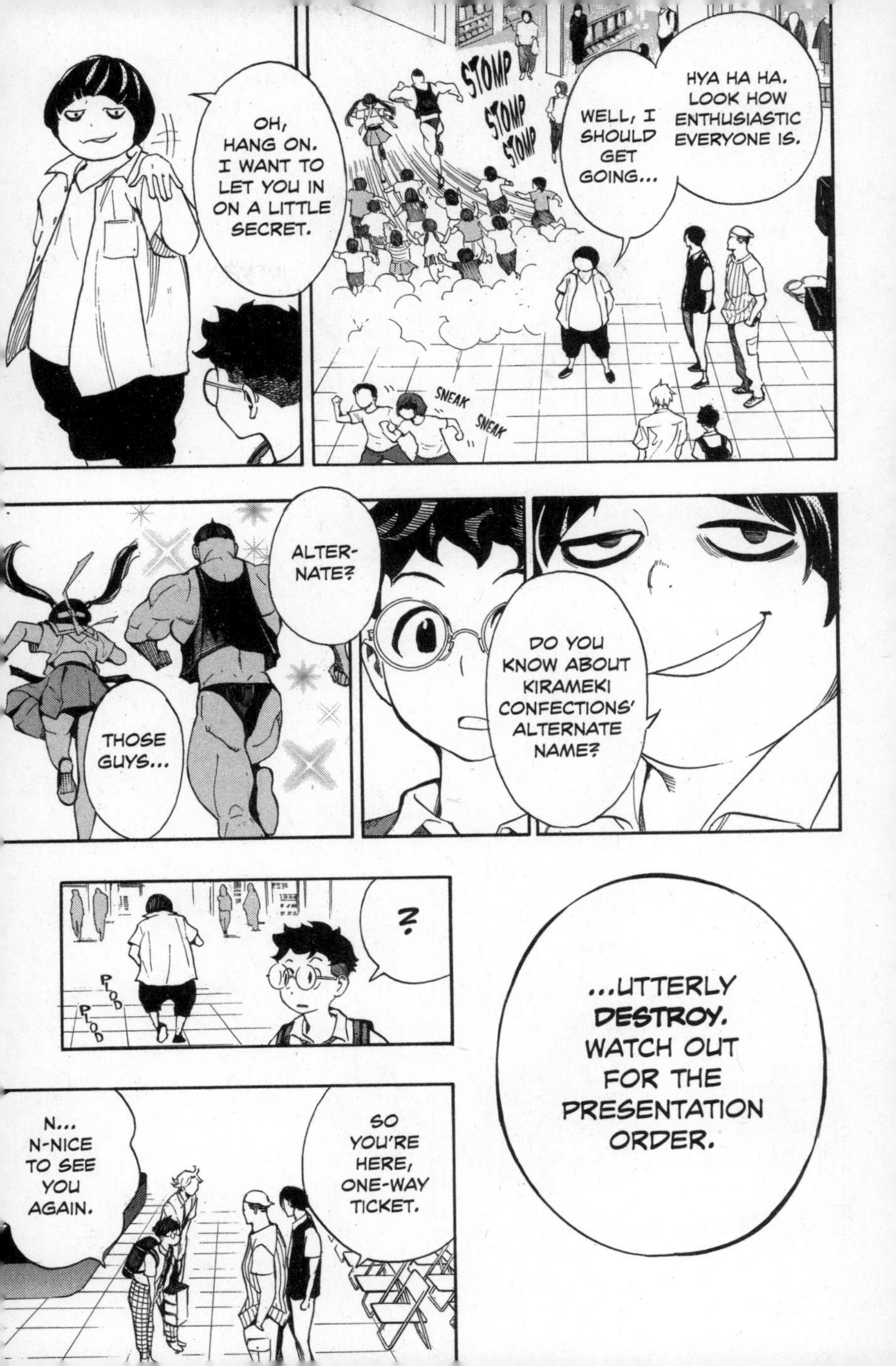
HYA HA HA. LOOK HOW ENTHUSIASTIC EVERYONE IS.
WELL, I SHOULD GET GOING...
STOMP
STOMP
STOMP
SNEAK
SNEAK
OH, HANG ON. I WANT TO LET YOU IN ON A LITTLE SECRET.
DO YOU KNOW ABOUT KIRAMEKI CONFECTIONS' ALTERNATE NAME?
ALTER-NATE?
THOSE GUYS...
...UTTERLY DESTROY. WATCH OUT FOR THE PRESENTATION ORDER.
?
PLOD
PLOD
SO YOU'RE HERE, ONE-WAY TICKET.
N... N-NICE TO SEE YOU AGAIN.

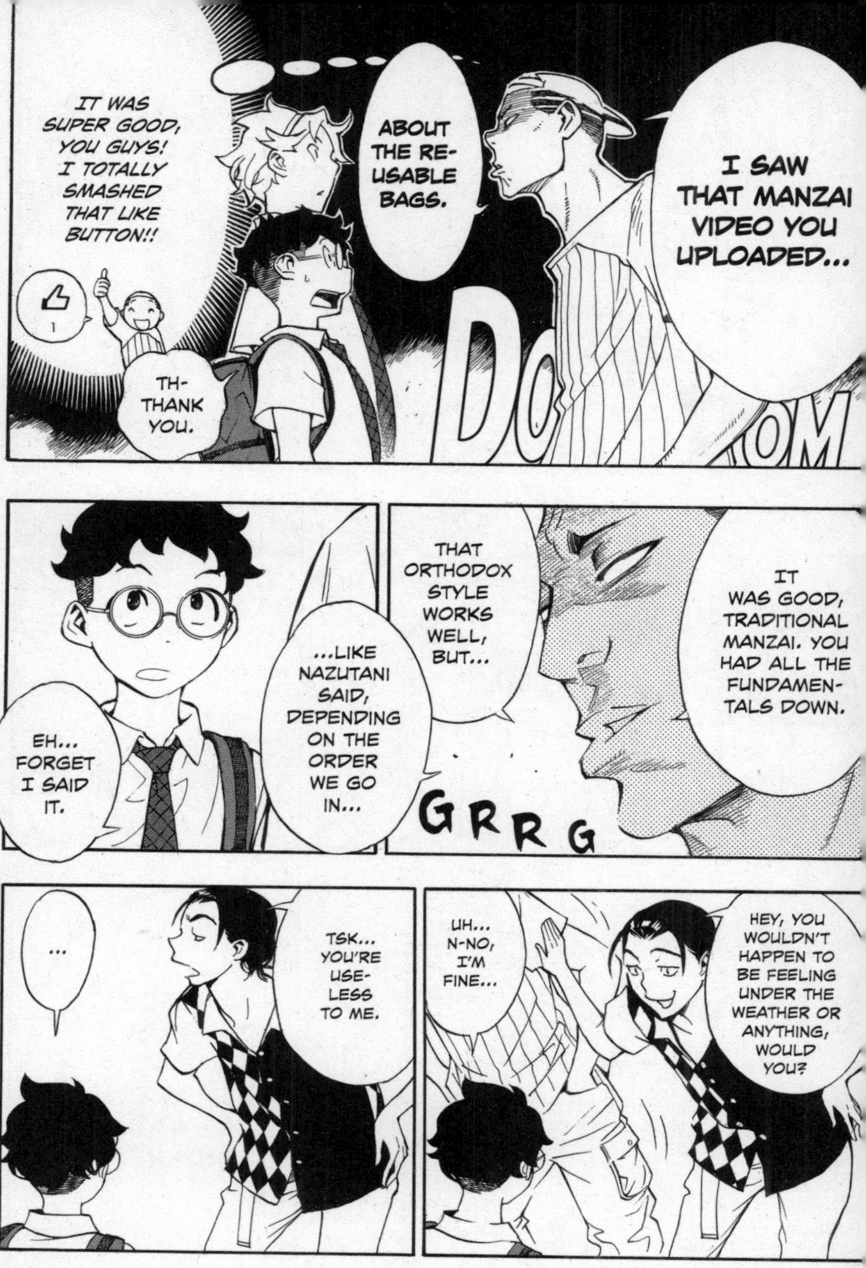
I SAW THAT MANZAI VIDEO YOU UPLOADED...
ABOUT THE RE-USABLE BAGS.
IT WAS SUPER GOOD, YOU GUYS! I TOTALLY SMASHED THAT LIKE BUTTON!!
1
TH-THANK YOU.
IT WAS GOOD, TRADITIONAL MANZAI. YOU HAD ALL THE FUNDAMENTALS DOWN.
THAT ORTHODOX STYLE WORKS WELL, BUT...
GRRG
...LIKE NAZUTANI SAID, DEPENDING ON THE ORDER WE GO IN...
EH... FORGET I SAID IT.
HEY, YOU WOULDN'T HAPPEN TO BE FEELING UNDER THE WEATHER OR ANYTHING, WOULD YOU?
UH... N-NO, I'M FINE...
TSK... YOU'RE USELESS TO ME.
...

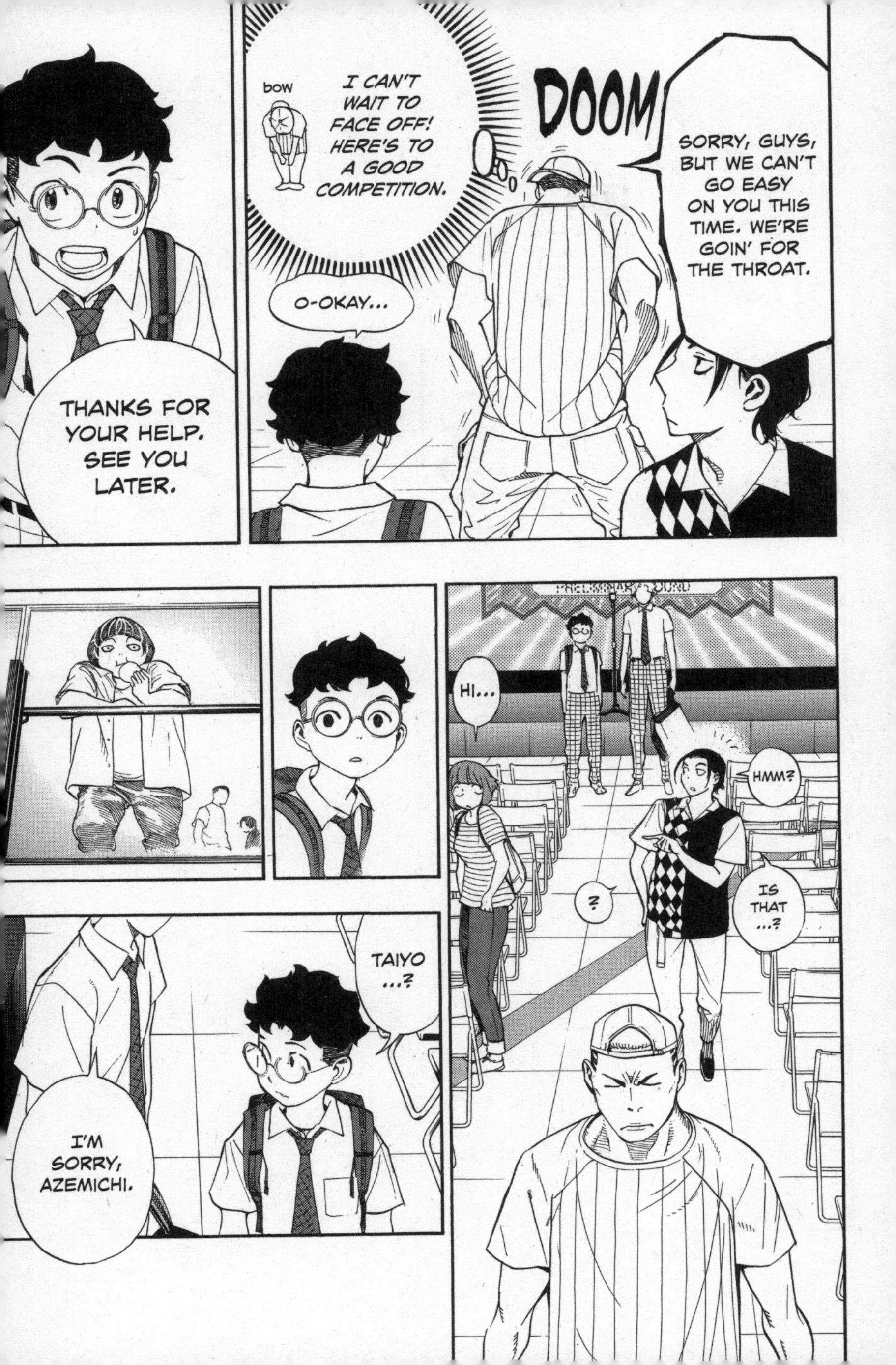
SORRY, GUYS, BUT WE CAN'T GO EASY ON YOU THIS TIME. WE'RE GOIN' FOR THE THROAT.
DOOM
I CAN'T WAIT TO FACE OFF! HERE'S TO A GOOD COMPETITION.
bow
O-OKAY...
THANKS FOR YOUR HELP. SEE YOU LATER.
HI...
HMM?
IS THAT ...?
?
TAIYO ...?
I'M SORRY, AZEMICHI.

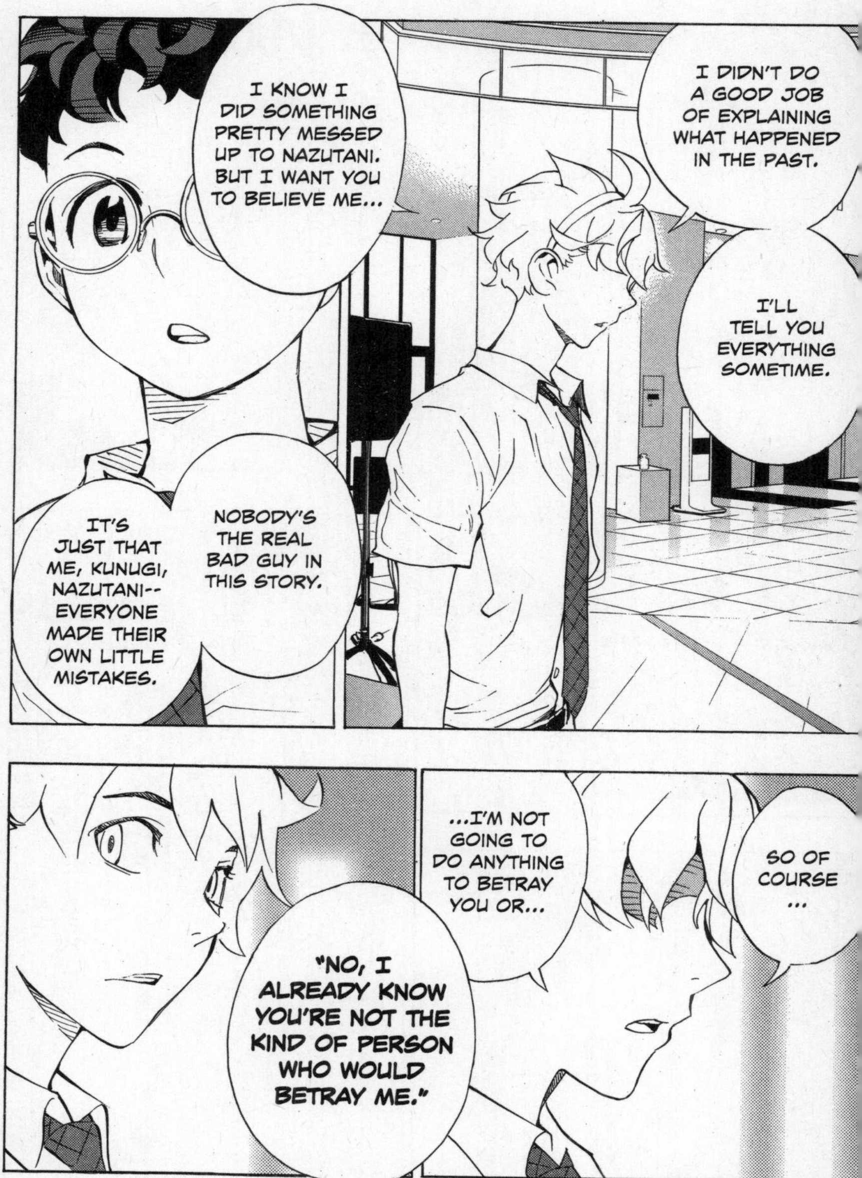
I DIDN'T DO A GOOD JOB OF EXPLAINING WHAT HAPPENED IN THE PAST.
I'LL TELL YOU EVERYTHING SOMETIME.
I KNOW I DID SOMETHING PRETTY MESSED UP TO NAZUTANI. BUT I WANT YOU TO BELIEVE ME...
NOBODY'S THE REAL BAD GUY IN THIS STORY.
IT'S JUST THAT ME, KUNUGI, NAZUTANI-- EVERYONE MADE THEIR OWN LITTLE MISTAKES.
SO OF COURSE ...
...I'M NOT GOING TO DO ANYTHING TO BETRAY YOU OR...
"NO, I ALREADY KNOW YOU'RE NOT THE KIND OF PERSON WHO WOULD BETRAY ME."

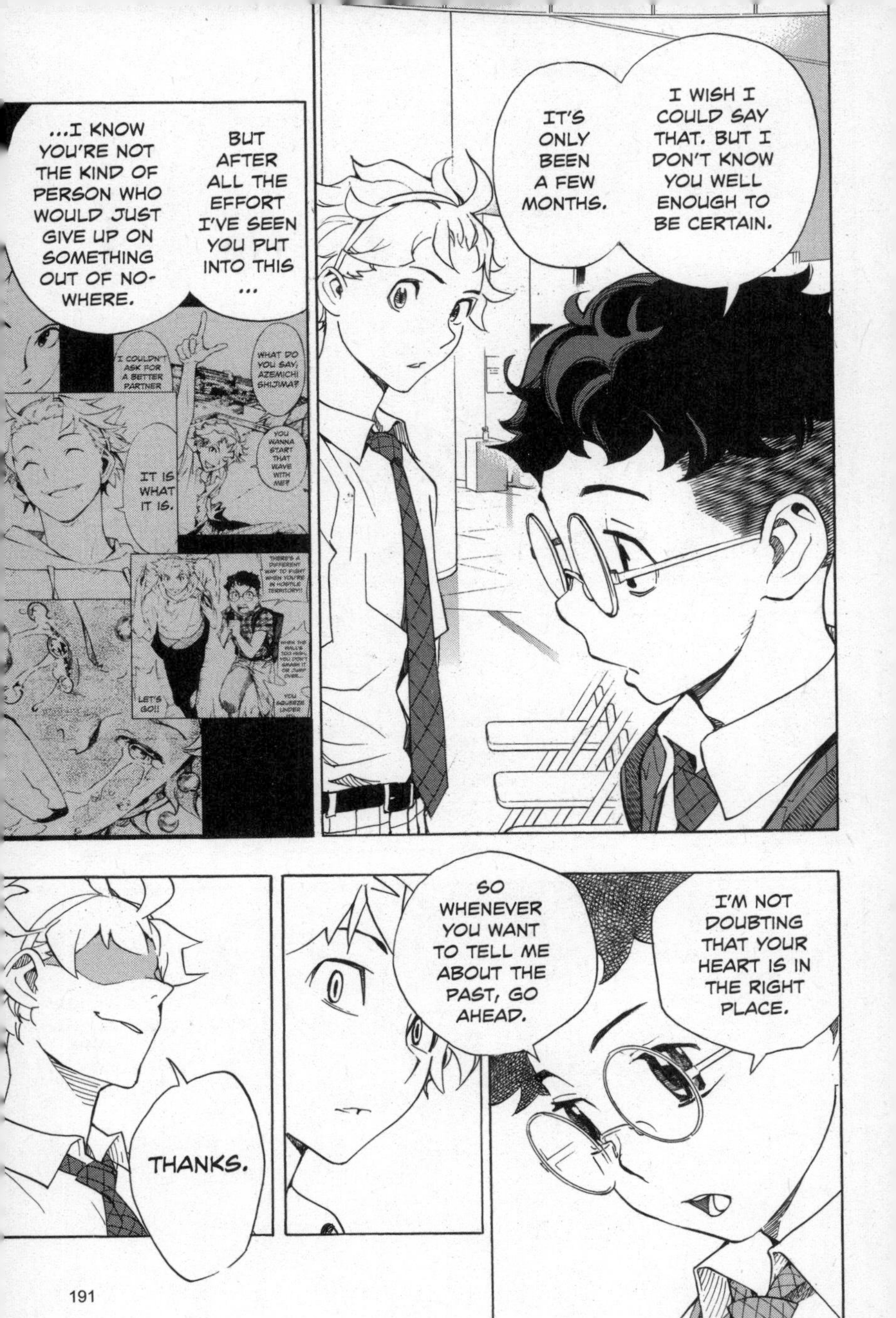
I WISH I COULD SAY THAT. BUT I DON'T KNOW YOU WELL ENOUGH TO BE CERTAIN.
IT'S ONLY BEEN A FEW MONTHS.
BUT AFTER ALL THE EFFORT I'VE SEEN YOU PUT INTO THIS ...
...I KNOW YOU'RE NOT THE KIND OF PERSON WHO WOULD JUST GIVE UP ON SOMETHING OUT OF NO-WHERE.
WHAT DO YOU SAY, AZEMICHI SHIJIMA?
YOU WANNA START THAT WAVE WITH ME?
I COULDN'T ASK FOR A BETTER PARTNER
IT IS WHAT IT IS.
THERE'S A DIFFERENT WAY TO FIGHT WHEN YOU'RE IN HOSTILE TERRITORY!!
LET'S GO!!
I'M NOT DOUBTING THAT YOUR HEART IS IN THE RIGHT PLACE.
SO WHENEVER YOU WANT TO TELL ME ABOUT THE PAST, GO AHEAD.
THANKS.

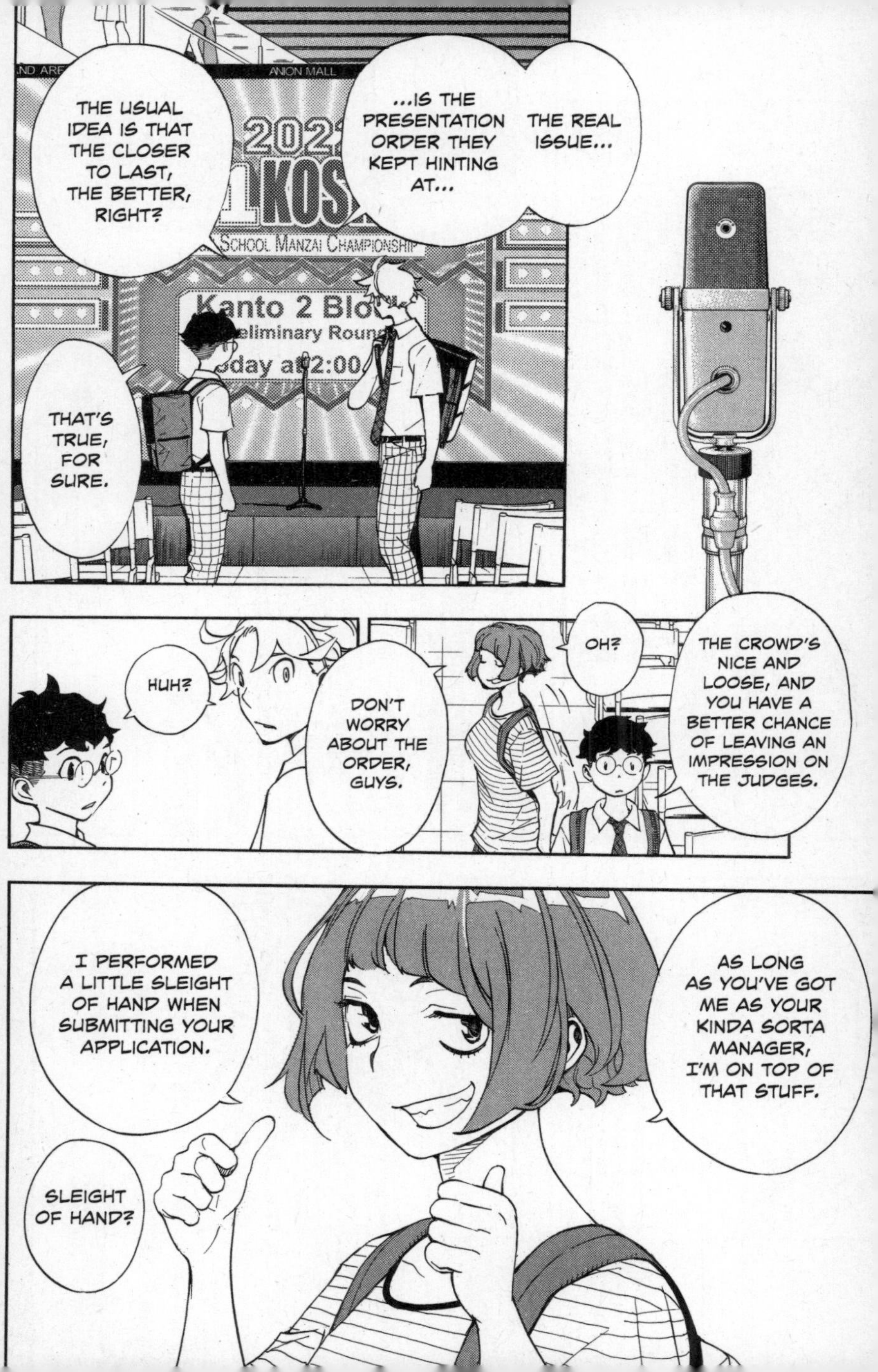
ANION MALL
SCHOOL MANZAI CHAMPIONSHIP
THE REAL ISSUE...
...IS THE PRESENTATION ORDER THEY KEPT HINTING AT...
THE USUAL IDEA IS THAT THE CLOSER TO LAST, THE BETTER, RIGHT?
THAT'S TRUE, FOR SURE.
THE CROWD'S NICE AND LOOSE, AND YOU HAVE A BETTER CHANCE OF LEAVING AN IMPRESSION ON THE JUDGES.
OH?
DON'T WORRY ABOUT THE ORDER, GUYS.
HUH?
AS LONG AS YOU'VE GOT ME AS YOUR KINDA SORTA MANAGER, I'M ON TOP OF THAT STUFF.
I PERFORMED A LITTLE SLEIGHT OF HAND WHEN SUBMITTING YOUR APPLICATION.
SLEIGHT OF HAND?

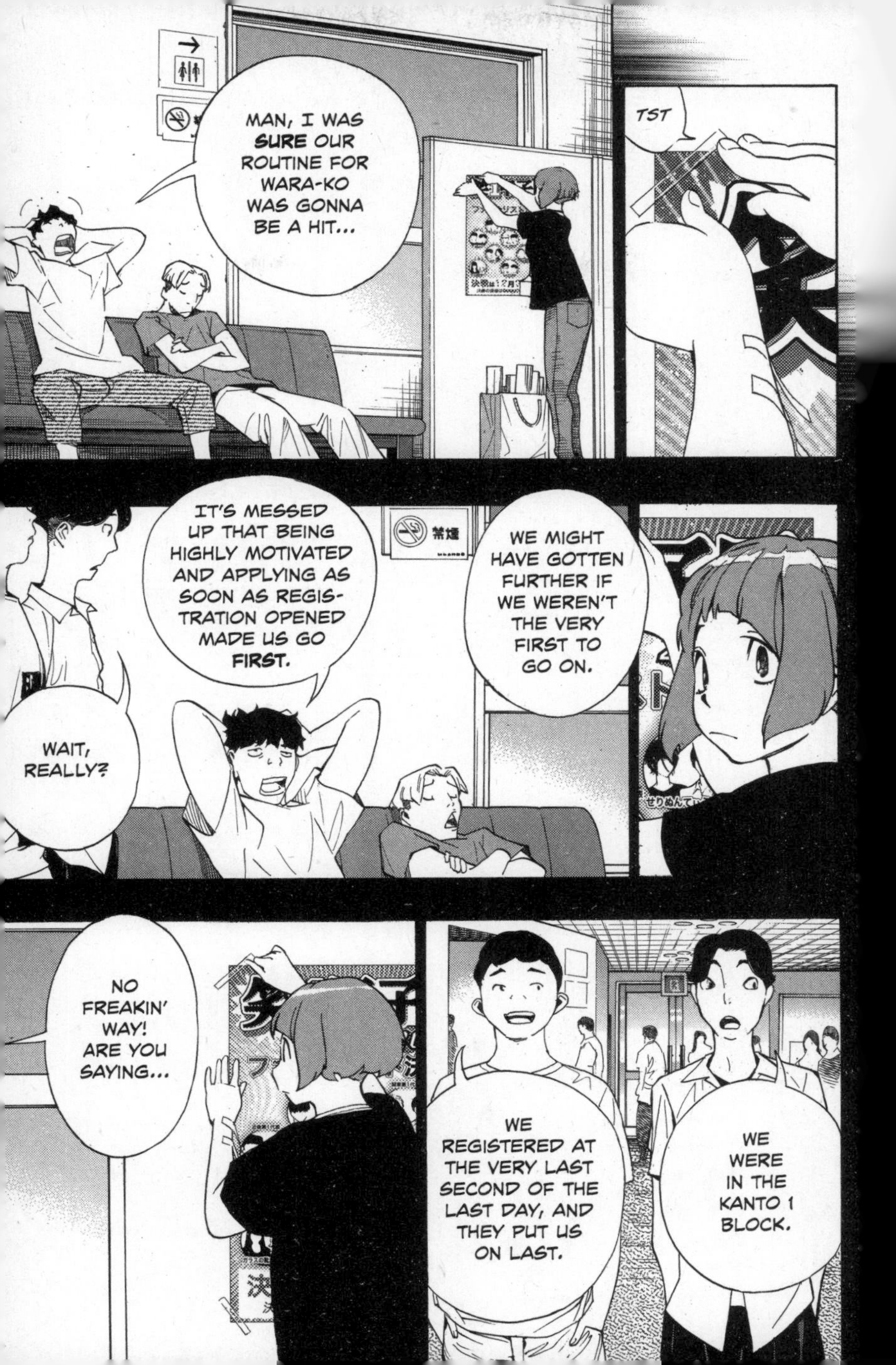
TST
MAN, I WAS SURE OUR ROUTINE FOR WARA-KO WAS GONNA BE A HIT...
禁煙
WE MIGHT HAVE GOTTEN FURTHER IF WE WEREN'T THE VERY FIRST TO GO ON.
IT'S MESSED UP THAT BEING HIGHLY MOTIVATED AND APPLYING AS SOON AS REGIS-TRATION OPENED MADE US GO FIRST.
WAIT, REALLY?
WE WERE IN THE KANTO 1 BLOCK.
WE REGISTERED AT THE VERY LAST SECOND OF THE LAST DAY, AND THEY PUT US ON LAST.
NO FREAKIN' WAY! ARE YOU SAYING...

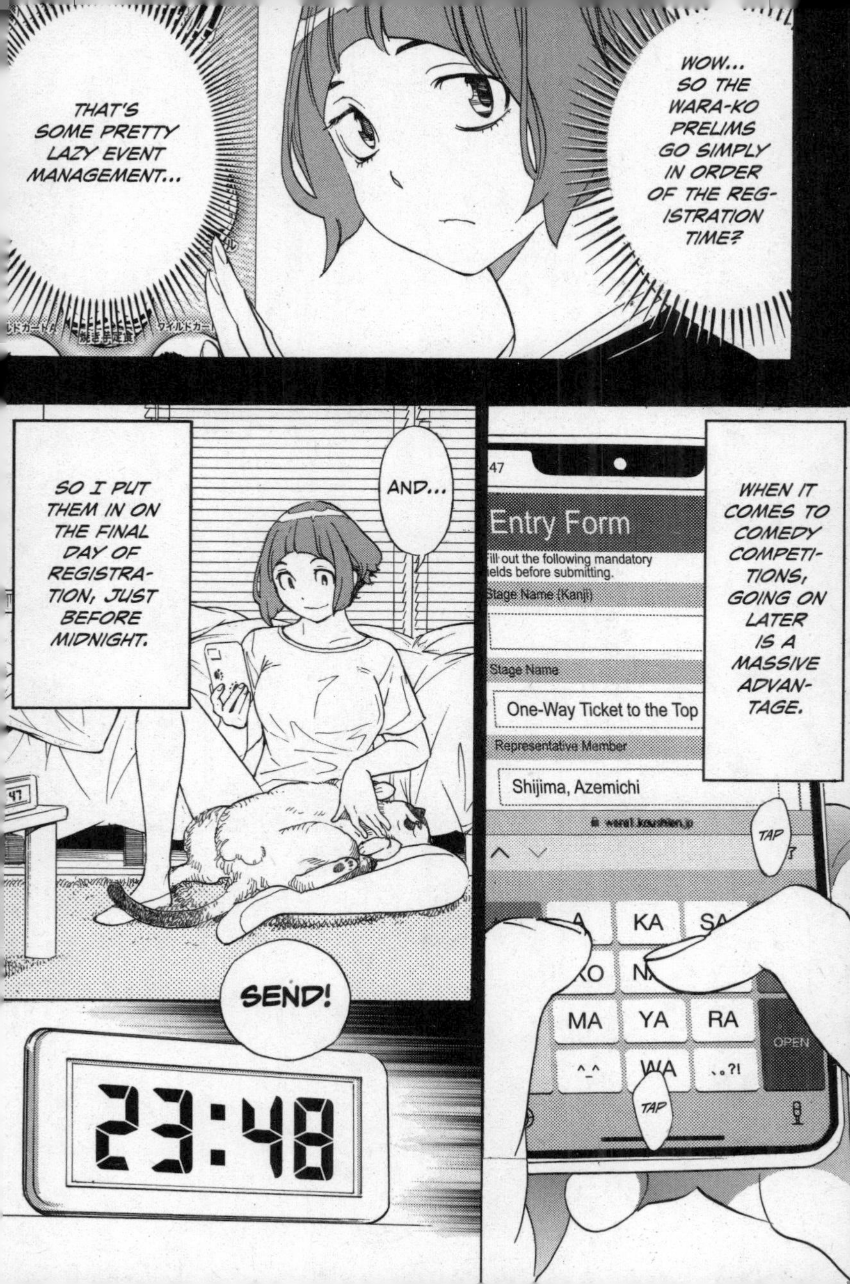

WOW... SO THE WARA-KO PRELIMS GO SIMPLY IN ORDER OF THE REGISTRATION TIME?
THAT'S SOME PRETTY LAZY EVENT MANAGEMENT...
WHEN IT COMES TO COMEDY COMPETITIONS, GOING ON LATER IS A MASSIVE ADVANTAGE.
Entry Form
Fill out the following mandatory fields before submitting.
Stage Name (Kanji)
Stage Name
One-Way Ticket to the Top
Representative Member
Shijima, Azemichi
TAP
A KA SA
KO NA
MA YA RA
OPEN
^_^ WA 、。?!
TAP
SO I PUT THEM IN ON THE FINAL DAY OF REGISTRATION, JUST BEFORE MIDNIGHT.
AND...
SEND!
23:48

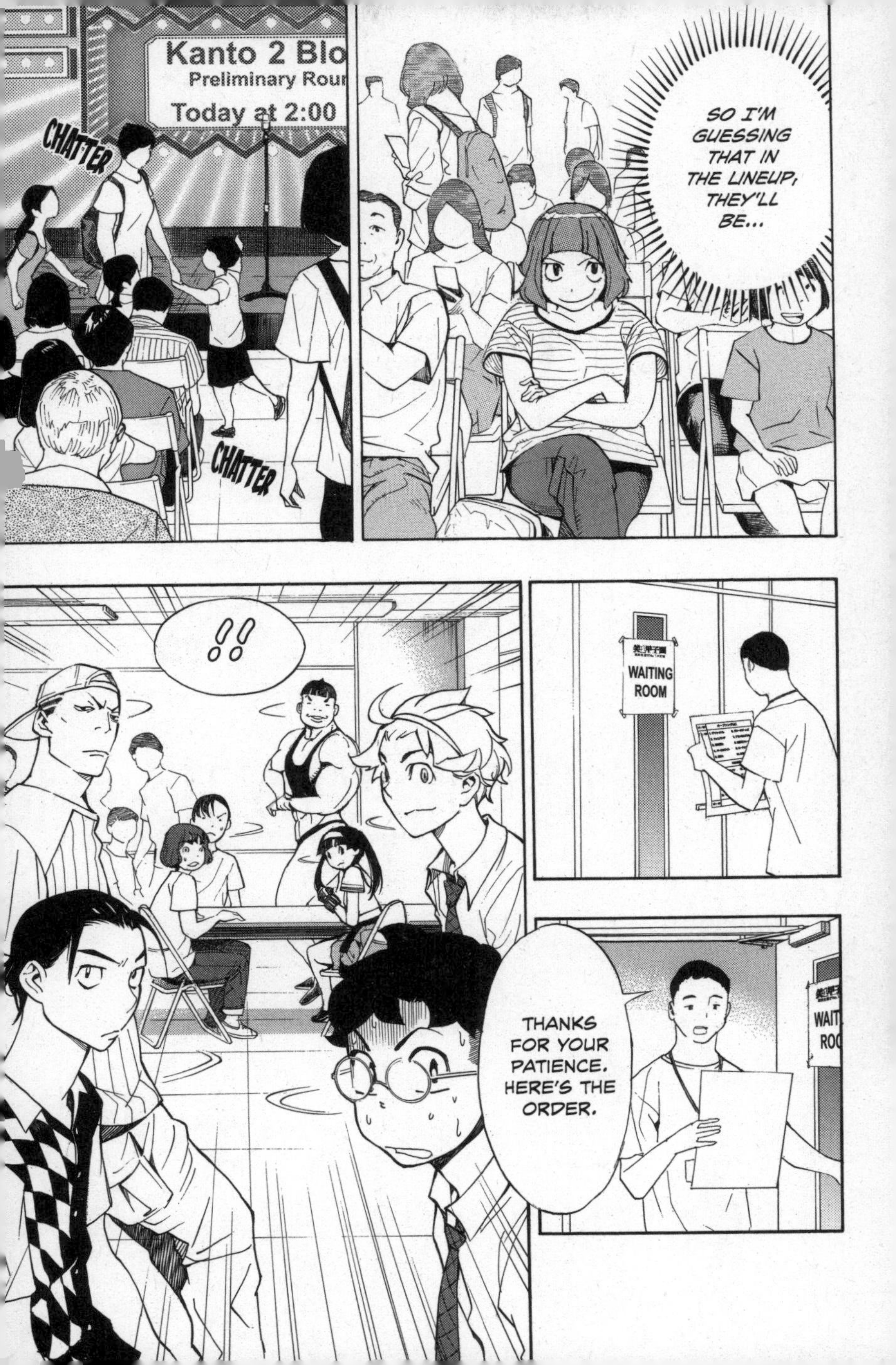
SO I'M GUESSING THAT IN THE LINEUP, THEY'LL BE...
Kanto 2 Blo
Preliminary Rour
Today at 2:00
CHATTER
CHATTER
WAITING ROOM
THANKS FOR YOUR PATIENCE. HERE'S THE ORDER.
WAIT
ROO
!!

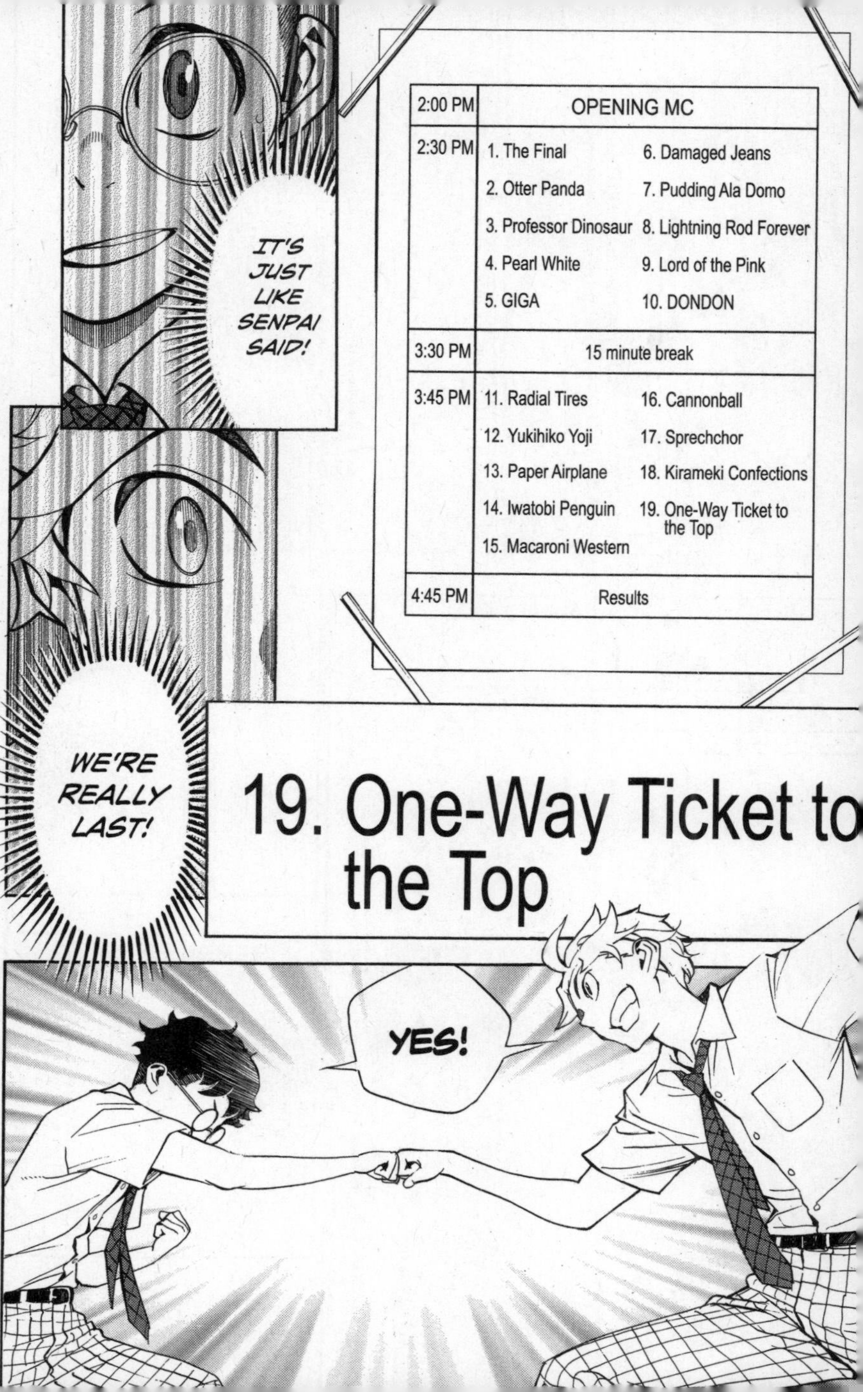
2:00 PM OPENING MC
2:30 PM 1. The Final 2. Otter Panda 3. Professor Dinosaur 4. Pearl White 5. GIGA 6. Damaged Jeans 7. Pudding Ala Domo 8. Lightning Rod Forever 9. Lord of the Pink 10. DONDON
3:30 PM 15 minute break
3:45 PM 11. Radial Tires 12. Yukihiko Yoji 13. Paper Airplane 14. Iwatobi Penguin 15. Macaroni Western 16. Cannonball 17. Sprechchor 18. Kirameki Confections 19. One-Way Ticket to the Top
4:45 PM Results
19. One-Way Ticket to the Top
IT'S JUST LIKE SENPAI SAID!
WE'RE REALLY LAST!
YES!

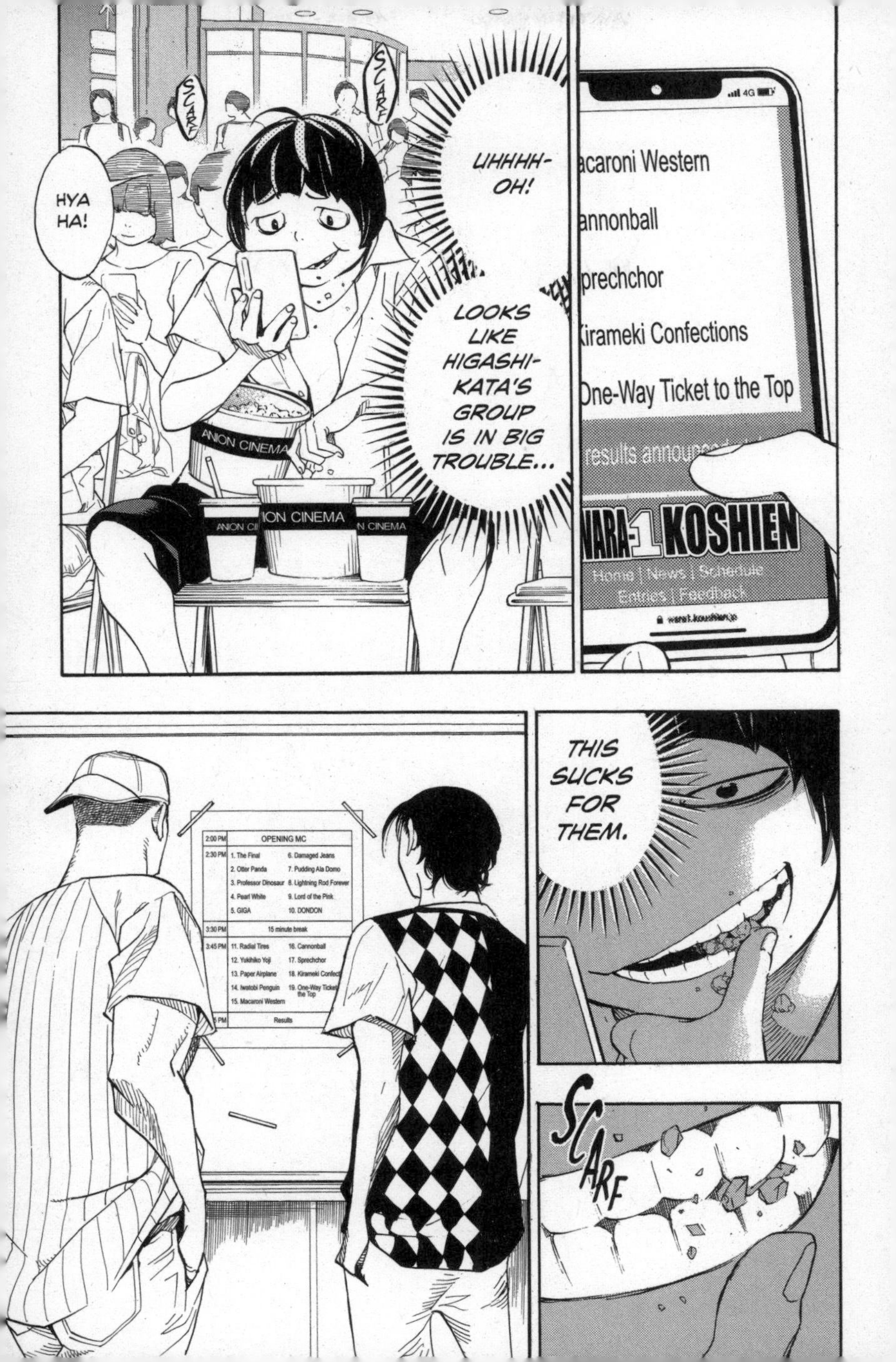
acaroni Western
annonball
prechchor
irameki Confections
One-Way Ticket to the Top
results announce
NARA-1 KOSHIEN
Home | News | Schedule
Entries | Feedback
UHHHH-OH!
LOOKS LIKE HIGASHI-KATA'S GROUP IS IN BIG TROUBLE...
SCARF
SCARF
HYA HA!
ANION CINEMA
ANION CINEMA
ANION CI
ANION CINEMA
THIS SUCKS FOR THEM.
SCARF
2:00 PM OPENING MC
2:30 PM 1. The Final 6. Damaged Jeans
2. Otter Panda 7. Pudding Ala Domo
3. Professor Dinosaur 8. Lightning Rod Forever
4. Pearl White 9. Lord of the Pink
5. GIGA 10. DONDON
3:30 PM 15 minute break
3:45 PM 11. Radial Tires 16. Cannonball
12. Yukihiko Yoji 17. Sprechchor
13. Paper Airplane 18. Kirameki Confect
14. Iwatobi Penguin 19. One-Way Ticket the Top
15. Macaroni Western
PM Results

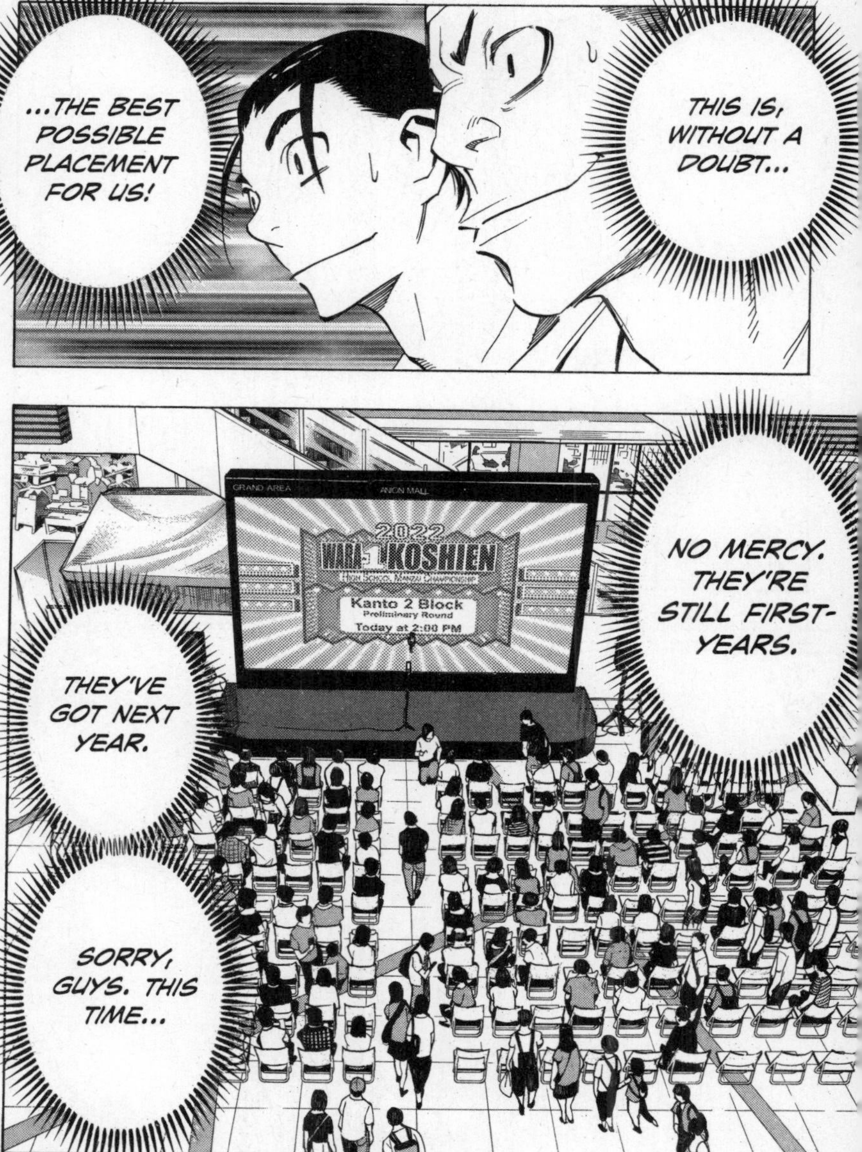
THIS IS, WITHOUT A DOUBT...
...THE BEST POSSIBLE PLACEMENT FOR US!
GRAND AREA
ANION MALL
2022
WARA-1 KOSHIEN
HIGH SCHOOL MANZAI CHAMPIONSHIP
Kanto 2 Block
Preliminary Round
Today at 2:00 PM
NO MERCY. THEY'RE STILL FIRST-YEARS.
THEY'VE GOT NEXT YEAR.
SORRY, GUYS. THIS TIME...

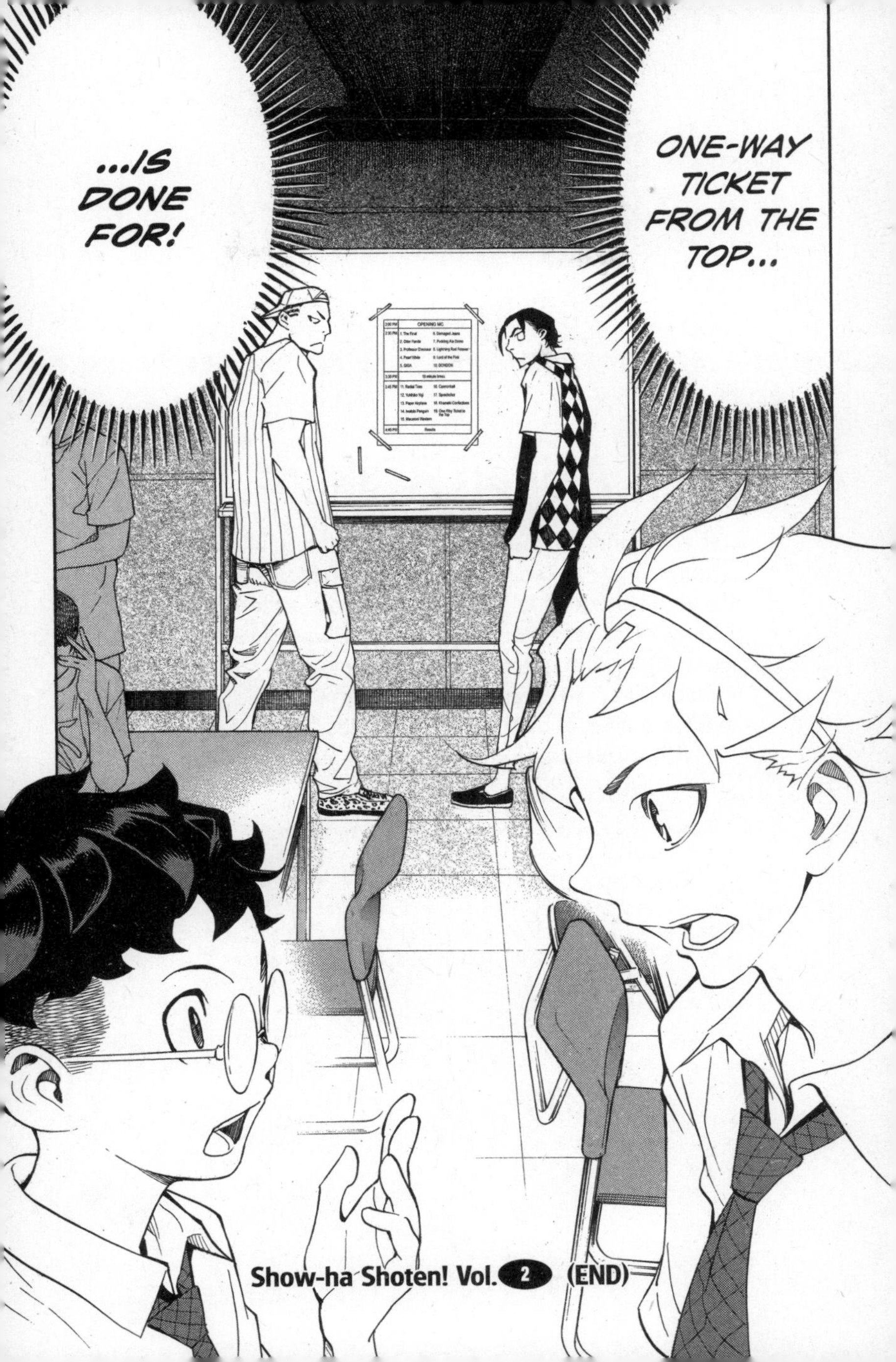
ONE-WAY TICKET FROM THE TOP...
...IS DONE FOR!
Show-ha Shoten! Vol. 2 (END)

About the Writer

Akinari Asakura

I was thinking, half-jokingly, of coming up with a numerical "battle value" for the characters, but it made me think of an old comedy show called *Bakusho On-Air Battle*. That show was a brilliant example of quantifying the amount of laughter a joke received in "kilobattles." I remember hearing the phrase, "A joke with a power of over 500 kilobattles," and trembling with the thought, "M-my god, it's a monster..."

Akinari Asakura is a novelist whose previous works include the mysteries *Ore de wa nai Enjou* (I'm Not the One Being Flamed), *Kyoushitsu ga, Hitori ni naru made* (Until I'm Alone in the Classroom), *Noir Revenant*, and the critically acclaimed *Rokunin no Usotsuki na Daigakusei* (Six Lying College Students). This is his first full-length work as a manga writer.

About the Artist

Takeshi Obata

When I'm typing out the dialogue for the manga, I get annoyed with how many mistakes I make, using the wrong kanji or missing kanji altogether. But Asakura Sensei's original storyboards have no mistakes at all in the text. And there's so much text! It's astonishing. It's enough to make you secretly hope you'll spot a mistake someday, but I don't. I never do.

Takeshi Obata was born in 1969 in Niigata, Japan, and first achieved international recognition as the artist of the wildly popular Shonen Jump title *Hikaru no Go*, which won the 2003 Tezuka Osamu Cultural Prize: Shinsei "New Hope" Award and the 2000 Shogakukan Manga Award. He went on to illustrate the smash hit *Death Note* as well as the hugely successful manga *Bakuman。* and *All You Need Is Kill*.

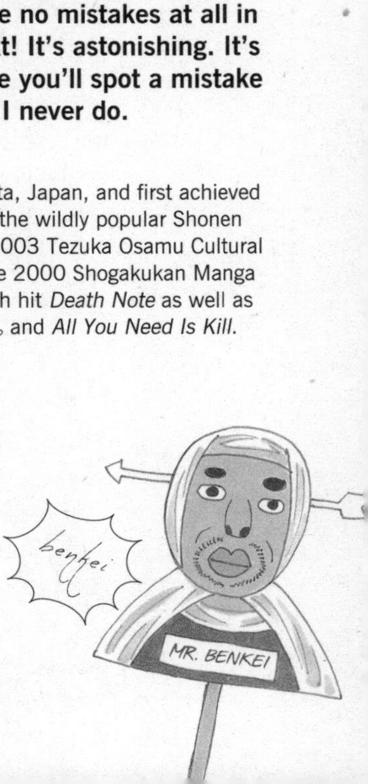
benkei
MR. BENKEI

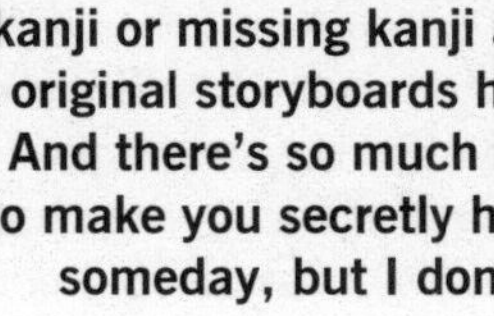
scissors

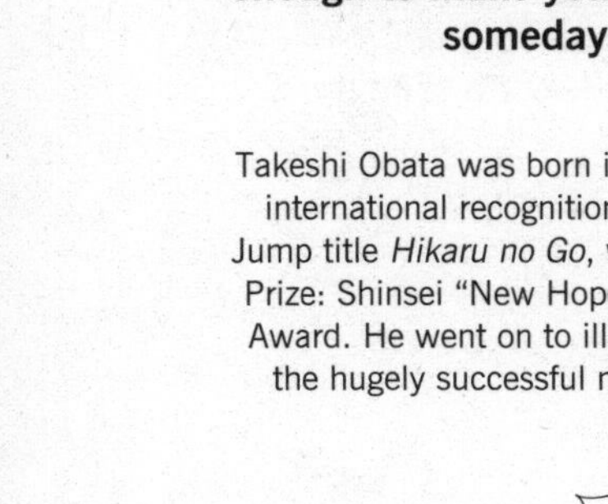
cat

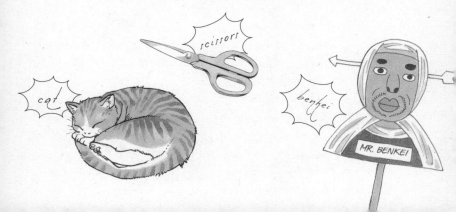

SHOW-HA SHOTEN!

Volume 2
SHONEN JUMP Edition

**STORY BY AKINARI ASAKURA
ART BY TAKESHI OBATA**

Translation / **Stephen Paul**
Touch-Up Art & Lettering / **James Gaubatz**
Designer / **Kam Li**
Shonen Jump Editor / **Alexis Kirsch**
Graphic Novel Editor / **Holly Fisher**

Printed in the U.S.A.

Published by VIZ Media, LLC
P.O. Box 77010
San Francisco, CA 94107

10 9 8 7 6 5 4 3 2 1
First printing, May 2023

VIZ MEDIA
VIZ.COM

SHONEN JUMP

Kuroko's BASKETBALL

TADATOSHI FUJIMAKI

When incoming first-year student Taiga Kagami joins the Seirin High basketball team, he meets Tetsuya Kuroko, a mysterious boy who's plain beyond words. But Kagami's in for the shock of his life when he learns that the practically invisible Kuroko was once a member of "the Miracle Generation"—the undefeated legendary team—and he wants Kagami's help taking down each of his old teammates!

SHOYO HINATA IS OUT TO PROVE THAT IN VOLLEYBALL YOU DON'T NEED TO BE TALL TO FLY!

HAIKYU!!

Story and Art by **HARUICHI FURUDATE**

Ever since he saw the legendary player known as the "Little Giant" compete at the national volleyball finals, Shoyo Hinata has been aiming to be the best volleyball player ever! He decides to join the team at the high school the Little Giant went to—and then surpass him. Who says you need to be tall to play volleyball when you can jump higher than anyone else?

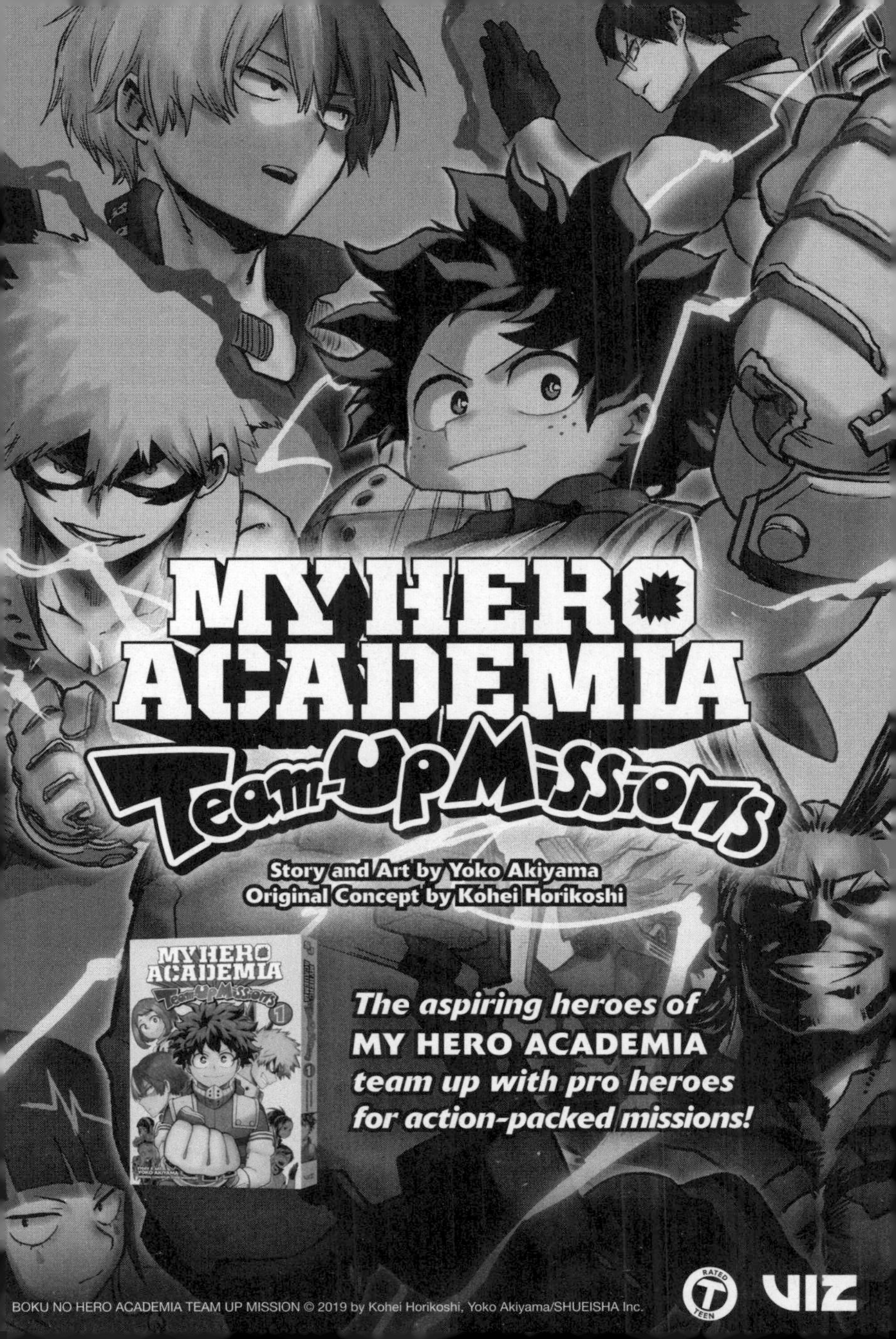

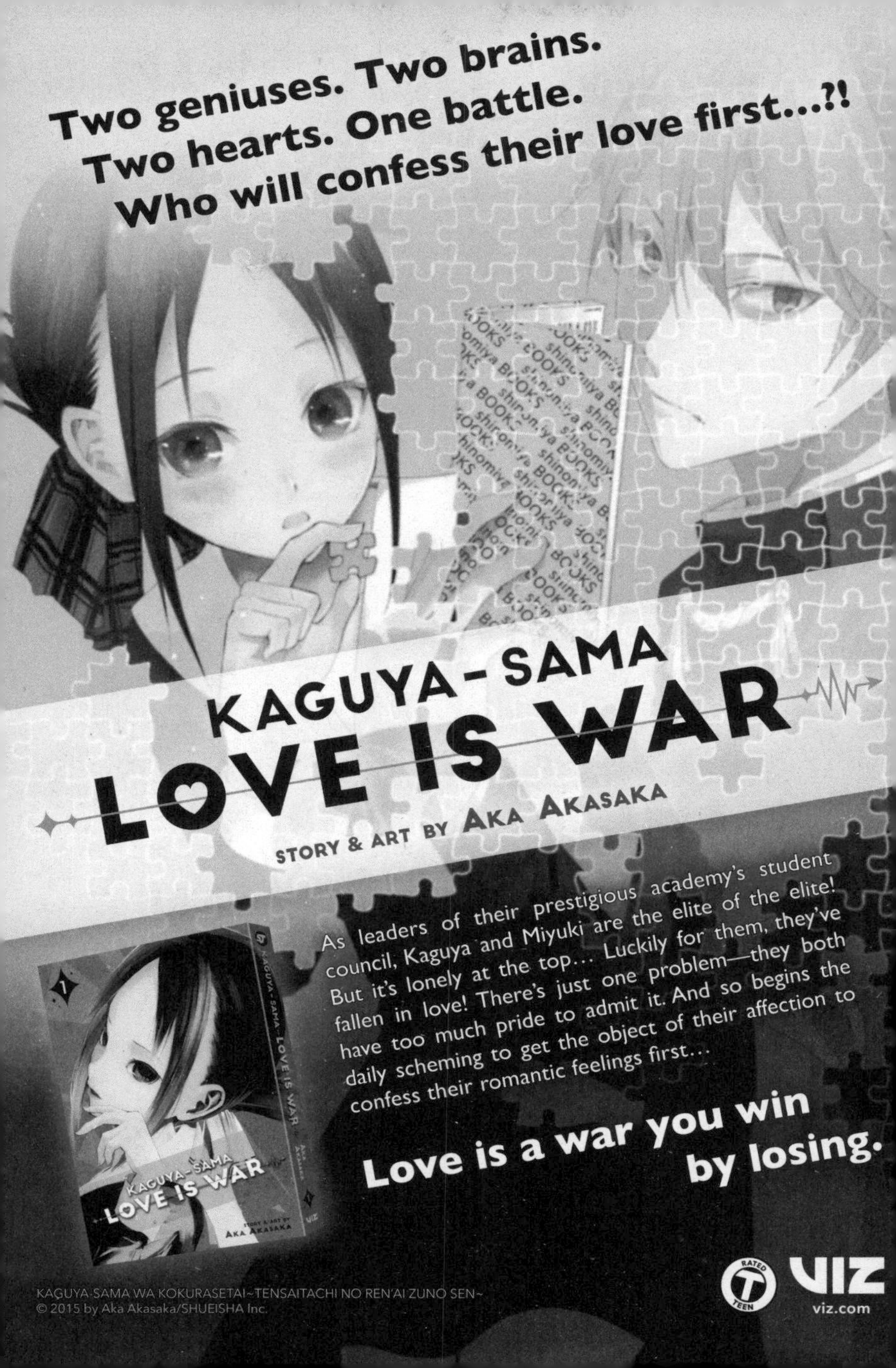
Two geniuses. Two brains.
Two hearts. One battle.
Who will confess their love first...?!
KAGUYA-SAMA
LOVE IS WAR
STORY & ART BY AKA AKASAKA
As leaders of their prestigious academy's student council, Kaguya and Miyuki are the elite of the elite! But it's lonely at the top… Luckily for them, they've fallen in love! There's just one problem—they both have too much pride to admit it. And so begins the daily scheming to get the object of their affection to confess their romantic feelings first…
Love is a war you win by losing.
1
KAGUYA-SAMA LOVE IS WAR
STORY & ART BY AKA AKASAKA
RATED T TEEN
VIZ
viz.com
KAGUYA-SAMA WA KOKURASETAI~TENSAITACHI NO REN'AI ZUNO SEN~
© 2015 by Aka Akasaka/SHUEISHA Inc.

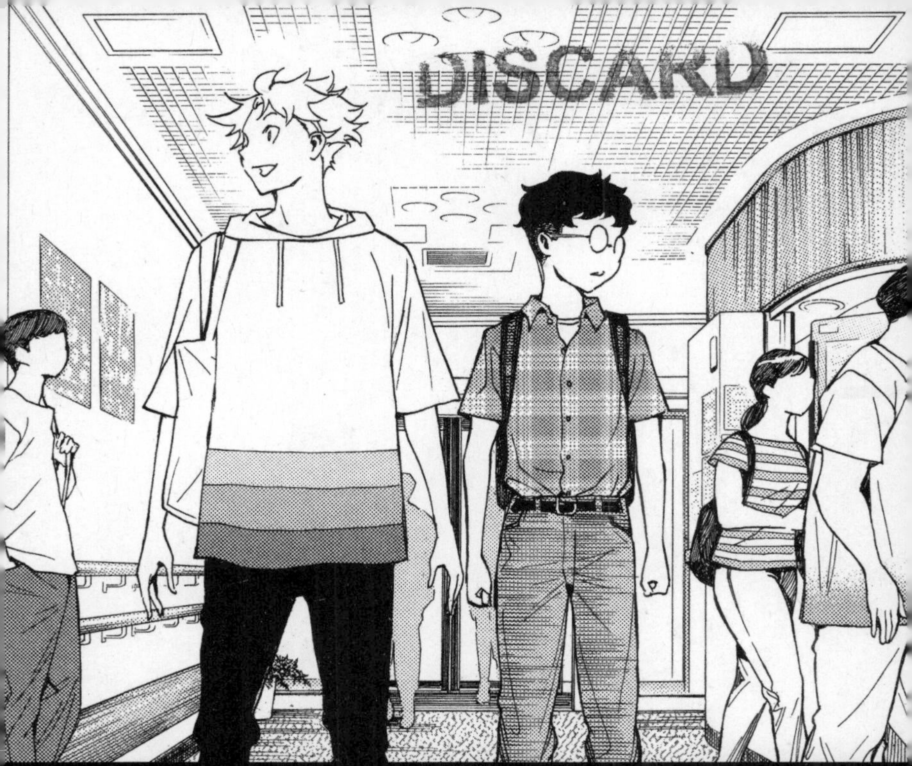

YOU'RE READING THE WRONG WAY!

Show-ha Shoten!
reads right to left, starting in the upper-right corner. Japanese is read right to left, meaning that action, sound effects, and word balloon order are completely reversed from English order.

Turn to the other side of the book to get started on the comedy journey!

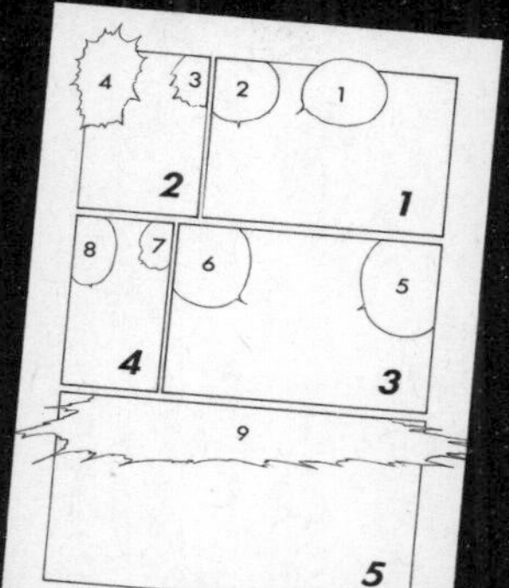
1
2
3
4
1
2
5
6
7
8
3
4
9
5